Chronicling the period from April thr[ough] 1861, Volume 2 of *The Papers of Ulysses S. Grant* leaves behind the ebbing fortunes of the prewar years and deals with Grant's assumption of a Civil War role during the critical half-year following the surrender of Fort Sumter. The headquarters records kept by the general as well as the letters received by him form the substance of this volume and are either reproduced *in extenso* or described in the notes and *Calendar*. Since the bulk of this material has not been published previously this volume lays open a store of information that sheds new light on many obscure aspects of the initial phase of the War. Of singular interest is the appearance in print for the first time of thirty letters addressed to his wife Julia—warm, affectionate letters touched with a deep concern that his performance reflect well upon his family.

With the aid of these records and letters, the reader can now chart, step by step, the unfolding of Grant's activities: the "decayed soldier" diffidently tendering his services to the government, his work in the state adjutant general's office, his appointment as colonel of the Twenty-first Illinois Volunteers, and finally his promotion to the rank of brigadier general with a territorial command which he himself ranked "third in importance in the country."

In the stark and unadorned detail of the records, these months of preparation assume a dramatic importance in the development of a strategy that presaged ultimate failure for the Confederacy. Grant understood the importance of the District of Southeast Missouri in commanding the rivers vital to northern success. Further, he had the difficult task of creating the army to implement his plan of action. The early records detail the problems of turning recruits and disorganized units with unreliable fire power into an effective fighting force; the difficulties of moving an army over uncharted terrain; the hazards of relying on local residents "conversant with all the roads"; and the drive to maintain the discipline and morale of troops quartered in an area of hostile "secessionists." Growing recognition of Grant's success is seen in the eventually attacking the fortifications on the Tennessee and Cumberland rivers which occupied a commanding position over the labyrinth of waterways fanning out to the very heart of the Confederacy.

These documents are valuable not only for the military aspects of the Civil War. There is much in these pages of interest to the social historian. The wavering sectional groups embittered by the dislocations of war, perplexed by the dimly understood objectives of the hostilities, but accepting the dissolution of the Union as the lesser of the evils confronting them, come through clearly in the terse accounts. The unmistakable impact of this volume, however, is the new personality of Grant himself. A new and deepening picture of Grant continues to emerge with the publication of these letters. Though they are important as original history, they deserve reading for their own sake.

THE PAPERS OF ULYSSES S. GRANT

THE PAPERS OF

ULYSSES S. GRANT

Volume 2 : April–September 1861

Edited by
John Y. Simon

━━━

SOUTHERN ILLINOIS UNIVERSITY PRESS

CARBONDALE AND EDWARDSVILLE

FEFFER & SIMONS, INC.

LONDON AND AMSTERDAM

Copyright © 1969, by the Ulysses S. Grant Association
All rights reserved
Printed in the United States of America
Designed by Bert Clarke
Standard Book Number 8093–0366–3
Library of Congress Catalog Card Number 67–10725

To Newton Camp Farr
(1887–1967)

Contents

Foreword

BY RALPH G. NEWMAN

====

As THIS VOLUME neared completion in August, 1968, the officers of the Grant Association were saddened to learn of the death of Major General Ulysses S. Grant 3rd, to whom our first volume was dedicated. He had always played a vital role in our project as patron, friend, adviser, and critic. His generosity to three generations of Grant scholars will be long remembered. President Grant's oldest grandson, who served for more than forty years in the U.S. Army, was both the inheritor and worthy guardian of a tradition of distinguished service to the American people. I recall with deep sentiment and much satisfaction the dinner-ceremony which took place in Washington not long after the publication of Volume 1 of *The Papers of Ulysses S. Grant* when we were able to present one of the first copies of the work to General Grant in the presence of members of his family and representatives of Southern Illinois University and the Grant Association. Our board of directors was much richer for the presence of one man who had a first-hand knowledge of President Grant.

An earlier loss to the Grant Association was the death in November, 1967, of Newton C. Farr of Chicago, a member of the board since its beginning. One of the founders of the Civil War Round Table and a former president of the Illinois State Historical Society, his interest in history was strong and backed by extensive knowledge. Like General Grant 3rd, he bridged the gap between our generation and those who knew the main participants in the Civil War intimately. His counsel will be missed.

In addition to renewing our thanks to those people whose assistance was acknowledged in our first volume, the officers of the

Grant Association wish to express their gratitude to: Clifford R. Burger, Southern Illinois University; Mabel Deutrich, National Archives; Dr. James E. Gleichert, Dallas, Tex.; Charles Holliday, Southern Illinois University Libraries; Sara D. Jackson, National Archives; Maizie Johnson, National Archives; Robert W. MacVicar, Southern Illinois University; Kathryn Oestreich, Galena, Ill.; Elmer Parker, National Archives; Gary Ryan, National Archives; and Gretchen Singles, Arlington, Va.

To supplement our thanks to individual members of the staff of the National Archives in the first volume and this, we should express our thanks to the Archives staff collectively. Our project has received every courtesy in the Archives and, from the first staff trip concerning places where Grant letters might be hiding to the filming of the last frame of microfilm, the level of assistance has been excellent.

We are indebted to C. Percy Powell, Karl L. Trever, and Almon R. Wright for searching the National Archives; to Barbara Long for maps; to Kathryn Overturf and Harriet Simon for typing; to Egon Kamarasy and Stephen Olah for translations of Hungarian texts; and to E. B. Long for invaluable editorial consultation. Last, though far from least, financial support for the preparation of this volume has come from Southern Illinois University, the National Historical Publications Commission, and the National Endowment for the Humanities.

Preface

BY T. HARRY WILLIAMS

——

IT WAS late July, 1863, and the loyal states were ringing with praises of U. S. Grant, the conqueror of Vicksburg. But one man was somewhat irked at the hero—General Ambrose E. Burnside, who had lent Grant a corps for the campaign against the river fortress and felt that he had contributed something to its success. Burnside did not want any public credit for his cooperation, but now that the operation was concluded he thought that he should get his troops back. They had not been returned, however, and he finally complained to Washington about the matter. What seemed to irritate him above all else was that he could secure no information as to the whereabouts of his corps.

The issue was deemed to be of sufficient importance to be laid before President Lincoln, who wrote Burnside a soothing letter. Grant had undoubtedly meant to return the troops but had probably found some use for them and had forgotten to tell the government, Lincoln explained. The President added: "Gen. Grant is a copious worker, and fighter, but a very meagre writer, or telegrapher."

Lincoln probably wrote the above sentence with relish. He was taking a dig at Burnside and other generals of his type, of whom there were many in the Civil War—the generals who were better with their pens than with their swords, who wrote much and fought little, who asked in letter after letter for more and more troops and then in other letters made excuses for not accomplishing anything with the troops they had received. Grant was not this kind of general, Lincoln told a friend. "He doesn't worry and bother me," the President said. "He isn't shrieking for reinforcements all the time. He takes what troops we can safely give him . . . and does the best he can with what he has got."

Lincoln could appreciate a general who was spare with the pen, and this was one of the several reasons that he appreciated Grant. In his letter he was expressing this esteem, but he was also revealing that he was influenced by a popular conception of the general, one that took shape early in the war and that would after it become one of the myths of American history—the myth of Grant the Silent, the taciturn man who said little and wrote less and did both rather badly. It was a conception that influenced even persons sympathetic to Grant. Charles A. Dana, former New York *Tribune* executive who was sent as a War Department observer to Grant's headquarters, reported with disgust that nobody around the general—his staff or generals or regimental officers—could write or seemed to be interested in writing. Illiteracy was the pervading style, Dana sneered, seeming by implication, at least, to include Grant in his condemnation.

Modern scholars who have studied Grant know that the myth is grossly exaggerated. Take the matter of his talking. It is true that he was given to long silences and that often when he broke these, he spoke haltingly or with seeming embarrassment. But there were other times when he spoke at length and with animation and force and even eloquence. The words poured forth when he was aroused about something, and he was most likely to be aroused by a military situation or crisis. He talked, in fact, much like he fought, and his speech and fighting were both reflections of his character. This character, as an astute English writer, C. F. Atkinson, noted, was under the direction of a powerful will that came into action only when stimulated by an unusual circumstance, such as battle. Then Grant acted, or talked, suddenly, usually ably, and sometimes magnificently.

The myth is even more inaccurate as an indicator of Grant's writing. Anyone who has dug into the source documents of the war knows that the general wrote as much as he was supposed to write— orders, dispatches, reports—and that in the military sense he wrote well. That is to say, although Grant sometimes misspelled words or was guilty of awkward grammatical constructions, he was nearly always lucid. As Bruce Catton has observed, the researcher in the *Official Records* comes eventually to the point where he can recognize a Grant document without waiting to see the signature: "it gets to the point, avoids unnecessary verbiage, and tells the recipient exactly what the recipient needs to know." This quality of clarity appears in other Grant compositions: in his personal letters, of which before the publication of these volumes we had only skimpy selections in two unsatisfactory books, and in his *Memoirs,* which is surely one of the superior reminiscent accounts of the war. Grant does not always tell us as much about himself as we would like to know—he preserved a certain reticence in writing even to his wife—but there is never any doubt as to the meaning of what he does tell.

With the publication of these volumes of the *Grant Papers* we have additional and abundant evidence of a truth that we glimpsed in the preceding first volume—that, to quote Catton again, Grant was "one of the most articulate of all American soldiers." We have, for the first time, full and authoritative texts of the discoverable documents that Grant wrote during the war and the Reconstruction. The number and range of these documents is amazing. In addition to the military communications that Grant penned—reports and letters to his superiors and orders and dispatches to his subordinates—he wrote many personal letters, to his wife, his father, and other members of his family. In 1861 he told Mrs. Grant, who had complained of not receiving mail from him, that he wrote to her at least once or twice a week. He went on to say that he wrote these and other personal letters late at night after finishing his official correspondence and that often his hand was so badly cramped that he could hardly hold a pen.

If the documents in these volumes demonstrated only that Grant was articulate, we would not learn anything from them that we did not already know. But they prove much more. In them we can see the evolution of a general and the formation finally of a commander. The word evolution is subject to a qualification. Grant most certainly grew as a general, learning from experience and from others and from his own mistakes. But, significantly, the ingredients that made up Grant's character, that character that enabled him to become a great general, were manifested in 1861, almost from the time that he entered the service. They shine forth in both the personal and the official documents.

The Grant of 1861 had the same grasp of reality that the later general had. He was keenly conscious, for example, of the vital relationship between war and, in the highest meaning of the word, politics. He told his Missouri father-in-law not to be victimized by the southern conception that the North would not fight. The northern people would unite to preserve the Union, he declared. "I tell you there is no mistaking the feelings of the people," he wrote. "It is all a mistake about the Northern pocket being so sensative." In remarkably prophetic language he warned the older man, who inclined to southern sympathies, of the inevitable result of war for the South: "In all this I can but see the doom of Slavery. The North do not want, nor will they want, to interfere with the institution. But they will refuse for all time to give it protection unless the South shall return soon to their allegiance."

Grant again showed a sense of reality in estimating the probable length of the war. At first he had succumbed to the popular notion that the struggle would be a short one—there would be one or two big battles and perhaps a slave revolt and then the South would quit. But as early as August, 1861, he was revising his opinion about the will of the "rebels" to resist. "They are so dogged that there is no telling when they may be subdued," he wrote dolefully, and a little later he confessed: "This war however is formidable and I regret to say cannot end so soon as I anticipated at first."

The Grant of 1861 was a man of quiet determination, ambitious to further his career, to make a name for himself, but always conscious that he had limitations and that he was only one of many human instruments serving the national cause. In May he was in Springfield, serving as an assistant to Governor Yates, and writing to his wife he made light of his duties, which he described as "principally smoking and occationally giving advice as to how an order should be communicated." But he added: "However I am in to do all I can and will do my best." One thing he would not do was to seek political support to advance his promotion. He wrote to his father: "I might have got the Colonelcy of a Regiment possibly, but I was perfectly sickened at the political wire pulling for all these commissions and would not engage in it."

He did secure the command of a regiment eventually, the Twenty-first Illinois, a disorganized unit when he took it. He whipped it into shape quickly and was immensely proud of it and his own role in transforming it. But in describing his accomplishment to his father he added a cautionary note that was almost unique for a Civil War volunteer or regular officer: "This I dont want you to read to others for I very much dislike speaking of myself." He exhibited a similar withdrawal and also, perhaps, something of a doubt of himself in informing his wife that he was directed to report to General John C. Frémont at

St. Louis for a larger duty. He wrote almost pleadingly: "You should be cheerful and try to encourage me. I have a task before me of no trifling moment and want all the encouragement possible. Remember that my success will depend a greatdeel upon myself and that the safety of the country, to some extent, and my reputation and that of our children greatly depends upon my acts."

The Grant of 1861 is, above all, a soldier of calmness and fortitude who evaluates reports of an enemy presence with sceptical realism and is not thrown off balance by rumors. In August he assumed command at Ironton, Missouri, in the center of an area reported to be swarming with enemies. He wrote his wife: "When I come there was great talk of an attack upon this place and it was represented that there was 8000 rebels within a few miles but I am not ready to credit the report." In Missouri and later at Cairo, Illinois, he made requests on his superiors for more troops. But these requests were not made in a spirit of panic: Give me more men or I will be crushed. Rather, they expressed a spirit of quiet, calculated confidence: Give me more men and I will do more.

This Grant of 1861 is, to anybody who knows him, the Grant of the later war years. With the publication of these volumes, we are enabled to know him much better than we have before as we follow him from Henry and Donelson to Shiloh, Vicksburg, Chattanooga, the Wilderness, Petersburg, and finally Appomattox. We can see unfolding in fuller flower the character of the man and the general. Here is the Grant who in asking Lincoln for more troops said humbly: "The greater number of men we have, the shorter and less sanguinary will be the war. I give this entirely as my view and not in any spirit of dictation, always holding myself in readiness to use the material given me to the best advantage I know how." Here is the Grant who in informing Lincoln that he would do all he could to further the government's program of enlisting Negro soldiers said: "I would do this whether the arming the negro seemed to me a wise policy or not, because it is an order that I am bound to obey and do not feel that in my position I have a right to question any policy of the Government." Here finally is the Grant of whom his friend Sherman said: "I know a great deal more about war, military history, strategy, and grand tactics than he does; I know more about organization, supply, and administration and about everything else than he does; but I tell you where he beats me and where he beats the world. He don't care a damn

for what the enemy does out of his sight, but it scares me like hell! . . .
I am more nervous than he is. I am more likely to change my orders,
or to countermarch my command than he is. He uses such information
as he has according to his best judgment; he issues his orders and does
his level best to carry them out without much reference to what is
going on about him."

In this series we follow Grant past the war years and into the
Reconstruction years. The new documents for this period indicate that
Grant played a greater and more active role in the determination of
policies than has been thought. They sharpen our anticipation for the
appearance of the volumes on the Presidential years.

Introduction

BY JOHN Y. SIMON

A T THE OUTBREAK of the Civil War, Ulysses S. Grant, a few weeks short of his thirty-ninth birthday, was earning a modest living in his father's leather business in Galena. Within eight years a rapid series of promotions carried him to the highest rank in the U.S. Army and from there to the White House, the youngest man inaugurated President to that time. In these crowded years, he was pre-eminently a man of deeds, but he was a man of words as well.

In April, 1861, Grant's experience with army paperwork, acquired during fifteen years of service, brought him his first Civil War appointment from Governor Richard Yates of Illinois. His competent work as aide to the Governor, assigned to the state adjutant general's office, led to a commission as colonel of an Illinois volunteer regiment. After his promotion to brigadier general in August, Grant inaugurated a system of meticulous letterbook records of his orders and correspondence based on conventional army practice which he maintained throughout the war.

The system of letterbooks was based on a fairly simple concept of separating documents by classes. Different letterbooks held copies of general orders, special orders, correspondence with superior officers, and correspondence with subordinate officers. Letters and telegrams received from superior officers were usually copied in the same book with letters addressed to them in order to form an integrated record of correspondence. Letters received from subordinate officers were described in a register of letters received, then the letters themselves were filed for reference.

During his first month of general command, Grant moved his

headquarters from Ironton to Jefferson City, to Cape Girardeau, then to Cairo, and during this eventful month had an inadequate staff. Consequently, some of the documents which should have been copied in the letterbooks were omitted. Within a week after his arrival at Cairo, however, the system was so firmly established that thereafter the books may be regarded as a reliable guide to the official correspondence of Grant's headquarters. Brief letters to subordinates were sometimes considered to be informal in nature and not copied, but communications regarded as official or important in a military sense were placed in the books. Grant regarded the District of Southeast Missouri as "quite an extensive and important command. . . . third in importance in the country," and this strengthened his concern for comprehensive records. As Grant's responsibilities increased during the war, he delegated more of the paperwork and record-keeping to his staff. For this reason it is important to remember that the records were begun before Grant had a staff and thus represent his own attention to detail and mastery of routine.

During the Civil War itself copies were made of some of the books. On the basis of those still in existence it is known that some books were eventually copied as many as four times. The original purpose of the copying was probably security: while Grant wanted his records with him, he could not afford to lose them. After the war, official records were collected by the War Department, and Grant turned over copies of all his letterbooks and those original letters he had received which were still in his possession. These are now in the National Archives. Some of the books were also copied for Adam Badeau, military secretary to Grant, for use in the preparation of his three-volume *Military History of Ulysses S. Grant*, and these were returned to the main collection when Badeau had finished using them. In addition, copies of early Grant wartime correspondence were made from War Department files for Badeau; these are now included with the letterbooks in the Grant collection in the Library of Congress. This is not the end of the duplication of Grant's Civil War communications, for letters to and from Grant found their way into letterbooks kept by other officers. Thus it is not unusual to find some half dozen copies of a Grant Civil War communication.

When only copies of Grant letters are available, we have tried to select the earliest for the text and to list all the others. As the letters were recopied, there were often alterations made in grammar, spelling, and punctuation. By using the earliest copies we are frequently under the necessity of perpetuating the errors of harassed army clerks, though at the same time we are closer to the missing original. When the original letter has been found, copies in the National Archives and Library of Congress are not cited. Those wishing to locate copies in the National Archives can do so by checking the citations for similar letters. Copies in the Library of Congress collection can be located through the *Index to the Ulysses S. Grant Papers* (Washington, 1965) prepared by the Library of Congress.

All letters located written by Grant during the first six months of the Civil War are printed in this volume, and those letters addressed to him are either printed or described in the notes or the calendar. Grant's orders are either printed or summarized, depending on their significance. Letters and orders written by members of Grant's staff have been included when significant in themselves or relevant to matters discussed by Grant and his correspondents. Letters and orders written by staff officers concerning such matters as leaves and furloughs, transfers and resignations, assignments to recruiting service or hospital duty, rations and supplies, and other matters of routine military housekeeping have been excluded. Enough of these communications were written by Grant himself to provide an idea of the contents of those excluded; it was not until September 11 that Grant wrote that his staff was "getting a little in the way of this kind of business," and many routine matters were handled by Grant himself afterwards.

The practice of not listing earlier printings of documents, begun in Volume 1, has been maintained, with the necessary exception of references to the 128 volumes of *The War of the Rebellion: A Compilation of the Official Records of the Union and Confederate Armies*—cited as *O.R.*— and the 31 volumes of its naval counterpart, *Official Records of the Union and Confederate Navies in the War of the Rebellion*—cited as *O.R.* (Navy). These mines of documentary wealth contain considerable information related to the Grant correspondence, yet too tangential for inclusion in this work. References to the pages on which Grant correspondence appears are designed to facilitate use of these massive compilations, which can never be superseded for research purposes.

Throughout his life Grant made no effort to save his personal correspondence: he disposed of the letters he received and made no copies of those he wrote. Few examples of his incoming personal correspondence survive. Beginning in 1861, many people began to save letters written by Grant, and the rate of retention increased as he rose in rank and fame. These letters are now widely scattered in public institutions and private collections. In addition, the distinction between private correspondence and official correspondence was not clearly drawn during the Civil War; much of Grant's military correspondence remained in the hands of the recipients and has been similarly scattered over the years. Undoubtedly there are letters in existence which have eluded our search, and we would appreciate learning of them for use in a supplement.

Although the responsibilities of command thrust an enormous amount of paperwork on Grant, he never lost sight of craftsmanship in writing. Often he crossed out words and added phrases not merely to correct slips of the pen or to provide accuracy, but to get the right balance or rhythm in his sentence. Clarity, brevity, informality of style, and a quiet sense of humor became his trademarks. His first report to headquarters from a demoralized outpost after his assignment to command as brigadier general stated that "at present our resistance would be in the inverse ratio of the number of troops to resist with." Grant used his detailed knowledge of the etiquette and forms of military correspondence in order to express himself with singular directness. When staff officers tried to ease his burden by writing for him, Grant repeatedly insisted on preparing his own letters, even if he had to stay up until two in the morning to complete the work. In his correspondence, Grant consistently speaks for himself.

In the early months of the Civil War, strange and irregular things happened in the Western Department. Old army officers chuckled when Major General John C. Frémont appointed a musical director to his staff, then gasped when he named four "acting major-generals." But in Grant's corner of the Western Department, business was transacted in a manner to warm the heart of the stiffest traditionalist. If Grant did something irregular, like occupying Paducah before formal authorization arrived, it made good military sense. He combined a well-developed sense of military professionalism with great flexibility, and was constantly interested in innovation. Only a man who knew the rules so well could have had such a sure touch in breaking them.

Editorial Procedure

1. Editorial Insertions

A.   Words or letters in roman type within brackets represent editorial reconstruction of parts of manuscripts torn, mutilated, or illegible.

B.   [. . .] or [— — —] within brackets represent lost material which cannot be reconstructed. The number of dots represents the approximate number of lost letters; dashes represent lost words.

C.   Words in *italic* type within brackets represent material such as dates which were not part of the original manuscript.

D.   Numbered notes marking passages crossed out in letters from USG to Julia Dent Grant represent material deleted by Mrs. Grant in later years. It is the wish of her descendants that this material remain unprinted. Most deletions involve minor personal matters and are not extensive.

E.   Other material crossed out is indicated by ~~cancelled~~ ~~type~~.

F.   Material raised in manuscript, as "4th," has been brought in line, as "4th."

2. Symbols Used to Describe Manuscripts

AD	Autograph Document
ADS	Autograph Document Signed
ADf	Autograph Draft
ADfS	Autograph Draft Signed
AES	Autograph Endorsement Signed
AL	Autograph Letter
ALS	Autograph Letter Signed
D	Document

DS	Document Signed
Df	Draft
DfS	Draft Signed
ES	Endorsement Signed
LS	Letter Signed

3. *Military Terms and Abbreviations*

Act.	Acting
Adjt.	Adjutant
AG	Adjutant General
AGO	Adjutant General's Office
Art.	Artillery
Asst.	Assistant
Bvt.	Brevet
Brig.	Brigadier
Capt.	Captain
Cav.	Cavalry
Col.	Colonel
Co.	Company
C.S.A.	Confederate States of America
Dept.	Department
Gen.	General
Hd. Qrs.	Headquarters
Inf.	Infantry
Lt.	Lieutenant
Maj.	Major
Q. M.	Quartermaster
Regt.	Regiment or regimental
Sgt.	Sergeant
USMA	United States Military Academy, West Point, N.Y.
Vols.	Volunteers

4. *Short Titles and Abbreviations*

ABPC	*American Book-Prices Current* (New York, 1895—)
CG	*Congressional Globe* Numbers following represent the Congress, session, and page.

J. G. Cramer	Jesse Grant Cramer, ed., *Letters of Ulysses S. Grant to his Father and his Youngest Sister, 1857–78* (New York and London, 1912)
DAB	*Dictionary of American Biography* (New York, 1928–36)
Garland	Hamlin Garland, *Ulysses S. Grant: His Life and Character* (New York, 1898)
HED	*House Executive Documents*
HMD	*House Miscellaneous Documents*
HRC	*House Reports of Committees* Numbers following *HED, HMD,* or *HRC* represent the number of the Congress, the session, and the document.
Ill. AG Report	J. N. Reece, ed., *Report of the Adjutant General of the State of Illinois* (Springfield, 1900)
Lewis	Lloyd Lewis, *Captain Sam Grant* (Boston, 1950)
Lincoln, Works	Roy P. Basler, Marion Dolores Pratt, and Lloyd A. Dunlap, eds., *The Collected Works of Abraham Lincoln* (New Brunswick, 1953–55)
Memoirs	*Personal Memoirs of U. S. Grant* (New York, 1885–86)
O.R.	*The War of the Rebellion: A Compilation of the Official Records of the Union and Confederate Armies* (Washington, 1880–1901)
O.R. (Navy)	*Official Records of the Union and Confederate Navies in the War of the Rebellion* (Washington, 1894–1927) Roman numerals following *O.R.* or *O.R.* (Navy) represent the series and the volume.
PUSG	John Y. Simon, ed., *The Papers of Ulysses S. Grant* (Carbondale and Edwardsville, 1967—)
Richardson	Albert D. Richardson, *A Personal History of Ulysses S. Grant* (Hartford, Conn., 1868)
SED	*Senate Executive Documents*
SMD	*Senate Miscellaneous Documents*
SRC	*Senate Reports of Committees* Numbers following *SED, SMD,* or *SRC* represent the number of the Congress, the session, and the document.
USGA Newsletter	*Ulysses S. Grant Association Newsletter*
Young	John Russell Young, *Around the World with General Grant* (New York, 1879)

5. Location Symbols

CSmH	Henry E. Huntington Library, San Marino, Calif.
CU-B	Bancroft Library, University of California, Berkeley, Calif.
DLC	Library of Congress, Washington, D.C. Numbers following DLC-USG represent the series and volume of military records in the USG papers.
DNA	National Archives, Washington, D.C. Additional numbers identify record groups.
IaHA	Iowa State Department of History and Archives, Des Moines, Iowa.
I-ar	Illinois State Archives, Springfield, Ill.
IC	Chicago Public Library, Chicago, Ill.
ICarbS	Southern Illinois University, Carbondale, Ill.
ICHi	Chicago Historical Society, Chicago, Ill.
ICN	Newberry Library, Chicago, Ill.
IHi	Illinois State Historical Library, Springfield, Ill.
InU	Indiana University, Bloomington, Ind.
KHi	Kansas State Historical Society, Topeka, Kan.
MHi	Massachusetts Historical Society, Boston, Mass.
MiD	Detroit Public Library, Detroit, Mich.
MoSHi	Missouri Historical Society, St. Louis, Mo.
NjP	Princeton University, Princeton, N.J.
NjR	Rutgers University, New Brunswick, N.J.
NN	New York Public Library, New York, N.Y.
OHi	Ohio Historical Society, Columbus, Ohio.
OrHi	Oregon Historical Society, Portland, Ore.
PHi	Historical Society of Pennsylvania, Philadelphia, Pa.
PPRF	Rosenbach Foundation, Philadelphia, Pa.
RPB	Brown University, Providence, R.I.
USG 3	Maj. Gen. Ulysses S. Grant 3rd, Clinton, N.Y.
USMA	United States Military Academy Library, West Point, N.Y.

Chronology

===

APRIL 12. Fort Sumter attacked.

APRIL 15. President Abraham Lincoln called for 75,000 vols.

APRIL 16. After a patriotic rally in Galena, Ill., USG decided to leave his father's leather goods store and to offer his services for the war.

APRIL 18. USG presided over a Galena rally held to recruit vols.

APRIL 25. USG accompanied the Jo Daviess Guards as they left Galena for Springfield, Ill.

APRIL 27. USG's thirty-ninth birthday.

APRIL 29. USG began to serve as aide to Governor Richard Yates.

MAY 4. USG became commanding officer at Camp Yates, Springfield.

MAY 8. USG ordered to muster regts. into state service at Mattoon, Belleville, and Anna, Ill.

MAY 9. USG in Mattoon found the 7th Congressional District Regt. not yet ready for muster.

MAY 10. USG witnessed disorders in St. Louis following the Federal capture of Camp Jackson.

MAY 11.   USG mustered into state service the 8th Congressional District Regt. at Belleville.

MAY 15.   USG mustered into state service the 7th Congressional District Regt. at Mattoon.

MAY 20.   USG mustered into state service the 9th Congressional District Regt. at Anna.

MAY 24.   Back in Galena, USG wrote to Washington for a commission.

MAY 30.   USG returned to Springfield.

JUNE 9.   USG arrived in Covington, Ky., to visit his parents, planning also to ask Maj. Gen. George B. McClellan in Cincinnati for a military appointment.

JUNE 16.   While visiting Col. Joseph J. Reynolds in La Fayette, Ind., on his way back to Springfield, USG learned of his appointment as col. of the 7th Congressional District Regt.

JUNE 18.   USG formally took command of his regt. at Camp Yates.

JUNE 21.   USG left Camp Yates for a visit to Galena.

JUNE 24.   USG returned to Springfield.

JUNE 28.   The 7th Congressional District Regt. mustered into U.S. service as the 21st Ill.

JULY 3.   The 21st Ill. began a march to Quincy, Ill.

JULY 5.   The 21st Ill. camped at Allinson's Grove, about seven miles west of Jacksonville, Ill.

JULY 8.   The 21st Ill. ordered to await transportation on the Illinois River to St. Louis.

JULY 10. The 21st Ill. ordered to proceed to Quincy by railroad due to guerrilla action in north Mo.

JULY 11. The 21st Ill. arrived at Quincy and camped at West Quincy, Mo.

JULY 12. The 21st Ill. stationed along the Quincy and Palmyra Railroad in Mo.

JULY 15. The 21st Ill. advanced to Salt River Bridge on the Hannibal and St. Joseph Railroad.

JULY 17. The 21st Ill. marched to Florida, Mo., in a fruitless search for rebels commanded by Brig. Gen. Thomas Harris, Mo. State Guard.

JULY 19. The 21st Ill. arrived at Macon City, Mo.

JULY 20. The 21st Ill. traveled by railroad to Mexico, Mo.

JULY 21. U.S. advance in Va. halted by defeat at the first battle of Bull Run or Manassas.

JULY 24. USG assigned command of all troops stationed near Mexico by Brig. Gen. John Pope, commanding District of North Mo.

JULY 25. Maj. Gen. John C. Frémont assumed command of the Western Dept.

JULY 31. USG nominated by Lincoln as brig. gen. The Senate confirmed the appointment on Aug. 5.

AUG. 5. USG sent by Pope to St. Louis to confer with Frémont.

AUG. 7. USG asked John A. Rawlins of Galena to serve on his staff.

AUG. 8. USG assumed command of Ironton, Mo., which was threatened by C.S.A. Brig. Gen. William J. Hardee.

Aug. 10. U.S. defeat at the battle of Wilson's Creek, Oak Hills, or Springfield, Mo., roused apprehension of the loss of the state.

Aug. 10. Skirmish at Potosi, Mo., near Ironton.

Aug. 17. Superseded by Brig. Gen. Benjamin M. Prentiss, USG left Ironton for St. Louis.

Aug. 19. USG assigned to command at Jefferson City, Mo.

Aug. 28. Called from Jefferson City to St. Louis, USG ordered to coordinate a movement against Brig. Gen. M. Jeff Thompson, Mo. State Guard, from hd. qrs. at Cape Girardeau, Mo.

Aug. 30. USG assumed command at Cape Girardeau.

Sept. 1. USG assumed command of the District of Southeast Mo.

Sept. 2. Due to the refusal of Prentiss to serve under USG, the expedition against Thompson collapsed, and USG went to Cairo, Ill., formally assuming command there on Sept. 4.

Sept. 3. Forces under C.S.A. Brig. Gen. Gideon Pillow entered Ky. to occupy Hickman and Columbus, violating the self-proclaimed neutrality of the state.

Sept. 4. Confederate troops occupied Columbus.

Sept. 6. USG occupied Paducah, Ky. Frémont assigned Brig. Gen. Charles F. Smith to command at Paducah.

Sept. 7. USG in Cape Girardeau arranged reinforcements for Paducah, then returned to Cairo.

Sept. 8. A gunboat reconnaissance engaged batteries at Lucas Bend, Mo., a few miles north of Columbus.

Sept. 10. USG directed a reconnaissance from Norfolk toward Belmont, Mo., supported by gunboats. After a skirmish at Beckwith Farm, U.S. troops returned to Norfolk, but advanced to another skirmish the next day.

Sept. 13. USG advanced his troops from Fort Holt, Ky., opposite Cairo, to Fort Jefferson, five miles farther down the Mississippi River.

Sept. 13. Death of Samuel Simpson Grant, brother of USG.

Sept. 15. USG ordered to send two regts. to Washington.

Sept. 17. USG temporarily withdrew his troops from Fort Jefferson to Fort Holt.

Sept. 20. The siege of Lexington, Mo., begun on Sept. 12 by Maj. Gen. Sterling Price, Mo. State Guard, ended in U.S. surrender.

Sept. 20. USG visited Cape Girardeau to inspect property taken for fortifications.

Sept. 21. USG directed a reconnaissance along the Ky. shore of the Mississippi River which encountered no Confederates closer than Columbus.

Sept. 22. Skirmish near Fort Jefferson.

Sept. 24. Under pressure from C.S.A. skirmishers in both Mo. and Ky., USG again withdrew his troops from Fort Jefferson to Fort Holt.

Sept. 26. Cavalry skirmish at Hunter's Farm below Norfolk.

Sept. 30. USG went to Paducah believing, incorrectly, that it was threatened by a Confederate army.

The Papers of Ulysses S. Grant

April–September 1861

To Frederick Dent

—————

Galena, April 19th 1861

Mr. F. Dent;
Dear Sir:

I have but very little time to write but as in these exciting times we are very anxious to hear from you, and know of no other way but but by writing first to you, I must make time.— We get but little news, by telegraph, from St. Louis but from most all other points of the Country we are hearing all the time. The times are indee[d] startling but now is the time, particularly in the border Slave states, for men to prove their love of country. I know it is hard for men to apparently work with the Republican party[1] but now all party distinctions should be lost sight of and evry true patriot be for maintaining the integrity of the glorious old *Stars & Stripes*, the Constitution and the Union. The North is responding to the Presidents call[2] in such a manner that the rebels may truly quaik. I tell you there is no mistaking the feel- ings of the people. The Government can call into the field not only 75000 troops but ten or twenty times 75000 if it should be necessary and find the means of maintaining them too. It is all a mistake about the Northern pocket being so sensative. In times like the present no people are more ready to give their own time or of their abundant mea[ns.] No impartial man can conceal from himself the fact that in all these troubles the South have been the aggressors and the Administration has stood purely on the defensive, more on the defensive than she would dared to have done but for her consiousness of strength and the certainty of right prevailing in the end. The news to-day is that Virginia has gone out of the Union.[3] But for the influance she will have on the other border slave states this is not much to be regreted. Her position, or rather that of Eastern Virginia, has been more reprehensible from the begining than that of South Carolina. She shoul[d] be made to bear a heavy portion of the burthen of the War for her guilt.—In all this I can but see the doom of Slavery. The North do not want, nor will they want, to interfere with the institution. But they will refuse for all time to give it protection unless the South shall return soon to their allegiance, and then too this disturbance will give such an impetus to the production of their staple, cotton, in other parts of the world that they can never recover the controll of the market again for that comodity. This will reduce the value of negroes so much that they will never be worth fighting over again.—I have just rec'd a letter from Fred.[4] He breathes fort[h] the most patriotic sentiments. He is for the old Flag as long as there is a Union of two states fighting under its banner and when they desolve he will go it alone. This is not his language but it is the idea not so well expressed as he expresses it.

Julia and the children[5] are all well and join me in love to you all. I forgot to mention that Fred. has another heir, with some novel name that I have forgotten.[6]

Yours Truly

U. S. GRANT

Get John or Lewis Sheets[7] to write to me.

ALS, Mrs. Walter Love, Flint, Mich. Frederick Dent was the father-in-law of USG.

1. USG here refers to the political views of his father-in-law, a native Marylander, a slaveholder most of his life, and an outspoken states rights Democrat. The extent to which USG includes his own views is unclear. His earliest political preference seems to have been the Whig Party (his father's choice) and this may have been confirmed by the Whig choice of his two commanders in the Mexican War, Zachary Taylor and Winfield Scott, as presidential nominees in 1848 and 1852. *Memoirs*, I, 212; *Young*, II, 269, 278. After USG resigned from the army in 1854 and began living in St. Louis County as a farmer at Hardscrabble and White Haven, he was closer to his father-in-law and used slaves. His only vote in a presidential campaign went to the Democratic nominee James Buchanan in 1856. *PUSG*, 1, 352; *Memoirs*, I, 214–15; *Young*, II, 268. In applying for the post of St. Louis County engineer in 1859, USG had the support of prominent St. Louisans of all parties. Only the two Democratic county commissioners, how-

ever, supported USG; the three Free-Soilers (pre-Republicans) gave the post to another. USG denied that he was a Democrat, but since he was generally known to St. Louisans as the son-in-law of Frederick Dent, he was apparently judged on the basis of Dent's politics. *PUSG*, 1, 348–55. USG's reaction to loss of the post of county engineer was an allegiance to the Democratic Party. His letters from 1859 and 1860 contain more political comment than any written previously, and his preference for the Democratic Party is unmistakable. *Ibid.*, 1, 350–60. In 1860 his choice for President was Stephen A. Douglas, candidate of the northern Democrats. In reporting this in his *Memoirs*, however, USG confused the issue by stating that he preferred the election of Abraham Lincoln to that of John C. Breckinridge, the candidate of the southern Democrats. *Memoirs*, I, 216–17. Since Breckinridge received only nine of 4,670 votes in Jo Daviess County, Ill., and under 1 per cent statewide, USG's comment is somewhat irrelevant. What is more significant is that USG was willing to drill the Galena Wide Awakes, a Republican marching society. *Ibid.*

Thus the evidence is strong that USG's political views in 1860 were those of a Douglas Democrat. He had freed a slave in 1859 at a time when he was financially hard-pressed and had never sympathized with southern states rights arguments. *PUSG*, 1, 347. See letter to Jesse Root Grant, July 13, 1861. When war came, he followed the lead of Senator Douglas in giving strong support to the maintenance of the Union. The point is important because of a traditional story in the Douglas family that the Senator met USG in Springfield, Ill., in April, 1861, and dissuaded him from accepting a commission in the Confederate army. George Fort Milton, *The Eve of Conflict: Stephen A. Douglas and the Needless War* (Boston and New York, 1934), p. 566. Although USG did meet Douglas in Springfield and later appointed his son a presidential secretary, the account is inconsistent with letters USG was writing at the time. USG may have become discouraged about his chances to obtain a commission by June, but his meeting with Douglas was definitely in April when he had no reason for dejection. *Memoirs*, I, 238.

During the congressional campaign of 1876, Daniel M. Frost, a St. Louis friend of USG before service in the C.S.A., stated that he possessed an original letter from USG offering his services to the Confederacy. *Chicago Times*, Sept. 27, 1876; *St. Louis Dispatch*, Oct. 3, 1876. Frost never, so far as is known, produced the letter. An account that pro-Confederate Governor Claiborne F. Jackson recommended USG for command of Mo. state troops "early in 1861" is equally implausible. Walter B. Stevens, *Centennial History of Missouri* (St. Louis and Chicago, 1921), I, 778.

Although USG was unquestionably a Democrat at the outbreak of the war, his assistance in raising, training, and equipping the Galena vols. brought him to the favorable attention of the local Republican Congressman Elihu B. Washburne and other prominent Galena Republicans. It was through their support that he received employment from the Republican Governor of Ill., Richard Yates. USG was surprised that Washburne would assist a man he knew to be a Democrat. James L. Crane, "Grant as a Colonel: Conversations between Grant and his Chaplain," *McClure's Magazine*, VII, 1 (June, 1896), 43. Through his connection with prominent Republicans, however, USG was becoming a Republican himself. At the same time, memories of his rejection for county engineer were still painful; USG rejected offers of political endorsement in his efforts to obtain a commission. See letters to Jesse Root Grant, May 2, 6, Aug. 3, 1861; *Memoirs*, I, 239. Once commissioned, the professionalism of USG as a soldier led him to avoid political statements and entanglements. Thus it is impossible to date his transfer to the Republican Party, though it is clear that by 1864 the change was complete.

2. On April 15, 1861, following the fall of Fort Sumter, President Abraham Lincoln issued a proclamation calling for 75,000 militia to enforce the laws of the United States. Lincoln, *Works*, IV, 331–32.

3. On April 17, a Va. state convention adopted an ordinance of secession. Va. did not technically leave the Union until the action of the convention was ratified by popular vote on May 23. Ratification, however, was inevitable; USG was correct in considering Va. out of the Union.

4. Capt. Frederick Tracy Dent of Mo., USMA 1843, 9th Inf., then stationed on the Pacific Coast, was a brother-in-law of USG.

5. USG had four children: Frederick Dent, born May 30, 1850; Ulysses S., Jr., born July 22, 1852; Ellen Wrenshall, born July 4, 1855; Jesse Root, Jr., born Feb. 6, 1858.

6. USG refers to Capt. Frederick T. Dent's third child, second son, Sidney Johnston Dent, presumably named for Bvt. Brig. Gen. Albert Sidney Johnston of La., USMA 1826, later C.S.A. gen. and USG's opponent at Shiloh. Sidney Dent was born Feb. 18, 1861, at Walla Walla, Washington Territory. Registration Book, United States Naval Academy, Annapolis, Md.

7. John Cromwell Dent was a brother-in-law of USG. Lewis Sheets was apparently connected with the Dent family. A relative of Frederick Dent who married Col. John O'Fallon of St. Louis had a maiden name variously given as Schütz, Schutz, and Sheets. In 1866, a subpoena for Lewis Sheets indicated his residence "at Mrs. Col. O'Fallons." Papers in the case of Ulysses S. Grant and Julia B. Grant vs. Joseph W. White, Circuit Court, Twenty-second Judicial Circuit of Missouri, St. Louis, Mo.

To Jesse Root Grant

———

Galena, April 21st 1861

DEAR FATHER;

We are now in the midst of trying times when evry one must be for or against his country, and show his colors too, by his every act. Having been educated for such an emergency, at the expense of the Government, I feel that it has upon me superior claims, such claims as no ordinary motives of self-interest can surmount. I do not wish to act hastily or unadvisadly in the matter, and as there are more than enough to respond to the first call of the President, I have not yet offered myself. I have promised and am giving all the assistance I can in organizing

the Company whose services have been accepted from this place.[1]
I have promised further to go with them to the state Capital and
if I can be of service to the Governer in organizing his state
troops to do so. What I ask now is your approval of the course
I am taking, or advice in the matter.[2] A letter written this week
will reach me in Springfield. I have not time to write you but a
hasty line for though Sunday as it is we are all busy here. In a few
minuets I shall be engaged in directing tailors in the style and
trim of uniforms for our men.[3]

Whatever may have been my political opinions before I have
but one sentiment now. That is we have a Government, and laws
and a flag and they must all be sustained. There are but two
parties now, Traitors & Patriots and I want hereafter to be
ranked with the latter, and I trust, the stronger party.—I do not
know but you may be placed in an awkward position, and a dangerous one pecuniarily, but costs can not now be counted. My
advice would be to leave where you are if you are not safe with
the veiws you entertain.[4] I would never stultify my opinions for
the sake of a little security.

I will say nothing about our business. Orvil & Lank[5] will
keep you posted as to that.

Write soon and direct as above.

Yours Truly

U. S. GRANT.

ALS (facsimile), *J. G. Cramer*, pp. 24–25.

1. USG's involvement with recruiting in Galena began when he attended a
public meeting on April 16, 1861, called in response to the news of the surrender
of Fort Sumter. A speech by Democratic Mayor Robert Brand advocating
compromise was badly received; militant resolutions by Republican Congressman Elihu B. Washburne were more popular. Among the patriotic orations was
a dramatic forty-five minute speech by Democratic lawyer John A. Rawlins
declaring "that the time for compromise had passed, and that we must appeal to
the God of Battles to vindicate our flag." *Galena Courier*, *Galena Advertiser*, April
17, 1861; *Galena Gazette*, April 23, 1861. Following the meeting, USG said that
he intended to volunteer for military service. *Richardson*, p. 179; *Lewis*, pp. 394–
400.

Two days later, April 18, another meeting was held to raise a co. USG was
chosen to preside, probably through the influence of Congressman Washburne.

See John Y. Simon, "From Galena to Appomattox: Grant and Washburne," *Journal of the Illinois State Historical Society*, LVIII, 2 (Summer, 1965), 167–68. In *Memoirs*, I, 230–31, USG telescoped the two meetings into one. USG declined to be a candidate for capt., but offered to assist in any other way. *Ibid.*

At the meeting, twenty-two men volunteered, and the co., named the Jo Daviess Guards, had forty by noon of the next day. *Galena Courier*, April 19, 1861. Through recruiting in nearby towns, the Guards had eighty men by April 20 and elected its officers. USG maintained his refusal to be a candidate for capt. and gave his support to the successful candidate, Augustus L. Chetlain. Chetlain, *Recollections of Seventy Years* (Galena, 1899), p. 71. Chetlain, formerly a wholesale grocer, relied on USG to drill the co. and advise on military procedure. USG said, "I never went into our leather store . . . to put up a package or do other business," and apparently gave all his time to the vols. *Memoirs*, I, 231–32.

2. Jesse R. Grant's favorable response may be inferred from USG's letter of May 2, 1861. On April 25, 1861, Jesse R. Grant wrote in his son's behalf to Attorney General Edward Bates. "Capt Grant graduated at West Point in 43—was through the whole of the Mexican war—was in every battle fought by Taylor & Scott except Buenavista—was never absent from his post during the war—The death of Col Bliss promoted him to the rank of Capt in 53—He was then in California & his family in St Louis. Seeing no probabilaty of leaving, & no prospect of taking his family there he resigned in 54 & came to St Louis. Seeing that many of the officers of Southern birth were resigning, & that the Government might need the servises of experianced officers; and believing that the Capt would be willing to serve his country & make himself usful, I wrote to Gen Scott some 8 or 10 days ago on this subject, but as yet have not recd any answer. ~~Cap~~ The Capt has been living at Galena Ill & I had not seen or written to him on the subject. Yesterday I recd a letter from him, he said as the Government had educated him for the military servis, & as it now needed his servises, he had again drawn his sword in its defence, & while his servises were needed they were at the disposal of his country—He had raised, uniformed & drilled a company, & should this week take them to Springfield & have them mustered into the servis. He said he would report himself to the Governor, & hold himself subject to his orders—I wish you would see Gen Scott, & if necessary the Pres & let me know soon if they can restore him again to the Reg Army Of course he would not be willing to return to the Army as a Capt. I hope Judge you will give this subject a little attention & *write* to me soon." ALS, IC.

3. The Jo Daviess Guards wore blue frock coats and dark grey pants with blue cords. Money to buy the cloth was advanced by the Galena banking firm of N. Corwith & Co. *Galena Courier*, April 22, 1861. After tailors cut the cloth, the ladies of Galena made up the uniforms. *Memoirs*, I, 231.

4. Jesse R. Grant continued to live in Covington, Ky., until his death in 1873. Although he held strong Republican views, there is no evidence that he was ever in danger during the Civil War. See *USGA Newsletter*, I, 4 (July, 1964), 22–23.

5. Orvil Grant, brother of USG. "Lank" probably refers to M. T. Burke of Galena, bookkeeper for the Grant leather store. Burke was the son-in-law of Ann Simpson Ross, sister of USG's mother. His initials, sometimes given as "W. T.," are clearly M. T. in a signature on a petition owned by Mrs. Lawrence Oestreich, Galena, Ill.

To Julia Dent Grant

———

Springfield, Apl. 27th / 61

Dear Julia;

On account of the cars not connecting promptly we did not arrive here until evening yesterday, and as no mail gets through as fast as passengers you will not probably get this until Tuesday morning.[1] I fully made up my mind last night, and had not changed it this morning, to start home to-day and consequently did not intend to write to you atall. Mr. Washburn[2] however come to me this morning and prevailed upon me to remain over for a day or two to see the result of a bill now before the legislature and which will no doubt pass to-day, authorizing the Governer to ration and pay the surplus troops now here, and to arrive, and to appoint suitable persons to take charge of them until such times as they may be organized into Companies and Regiments.[3] All the Companies that have arrived so far, and that is near the whole number called for, have brought with them from twenty to sixty men more each than the law allows. The overplus have as a matter of course, to be cut off. These are the men the Legislature are providing for. The Governer[4] told Mr Washburn last night that should the legislature pass the provision for them, he wanted me to take the command and drill them until they are organized into Companies and placed in Regiments. In case I should accept such a position I may remain here several weeks. In any event however I shall go home, if but for a day or two, so as to be there on next Sunday morning.—Our trip here was a perfect ovation, at evry station the whole population seemed to be out to greet the troops. There is such a feeling arroused through the country now as has not been known since the Revolution. Evry company called for in the Presidents proclimation has been organized, and filled to near double the amount that can be recieved.[5] In addition to that evry town of 1000 inhabitants and over has from one to four additional companies organized

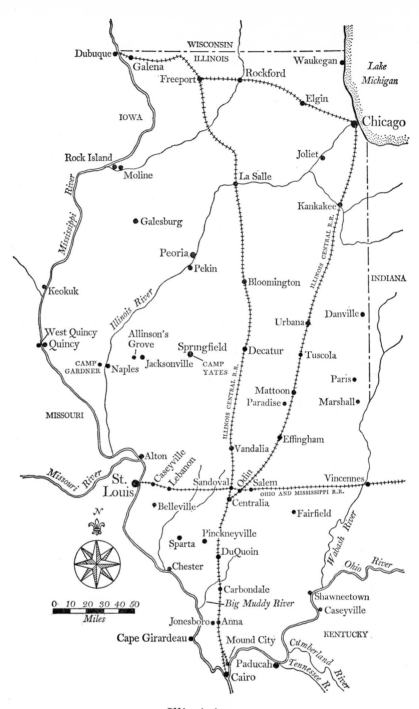

Illinois in 1861

ready to answer the next call that will be made.—I find but few old acquaintances here except from Galena. Capt. Pope[6] of the army is here mustering in the volunteers.—I see by Telegraphic dispatch that K McKenzie[7] died yesterday. So they go one at a time. I shall write to your father about Monday. Kiss all the children for me. Write as soon as you get this.

ULYS.

ALS, DLC-USG.

1. The letter is dated on Saturday. USG had accompanied the Jo Daviess Guards when they left Galena by train on Thursday, April 25, 1861. The Guards went to Camp Yates on the outskirts of Springfield.

2. Congressman Elihu B. Washburne, born in Livermore, Me., had studied at Maine Wesleyan Seminary and Harvard Law School before coming to Galena in 1840. Washburne was soon a successful lawyer and Whig politician. First elected to the House of Representatives in 1852, by 1861 he had the longest continuous service of any Republican on the floor of the House. Since his friendship with Abraham Lincoln dated from the winter of 1843–44, Washburne had considerable political influence. He was, however, not on friendly terms with Governor Richard Yates. Thomas J. McCormack, ed., *Memoirs of Gustave Koerner, 1809–1896* (Cedar Rapids, 1909), II, 127; Jack Junior Nortrup, "Richard Yates: Civil War Governor of Illinois," (unpublished doctoral dissertation, University of Illinois, 1960), p. 196. See letter of April 21, 1861, note 1.

3. On April 29, 1861, 1st Asst. Ill. AG John B. Wyman wrote to Yates that after the six authorized regts. were filled there would be 2,380 vols. still at Camp Yates. *Journal of the House of Representatives of the Twenty-Second General Assembly of the State of Illinois at their Second Session, Begun and Held at Springfield, April 23, 1861* (Springfield, 1861), p. 44. The legislature passed two bills, both approved May 2, concerning the additional vols. The first provided that vols. who had reported to Springfield or Cairo in response to the governor's proclamation but were not sworn into U.S. service would receive pay for one month. The second authorized the governor to accept ten regts. of inf. and one battalion of light art. for state service for thirty days. One regt. would be organized of the vols. then in Springfield and one other would be organized in each of the nine congressional districts. *Laws of the State of Illinois, Passed by the Twenty-Second General Assembly at its Extraordinary Session, Convened April 23, 1861* (Springfield, 1861), pp. 13–15.

4. Governor Richard Yates was born in Ky., graduated from Illinois College, and studied law at Transylvania University. During a career as an Ill. Whig lawyer-politician, he served three terms in the legislature and two terms in Congress (1851–55). The somewhat conservative nature of his Republican politics and his personal popularity contributed to his election as governor in 1860.

5. See letter of April 19, 1861.

6. Capt. John Pope of Ill., USMA 1842, was then in command at Camp Yates. Later, as maj. gen. of vols., he led the Army of Va. to defeat at Second Bull Run.

7. Both the *Illinois State Journal* and *Illinois State Register*, April 27, 1861, carried dispatches about the death of Kenneth MacKenzie, "one of the oldest merchants in St. Louis." MacKenzie had endorsed USG's 1859 application for St. Louis County engineer. *PUSG*, 1, 349*n*.

To Richard Yates

———

Springfield, Illinois,
April 29th, 1861.

To His Excellency Richard Yates,
    Governor and Commander-in-Chief, Illinois
    State Militia.

Sir: In compliance with your request, I have visited the State Armory and made careful examination of all the muskets now in possession of the State authorities, and beg leave to report:

Number of muskets that are in serviceable condition,		60
" " that require repairs,		262
" " that have been delivered to troops,		220
" musquetoons that are serviceable,		93
" " that require repairs,		40
" rifles issued to troops,		80
" Cadet rifles issued,		60
" Minnie rifles issued,		90

Making, altogether, nine hundred and five (905) pieces.

The muskets are the old army pattern changed from the flint lock, are in good order, but need cleaning. I do not know as to the practicability of rifling them, and have not a correct idea of their value.

Respectfully, your obedient servant,
U. S. Grant.

Journal of the House of Representatives of the Twenty-Second General Assembly of the State of Illinois at their Second Session, Begun and Held at Springfield, April 23, 1861 (Springfield, 1861), p. 62. On April 29, 1861, Governor Richard Yates wrote to Speaker of the House Shelby M. Cullom. "In compliance with the resolution of the House of Representatives of this day requesting this Department to report to that body the quantity and kind of muskets now in possession of the authorities of this State, whether the same be capable of being rifled, as is now being done by the United States at Pittsburgh, with similar arms, and what is the probable value and efficiency of muskets, so rifled, I have the honor to transmit herewith to your body the report of Capt. U. S. Grant, who was specially detailed by this Department to make the examination required by said resolution." *Ibid.* The resolution had been introduced by E. G. Johnson, representing Peoria and Stark counties. *Ibid.*, pp. 37–38. USG's letter was also printed in the *Missouri Republican*, May 1, 1861, attributed to "N. S. Grant." See letter of May 1, 1861, note 3.

To Mary Grant

Springfield, April 29th, 1861

DEAR SISTER;

I come to this place several days ago fully expecting to find a letter here for me from father.[1] As yet I have rec'd none. It was my intention to have returned to Galena last evening but the Governer detained, and I presume will want me to remain with him, until all the troops now called into service, or to be so called, are fully mustered in and completely organized.[2] The enthusiasm through this state surpasses anything that could have been imagined three weeks ago. Only six Regiments are called for here while at least thirty could be promptly raised. The Governer, and all others in authority, are harrassed from morning until night with Patriotic men, and such political influ-ance as they can bring, to obtain first promises of acceptance of their companies if there should be another call for troops. The eagerness to enter companies that were accepted by the Governer was so great that it has been impossible for commanders of companies to keep their numbers within the limits of the law consequently companies that have arrived here have all had from ten to sixty men more than can be accepted. The Legislature on Saturday last passed a bill providing for the maintenance and discipline of these surplus troops for one month, unless sooner mustered into service of the United States under a second call.[3] — I am convinced that if the South knew the entire unanimity of the

North for the Union and maintenance of Law, and how freely men and money are offered to the cause, they would lay down their arms at once in humble submission. There is no disposition to compromise now. Nearly every one is anxious to see the Government fully tested as to its strength, and see if it is not worth preserving. The conduct of eastern Virginia has been so abominable through the whole contest that there would be a great deal of disappointment here if matters should be settled before she is thoroughly punished. This is my feeling, and I believe it universal. Great allowance should be made for South Carolinians, for the last generation have been educated, from their infancy, to look upon their Government as oppressive and tyrannical and only to be endured till such time as they might have sufficient strength to strike it down. Virginia, and other border states, have no such excuse and are therefore traitors at heart as well as in act. I should like very much to see the letter Aunt Rachel wrote Clara![4] or a copy of it. Can't you send it?

When I left Galena, Julia and the children were very well. Jesse[5] had been very sick for a few days but was getting much better. I have been very anxious that you should spend the summer with us. You have never visited us and I don't see why you can't. Two of you often travel together, and you might do so again, and come out with Clara. I do not like to urge anything of the kind, lest you should think that I ignored entirely the question of economy, but I do not do so. The fact is I have had my doubts whether or not it would not be more prudent for all of you to lock up and leave, until the present excitement subsides.[6] If father were younger[7] and Simpson strong and healthy,[8] I would not advise such a course. On the contrary, I would like to see every Union man in the border slave states remain firm at his post. Every such man is equal to an armed volunteer at this time in defence of his country. There is very little that I can tell you that you do not get from the papers.

Remember me to all at home and write to me at once, to this place.

BROTHER ULYSSES.

J. G. Cramer, pp. 27–30. The first page is reproduced in the catalogue of the J. H. Benton sale, American Art Association, March 12, 1920. Mary Grant was the youngest sister of USG.

1. The letter was requested in USG's letter of April 21, 1861. It arrived the same day USG mailed this letter. See letter of May 2, 1861.

2. In his letter of April 27, USG spoke of the intention of Governor Richard Yates to have him drill the vols. at Camp Yates. What had changed these plans is unknown, but there may be a clue in a resolution introduced in the Ill. House of Representatives on April 26 by William C. Harrington of Adams County authorizing the state adjt. gen. to secure the services of three men as drill officers at Camp Yates. USG was not one of the persons named. *Journal of the House of Representatives of the Twenty-Second General Assembly of the State of Illinois at their Second Session . . .* (Springfield, 1861), p. 24.

3. See letter of April 27, 1861, note 3.

4. Rachel B. Grant, youngest of the nine children of Noah Grant, sister of Jesse Root Grant, married William Tompkins of Charleston in what is now W. Va. According to *J. G. Cramer*, p. 27, in the letter referred to by USG, Rachel Tompkins had asserted: "If you are with the accursed Lincolnites, the ties of consanguinity shall be forever severed." Although the letter to USG's oldest sister, Clara Grant, referred to by USG is not available in full, a long letter of June 5 has been printed. This letter was undoubtedly written by Rachel Tompkins, although signed "The Secretary of Your Aunt Rachel." In this letter the southern cause is defended and Lincoln condemned vigorously. "Mrs. Tompkins says," reports her secretary, "that if *you* can justify your Bro. Ulysses in drawing his sword against those connected by the ties of blood, and even boast of it, you are at liberty to do so, *but she can not.*" *Ibid.*, pp. 159–82.

5. Jesse Root Grant, Jr., youngest child of USG, was born Feb. 6, 1858.

6. See letter of April 21, 1861, note 4.

7. Jesse Root Grant was then sixty-seven years old.

8. Samuel Simpson Grant, oldest brother of USG, had been ill with tuberculosis for some time. *PUSG*, 1, 347*n*, 350, 356. He died in Sept., 1861.

To Julia Dent Grant

GENERAL HEAD QUARTERS—STATE OF ILLINOIS.
ADJUTANT GENERAL'S OFFICE,
SPRINGFIELD, May 1st *1861*.

DEAR JULIA;

I have an opportunity of sending a letter direct to Galena by Mr. Corwith[1] and as it will probably reach you a day or two earlyer than if sent by Mail I avail myself of the chance. I enclose also a letter from father for you to read. As I shall probably be home on Saturday[2] evening I shall say nothing about what my intentions are for the future, in fact my plans will have to mature from circumstances as they develop themselvs. At present I am on duty with the Governer, at his request, occupation principally smoking and occationally giving advice as to how an order should be communicated &c. I am going this morning however into the Adjutant General's Office[3] to remain until some regularity is established there, if I can bring about that regularity. The fact is however, as I told the Governer, my bump of order[4] is not largely developed and papers are not my forte and therefore my services may not be as valuable as he anticipates. However I am in to do all I can and will do my best.

We recieve the St. Louis morning papers here at 10 O'Clock a.m. evry day of the day issued and evry day some one is here from the city. The state of affairs there is terrible and no doubt a terrible calamity awaits them. Stationing Ill. Troops within striking distance of St Louis may possibly save the city. Business is entirely prostrated and the best houses are forced to close. I see by the Mo. Republican that Charless Blow & Co are among the number.[5] But for the little piece of stratagem used to get the arms out of the arsenal, to this place,[6] they would have fallen into the hands of the Secessionests and with their hands strengthened with these an attempt would have been made to take the city entirely under controll and terrible slaughter would have taken place. Great numbers of people are leaving Missouri now in evry direction, except South. In some of the Northern towns of the state merchants and business men are leaving with all their personal property. Missouri will be a great state ultimately but she is set back now for years. It will end in more rapid advancement however for she will be left a free state. Negroes are stampeding already and those who do not will be carried further South so that the destiny of the state, in that respect, may now be considered settled by fate and not political parties. Kiss the children for me. You need not write as I will be home so soon

Ulys.

ALS, DLC-USG.

1. Several members of the Corwith family were active in the commercial life of Galena. See letter of April 21, 1861, note 3. The recent visit of John Corwith, of the Bank of Galena, to Camp Yates in Springfield was noted in the *Galena Advertiser*, May 10, 1861.

2. Saturday, May 4, 1861.

3. USG does not appear on a "Statement of officers and employees of the Adjutant General's Department . . . from April 16, 1861, to January 1, 1863." Those assigned to the AGO when USG entered it were AG Thomas S. Mather, 1st Asst. AG John B. Wyman, 2nd Asst. AG John S. Loomis, and clerks M. A. T. McHugh, Chauncey Miller, and Benjamin F. Johnson. Two additional clerks, Robert B. Nay and John Belser, were hired on May 4 and May 6, 1861, respectively. [Allen C. Fuller], *Annual Report of the Adjutant General of the State of Illinois* (Springfield, 1863), pp. 84–85. When USG was paid on May 23, he received $130 for "services as aid to the Governer & Mustering Officer." DS, Auditor's Receipt Book, I-ar. It appears likely that USG officially remained an aide to Governor Richard Yates while serving down the hall in the AGO.

4. In speaking of his "bump of order," USG refers to the popular pseudoscience of phrenology which held that character could be discerned and the future predicted by study of the shape of the head. USG had als oreferred to phrenology in 1844. *PUSG*, 1, 24.

5. Charless, Blow & Co., wholesale drug merchants of St. Louis, announced on April 29, 1861, that "Circumstances have compelled us to relinquish business for the present . . ." *Missouri Republican*, April 30, 1861. One member of the firm, Taylor Blow, had signed USG's petition for St. Louis County engineer in 1859. *PUSG*, 1, 349n.

6. Capt. Nathaniel Lyon of Conn., USMA 1841, stationed at the U.S. Arsenal in St. Louis, had been fearful that its rich stores would be seized by secessionists. He arranged for a raid on the arsenal by Ill. militia on the night of April 25, during which weapons and ammunition were seized, carried across the Mississippi, and eventually transported to Springfield, Ill.

To Jesse Root Grant

GENERAL HEAD QUARTERS—STATE OF ILLINOIS.
ADJUTANT GENERAL'S OFFICE,
SPRINGFIELD, May 2nd, *1861*.

DEAR FATHER:

Your letter of the 24th inst was received the same evening one I had written to Mary was mailed.[1] I would have answered earlier but for the fact I had just written.

I am not a volunteer, and indeed could not be, now that I did not go into the first Company raised in Galena. The call of the President was so promptly responded to that only those companies that organized at once, and telegraphed their application to come in, were received. All other applications were filed, and there are enough of them to furnish Illinois quota if the Army should be raised to 300,000 men. I am serving on the Governor's staff at present at his request, but suppose I shall not be here long.

I should have offered myself for the Colonelcy of one of the Regiments, but I find all those places are wanted by politicians who are up to log-rolling, and I do not care to be under such persons.

The war feeling is not abating here much, although hostilities appear more remote than they did a few days ago. Three of the six Regiments mustered in from this state are now at Cairo, and probably will be reinforced with two others within a few days.[2]

Galena has several more companies organized but only one of them will be able to come in under a new call for ten regiments. Chicago has raised companies enough nearly to fill all the first call. The Northern feeling is so fully aroused that they will stop at no expense of money and men to insure the success of their cause.

I presume the feeling is just as strong on the other side, but they are infinitely in the minority in resources.

I have not heard from Galena since coming down here, but presume all is moving along smoothly. My advice was not to urge collections from such men as we knew to be good, and to make no efforts to sell in the present distracted state of our currency.[3] The money will not buy Eastern exchange and is liable to become worse; I think that thirty days from this we shall have specie, and the bills of good foreign banks to do business on, and then will be the time to collect.

If Mary writes to me any time next week she may direct here to

ULYSSES.

J. G. Cramer, pp. 31–33.

1. See letter of April 29, 1861.
2. The 8th, 9th, and 10th Ill. were then at Cairo. The 11th Ill. was ordered to Villa Ridge (near Cairo) on May 5, 1861, and the 7th Ill. left Alton for Cairo on June 3. *Ill. AG Report*, I, 9–10; D. Leib Ambrose, *History of the Seventh Regiment . . .* (Springfield, Ill., 1868), p. 8.
3. Secession caused a currency crisis in Ill., since many banks based their currency on southern securities. Arthur Charles Cole, *The Era of the Civil War* (Springfield, Ill., 1919), pp. 361–62; George William Dowrie, *The Development of Banking in Illinois, 1817–1863* (Urbana, Ill., 1913), pp. 166–71.

To Julia Dent Grant

Springfield, May 3d / 61

DEAR JULIA;

I thought I was going home this evening but when I told the Governer of it he objected because he had important duties for me in connexion with the organization of new Regiments provided for by the Legislature a day or two ago. I presume I shall be put on duty in Freeport mustering in a Regiment from that Congressional district.[1] If so I will be within a few hours travel of Galena and can go down most any afternoon and return in the morning. It may be that I will remain there two or three weeks and then retire from the service. This place is within four hours travel of St. Louis and the Cars run her[e] so that I could start at 5 o'clock a.m. be in St. Louis at 9, get a horse and buggy and go out and spend the day at your fathers[2] and return here for breakfast the next morning. If I can get sent down to Alton on business I will try and go out and spend one day. All is buzz and excitement here, as well as confusion, and I dont see really that I am doing any good. But when I speak of going it is objected to by not only Governer Yates, but others.—I imagine it will do me no harm the time I spend here, for it has enabled me to become acquainted with the principle men in the state. I do not know that I shall receive any benefit from this but it does no harm.

Orvil enquires what compensation I receive: I presume it will be the pay of Capt. or $140 00 per month.[3] At present I am at the Principle Hotel[4] where I presume my board will be 10 or 12 dollars per week but if I remain I shall leave it. I have not had a line from you since I come here, how does this happen?

Kiss all the children for me. Tell Mary Duncan[5] her beaux takes to soldiering very naturally. I have no doubt but he will send her a kiss by me when I go back.

Write to me Sunday the day you will get this.

Ulys.

ALS, DLC-USG.

1. USG was later assigned to muster regts. at Mattoon, Belleville, and Anna. See letter of April 27, 1861, note 3.

2. Frederick Dent was then living at Wish-ton-wish, the farm of his son Lewis Dent, adjacent to the Dent estate of White Haven in St. Louis County which USG had helped his father-in-law to dispose of in 1858. *PUSG*, 1, 344–45.

3. On May 23, 1861, USG was paid $130. See letter of May 1, 1861, note 3. If he received payment for the period between his first full day in Springfield, April 27, and the day he was paid, this would be compatible with the pay expected by USG.

4. Capt. Augustus L. Chetlain recalled that he had roomed with USG in a private apartment and they ate at the Chenery House. *Recollections of Seventy Years* (Galena, 1899), p. 73.

5. Mary E. Duncan of Galena, eighteen-year-old stepdaughter of G. W. Brownell, a grain merchant, was a neighbor of the Grant family. U.S. Census, 1860. Her "beaux" may have been Mr. King. See letter of June 1, 1861.

To Jesse Root Grant

Camp Yates, near Springfield
May 6th 1861

Dear Father;

Your second letter, dated the 1st of May has just come to hand. I commenced writing you a letter three or four days ago but was interrupted so often that I did not finish it.[1] I wrote one to Mary[2] which no doubt was duly recieved but do not rember whether it answers your questions or not.

At the time our first Galena company was raised I did not feel at liberty to engage in hot haste, but took an active interest in drilling them and emparting all the instruction I could, and at the request of the members of the company, and of Mr. Washburn, I come here for the purpose of assisting for a short time in camp, and, if necessary, my services for the War. The next two days after my arrival it was rainy and muddy so that the troops could not drill and I concluded to go home. Governer Yates heard it and requested me to remain.[3] Since that I have been acting in that capacity, and for the last few days have been in command of this camp.[4] The last of the six Regiments called for from this state will probably leave by to-morrow, or the day following,[5] and then I shall be relieved from this command.

The Legislature of this state provided for the raising of Eleven additional Regiments[6] and a Battalion of Artillery, and a portion of these the Governer will appoint me to muster into the service of the State, when I presume my services may end. I might have got the Colonelcy of a Regiment possibly, but I was perfectly sickened at the political wire pulling for all these commissions and would not engage in it. I shall be no ways backward in offering my services when and where they are required, but I feel that I have done more now than I could do serving as a Capt. under a green Colonel, and if this thing continues they will want more men at a later day.—

There has been full 30,000 more volunteers offered their services than can be accepted under the present call, without including the call made by the state; but I can go back to Galena and drill the three or four companies there and render them efficient for any future call.—My own opinion is that this War will be but of short duration. The Administration has acted moste prudently and sagaciously so far in not bringing on a conflict before it had its forces fully martialed. When they do strike our thoroughly loyal states will be fully protected and a few decisive victories in some of the southern ports will send the secession army howling and the leaders in the rebelion will flee the country. All the states will then be loyal for a generation to come, negroes will depreciate so rapidly in value that no body will want to own them and their masters will be the loudest in their declaimations against the institution in a political and economic view. The nigger will never disturb this country again. The worst that is to be apprehended from him is now; he may revolt and cause more destruction than any Northern man, except it be the ultra abolitionest, wants to see. A Northern army may be required in the next ninety days to go south to suppress a negro insurrection. As much as the South have vilified the North they would go on such a mission and with the purest motives.

I have just recieved a letter from Julia. All are well. Julia takes a very sensible vue of our present difficulties. She would be sorry to have me go but thinks the circumstances may warrent it and will not through a single obsticle in the way.

(There is no doubt but the *valiant* Pillow[7] has been planning an attac on Cairo, but as he will learn that that point is well Garrisoned and they have thei[r] ditch on the out side, filled with watter, he will probably desist. As however he would find it necessary to receive a wound, on the first discharge of fire arm[s] he would not be a formidable enemy. I do not say he would shoot himself, ah no! I am not so uncharitable as many who served under him in Mexico. I think however he might report himself wounded on the receipt of a very slight scratch, recieve[d] hastily in any way and might eritate the sore until he convinced himself that he had been wounded by the enemy.[8])

Tell Simp. that I hope he will be able to visit us this Summer. I should like very much to have him stay with us and I want him to make my house his home.

Remember me to all.

ULYSSES

ALS, PPRF.

1. USG had presumably forgotten that he did finish his letter to his father on May 2, 1861.

2. See letter of April 29, 1861.

3. Governor Richard Yates probably requested USG to remain on the advice of Congressman Elihu B. Washburne. See letter of April 27, 1861.

4. USG replaced Capt. John Pope as commanding officer of Camp Yates probably on May 4. *Richardson*, p. 183; *Galena Advertiser*, May 10, 1861. The *Chicago Tribune*, May 11, 1861, reported that USG had been replaced in command of Camp Yates. On May 8, Yates wrote to Secretary of War Simon Cameron. "I have requested Captain Pope U. S. Army who has completed mustering in the troops of this state called out under the President's Proclamation of April 15th to proceed to Washington and explain to you the condition of affairs in this state and to suggest to you what is considered desirable to be done to render the forces in the field at Cairo and elsewhere most efficient." LS, DLC-Robert T. Lincoln.

5. The 12th Ill. Vols. left Camp Yates for Caseyville on May 10. George L. Paddock, "The Beginnings of an Illinois Volunteer Regiment in 1861," *Military Essays and Recollections* (Chicago, 1891–1907), II, 261.

6. Ten regts. See letter of April 27, 1861, note 3.

7. Gideon J. Pillow of Tenn., former law partner of President James K. Polk, served as maj. gen. of vols. in the Mexican War. His error in having a ditch dug on the wrong side of his own breastworks amused USG considerably. His quarrelsome disposition and military ineptitude won him USG's contempt. *Memoirs*, I, 294, 309. Pillow, then C.S.A. brig. gen. of vols., made no attack on Cairo.

8. During the assault on Chapultepec, Sept. 13, 1847, Pillow's foot had been bruised by a grazing ball; his report stated that he had been "cut down by a grape shot." Charles Winslow Elliott, *Winfield Scott: The Soldier and the Man* (New York, 1937), pp. 544–45; *SED* 30–1–1, p. 404.

To Julia Dent Grant

Camp Yates, May 6th 1861

DEAR JULIA;

There is nothing special to write but you will want to hear often from me during my absence. I too would like to hear from you but so far I have not had the scrape of a pen from you. I presume by Thirsday[1] I shall be on duty in Freeport, mustering in a Regiment there, and if so will be within three hours of Galena and of course will go home. How soon I shall be relieved entirely I do not know. There is no necessity for any volunteers who feel the slightest reluctance about going for already near thirty thousand more have offered their services from this state than can be accepted. There is no doubt but the secessionest contemplated making an attack upon this state but the preperations that have been made here will probably prevent it. We expect here that the next few days will develop a decidedly active policy on the part of the Administration, not perhaps in the way of direct attack, but in stoping all communication with the rebels.

Evrything has been managed most admirably so far in not bringing on a conflict whilst our troops were entirely without drill and totaly unaccustomed to camp life and the proper use of fire arms.—As people from the Southern states are allowed to travel freely through all parts of the North and cannot fail to see the entire unanimity of the people to support the Government, and see their strength in men and means, they must become soon dishartened and lay down their arms. My own opinion is there will be much less bloodshed than is generally anticipated. I believe there will be an attack made on some of the Southern forts and a few decided victories gained when the masses in the south will lay down their arms and the leaders in the rebelion flee to other parts, for their country's good. The worst to be apprehended is from negro revolts. Such would be deeply deplorable and I have no doubt but a Northern army would hasten South to suppress anything of the kind.—Kiss all the children for me. Tell Orvil that when I draw pay here it may be better than our currency, at all events I shall not draw anything until I am relieved, and as I did not bring enough with me to pay my board until my return I shall have to draw for from 10 to 20 dollars, depending upon how long I may have to remain. This place, during its present crouded state is more expensive than New York and living abominable.

Love to all

ULYS.

ALS, DLC-USG.

1. May 9, 1861.

To Julia Dent Grant

ESSEX HOUSE,
GEO. E. VAN SICKLE, PROPRIETOR.
MATTOON, ILLS., May 9th *1861*

DEAR JULIA;

Here I am down in Egipt[1] mustering in a Regiment of Volunteers.[2] Saturday I muster in one at Bellville and next week one at Anna, near Cairo. I think then the Governor will let me go home. I am very well. Your letter directed to Mr. Grant was received the same day I wrote last. I have no time to write much because I want to get off at 10 o'clock so as t[o] [——] Cars for St. Louis and spend the time [——] this until Saturday with your fath[er] [———] a goodeal to do in the mean time.— [———] of your letter never made me [———]

I saw Mary Duncan's be[au] [———] or two. Told him day before yes[terday] [———] heard from his sweet heart who [———] hear from him. Kiss all th[e] [———] papa and have them kiss you [———] me. If you write to me as soon [———] and direct to Anna Ill. I will [———] shall be there next week and r[———] the 18th.

Love to all.

AL, DLC-USG. Approximately a sixth of the sheet, on the lower right, is torn away.

On May 8, 1861, Ill. Asst. AG J. B. Wyman issued General Orders No. 52, addressed to USG. "I am instructed by the Commander-in-Chief to authorize you to proceed to Mattoon Coles Co. and on Thursday May 9th muster into the service of the State under the provisions of the Ten Regiment act ten companies of Volunteers who will report themselves to you, and who are to form the Regiment for the Seventh Congressional District. From thence you will proceed to Belleville, St. Clair Co and on the 11th of May perform the same duty by organizing the Regiment for the eighth Congressional District. From thence you will proceed to Anna, Union Co. and on the 16th of May perform the same duty by organizing the Regiment for the ninth Congressional District. You will find enclosed the proclamation of the Commander in Chief which will be your guide in the performance of these, your duties." Copy, AG Letterbook, I-ar.

1. The term "Egypt" describing southern Ill. usually refers to an area south of a line from St. Louis, Mo., to Vincennes, Ind. Mattoon is at least fifty miles north of this line.

2. The 7th Congressional District Regt. was not ready for muster. USG went to St. Louis and returned to Mattoon on May 14.

To Julia Dent Grant

———

Wish-ton-Wish
May 10th 1861

Dear Julia;

You see by the above that I am writing from your old home.[1] Your father is in the room, absorbed in his paper. Lewis Sheets[2] is fixing a segarita to smoke and Aunt Fanny[3] is seting by me busy with her work. All are well. Soon your father & Lewis Sheets will be left to themselvs at the mercy of Mary[4] and the rest of the darkeys. Aunt Fanny is going back to Ohio and will start in a few days. John[5] is staying at Bill Barnards[6] and only comes out here occationaly. I believe he thinks of a colonelcy in the secession army. Your father says he is for the Union but is opposed to having army to sustain it. He would have a secession force march where they please uninterupted and is really what I would call a secessionest. Aunt Fanny is strong for the Union and is distressed that your father is not so also. Great numbers of people are leaving St. Louis and Missouri generally. There are two armies now occupying the city, hostile to each other, and I fear there is great danger of a conflict which, if commenced must terminate in great blood shed and destruction of property without advancing the cause of either party.

I called on Mrs. Barrett a few minuets this morning. ~~Her~~ She and children are well. She says that she will write to you and let you hear from home if you will answer her letters.—Nelly[7] has another little girl. Emma[8] is with her and talks of going up to see you. Your father has given up all notion of going up but I will try and perswade him to change his mind. He is bothered about his June payment to Mitchel: The latter has told him that he must have his money.—I advize to throw the matter into the courts under the Usury laws and stave it off as long as possible.— Sam. Sale[9] is back here and it is said is courting his old wife who has a divorce. His sister-in-law is also back. Miss Enas Pipkins is married to young Poindexter[10] and has gone to California. Jo Pipkins (dont read this out loud) became intimate with a Dutch girl in the neighborhood who was so sensitive to infection as to become a mother without any ceremony from Preacher or Squire. Jo sent her to the city and kept her there for some time but tiring of the seperation he took occation one day, when in the city, to take her some place and have the not tied which made them one, and the heir all right—In the evening he returned bringing his bride with him and the old lady flare up, as you can imagine, and put them both out of the house. All the other neighbors are about as when we left with exception of the changes we have heard of from time to time.

Old Man Rush is still living at White Haven. Does not make enough to pay his rent. White[11] paid $150 00 on his interest. That and the rent of our house in town and the hire of the negroes I expect helps your father very much. He requires them all. He still has Brooks idyling about. Old Bob, Bon, the Mules Dun colt and now another colt are still roaming at large.

As soon as I get through this letter I am going to leave and will carry the letter with me and mail it. To-morrow I have to be in Belleville. I understand the Regiment to be mustered in there cannot possibly be there so I will have to return again.[12] I have to go back to Mattoon on Monday and on Thursday be at Anna, near Cairo, so that probably it will be about Saturday week[13] before I get back again to Belleville. Once through there and I hope there will be no further need of me. Tell Orvil that he need not be surprised if I should have to draw again for some money, because paying for my meals, and tobacco, (I have not spent a dollar otherwise and have gone without my dinner sometimes to save four bits) takes a goodeal. It will all be made up to me when I start home.

Kiss all the children for me. I think of nothing more that I heard here to write to you.—Aunt Fanny is going to Ohio in company with Jeff Sappington and wife.[14]

Your Husband
U. S.

Since coming into the city I find about 4000. Union troops marching out to the secession encampment to break it up. I very much fear bloodshed.[15]

ALS, DLC-USG.

1. The Grant family had lived at Wish-ton-wish in 1855–56. See letter of May 3, 1861, note 2.

2. See letter of April 19, 1861, note 7.

3. Frederick Dent's sister Frances had married a man named Gwinn. Harry Wright Newman, *The Maryland Dents* (Richmond, 1963), p. 70. It is not certain that she is the "Aunt Fanny" discussed.

4. Mary Robinson was a slave owned by the Dents. *Lewis*, p. 104; J. L. Ringwalt, *Anecdotes of General Ulysses S. Grant* (Philadelphia, 1886), pp. 26–27.

5. John Dent, brother-in-law of USG. See letter of May 15, 1861.

6. William D. W. Barnard of St. Louis, a friend of USG, was connected with the Dent family through his wife, whose two sisters had married sons of Frederick Dent. *PUSG*, 1, 342. John Dent was his brother-in-law. Barnard lived in St. Louis on Merrimac Street at the intersection of Stringtown Road.

7. Ellen (Nellie) Dent Sharp, sister-in-law of USG.

8. Emily (Emma) Dent Casey, sister-in-law of USG, had married James F. Casey on Feb. 14, 1861.

9. Probably Waller Semple Sale, son of Judge Joseph Sale of the Gravois area. He married, successively, Katherine and Martha Ferris. Genealogical notes, Sale Family Papers, MoSHi.

10. Phoebe Jane Sale, daughter of Judge Joseph Sale, married Enos Pipkin. Phil and Tom Poindexter, stepsons of Judge Sale by his second marriage, married two of his granddaughters. *Ibid.*

11. In 1859, Joseph W. White had acquired USG's Hardscrabble property in exchange for a house and two lots in St. Louis, and a note for $3,000. White's mortgage on the St. Louis property was secured by a deed of trust on Hardscrabble. When White was unable to meet his obligations, USG lost the St. Louis property, but eventually recovered Hardscrabble after litigation ending in 1867. *PUSG*, 1, 353; papers in the case of Ulysses S. Grant and Julia B. Grant vs. Joseph W. White, Circuit Court, Twenty-second Judicial Circuit of Missouri, St. Louis, Mo.

12. USG did muster in the 8th Congressional District Regt. on May 11, 1861.

13. Saturday, May 18.

14. Thomas Jefferson Sappington (1832–97), son of John Sappington, farmed in the Gravois area.

15. On May 10, Capt. Nathaniel Lyon led a force of a few regular troops and several regts. of home guards organized by Representative Francis P. Blair, Jr., to capture Mo. militia commanded by Brig. Gen. Daniel M. Frost at Camp Jackson. Lyon believed, correctly, that Mo. Governor Claiborne Jackson had assembled the militia originally to seize munitions in the U.S. Arsenal, and that the purpose of the encampment on the western edge of St. Louis was to further the secession of Mo. Confused by the legal ambiguities of his position and aware of the superiority of Lyon's forces, Frost surrendered without forcible resistance. *O.R.*, I, iii, 4–8; *ibid.*, II, i, 107–16. While the militia were marching as prisoners under guard from Camp Jackson to the U.S. Arsenal, spectators began a riot which resulted in twenty-eight deaths. William E. Parrish, *Turbulent Partnership: Missouri and the Union, 1861–1865* (Columbia, Mo., 1963), p. 24. In the morning, USG had gone to the arsenal as the troops were leaving, introduced himself to Blair, and expressed "sympathy with his purpose." *Memoirs*, I, 235. USG later returned to watch the prisoners marched to the arsenal. *Ibid.*, I, 236; *Young*, II, 468.

According to Augustus L. Chetlain, USG had visited St. Louis hoping to secure military employment through Lyon. *Recollections of Seventy Years* (Galena, 1899), p. 76; "Recollections of General U. S. Grant, 1861–1863," *Military Essays and Recollections* (Chicago, 1891–1907), I, 15–16.

Orders

Head Quarters
Regt 7th Consl Dist
May 14th 1861

ORDERS

An Election for one Colonel one Lieutenat Colonl and one Major for the 7th Congressional District Regiment of Illinois Volunteers Militia will take place at this camp to-morrow the 15th ~~day~~ of May commencing at 1 o clock P. M. The Election will be by ballot each ballot bearing the names of Candidates for Colonel Lieutenant and Major. Capts J Love J E Calloway and J. P. H. Stevenson are appointed Judges of Election. The will cause Poll Lists to be opened and appoint necessary clerks. The Election will be held at the Officers Quarters

U. S. GRANT
Acting Mustering Officer

Copy, Records of 21st Ill., I-ar. USG wrote this order at the Coles County Fairgrounds, about one mile northeast of Mattoon. The three judges, John Love of
Sullivan, Moultrie County; James E. Calloway of Tuscola, Douglas County; and
Jesse P. H. Stevenson of Paradise, Cumberland County, had already been elected
capts. by the vols. In the election, Simon S. Goode, city clerk of Decatur, Macon
County, who had already been elected a capt., was elected col. with 466 votes to
392 for Thomas A. Apperson. John W. S. Alexander of Paris, Edgar County, was,
elected lt. col. with 468 votes; and Warren E. McMackin of Salem, Clay County,
was elected maj. with 332 votes. Tally sheet, *ibid.* The judges compiled a list of
voters or poll book of the 879 vols. voting which they certified as correct. Below
their certification USG wrote: "I certify that the above judges were duly detailed,
and sworn, by me." AES, *ibid.*

   USG left the camp after the election and returned to his hotel in Mattoon to
wait for his train, thus missing the speeches made by the newly elected officers to
their men. *Garland*, p. 166; letter of "Orion," May 16, 1861, in *Missouri Democrat*
May 20, 1861. The following day, the camp was named Camp Grant. *Ibid.; Mattoon Gazette*, May 17, 1861.

To Julia Dent Grant

————

Camp Near Mattoon
May 15th 1861

DEAR JULIA;

   I am now nearly through at this place and will get away to-
morrow for Anna, a town about forty miles from Cairo. As I will
then be where it may be impracticable to draw any money, and as
I do not expect to be back for two weeks[1] and have not got
sufficient money to pay my board for that time, I shall draw for
about $15 00 before leaving here. Tell Orvil of this. I enjoy first
rate health and am geting a fine opportunity of seeing a greatdeel
of this very fine state. It is truly an empire within itself. I am
more out of the way of War news here than you are and of course
can give you nothing in that way. You have seen from the papers
that they had terrible times in St. Louis the day I wrote you from
there.[2] The statements given in St. St. Louis Herald were not
strictly, though substantially correct. The troops did not fire
until they had been grossly abused and fired upon and two or
three of their number killed besides some wounded.[3] I staid at

Lynches that night. St. Louis is said now to be restored to perfect quiet. It is truly a deserted city. I noticed in going through that about three stores in four were unoccupied. How different that from what it was a few years ago when it was so difficult to get a place.[4]—I have received two letters from father[5] and one from Mary since leaving Galena. They are no ways alarmed for their safety. Mary would like but does not expect to be able to visit Galena this Summer.—One piece of news I forgot to mention in writing from St. Louis! William Gibson[6] died two or three weeks ago.

I begin to want to see you and the children very much. Little Jesse does he talk any about his pa. Two weeks now is the earlyest day now that I set for geting back to Galena. I have tickets to carry around by St. Louis again if I choose to go that way but I think I shall not go.—Tell Mary Duncan that I spent last Saturday night at Caseyville,[7] Illinois, seven miles East of St. Louis, where her beaux is stationed. He professes not to be tired of the War and looks well. He wanted to send his love I know but he is modest and only told me to remember him &c.

If you write to me when you receive this, promptly direct to Anna, if you put it off for a few days direct to Springfield.—I hope by this time you feel as loyal to the Union as Aunt Fanny[8] does. As I told you your father professes to be a Union man yet condemns evry measure for the preservation of the Union. He says he is ruined and I fear it is too true. He says no money can be borrowed there and Mitchel will listen to no arrangement. I advised him to raise the plea of Usury and get it into the Courts and contest the thing, if possible, until times mend. He will do it. As I come to St. Louis I stoped at Barnards to see John & Amanda[9] and sent my name up and waited until I got tired and as no body come down I retired, leaving word however that I expected to be back. John was out however. Your father says he will take a Regiment. I would advise him to let it alone. Secession has met its last success and a few months will see the bigest stampede of political Refugees from this country that the world ever witnessed. He might find himself one of the *N. R* s, (you remember the joke) without the capacity to turn his position to account. He had better keep cool and claim to have always been for the Union.

To say so little I have written you a long letter. Remember me to all our friends, relations. Kiss the children for me and accept a dozen for yourself.

ULYS.

ALS, DLC-USG.

1. USG was back in Galena on May 24, 1861.
2. See letter of May 10, 1861.
3. *Ibid.*
4. In 1859, USG had been a partner in a real estate firm in St. Louis. *PUSG,* 1, 345–47.
5. See letters of May 2, 6, 1861.
6. See *PUSG,* 1, 357.
7. On Saturday, May 11, USG had mustered in the 8th Congressional District Regt. at Belleville, Ill. He probably went to Caseyville, about ten miles north of Belleville, in order to make railroad connections with Mattoon. While in Caseyville, he visited the 12th Ill., Co. F of which was composed of the former Jo Daviess Guards. Augustus L. Chetlain, *Recollections of Seventy Years* (Galena, 1899), p. 76; Thomas J. McCormack, ed., *Memoirs of Gustave Koerner, 1809–1896* (Cedar Rapids, 1909), II, 146.
8. See letter of May 10, 1861.
9. *Ibid.*

To Julia Dent Grant

Anna, Ill.
May 21st 1861

DEAR JULIA;

I am through at this place[1] and will leave in about one hour for Cairo, where I shall only remain until evening. I will then return to Springfield when I may be released from further duty. I am not however by any means certain of that for I know that I have been applied for for other service.[2] I will write you again on Thirsday[3] if I am not at home. I might about as well volunteered in the first instance as to be detained the way I have and then I should have got the Colonelcy of a Regt. However my services have been quite as valuable, I presume the state thinks, as if I had been at the head of a Regt. and the duties are much more pleasant to me.—I have been ~~disagreeably~~ disappointed in the people of Egypt. It is the prevailing opinion abroad that the people of this section of the State are ignorant, disloyal, intemperate and generally heathenish. The fact is the Regt. formed here is the equal, if not the superior, of any of the Regiments raised in the State, for all the virtues of which they are charged with being deficient. I have had no letter from you here but expect to find one at Springfield when I get there. I am anxious to hear from you and the children as well as see you. Somehow though I feel as if I was in for the War and cannot divest myself of the feeling. I will not go though for a position which I look upon as inferior to that of Col. of a Regt. and will not seek that. How much soever I might deem it my duty to give my services at this time I do not feel that the obligation, at present, calls for me to accept a lower position.—I see Jo Reynolds[4] is in with the Indiana Volunteers. I do not expect to see Emma at Cairo but presume Jim. is there.[5] My stay will be but about five hours there and my duties will occupy about half that time.

I hope you are geting along happily without me. I presume the last crash among the banks[6] has startled Orvil. I expected it to come and when they wrote me that business was dull and collections ditto I was glad of it. No debts can be paid with the money they are geting and there is no use holding the depreciated stuff. Kiss the children for me and give my love to all our relations.

ULYS.

ALS, DLC-USG.

1. USG had mustered in the 9th Congressional District Regt., later the 18th Ill., at Anna. In addition to the usual duties of mustering in the vols. and supervising the election of field officers, USG became involved in the problem created when more men than authorized offered their services. On May 16, 1861, the Ill. AGO sent a telegram to Anna. "No company can be accepted from Johnson Co—

the compliment is full without it—The company from Union is accepted—Full instructions to Capt Grant by letter of yesterday—" Copy, Records of 18th Ill., I-ar. On May 17, USG telegraphed to 1st Asst. AG John B. Wyman. "No compromise between Capts. Marks & Cormick. Marks' company is in camp; the other is disbanded but would be here the officer says tomorrow night if accepted. Can rifles be be furnished two (2) cos.? There is fine material here to use them. Answer." Telegram received (punctuation added), *ibid*. On May 18, Ill. Auditor Jesse K. Dubois telegraphed to Governor Richard Yates. "I have just received this despatch: 'Capt. Markes' Company is here and ought to be accepted. S. F. McCrellis.' I am satisfied to have it done. Answer." Telegram received, *ibid*. The regt. as finally organized contained the cos. commanded by Joseph T. Cormick of Centralia and Samuel B. Marks of Anna, and no co. from Johnson County.

2. On May 20, Col. Michael K. Lawler of the 9th Congressional District Regt. wrote to Ill. AG Thomas S. Mather. "I desire the assistance of Capt. U. S. Grant, in drilling the Regiment, and will be under obligation to the Governor if he will cause him to return here for a short time." LS, *ibid*. It is not certain, however, that this is the "other service" USG mentions. In any case, USG was not assigned to Anna, and returned to Galena from Springfield.

3. May 23.

4. Col. Joseph Jones Reynolds of Ind., USMA 1843, was then commanding the 10th Ind. While a professor at Washington University, St. Louis, in 1859, Reynolds had endorsed USG's application for St. Louis County engineer. *PUSG*, 1, 348n–49n.

5. On Feb. 14, 1861, Emma Dent, sister-in-law of USG, had married James F. Casey.

6. See letter of May 2, 1861, note 3.

To Col. Thomas S. Mather

General Head Quarters—State of Illinois.
Adjutant General's Office,
~~Springfield,~~
Camp Near Anna Ill. May 22d *1861*.

Col. T. S. Mather
Adj. Gen I.V.M.
Springfield Ill.
Sir:

Enclosed find Muster Rolls & Election returns for the Regt. of Ill. Vol. Militia mustered into state service at this place.

Where certificates of election of Comp.y officers do not accompany the Muster Roll they have been sent direct to your office.

Very Respectfully
Your Obt. Svt.
U. S. GRANT
Mustering Officer

ALS, Records of 18th Ill., I-ar. In conducting elections for the 9th Congressional
District Regt., USG apparently followed the procedure used at Mattoon. See
Orders of May 14, 1861. Three capts., James Baird of Pinckneyville, Wilson M.
Cooper of Fairfield, and George R. Fitch of Edwards County, were appointed
judges, and two clerks were also appointed. On May 20, 1861, all five swore to
perform their duties "according to Law and the best of our abilities," and USG
witnessed their signatures. DS, Records of 18th Ill., I-ar. The judges later reported that Michael K. Lawler of Gallatin County had been elected col. with 624
votes to 304 for his opponent, Stephen G. Hicks; Thomas H. Burgess of Du Quoin
was elected lt. col. with 684 votes to 244 for T. M. Heite; Samuel Eaton was
elected maj. with 211 votes in a field of six. *Ibid.*

To Bvt. Brig. Gen. Lorenzo Thomas

Galena,¹ Ill.
May 24th 1861

COL. L. THOMAS,
ADJT. GEN. U.S.A.
WASHINGTON D.C.
SIR:

Having served for fifteen years in the regular army, including
four years at West Point, and feeling it the duty of evry one who
has been educated at the Government expense to offer their
services for the support of that Government, I have the honor,
very respectfully, to tender my services, until the close of the
War, in such capacity as may be offered. I would say that in view
of my present age, and length of service, I feel myself competent
to command a Regiment if the President, in his judgement, should
see fit to entrust one to me.²

Since the first call of the President I have been serving on the Staff of the Governer of this state rendering such aid as I could in the organization of our state Militia, and am still engaged in that capacity.[3] A letter addressed to me at Springfield Ill. will reach me.

> I am very Respectfully
> Your Obt. Svt.
> U. S. GRANT

ALS, DNA, RG 94, ACP 4754/1885. *O.R.*, III, i, 234. Bvt. Brig. Gen. Lorenzo Thomas of Del., USMA 1823, had been promoted to AG on March 7, 1861, following the resignation of Col. Samuel Cooper. "This letter failed to elicit an answer from the Adjutant-General of the Army. I presume it was hardly read by him, and certainly it could not have been submitted to higher authority. Subsequent to the war General Badeau having heard of this letter applied to the War Department for a copy of it. The letter could not be found and no one recollected ever having seen it. I took no copy when it was written. Long after the application of General Badeau, General Townsend, who had become Adjutant-General of the Army, while packing up papers preparatory to the removal of his office, found this letter in some out-of-the-way place. It had not been destroyed, but it had not been regularly filed away." *Memoirs*, I, 240. Clerical markings on the back of the letter indicate that it was prepared for regular filing by the AGO, although it was not registered until 1876. On Dec. 19, 1876, AG Edward D. Townsend prepared an official copy of the letter for USG. An official copy of this date is in RPB.

1. USG had drawn his pay in Springfield the previous day. See letter of May 1, 1861, note 3.
2. At this point, all cols. of vol. regts. were appointed through the states, and the only regts. for which President Abraham Lincoln could appoint cols. were the regulars. On May 3, Lincoln had directed "that the regular army of the United States be increased by the addition of eight regiments of infantry, one regiment of cavalry, and one regiment of artillery . . ." Lincoln, *Works*, IV, 353.
3. On June 26, USG signed a warrant for $100.80 "for 24 days actual service as acting aid to Governer, as Mustering officer @ $4.20 per day—" DS, Auditor's Receipt Book, I-ar. This means that USG remained in state service May 24–June 16. Since there is no record of services performed by USG for the state in this period, his appointment may represent the method used by Governor Richard Yates to keep him available for service.

To Jesse Root Grant

———

Galena, May 30th 1861

DEAR FATHER;

I have now been home near a week but return to Springfield to-day. I have tendered my services to the Government[1] and go to-day to make myself useful, if possible, from this until all our national difficulties are ended. During the six days I have been at home I have felt all the time as if a duty was being neglected that was paramount to any other duty I ever owed. I have evry reason to be well satisfied with myself for the services already rendered but to stop now would not do.

All here are well. Orvil or Lank will write to you in a day or two and tell you how business matters stand. Write to me at Springfield.

Yours Truly
U. S. GRANT

ALS, PPRF.

1. See letter of May 24, 1861.

To Julia Dent Grant

———

Springfield June 1st / 61

DEAR JULIA;

I arrived here last evening and was some what disappointed at finding that the Governer had not yet returned from Washington. What I may do I can not yet know but on my arrival here I find that I had been spoken of for the Colonelcy of a Regiment now partly made up.[1] In a few days all will be determined and then I will either go home to stay or will know what I am to do.

I am thinking a little of going down to St. Louis tonight and spend until Teusday[2] with your father but have not fully determined. Next week, if I can, I want to get ordered to Cincinnati to visit them[3] there but do not know that I shall succeed. There is nothing to write about from here so you must be satisfied with a short letter. I found a letter here from you, one that had not arrived when I left. Kiss the [children] for me and accept the same for your[self. Tell] Mary Duncan that I do not know [——] shall see Mr. King[4] soon. I would have taken th[e] kiss she was going to send but you were looking. Was not that clever in me to abstain. I will write again in a few days. On the other half page I will write a few lines to Mr. Felt[5] which I wish you would tear off and send to him.

ULYS.

ALS, DLC-USG.

1. This regt. has not been identified. It is not unlikely, however, that the dissatisfaction in the 7th Congressional District Regt. at Mattoon was already known in Springfield and that plans were already underway which would culminate two weeks later in USG's appointment as col.
2. Tuesday, June 4, 1861.
3. USG refers to his parents in Covington, Ky.
4. See letter of May 3, 1861, note 5.
5. Lewis S. Felt, a partner with his brother, Benjamin F. Felt, in a wholesale grocery concern in Galena.

To Julia Dent Grant

———

Springfield, June 6th / 61

DEAR JULIA;

I am still here and uncertain about what I shall do. The Governor has just returned and as I have had nothing to do in his absence I might just as well be at home up to this time. It is probable now that I shall be ordered to the South part of the state[1] for a few days but will be back here ~~probably~~ again. There

is no special news from here. All the War news we get would
rather indicate that the South have determined to risk the success
of their cause to one or two grand battles and then settle our
difficulties. The question is being continually asked, What is
Government going to do? Of course the plans of the Administration are not known outside of their own circle but it looks to
me as if the determination was strong to take possession of
Eastern Virginia and Memphis Tennessee[2] this Summer. Further
I do not believe troops will be carried during the hot months.
Of course circumstances may compell a further movement.

How do you all get on? I hope you will content yourself
without me for I may be absent for several months this time, or
may be back in a week, there is no telling. If I take a regiment
however I shall try and go home for a few days. I should like
very much to go to Covington[3] for a few days if I can manage it
but fear I shall not be able to do it. If I should remain absent however I will send you money to take you and the children there if
you feel like making the visit during the vacation. It is hard for
me to fill up a sheet with anything that would interest you. I hear
or see nothing but matters pertaining to the Military; do not go
out any or visit even other hotels than the one I stop at.

Kiss all the children for me. Does Jesse talk about me? The
little rascal I would like to see him. I hope you are all well and
enjoying yourselvs. Kisses for yourself. Write to me soon.

ULYS.

ALS, DLC-USG.

1. USG may refer to an assignment to Cairo at the southernmost tip of the
state where most of the Ill. vols. were stationed, or he may refer to the request of
Col. Michael K. Lawler that he drill the 9th Congressional District Regt. See
letter of May 21, 1861, note 2.
2. The advance in eastern Va. ended with Union defeat at First Bull Run,
July 21, 1861. Memphis, Tenn., remained in Confederate hands until June 6,
1862.
3. See letter of June 1, 1861.

To Julia Dent Grant

Covington, June 10th / 61

DEAR JULIA;

I arrived here yesterday, Sunday, morning and found all well except Simp.[1] He seems as well as could be expected but yet a change is visable in the last year. His face is begining to wear a pinched appearance. Mother and him will probably be out to see you next week.—I am going over to the city to-day with Mary to make some calls and to see some of the military there,[2] and to-morrow Simp. and myself will go out to Camp Dennison. I shall not be able to go to Georgetown[3] this trip as I am liable to be telegraphed any day to return to Springfield, and must return by Saturday. Mary would like very much to go out and spend the Summer with you but it is hardly probable that she and mother will both go.

This town, like St. Louis, is a greatdeelly deserted city, but Union sentiments prevail almost unanimously. I called yesterday on Col. Whistler.[4] Mrs. Whistler was so unwell that she could not see me. The Col. is geting quite infirm. Louisa[5] is there looking well. She has been fed on Government pap all her life, since marriage as well as before, and now she would like to see that Government broken up. Such is human nature.

I will write to Orvil to-morrow and give him what they say here. Father thinks it is a necessity that he should go out this Summer.[6] Simp. says that he has as much time to read the papers here as he would have there and had better remain, because he can get them earlier. I think he will be overruled and will remain at home.

Strawberries have been selling here two quarts for 5 cts and evry thing in proportion. It only takes about 10 cts. to buy two days marketing of peas, cucumbers, lettuce, strawberries radishes &c. They had a big mess of green peas on the table yesterday for dinner, so many that quite a dishfull was left and set on the table at supper, and Clara informed me (I dont know that any other member of the family would have been thoughtful enough to have reminded me of the fact) that the whole cost two cents. They are without a girl again. They have only been without a few days however.

The very day I mailed my last letter to you I received yours saying that Jess. had had an attack of croup. I did not feel much al+armed however as you wrote the last of your letter the next morning after and said that he was better. Poor little fellow I hope he is well. Tell him that his pa will try and come and see him soon. Kiss all the children for me and accept the same for yourself.

ULYS.

ALS, DLC-USG.

1. For earlier comment on the health of USG's brother, Samuel Simpson Grant, see letter to Mary Grant, April 29, 1861.
2. "Having but little to do after the muster of the last of the regiments authorized by the State legislature, I asked and obtained of the governor leave of absence for a week to visit my parents in Covington, Kentucky, immediately opposite Cincinnati. General McClellan had been made a major-general and had his headquarters at Cincinnati. In reality I wanted to see him. I had known him slightly at West Point, where we served one year together, and in the Mexican war. I was in hopes that when he saw me he would offer me a position on his staff. I called on two successive days at his office but failed to see him on either occasion, and returned to Springfield." *Memoirs*, I, 241. Maj. Gen. George B. McClellan later explained that USG may have visited his office while he was inspecting troops in Indianapolis. "[*Randolph B.*] Marcy or Seth Williams saw him and told him that if he would await my return, doubtless I would do something for him; but before I got back he was telegraphed that he could have a regiment in Illinois, and at once returned thither, so that I did not see him. This was his good luck; for had I been there I would no doubt have given him a place on my staff, and he would probably have remained with me and shared my fate." George B. McClellan, *McClellan's Own Story* (New York, 1887), p. 47. USG did not learn of his Ill. appointment, however, until he had left Cincinnati. It seems implausible that nobody at McClellan's hd. qrs. would tell USG that he was out of town. In another place USG makes it clear that he was told the opposite. *Young*, II, 214–15.

A Cincinnati newspaper reported that McClellan left for Cairo, Ill., on the evening of Wednesday, June 12, 1861, went from Cairo to St. Louis on June 14, and returned to Cincinnati on June 17. *Cincinnati Enquirer*, June 13, 16, 18, 1861. McClellan was in Springfield, Ill., on June 15, visited Camp Yates, and "expressed his satisfaction at the military proficiency of the troops there encamped, under the command of Col. Goode." *Illinois State Register*, June 17, 1861. This was doubly ironic because the disorganization of the regt. led to USG's appointment as col. The conflicting accounts of USG's visit to McClellan's office cannot be reconciled without definite information about the dates of these visits. USG's letter does indicate that he may have planned a visit on June 11, when McClellan was still in town.

3. Carr B. White later recalled that USG had visited his boyhood home of Georgetown, Ohio, at this time. *Garland*, p. 168.

4. Col. William Whistler commanded the 4th Inf. from July 15, 1845, until his retirement on Oct. 9, 1861. USG served at the same post with him at Detroit and Sackets Harbor, N.Y., 1849–52.

5. The daughter of Col. and Mrs. William Whistler.

6. This is probably another reference to the banking crisis. See letter of May 2, 1861, note 3.

To Julia Dent Grant

Springfield, June 17th 1861

DEAR JULIA;

At last I am back at this place after a very pleasant visit at home. I found all well except Simp. who is geting gradually weaker evry day. He and either father or mother will be out before many days. Simp. will make his home with you during his stay.—You have probably seen that I have been appointed to a Colonelcy?[1] My Regiment is stationed at this place for the present but will go into summer encampment near Quincy[2] probably next week. I shall be at home in four or five days after you receive this[3] so this will be my last letter before you see me. Tell Orvil that I am compelled to keep a horse now and want him to keep his eyes open from now until I get home and see if he can get his eye on a good one for me. I would prefer buying about Galena if I can.[4] I would like to bring Fred. & Buck[5] down to Quincy with me to spend about a month of their vacation if you will let them come. If you conclude to you had better get them some clothes ready for I shall only remain at home two days when I go. It seems to be thought that the Regiments that are now going into camp will be left until the Fall frosts. This however cannot be calculated upon. I spent Sunday in Lafayette with Jo Reynolds.[6] Mrs. Reynolds enquired very particularly about you. Jo has just the nicest family of brothers you ever saw. Jo is off soldiering too but one peg higher[7] than I am. That is he is likely to be. Up to now his position has been just the same.

Kiss the children for their pa and accept the same for yourself.

ULYS.

ALS, DLC-USG.

1. On June 15, 1861, by executive order, Governor Richard Yates appointed USG to command the 7th Congressional District Regt. which USG had mustered into state service one month earlier at Mattoon. Executive Register, I-ar; *Chicago Tribune,* June 16, 1861; *Illinois State Journal, Illinois State Register,* June 17, 1861. The *Illinois State Journal* referred to former Col. Simon S. Goode as "acting Colonel." The *Chicago Tribune* stated that Goode had been "deposed," and that Yates was "acting under the instructions of the War Department in the business." AGO General Orders No. 15, May 4, 1861, stated that "The field officers of the Regiment will be appointed by the Governor of the State which furnishes the Regiment." Congress later provided, July 22, 1861, that governors would commission field, staff, and company officers of new regts. of vols., and that vacancies above the rank of capt. would be filled by vote of the commissioned officers of the regt. The latter provision was repealed by Congress, Aug. 6, 1861, in favor of appointment by the governor. *U.S. Statutes at Large,* XII, 269–70, 318. Under the terms of the Ill. act providing for raising the regt., the col. was to be elected by the vols. *Laws of the State of Illinois, Passed by the Twenty-Second General Assembly, at its Extraordinary Session, Convened April 23, 1861* (Springfield, 1861), p. 15. The legislature, however, provided that the vols. were to be in state service for one month; the 7th Congressional District Regt. was mustered into state service by USG on May 15, and exactly one month later a new col. was appointed. If Yates had been waiting for the expiration of the month state enlistment this would explain intimations in earlier USG letters of an impending commission. In any case, the normal expectation of the vols. was that they would enter U.S. service under the col. they had elected, and USG's appointment by Yates can only be explained in terms of the peculiarly demoralized state of the regt.

The regt. was encamped on the eighty acres of the Coles County Fairgrounds, housed in structures referred to as stalls or sheds which were in constant danger of catching fire from the stoves used for heat. It was several days before the first blankets arrived and a week later before the first muskets appeared— enough for half the men. There were no uniforms at all. Letters of "Orion," May 16, 24, 31, 1861, in *Missouri Democrat,* May 20, 27, June 3, 1861; *Mattoon Gazette,* May 24, 30, 1861; Col. Simon S. Goode to AG Thomas S. Mather, June 8, 1861, Records of 21st Ill., I-ar.

Goode, formerly city clerk of Decatur, had no military experience except service in a Central American filibustering expedition. Goode carried three revolvers and a bowie knife, tried to convince his men that he never slept, and once made a speech to the regt. proposing to challenge Jefferson Davis to a field fight with an equal number of men on each side and Davis to have the choice of ground. Goode soon lost the confidence of the other officers. *Garland,* p. 165;

Mattoon Gazette, May 24, 1861; letter of "Orion," May 31, 1861, in *Missouri Democrat*, June 3, 1861.

Goode was also unable to maintain discipline. The vols. frequently tunneled under the wooden fence at night for drunken carousing in Mattoon and foraging raids on neighboring farms. When Goode attempted to enforce discipline, the vols. burned the guardhouse and staged a bread riot. Goode vacillated between expecting too much of his men (as when he ordered drill daily from 8:30 A.M. to 11:00 A.M. and from 2:00 P.M. to 5:00 P.M.) and too little (as when he joined the men assigned to guard duty one night in a visit to a tavern). The unruly behavior of the officers and men soon outraged the authorities of nearby Mattoon, while the AGO in Springfield received ominous reports of desertion. The final blow to morale came when the vols. learned that they would be expected to enlist for three years instead of the ninety days they had originally anticipated. *Mattoon Gazette*, May 24, 30, June 7, 14, 1861; letters of "Orion," May 24, 31, 1861, in *Missouri Democrat*, May 27, June 3, 1861; Philip Welshimer to wife, June 6, 1861, *USGA Newsletter*, IV, 1 (Oct., 1966), 2; Records of 21st Ill., I-ar; DNA, RG 94, 21st Ill., Order Book; *Memoirs*, I, 243; *Garland*, p. 169.

On June 14, the regt. left Mattoon for Springfield. The vols. were unruly on the train and a Springfield newspaper noted that they needed "more proficiency in drill." *Jonesboro Gazette*, June 29, 1861; *Illinois State Journal*, June 15, 1861. One officer later recalled that all the commissioned officers in a conference with Yates had decided by vote on USG for their new col. *Garland*, pp. 169–70; *New-York Tribune*, Sept. 27, 1885. Yates stated only that he had appointed USG after consultation with Auditor Jesse K. Dubois and 2nd Asst. AG John S. Loomis. Richard Yates and Catharine Yates Pickering, *Richard Yates: Civil War Governor* (Danville, Ill., 1966), p. 205. USG's appointment was generally believed necessary to encourage the men to enlist for three years and received favorable newspaper comment. *Chicago Tribune*, June 16, 1861; *Illinois State Register*, June 19, 1861; *Galena Advertiser*, June 18, 19, 1861; *Mattoon Gazette*, June 22, 1861.

No documentary evidence has been found substantiating an account that about the same time USG received a commission from Yates he received an offer to command the 12th Ohio from Governor William Dennison. *Galena Advertiser*, June 20, 1861; *Garland*, p. 169; *Chicago Tribune*, Nov. 8, 1885. All of the original field officers of the 12th Ohio were friends of USG. Col. John W. Lowe of Xenia, Ohio, had corresponded with him during the Mexican War. *PUSG*, 1, 94–98, 135–37. Lt. Col. Jacob Ammen was the son of David Ammen, publisher of *The Castigator* in Georgetown, Ohio. Maj. Carr B. White, a boyhood friend of USG, was the son of John D. White, USG's schoolmaster in Georgetown. Competition between Lowe and Ammen for command caused trouble in the regt. in spring, 1861, until Governor Dennison transferred Ammen to command of the 24th Ohio. Diary of Jacob Ammen, June 22, 1861, IHi; Carl M. Becker, "John W. Lowe: Failure in Inner-Direction," *Ohio History*, 73, 2 (Spring, 1964), 84. Lowe continued as col. of the 12th Ohio until killed at the battle of Carnifix Ferry, Sept. 10, 1861.

2. The regt. did not leave for Quincy, Ill., until July 3.

3. USG left Springfield on June 21. Letter of "Orion," June 30, 1861, in *Missouri Democrat*, July 4, 1861.

4. During USG's trip to Galena he borrowed money from E. A. Collins, his father's partner in the leather business, 1840–53, to purchase a horse and other equipment. "One of the many absurdly false stories relating to Grant, which have

become part of popular tradition, is that when he was made colonel he did not have the means with which to purchase a horse and accoutrements, and that his father having refused to give him the money he was compelled to borrow it of a friend, whom he never repaid. The truth is that the outfit could not advantageously be bought without the gold, which could not be obtained short of the bank. He accordingly gave his note indorsed by E. A. Collins and Samuel Hughlette [*Hughlett*], and receiving the specie purchased with it a horse of John C. Calderwood, in this city, and other necessaries demanded by his position. The note was paid in full some time before it became due, the money having been sent by Grant to his friend, Major Rowley, for that purpose. Your correspondent has been shown the letter of instruction written by Grant while at Cairo." *New York Evening Telegram,* Aug. 8, 1885. John C. Collins, son of E. A. Collins, later recalled that USG had stated that his father and brother Orvil refused to loan him the money and that E. A. Collins had endorsed a note for $500 since he had frequently advanced money to USG previously and had been reimbursed by Jesse R. Grant. John C. Collins to Hamlin Garland, Oct. 22, 1896, Garland Papers, University of Southern California. See also *Richardson*, p. 186.

5. Ulysses S. Grant, Jr., second son of USG, born July 22, 1852, was nicknamed Buck. According to family tradition, he was originally nicknamed "Buckeye" by slaves at his grandfather's estate of White Haven because he was born in Ohio.

6. Col. Joseph J. Reynolds. See letter of May 21, 1861, note 4. The telegram from Yates offering USG command of the 7th Congressional District Regt. arrived in Covington, Ky., after USG had left. Jesse R. Grant, "The Early Life of Gen. Grant," *New York Ledger*, March 21, 1868; *Young*, II, 215. There was a traditional account in the Reynolds family that when USG was notified of his appointment in La Fayette, Ind., he planned to decline the commission but was dissuaded by William F. Reynolds, brother of Joseph J. Reynolds. R. P. DeHart, *Past and Present of Tippecanoe County, Indiana* (Indianapolis, 1909), I, 227–28.

7. Reynolds was later promoted to brig. gen.

Orders No. 7

Head Quarters, Camp Yates June 18 1861.

Orders No. 7.

The undersigned having been duly appointed Colonel of the 7th Congl Dist Regt. of Ills Volts. Militia by order of Govr Richard Yates, duly promulgated hereby assumes command.

In accepting this command, your Commander will require the co-operation of all the commissioned and non-commissioned Officers in instructing the command, and in maintaining discipline, and hopes to receive also the hearty support of every enlisted man.

All orders now in force at this camp will be continued until countermanded.

By Order
U. S Grant Col. Comdg.

Copy, DNA, RG 94, 21st Ill., Order Book.

Orders No. 8

———

Head Quarters Camp Yates June 19.61

Orders No. 8

Hereafter no Passes to soldiers to be out of Camp after Sun down will be valid unless approved by the Commanding Officer of the Regt.

From Revielle until Retreat no passes will be required. In extending this privilege to the men of this command the Col Commanding hopes that his leniency will not be so abused as to make it necessary to retract it. All men when out of Camp should reflect that they are gentlemen—in camp soldiers; and the Commanding Officer hopes that all of his command, will sustain these two characters with fidelity.

Absence from Camp will not be received as a paliation for any absence from duty, on the contrary will be regarded as an aggrivation of the offence, and will be punished accordingly.

The Guards are required in all cases to arrest all men coming into camp after retreat unless provided with a Pass countersigned by the Regimental Commander[1]

U. S Grant
Col. Comdg. 21st Regt I V M[2]

Copy, DNA, RG 94, 21st Ill., Order Book.

1. On June 25, 1861, 1st Lt. Philip Welshimer wrote to his wife. "We have certain hours for drill each day, and evry man must be on hands. If he is not as soon

as he gets back into the Gard House he goes pop sure and hours that they are not required to drill they can go where they please. The gard house was not large enough for the first fiew nights and days but yesterday there was but two or three in and to day none. No person is allowed out of Camp after dar[k] unless by permission of the Col. So you see we have the best of order and every thing mooves off pleasantly." *USGA Newsletter*, IV, 1 (Oct., 1966), 3.

2. Ill. Vol. Militia. Although the 7th Congressional District Regt. did not officially become the 21st Ill. until mustered into U.S. service on June 28, the new designation was used on June 19.

Orders No. 9

————

Head Quarters Camp Yates June 19, 1861.

ORDERS No. 9,

Until otherwise ordered there will be daily Drill as follows:
Squad Drill from 6. A M to 7. a m, Sundays excepted.

Company Commanders will have their companies divided into convenient squads, and appoint suitable persons to Drill them. The Officers of Companies are expected to be present, and give their personal supervision to the Drills, and see that all their men, not on duty are present.

Company Drill from 10 to 11 o clock a m, and from 5 to 6 o clock P. M.

> By order
> U S. GRANT Col
> Commanding 21st Regt.

Copy, DNA, RG 94, 21st Ill., Order Book.

Orders No. 10

————

Head Quarters Camp Yates June 25 1861.

ORDERS No 10.

Capt R. Madisons[1] Company of Artillery will hereafter turn out at Parade with the other Troops. Their position for this purpose will be on the left of the left Company, and three paces distant

There will be three Drills daily of this Company at such hours as the Company Commanders may direct, at which one at least must be as Infantry.

U. S. GRANT
Col. Commanding

Copy, DNA, RG 94, 21st Ill., Order Book.

1. The battery led by Capt. Relly Madison of Marshall, Ill., was later designated Battery B, 2nd Ill. Light Art.

Orders No. 14

Head Quarters Camp Yates June 26, 1861.
ORDERS NO. 14.

The following is published for the benefit of this command. It is with regret that the commanding officer learns that a number of the men composing the Guard of last night deserted their posts, and their guard. This is an offence against all military rule and law, which no punishment can be prescribed for by a commanding officer, at his discretion but must be the subject for a General Court Martial to decide upon. It cannot, in time peace, be accompanied, with a punishment less than the forfeiture of 10$ from the pay of the soldier, together with corporal punishment such as confinement for thirty days with ball & chain at hard labor. In time of war the punishment of this is death.

The Col Commanding beleiving that the men of his command, now in confinement for this offence, were ignorant of the magnitude of it, is not disposed to visit them with all the rigor of the law, provided for such cases, but would admonish them, and the whole command against a repetition of the offence, as it will not be excused again in this Regt.

U. S. Grant, Col Comdg
J W. VANCE 1st Lieut & Act. Adjt[1]

Copy, DNA, RG 94, 21st Ill., Order Book. In the regt. records this order follows Orders No. 12 and is itself followed by Orders No. 13 and a different Orders No. 14.

1. 1st Lt. Joseph W. Vance of Paris Ill., a nongraduate of USMA 1862.

Orders No. 13

Head Quarters Camp Yates June 26 1861.
ORDERS NO. 13.

Hereafter Compy Commanders, are required to be present in person, or to have present one Commissioned Officer at all Roll Calls. The Officer present will see that all absentees not properly excused are reported. All Officers not reported sick, or otherwise excused by competent authority, will attend all Drills and Parades. They will give strict attention that the men of their respective commands receive proper instruction. Officers wishing to be absent from Camp at night are required to get the counter-sign from the Comdg. Officer of the Camp. No one having the countersign will be permitted to communicate it to another for the purpose of enabling him to pass the Guards.

By order U S GRANT Col Comdg

Copy, DNA, RG 94, 21st Ill., Order Book.

To Julia Dent Grant

Camp Yates, June 26th 1861
DEAR JULIA;

We arrived here on Monday evening[1] all well. Fred.[2] was delighted with his trip but I think is not so pleased here as while traveling. When I get a horse however so that he can ride out with me he will make up.

The probabilities are that we will not remain here longer than next [*week*]. I will write again before leaving here.—I am very much pleased with my officers generally. They are sober and attentive and anxious to learn their duties.³ The men I believe are pleased with the change that has taken place in their commander, or at least the greatest change has taken [*place*] in the order in camp.⁴ For Lieut. Colonel and Major⁵ I have two men that I think a greatdeal of but I can never have a game of Eucre with them. One is a preacher and the other a member of Church. For the Field officers of my regt. the 21st Ill. Volunteers one pint of liquor will do to the end of the war.

I am kept very busy from morning until night and no time for making acquaintances. No ladies have yet been to see me in camp and although I have been here most of the time for over two months I have not made the acquaintance of a single family.

Has Buck got used to being without Fred? When we get over to Quincy all of you will have an opportunity of trying camp life for a while.

Tell Orvil that I shall not buy another horse until I get to Quincy, in the mean time if he should see a very fine one in Galena I would rather buy there. Rondy⁶ will do me for the march, if we should make it which is by no means certain. Fred. will ride in a waggon if we should march. That part he will enjoy very much. It is a very uphill business for me to write this evening.—Is Simp. & Mother with you yet? When they come be sure and write me at once and tell me how Simp. stood the trip. I am very anxious that he should get out for I believe the trip will do him good if he can stand it.—Have you heard from any of your people since I left? I should like to hear from Dr. Sharp.⁷ I feel a little anxious to his sentiments on the present issues.

If you have an opportunity I wish you would send me McClellands report of battles in the Crimea.⁸ You will find it about the house.—Kiss all the children for me. Tell Mary Duncan to give you back that kiss you caught me giving her. The next time I write you may take back the one from Hellen.[9]

This is a very poor letter but I have not written scarsely a single sentence without interruption.

Your Dodo

ALS, DLC-USG.

1. June 24, 1861.

2. Frederick Dent Grant, oldest son of USG, born May 30, 1850, accompanied his father to Springfield, traveled with the 21st Ill. across the state, and returned from Quincy to Galena on July 12. See letter to Jesse Root Grant, July 13, 1861.

3. On June 25, 1st Lt. Philip Welshimer wrote to his wife. "Evry thing goes off much smoother and better since our new Colonel has got command." *USGA Newsletter*, IV, 1 (Oct., 1966), 3.

4. On June 17, a correspondent noted that "insubordination is rapidly disappearing." *Chicago Tribune*, June 18, 1861. The next day the vols. were "in buoyant spirits." *Illinois State Register*, June 19, 1861. The same newspaper, three days later, reported: "they are good soldiers in the camp, and present the strongest evidence of a willingness to do their duty well at all times."

5. Lt. Col. John W. S. Alexander of Paris, Ill., and Maj. Warren E. McMackin of Salem, Ill. Alexander, 2nd lt., 4th Ill. Vols., in the Mexican War, later succeeded USG as col. and was killed at Chickamauga, Sept. 20, 1863. McMackin was previously a minister. "The Colonel, Lieutenant-Colonel and Major of the Seventh Congressional District Regiment of Illinois Volunteers were at the battle of Cerro Gordo, and together at numerous other engagements in Mexico. They are all total abstinence men and bitterly opposed to profane swearing." *Illinois State Journal*, June 29, 1861.

6. Rondy was the horse purchased by USG in Galena.

7. Dr. Alexander Sharp of Lincoln County, Mo., had married Ellen Dent, sister-in-law of USG. *PUSG*, 1, 337. See letter to Brig. Gen. Lorenzo Thomas, Aug. 31, 1861.

8. "Report of the Secretary of War, communicating the Report of Captain George B. McClellan (First Regiment United States Cavalry.) one of the Officers sent to the Seat of War in Europe in 1855 and 1856." *SED*, 35–special–1.

9. Possibly Helen Burke. See letter of June 27, 1861, note 1.

Orders No. 14

———

Head Quarters Camp Yates June 27, 61

ORDERS NO 14

To-morrow June 28, no Officers or men will be permitted to pass out of the camp, as the Regt. will probably be sworn into the United States service

> By order of
> U S Grant Col Comdg 21st Regt
> Lt VANCE Act Adjt.

Copy, DNA, RG 94, 21st Ill., Order Book.

To Julia Dent Grant

———

Camp Yates, Ill.
June 27th 1861

DR. JULIA;

Orly[1] has just arrived and delivered your letter. My Regt. was just being sworn into the service[2] when he come dashing into Camp, on horseback with the fine trappings Orvil sent to me, not on Rondy[3] but a showey Livery horse hired for the occation. I have been here most of the time for two months and between here and Springfield, one mile, I have yet to pay the first dime for a conveyance to carry me.[4] I was so disgusted that I passed him with but little ceremony. I give him an order to one of the Captains assigning him to his comp.y for rations and quarters with his comp.y.

Rondy has come at a cost of $23 50 to me besides 7 50 for Orly. Dont let Aunt Ann and Hellen[5] annoy you. I am certain Orly will not me. He will soon learn too the difference in amount of baggage carried by different people. I am kept very busy now and expect to be for the next month. On ~~Teusday~~ Wednesday[6] we will get away from here, or at least hope to. Fred. is better contented now than for the first few days and when he heard that the horse had arrive was perfectly jubilant. He rec'd Susy Felts[7] letter which I had to read for him. I will try and have him answer it soon. He has been writing to you for several days. This is the fourth letter I have written this evening besides considerable in an official way, and as I was on my feet from 3 o'clock 'til supper I will stop for daylight.

June 29th. For several days back it has rained all the time making it very disagreeable in camp, and there are quite a number on the sick list. Nothing serious however but so long as we stay here we must expect sickness. O̶u̶r̶ The water is very bad[8] and during this wet weather the men are but little more protected than if out of doors. My quarters are good however. It is impossible for me to write one sentence without interruption and necessarily my letter must be disconnected and uninteresting. From present indications there will be but little chance for me to take any more leave of absence to go home. You however can come down to Quincy.

I will enclose you ten dollars in this letter which will probably be the last f̶o̶r̶ ̶s̶o̶m̶e̶ until I draw some pay. I will then send you a good supply.

Kiss all the children for me and I send the same to you. Write to me soon. If we should be away from here your letter will follow. Remember me to all our friends.

ULYS.

ALS, DLC-USG.

1. Orlando H. Ross, cousin of USG, was the son of USG's mother's sister, Ann Simpson Ross. His father, James Ross, died in 1849 at Bethel, Ohio. Orlando Ross was employed at the J. R. Grant leather store in Galena along with his brother-in-law, M. T. Burke, who had married Ross's sister Helen.

2. All official records state that the 7th Congressional District Regt. was mustered into U.S. service as the 21st Ill. Vols. on June 28, 1861. Since USG dates the continuation of his letter June 29, it is possible that he misdated the first section.

Some confusion about mustering exists because the 7th Congressional District Regt. had been remustered into state service soon after USG took command. The regt. had been mustered into state service for one month on May 15; one month later it was not yet ready for U.S. service. 2nd Asst. AG John S. Loomis remustered half the regt. into state service on June 17, the day USG took command. *Chicago Tribune*, June 18, 1861. In *Memoirs*, I, 244–46, USG discusses speeches made to his regt. by Ill. Democratic Congressmen John A. McClernand and John A. Logan which inspired his men to enter U.S. service. Logan made his speech on June 19. *Illinois State Journal*, June 20, 1861. Cf. *Garland*, pp. 171–72. The date indicates that the occasion was remuster into state service.

In a biographical sketch of USG, Isaac N. Morris wrote "that upon being tendered the command of a regiment . . . he declined to accept it until the regiment had made him their choice by a unanimous vote." *National Intelligencer* (Washington, D.C.), March 21, 1864. Since remuster into state service coincided with the appointment of USG, a vote on the new col. may have been implicit in the decision to accept remuster; otherwise the statement is not correct. "There was some dissatisfaction in the regiment at the time of the appointment of Col. Grant. Although he was admitted to be both an able and efficient commander, the members of the regiment deemed that they were yet American citizens, and entitled to that most sacred of rights, the privilege of choosing their own rulers, by the rightful test of the ballot." Letter of "Orion," Aug. 1, 1861, in *Missouri Democrat*, Aug. 3, 1861.

3. See letter of June 26, 1861, note 6.

4. The *Illinois State Register*, April 26, 1861, announced the start of a line of omnibuses between downtown Springfield and Camp Yates. This or a rented horse would have been the "conveyance" available.

5. See note 1.

6. Wednesday, July 3.

7. Susan M. Felt, eight-year-old daughter of Lewis S. Felt. See letter of June 1, 1861, note 5.

8. In a letter to his wife, June 26, 1861, 1st Lt. Philip Welshimer of USG's regt. wrote, "I think it is the water here that effects me and quite a number of others as it is limestone . . ." *USGA Newsletter*, IV, 1 (Oct., 1966), 3. The *Chicago Tribune*, June 27, 1861, attributed the bad water to the proximity of a coal seam.

Orders No. 16

———

Head Quarters, Camp Yates, July [*June*] 28, 1861.

ORDERS No. 16

Company Commanders will have their Companies paraded for muster, at 2 ½ o.clock PM to day. The Regt. will be ~~releived~~ formed on the Regt. Parade ground, as for evening parade.

The guard will be relieved, and required to join their respective Companies at the call for assembling the Compys. with the exceptions of the men from Co. K. These latter will be posted at the guard House, gate & compy store.

As fast as a Company has been mustered into the service the Guard from such companies will immediately join their guard, and be posted as before being releived.

As soon as relieved the members of the Guard from "K" Company, will join their company and as soon as mustered rejoin their guard.

> By order
> U. S. GRANT
> Col Comdg.

Copy, DNA, RG 94, 21st Ill., Order Book.

Orders No. 17

———

Head Quarters Camp Yates June 28 [*1861*].

ORDERS No 17

Commandants of Companies will immediately make requisition for three months allowance of Stationery, and Regulation allowance of Company Books, Knapsacks, Haversacks, Camp Kettles and Mess Pans.

The Uniform Jackets and Pants, except such as are absolutely necessary will be packed by each Company in good order, and sent by Rail Road.

Bayonets will be delivered at the Qr Masters Office, for transportation by Rail Road.

> By order
> U. S. GRANT Col. Comdg.

Copy, DNA, RG 94, 21st Ill., Order Book.

Orders No. 18

Head Quarters 21st Inft I. V. M. Camp Yates June 28, 1861.
ORDERS No. 18.

Appointment

On the recommendation of a majority of the Captains of this
Regt. the Revd Jas. L. Crane, of Urbana Ills. is appointed
chaplain of this Regt. to take effect from this date.

U. S. GRANT Col Comdg

Copy, DNA, RG 94, 21st Ill., Order Book. James L. Crane, of the Methodist
Episcopal Church, served as chaplain until Sept. 20, 1861. He later wrote "Grant
as a Colonel," *McClure's Magazine*, VII, 1 (June, 1896), 40–45. Some back-
ground on Crane is available in his novel concerning a young Methodist minister,
The Two Circuits: A Story of Illinois Life (Chicago, 1878), which, though not
autobiographical, draws on his own experiences.

Orders No. 19

Head Quarters Camp Yates July 1, 1861
ORDERS No. 19.

Commandants of Companies will immediately make out a
Roll of all their sick in Hospital, and such others of their Companies as they deem unable to make the march to Quincy, and
report the same at this Office.

Company Commanders, being accountable for the muskets
they have received from the State, they will at once with draw
such as they have stored with the Regt Qr Mast. and assign them
to the best drilled men of their respective companies who they
will hold responsible for their safe keeping

U. S. GRANT, Col. Comdg.

Copy, DNA, RG 94, 21st Ill., Order Book. The transfer of the 21st Ill. to Quincy,
Ill., had been planned before USG took command. The *Chicago Tribune*, June 22,
1861, reported that USG would, if permitted, march his men instead of traveling
by railroad as the other regts. had done. The *Illinois State Journal*, July 2, 1861,

credits the decision to march to Ill. Q. M. John Wood, but the earlier news story and USG's statement in his *Memoirs*, I, 246–47, show that it was USG's decision. In 1866, USG reported to the Ill. AG. "I thought for the purpose of discipline and speedy efficiency for the field it would be well to march the regiment across the country instead of transporting by rail." ADS, ICHi. See *Galena Gazette*, July 8, 1861. The march began on July 3.

General Orders No. 22

——

July 2nd 1861.

GEN ORDER No 22

On Wendesday morning at the beating of the Assembly, in front of the Guard House the Guards will join their respective Companies. All nesessary clothing will be packed in knapsacks and Blankets Rolled and Strapped. The following duty is assigned to each Company whilst en route for Quincy. Company "A" will form the Guard and march in rear of the Waggons on Wednesday Compy B will do Camp Guard duty Wednesday night and march in rear of the Waggons Thursday. Compy "C" will do camp Guard Duty Thursday night and march in rear of the Waggons Friday. Comp "D" will do camp Guard duty Friday night and march in rear of the Waggons Saturday. Comp "E" will do Camp Guard Duty Saturday night and camp Guard Sunday. Compy F will do Camp Guard duty Sunday night and march in rear of Waggons Monday. Compy G will do Camp guard duty monday night and march in rear of Waggons Tuesday. Comp H will do camp duty Tuesday night and march in rear of Waggons Wednesday. Compy I will do Camp Guard duty Wednesday night and march in rear of Waggons Thursday. Compy K will do Camp Guard duty Thu[rs]day night and march in rear of Waggons Friday.

No Officers nor men, will be allowed to leave camp after Tuesday Evening.

U S GRANT Col Com 21st Regt

Copy, DNA, RG 94, 21st Ill., Order Book.

To Col. Thomas S. Mather

———

                                        Head Quarters, 21st Ill. V. Militia
                                            Camp Yates, July 2d 1861
COL. T. S. MATHER
ADJT. GEN. ILL. STATE TROOPS
SPRINGFIELD ILL.
SIR:

Having neither Surgeon or Assistant Surgeon attached to the regiment under my command I would respectfully request that Surgeon Amassa Blake, and Assistant Surgeon James Maddison, should he pass the prescribed examination, be appointed to fill these positions respectively.

In case of the failure of Dr. Maddison to pass his examination I would recommend Dr. Jas. Hamilton for the latter position.

                                        Respectfully
                                        Your Obt. Svt.
                                        U. S. GRANT
                                        Col. Comd.g 21st Regt. I.V.M.

ALS, deCoppet Collection, NjP. James Madison was serving as asst. surgeon a few weeks later. *Quincy Whig*, July 19, 1861. On August 11, 1861, USG issued Special Orders No. 18 for Lt. Col. John W. S. Alexander. "You will upon Reciept of this order send Surgeon Blake of your Regt. with his wife to Quincy, and St. Louis for the purpose of bringing all the sick of your Regiment from those Cities to your Camp at this place" Copy, DNA, RG 94, 21st Ill., Order Book.

Orders

———

                                        Camp Allison[1] July 6th 1861
The Col Commanding regrets that it becomes his duty, to notice the fact, that some of the Officers of this command fell out of ranks yesterday, in passing through Jacksonville without authority to do so; and this whilst the rank & file were guarded

most strictly. This being the first offence is overlooked, but in future no Excuse will be recieved

U. S. GRANT Col Comdg

Copy, DNA, RG 94, 21st Ill., Order Book. This order may also have reflected USG's experience the previous day with a citizen of Jacksonville, Ill., who attempted to sell liquor to the troops. "Having got Mingle's light wagon, he loaded it with full jugs and started out to camp, about seven miles west of town. On his arrival he pulled off his coat and arranged his stock for doing business. Col. Grant, however, having out his scouting parties, our speculator was duly reported at head quarters, whereupon the Col. ordered the confiscation of the jugs and the speedy retreat of the owner, giving him one minute to 'hitch up' and make tracks, all of which he did in double-quick time, not even taking the trouble to pick up his coat, but leaving it as a trophy in the hands of the victors." *Jacksonville Journal*, July 11, 1861.

1. The order was written before the march of July 6, 1861, from camp in Allinson's Grove, about seven miles west of Jacksonville. Ensley Moore, "Grant's First March," *Transactions of the Illinois State Historical Society for the Year 1910* (Springfield, 1912), p. 59.

To Julia Dent Grant

Naples, Ill.
July 7th 1861

DEAR JULIA;

We are now laying in camp on the Illinois river spending sunday and will leave to-morrow on our way to Quincy. Up to this time my regiment have made their marches as well as troops ever do and the men have been very orderly. There have been a few men who show a disposition to not to respect private property such as hen roosts and gardens, but I have kept such a watch on them, and punished offenders so, that I will venture that the same number of troops never marched through a thickly settled country like this committing fewer depridations. Fred. enjoys it hugely. Our Lieut. Col.[1] was left behind and I am riding his horse so that Fred. has Rondy to ride. The Soldiers and officers call him Colonel and he seems to be quite a favorite.

From Springfield here is one of the most beautiful countries in the world. It is all settled and highly improved. It is all of it the district of the State that sends so much fine stock to St. Louis fair.

Passing through the towns the whole populat[ion] would turn out to receive us. At Jacksonville, one of the prettyest towns with the most tasty houses that I ever saw, the ladies were all out waving their handkerchiefs, and one of them (I know she must be pretty) made up a boquet and sent me with her name, which by the way the messenger forgot before it come to me. So you see I shall probably never find who the fair donor was.

From present indications we will not remain long at Quincy. There was four regiments ordered there with the expectation of remaining until frost. Two have arrived and been ordered into Missouri.[2] I think my regiment cannot be ordered so soon because we have yet to get all our uniforms & equipments and a part of our arms. It will be at least two weeks before my regt. can be of much service and a month before it can do good service. It was in a terribly disorganized state when I took it but a very great change has taken place. Evry one says so and to me it is very observable. I dont believe there is a more orderly set of troops now in the volunteer service. I have been very strict with them and the men seem to like it. They appreciate that it is all for their own benefit.—Kiss the children for me. Fred. would send his love to all of you but he is out. He says he will answer Susy Felts[3] letter but I am affraid that he will be slow about it. He writes sometimes but never copys letter.

Kisses to you.

ULYS.

ALS, DLC-USG.

1. Lt. Col. John W. S. Alexander.
2. The 16th Ill., Col. Robert F. Smith, and the 14th Ill., Col. John M. Palmer, were already in Mo. The two additional regts. ordered to Quincy were the 21st Ill. and the 19th Ill., Col. John B. Turchin.
3. See letter of June 27, 1861.

Orders No. 23

Camp Gardner[1] Ills July 9th 1861

Orders No 23

The progress of this command towards Quincy Ills, having been stopped by orders recieved yesterday,[2] will return to the West Bank of the Ills River, and then go in to camp to await transportation. During the stay of the Regt. at the encampment all order ~~thus~~ established & existing at Camp Yates on the departure of the Regt. from there, at all aplicable, will be in force unless changed

There will be a daily Battallion drill commencing at 4 o'clock P M Squad and company drills at least twice each day commencing at 6 & 10 o clock a m respectvly will be held.

It is enjoi[n]ed upon Officers and men, to give the strictest attention to all their Military duties and the commanding Officer has evry confidence that this injunction will be cordialy recieved when it is reflected upon, how soon we may be called into actual service, and how important it is that evry one should know his duty. This is not only important for the credit and reputation of the Regiment, but for their security.

U S Grant Col Comdg

Copy, DNA, RG 94, 21st Ill., Order Book.

1. Camp Gardner was about four miles west of Naples, Ill. It was named for a nearby octagonal house known as Gardner's. Ensley Moore, "Grant's First March," *Transactions of the Illinois State Historical Society for the Year 1910* (Springfield, 1912), p. 62.

2. The 21st Ill. had been ordered to return to the Illinois River to await a steamer which would carry it to St. Louis. From there the regt. would go to Ironton, Mo. *Memoirs*, I, 247; *Illinois State Journal*, July 9, 1861; letter of "Orion," July 9, 1861, in *Missouri Democrat*, July 12, 1861. The orders to USG to proceed to Ironton have not been located, but the matter is clarified by other corespondence. On July 5, 1861, Maj. Gen. George B. McClellan, commanding the Dept. of Ohio, wrote to Lt. Col. Chester Harding. "Telegraph to General Pope, at Alton, to give you a regiment; and to Hurlbut, at Quincy, to give you another." *O.R.*, I, iii, 390. Harding replied to McClellan the next day. "The Quincy regiment will go to Ironton, and thence to Greenville." *Ibid.*, p. 391. On July 7,

Harding reported to Bvt. Brig. Gen. Lorenzo Thomas. "General McClellan has placed at the disposal of General Lyon one of the regiments at Quincy. Orders have been sent for it to come here [*St. Louis*], where it will be equipped, and then sent down the Iron Mountain Railroad to Ironton, from whence it will proceed to Greenville, in Wayne County." *Ibid.* On July 11, Harding wrote to Bvt. Maj. Seth Williams, asst. adjt. gen. for McClellan. "I hope Grant's regiment will be allowed to come. He and Marsh can aid Cairo and Bird's Point effectually by operations in Cape Girardeau, Scott, Stoddard, Wayne, and Butler counties." *HRC*, 37–3–108, III, 84. On July 19, Harding wrote to Maj. Gen. John C. Frémont. "Grant was under orders, but his orders were countermanded. Marsh is at Cape Girardeau, instructed to keep open communication with Bloomfield, where Grant was to be." *O.R.*, I, iii, 399. See also Harding to Brig. Gen. Nathaniel Lyon, July 21, 1861, *ibid.*, pp. 400–401. Whether USG was to go to Greenville or Bloomfield is unknown. Greenville, Mo., is about thirty-seven miles south of Ironton; Bloomfield, Mo., about thirty-two miles southeast of Greenville, and about thirty-seven miles southwest of Cape Girardeau.

General Orders No. 24

Hd Quarters Camp Gardner
July 9th 1861

Gᴇɴ Oʀᴅ Nᴏ 24

The Col commanding this Regiment, deems it his duty at this pe[ri]od of the march to return his thanks to the Officers and men composing the command on their general Obedience and Military disipline. Having for a Period of years been accostomed to strict military duties and disipline he deems it not inapropriate at this time to make a most favorable comparison of this command with that of veteran troops in point of Soldierly ~~learning~~ bearing general good Order, and cheerfull~~ness~~ execution of commands; ~~and~~ making the real necescity of a Guard ~~particularly~~ally unnessesary Although discipline has been generaly enforced, yet, the same strictness would have been unnessary, but for a few unruly men, who have caused the Regt. to be more strictly under regulation for their misdemeaniors

The Col. Comdg trusts that a repetition of disorder on their part may never occur again; but that all may prove themselves

The Civil War in Missouri, 1861

Soldiers, fit for duty without any unnessary means being pursued by him to make them such.

                                        U. S. GRANT Col. Condg

Copy, DNA, RG 94, 21st Ill., Order Book.

To Brig. Gen. John Pope

                    BY TELEGRAPH FROM Quincy [*July*] 11 *1861*
To GEN J POPE

Palmer[1] has moved on Palmyra[2] with his Regiment, one company of mine, & company of cavelry.[3] One company of my regiment guards a bridge four miles west.[4] Will move along the road commencing about ten 10 tomorrow with the balance.

                                        U S GRANT
                                        Col 21st I V

Telegram received (punctuation added), DNA, RG 94, 21st Ill. On July 4, 1861, Brig. Gen. John Pope was ordered to assume command of the troops at Alton, Ill. *O.R.*, I, iii, 390. See letter of April 27, 1861, note 6.

On July 9, USG had taken his regt. to the Illinois River to await a steamer to St. Louis. See Orders No. 23, July 9, 1861, note 2. The steamer stuck on a sandbar before reaching the 21st Ill., and new orders were received on July 10 ordering the regt. to proceed to Quincy, Ill., by railroad. On July 10, Pope wrote to USG. "Immediately upon your arrival at Quincy Ills you will move your Regiment to Palmyra Missouri and from thence to points on or near the line of Hannibal & St Jo R. R. directed by Col R F Smith or the Officer of his Regiment in command and dispose your command in such a manner as will Effectualy reinforce and sustain him in his present position or any that may hereafter be taken by him— Untill you are relieved from such Service or ordered to return to Quincy and proceed from there to St. Louis as heretofore directed as far as practicable, considering the Nature of Service & you will prevent a the dividing of you Regiment into small detachments, but hold it for the execution of above order alluded to Capt. John Rurnap is ordered to report his company the Yates Draggoons to you and and you are hereby commissioned to attach the same to your command during this Expidition and issue directly such Orders as you may Deem best" Copy, DNA, RG 94, 21st Ill., Order Book. Virtually the same orders were sent from Pope's hd. qrs. in Chicago to USG on July 11, probably by telegraph. "General Pope orders that you go with your regiment to relieve Colonel Smith, on H. and St Joe R. R. and that you issue orders to Capt Burnap who is to report to you.

That you hold yourself in readiness, when so ordered, to return to Quincy and re-turn as soon as practicable, and move as before directed, to Saint Louis. Tell me the position of your command after reporting to Smith, and I will send further orders. Letter enclosing warrant received. Will convert and send to where you wish." Copy, *ibid.*, RG 393, District of North Mo., Letters Sent. The 21st Ill. arrived in Quincy at noon, July 11. *Ibid.*, RG 94, 21st Ill., Records of Events; *Quincy Herald, Quincy Whig*, July 12, 1861.

The change in orders was caused by increased secessionist guerrilla activity along the line of the Hannibal and St. Joseph Railroad. On July 9, six cos. com-manded by Col. Robert F. Smith, 16th Ill., were attacked about twelve miles south of Monroe Station, Mo. The next day, Smith proceeded to Monroe, where he found secessionists destroying railroad property. They left as Smith ap-proached, and he moved into a brick building. The next morning, July 11, the building was surrounded by a force, estimated by Smith as high as 2,000 men, which fired on the building until late in the afternoon, when reinforcements of the 16th Ill. arrived by train. Smith to Brig. Gen. Nathaniel Lyon, July 14, 1861, *O.R.*, I, iii, 40–41; *Chicago Times*, July 11, 1861; *Quincy Herald*, July 11, 12, 13, 16, 27, 1861; *Illinois State Register*, July 12, 1861; *Missouri Republican*, July 12, 13, 18, 1861; *Missouri Democrat*, July 13, 1861; Walter Williams, *A History of Northeast Missouri* (Chicago and New York, 1913), pp. 55, 486–87.

On his arrival at Quincy, USG learned that the 16th Ill. was in less danger than supposed. *Memoirs*, I, 248. The bulk of the 21st Ill. crossed the Mississippi River and encamped at West Quincy, awaiting the repair of bridges to permit an advance. DNA, RG 94, 21st Ill., Records of Events.

1. Col. John M. Palmer, 14th Ill.
2. Palmyra, Mo., about ten miles southwest of Quincy.
3. Co. A, 21st Ill., Capt. George H. Dunning, accompanied cav. brought from Springfield, Ill., by former Governor John Wood. Letter of "Orion," July 19, 1861, in *Missouri Democrat*, July 22, 1861.
4. Co. I, 21st Ill., Capt. George W. Peck, probably guarded the bridge. DNA, RG 94, 21st Ill., Records of Events.

To Brig. Gen. John Pope

Quincy, July 12th, 1861

Col. Palmer is occupying the road from Hannibal out. Three companies of my regiment from here to Palmyra. Col. Smith is relieved. When the Chicago troops[1] arrive shall I come in?

Telegram, copy (punctuation added), DNA, RG 393, District of North Mo., Register of Letters Received. On July 12, 1861, Brig. Gen. John Pope's hd. qrs. replied. "General Pope's last instructions were for you to wait further orders. Will ask him when you are to move." Copy, *ibid.*, Letters Sent. On July 12, Pope wrote to John S. Loomis of the Ill. AGO. "Grant had best remain where he is until Turchin relieves him which will be a day or two yet. By that time, Frémont will be here and things can be definitely arranged I have telegraphed Harding to send arms to Quincy or Hannibal for Grant and Turchin. You had best telegraph him also to same effect." Copy, *ibid*. On the same day, Pope also wrote directly to USG. "You will remain where you are until the arrival of Colonel Turchin to relieve you, which will be in a day or two. How many arms have you and how many do you need? Will have them sent you from Saint Louis." Copy, *ibid*. On July 13, USG reported to Pope. "The steamer Jennie Deans is here prepared to move troops at short notice Col Turchin command is to arrive at three 3 P. M." *Ibid*., Register of Letters Received.

1. The 19th Ill., Col. John B. Turchin, was recruited primarily in Cook County.

To Jesse Root Grant

———

East Quincy, Mo.,[1]
July 13th, 1861.

DEAR FATHER:

I have just received yours and Mary's letters and really did not know that I had been so negligent as not to have written to you before. I did write from Camp Yates, but since receiving yours remember that I did not get to finish it at the time, and have neglected it since. The fact is that since I took command of this regiment I have had no spare time, and flatter myself, and believe I am sustained in my judgment by my officers and men, that I have done as much for the improvement and efficiency of this regiment as was ever done for a command in the same length of time.—You will see that I am in Missouri. Yesterday I went out as far as Palmyra and stationed my regiment along the railroad for the protection of the bridges, trestle work, etc.[2] The day before I sent a small command, all I could spare, to relieve Colonel Smith who was surrounded by secessionists. He effected his relief, however, before they got there.[3] Tomorrow I start for Monroe,[4] where I shall fall in with Colonel Palmer and one company of horse and two pieces of artillery. One regiment and a battalion of infantry will move on to Mexico,[5] North Missouri road, and all of us together will try to nab the notorious Tom Harris[6] with his 1200 secessionists. His men are mounted, and I have but little faith in getting many of them. The notorious Jim Green[7] who was let off on his parole of honor but a few days ago, has gone towards them with a strong company well armed. If he is caught it will prove bad work for him.

You no doubt saw from the papers that I started to march across the country for Quincy. My men behaved admirably, and the lesson has been a good one for them. They can now go into camp after a day's march with as much promptness as veteran troops; they can strike their tents and be on the march with equal celerity. At the Illinois River, I received a dispatch at eleven o'clock at night[8] that a train of cars would arrive at half past eleven to move my regiment. All the men were of course asleep, but I had the drum beaten, and in forty minutes every tent and all the baggage was at the water's edge ready to put aboard the ferry to cross the river.

I will try to keep you posted from time to time, by writing either to you or to Mary, of my whereabouts and what I am doing. I hope you will have only a good account of me and the command under my charge. I assure you my heart is in the cause I have espoused, and however I may have disliked party Republicanism there has never been a day that I would not have taken up arms for a Constitutional Administration.[9]

You ask if I should not like to go in the regular army. I should not. I want to bring my children up to useful employment, and in the army the chance is poor. There is at least the same objection that you find where slavery exists. Fred. has been with me until yesterday; I sent him home on a boat.[10]

> Yours &c.
> U. S. Grant.

J. G. Cramer, pp. 40–42.

1. "East Quincy, Mo." must be either an inadvertent error by USG or an error in transcription. USG was encamped at West Quincy.
2. At least four cos. of the 21st Ill. were stationed between Quincy and

Palmyra; the remainder were encamped at West Quincy. DNA, RG 94, 21st Ill., Records of Events. USG and Col. Thomas S. Mather had traveled by railroad to Palmyra. *Chicago Tribune*, July 13, 1861.

3. See telegram of July 11, 1861.

4. On July 14, 1861, the 21st Ill. consolidated at Palmyra. DNA, RG 94, 21st Ill., Records of Events. On July 13, Brig. Gen. Stephen A. Hurlbut, commanding at Quincy, issued orders for a movement to Monroe, about fifteen miles southwest of Palmyra. "Col U S Grant will proceed with his Regt at an early hour in the morning as he can make the nessesary arangments by the cars of Quincy & Palmyra R. Road to Palmyra accompanied by two ~~Reg~~ Companies detailed from the 19th Regt. He will call in as he passes his Companies now on guard on said road replacing them with the Companies from Col. Turchens Regt. and giving the officer in Command all the information he has in his posession as to the state of affairs on the line of the Road. At Palmyra he will await the arrival of Col. Turchins with five companies of the 19th who will relieve the remaining companies of the 21st. As soon as relieved Col Grant will push on as rapidly as possible to Monroe, Effect a junction with Col Palmer and deliver to him for his action the Telegraphic Orders here~~after~~with and be governed afterwards by his discretion as to further advances.

2nd   Col Turchin will proceed at the earliest hour practicable to morrow morning with the five Companies of his Regt. on the Str Black Hawk to Hannibal where he will demand and recieve from the Hannibal and St Joseph R Road Company transportation for One Thousand men and Stores and proceed to Palmyra, where he will Establish the present Head Quarters of his Regt. and Establish and keep open communications with Col Smith at Monroe

The last five Companies will cross the River on the Ferry Boat by 8 A. M. July 14th

3   Each Regiment will take with them forty Rounds of of Amunition and rations as follows: —Col Grants for Six days, and Col Tuchins for three days inclusive. of what they may have on on hand

4   A Supply train of amunition and provisions for Col Turchins Command will be in charge of Col Grant, who will see to their delivery.

5   If on consultation at Monroe Cols Grant & Palmer shall be of opinion that that point can be held safely by Col Smith's command they will both proceed on the special duty assigned them. If not, Col Palmer will detach so many of his men as shall render that point secure and maintan the communication with the Iowa Regt on the west and the detachment at Palmyra on the East with out any question, but Col Grants Regt. to make part of the advancing force at all Events

6   After fulfulling the duty assigned by Telegraphic orders—Col Grant will make the best of his way by the shortest and best route to Alton and report for duty to Brig Genl Pope. Col Palmer will return to Monroe and report to me for Orders. The Officer in charge of the Expedition will take with him if if he thinks proper the Troops of Cavalry and two pieces of Artillery from Monroe and either hire from Loyal Citizens or impress into the Service of the U States such Means of transportation as he may require, giving vouchers therefor

7th   The General takes this occasion to remind the Officers in charge of this movement that all nessesary precaution against supprise by proper advanced & Rear Gards and light troop must be vigilantly made, but would futher ~~caution~~ remind them that caution is no impediment to rapid & Effective action." Copy, *ibid.*, 21st Ill., Order Book. On July 14, Hurlbut wrote to Col. John M. Palmer,

14th Ill. "Your regiment is ordered back to morrow to be joined by Col Grants who will bring you detailed orders and meet you at Palmyra" Copy, *ibid.*, RG 393, Records of Brigade Hd. Qrs., Quincy, Ill., Letters Sent. *O.R.*, II, i, 185.

5. The 21st Ill. moved to Mexico, Mo., about thirty-five miles south of Monroe, on July 19–20, 1861. DNA, RG 94, 21st Ill., Records of Events.

6. Brig. Gen. Thomas A. Harris commanded the pro-Confederate Mo. State Guard in northern Mo.

7. James Stephen Green of Canton, Mo., completed a term in the U.S. Senate on March 3, 1861, then took a prominent role in the C.S.A. He had been captured and paroled by the 14th Ill. *Ill. AG Report*, I, 632.

8. July 10.

9. See letter of April 19, 1861, note 1.

10. Frederick Dent Grant went by boat to Dubuque, Iowa, then by railroad to Galena. *Memoirs*, I, 248.

To Julia Dent Grant

West Quincy, Mo.
July 13th 1861

Dear Julia;

A letter from you has just reached me. I join you in disappointment that you will not likely be able to make a trip to visit me this Summer. But our country calls me elswhere and I must obey. Secessionests are thick through this part of Missouri but so far they show themselves very scary about attacking. Their depridations are confined more to burning R. R. bridges, tearing up the track and where they can, surround small parties of Union troops. I come here to release Col. Smith who was surrounded but he effected his release too soon for me to assist him. Yesterday I went out as far as Palmyra and stationed my Regt. along at different points for the protection of the road. To-morrow I will be relieved by Col. Terchin[1] and will start for Monroe where I will meet Col. Palmer with his Regt. and one company of horse & two pieces of Artillery. There will also be a Regt. & a half over at Mexico on the North Missouri road and all of us together will try and surround the notorious Tom Harris and his band. After that my Regt. goes down to St. Charles where we take a steamer for Alton there to go into Camp.[2] I have no idea however that we will be allowed to remain long. I am kept very busy but with such a set of officers as I have they will learn their duties rapidly and relieve me of many of the cares I now have. My Regt. is a good one and deserves great credit for the progress it has made in the last three weeks. Our March from Springfield was conducted with as much dicipline, and our geting into camp at night and starting in the morning, was as prompt as I ever saw with regular troops. I have been strict with my men but it seems to have met with the approbation of them all.—Fred. started home yesterday and I did not telegraph you because I thought you would be in a perfect stew until he arrived. He did not want to go atall and I felt lothe at sending him but now that we are in the enemies country ~~country~~ I thought you would be alarmed if he was with me.[3] Fred. is a good boy and behaved very manly. Last night we had an alarm which kept me out all night with one of those terrible headaches which you know I am subject to. To-day I have laid up all day and taken medicine so that I feel pretty well.

Write your next letter to me at Alton. Fred. will have a budget of news to tell you. You must not fret about me. Of course there is more or less exposure in a call of the kind I am now obeying but the justness of it is a consolation.—It is geting late and I must go to bed. give my love to all at home. I hope Simp. will not abandon the idea of going to Lake Superior.[4] I think it will do him a greatdeel of good. Kisses for yourself & children.

ULYS.

ALS, DLC-USG.

1. Col. John B. Turchin, 19th Ill.
2. See preceding letter. St. Charles, Mo., is on the Missouri River a few miles northwest of St. Louis.
3. Julia Dent Grant later told USG that she would have preferred to have Frederick Dent Grant remain with his father. *Memoirs*, I, 247–48.
4. Samuel Simpson Grant died on Sept. 13, 1861, near St. Paul, Minn.

To Brig. Gen. Stephen A. Hurlbut

———

Head Quarters, 21st Ill. Vols
Camp Salt River, Mo.[1]
July 16th 1861

Gen. S. A. Hurlbut
Comd.g Ill. Vols
Quincy, Ill.

The troops under Col. Palmers command arrived here yesterday and crossed the baggage of the 14th Ill. V.s ready to take the cars at an early hour this morning. In consequence of information received by Col. Palmer, of which no doubt he has informed you, he felt it necessary that he should proceed, without delay, for the protection of more Westerly points on the road, with his entire regiment. This necessarily changed the programe for my command. I am now fiting out teams to start from this point to Florida, where it was said Harris has his encampment,[2] and after breaking him up will return to this point where I shall leave most of my camp equipage under a sufficient guard.

On finally breaking up here I shall proceed to Hannibal to await transportation should no orders be received in the mean time changing my destination.[3]

From the best evidence that can be obtained here Harris' command is not likely to be found at Florida, nor at any other point where a regiment of Federal troops are together.

Respectfully
Your Obt. Svt.
U. S. Grant
Col. 21st Ill. Vols

ALS, Stephenson County Historical Society, Freeport, Ill. Brig. Gen. Stephen A. Hurlbut, born and raised in S.C., practiced law in Belvidere, Ill., and served two terms in the Ill. General Assembly. On July 4, 1861, he was ordered by Maj. Gen. George B. McClellan to take command of the troops at Quincy. *O.R.*, I, iii, 390. His assignment was to protect the Hannibal and St. Joseph Railroad. *Ibid.*, pp. 396–97. Hurlbut had sent USG an order on July 15, via C. J. Sellon, correspondent for the *Illinois State Journal. Chicago Tribune*, July 17, 1861. This order has not been located.

1. On July 15–16, the 21st Ill. moved to Salt River Bridge on the Hannibal and St. Joseph Railroad. The bridge had been destroyed by rebels, and the 21st Ill. guarded the workmen repairing it. DNA, RG 94, 21st Ill., Records of Events; *Memoirs*, I, 248.

2. On July 17, USG led six cos. of the 21st Ill. about twenty miles south to Florida, Mo. Mo. State Guards commanded by Brig. Gen. Thomas A. Harris left before USG arrived, and USG returned to Camp Salt River the following day. DNA, RG 94, 21st Ill., Records of Events; *Memoirs*, I, 249–51.

3. After leaving Camp Salt River, USG proceeded to Macon City, then to Mexico, Mo.

To Julia Dent Grant

Macon City, Mo.
July 19th 1861

DEAR JULIA;

For the last week I have been kept troting around so that I have neither had time to write nor a place to mail a letter from. I arrived with my Regt. at this place, the junction of the North Missouri road with the Hannibal & St. Jo, about 1 o'clock this afternoon, and will leave to-morrow for Alton unless counter orders should be received in the mean time.[1] For the last two weeks however there has been so little stability in the orders we receive that I make no calculation one day ahead where I may be. I have now been on the road between here & Quincy, and marching South of the road for nine days. When we first come there was a terrible state of fear existing among the people. They thought that evry horror known in the whole catalogue of disa[sters] following a state of war was going to be their portion at once. But they are now becoming much more reassured. They find that all troops are not the desperate characters they took them for. Some troops have behaved badly in this part of the state and given good grounds for fe[ar] but they have behaved no worse than their own people. The Secessionest commit evry outrage upon the Unionests. They seize their property, drive them out of the state &c. and destroy the railroad track wherever they find it without a guard. Yesterday I returned to camp on the line of the R. R. from a little march south as far as the town of Florida. As we went down houses all appeared to be deserted. People of the town, many of them, left on our approach but finding that we behave respectfully and respected private property they returned and before we left nearly evry lady and child visited Camp and no doubt felt as much regret at our departure as they did at our arrival. On our re[turn] evry farm house seemed occupied and all the people turned out to greet us. I am fully convinced that if orderly troops could be marched through this country, and none others, it would create a very different state of feeling from what exists now. I have been very well and enjoy myself well. Fred. has told you, no doubt, a long history of his camp. I should like very much to go into Camp some place where you could visit me.

I should like to hear from you and the children oftener. I got one letter from you since I left Springfield ~~but~~ and no doubt you have writ[ten] others. But I am kept so on the wing tha[t] they do not reach me. They will all come to hand when I reach Alton.

Give my love to all at Galena. Write all about the children and direct to Alton un[less] I advise you differently.

ULYS.

ALS, DLC-USG.

1. On July 19, 1861, Brig. Gen. Stephen A. Hurlbut issued new orders to USG. "Col Grant 21st Regt Ills will with his entire Regt. ~~will~~ take train of N. M. R Road and proceed at 4 A. M. tomorrow 20th to Mexico to the aid of Col Morgan L Smith, and Effect a junction with his force and afterwards report to Brig. Gen. Pope who is at some point south on that Road A pilot Engine will proceed the train and Col Grant will arrange the nessesary Signals so as to prepare the main cars for any attack. Evry caution will be taken to prevent supprise and the supretendent Pro tem Capt Purdy will obey any orders from Col Grant the Brigadier General desires. In taking leave of the Regt which now probaly leaves his command he desires to render his thanks for orderly and Soldierlike deportment which has given the Regiment a most desirable reputation—no complaint has been made to any Citizen against the 21st Regt. and their Obedience to all Orders and promptness of movement are the best evidence of the attention of the Officers" Copy, DNA, RG 94, 21st Ill., Order Book. See also *O.R.*, II, i, 188.

Orders No. 25

———

                                    Camp Near Mexico Mo July 23rd 1861
ORDER No 25

Hereafter the guard detailed will be marched by the 1st
Sergeants of their respective Comps. to the front of the Commanding Officers Quarters, where the guard will be formed and
marched to the guard tents. All instructions to the guard must be
communicated by the Officer of the day Officer of the guard and
Sergeants of the guard. All Officers will be required to be present
at guard mounting untill they are thouroughly aquanted with the
ceremony of mounting guard correctly.

The right wing of the Battallion when form[ed] for Comps
roll call will form with the right of Companies towards the rear
of the encampment The Officer of the ~~guard~~ day must visit
frequently through the day and once at least after 12 Oclock at
night, and see that they are thouroghly instructed in their duties
to insure their instruction being correctly given. All Officers are
advised to consult the army Regulations. The Officer of the guard
will be required to visit each relief or post during his whole tour
of duty

                                    U. S. GRANT
                                    Col Comdg 21st Regt
                                    Inft. U. S. V.

Copy, DNA, RG 94, 21st Ill., Order Book.

General Orders No. 1

———

                                    Head Quarters Military District
                                    Mexico Mo July 25th 1861
GEN ORDER No 1

In pursuance of Genl. Order No 1 Hd Qurs. Dist. Mos the
undersigned assumes command of all the Troops now Encamped

in this vicinity. for the guidance of all conserned the following orders will be published to the several commands composing the force of this place No wandering will be permited and evry violation of this order will be summarrily & severly punished

No Soldier will be allowed to go more than one mile beyon his camp except under order or by special permission on pain of being dalt with as a deserter No Expeditions will be fitted out for the purpose of arresting suspected persons without first getting authourity from these Hed Quarters[1] Soldiers will not be permited to be out of their camps after retreat roll call and all such absentees will be punished by confinement and Extra tours of Guard Duty

To see that this Order is more fully carried out sentinels will ~~be allowed~~ have conducted to the Guard tents all Soldiers returning to camp through the night and company commanders will inspect the tents of their tents of their companies between Tattoo & 12 Ock at night to see that all of their companies are present Men leaving camp will not be permited to carry fire arms and no firing will be allowed in or around the camp

U. S. GRANT Col Comdg
21st Regt Ills Volt

Copy, DNA, RG 94, 21st Ill., Order Book. On July 24, 1861, Brig. Gen. John Pope issued an order assuming command of the District of North Mo. and assigning USG to command at Mexico, Mo. *Ibid.* Misdated July 29 in *O.R.*, I, iii, 415–16.

"My arrival in Mexico had been preceded by that of two or three regiments in which proper discipline had not been maintained, and the men had been in the habit of visiting houses without invitation and helping themselves to food and drink, or demanding them from the occupants. They carried their muskets while out of camp and made every man they found take the oath of allegiance to the government. I at once published orders prohibiting the soldiers from going into private houses unless invited by the inhabitants, and from appropriating private property to their own or to government uses. The people were no longer molested or made afraid. I received the most marked courtesy from the citizens of Mexico as long as I remained there." *Memoirs,* I, 252.

1. USG had punished two men at Salt River Bridge who had brought into camp a "secesher" on their own initiative. James L. Crane, "Grant as a Colonel," *McClure's Magazine,* VII, 1 (June, 1896), 42.

Special Orders

Head Quarters District of Mexico
July 26th 1861

SPECIAL ORDER

One company of cavalry from the 1st Regt Ills and one compy of Infantry from the 15 Ills Vol will be detailed at once to proceed to Montgomery City Mo there to act in conjunction with the Home Guards in repelling a threatened attack upon that point If they find upon reliable information that the enemy are encamped in any place in the neighborhood they will then proceed at once to break up the camp should this fource not be deemed sufficient they will immediately report to these Hd Quarters all the fact learned by them Rations will be sent to-morrow if it is deemed advisable to keep this force detached for a longer than one day

U. S. GRANT, Col. Comdg.

Copy, DNA, RG 94, 21st Ill., Order Book. USG Special Orders No. 4, July 26, and Special Orders No. 3, July 27, 1861, concerned supplies for troops at Montgomery City, Mo., about twenty-five miles southeast of Mexico. Copies, *ibid*. On July 28, USG issued Special Orders No. 5. "In pursuance of directions from the Department of the West, to send a Battallion from this command to occupy Fulton, Mo. the 15th Ills. Volunteers, Lt. Col. E. F. W. Ellis, Commanding, will furnish the detail. The Company now at Montgomery City, Mo. will form ~~these~~ part of the detail and orders will emanate from these Head Quarters to that effect." Copy, *ibid*. Fulton, Mo., is about twenty-four miles south of Mexico.

Special Orders No. 1

Head Quarters Military District
Mexico Mo July 27th 1861

SPECIAL ORDER No 1

By command of Brig. Genl Pope the 24 Ills Voll will move with dispach to St. Louis Mo by way of North M. R. R¹ and

upon arrival at the place to report your Regt. to Major Genl.
Freemont[2] for Service

By Order of

U S Grant Col. Comdg

C. H. FULLER Asist Act Adjut

Copies, DNA, RG 94, 21st Ill., Order Book. The 24th Ill., Col. Friedrich Hecker,
was transferred to Ironton, Mo. Special Orders No. 2 of the same date was similarly worded for a command of light art. *Ibid.* Both are marked "Void."

1. North Missouri Railroad.
2. John C. Frémont of S.C. served in the U.S. Topographical Corps, 1838–
46, winning distinction as an explorer of the West and in the U.S. acquisition of
Calif. He then was U.S. Senator from Calif. and the 1856 Republican presidential
nominee. On July 3, 1861, he was appointed maj. gen. and assigned to command
the Western Dept., which included all territory from the Mississippi River to the
Rocky Mountains and Ill. *O.R.*, I, iii, 390. He did not arrive in St. Louis to take
command until July 25. *Ibid.*, p. 406.

Special Orders No. 28

———

Head Quarters Military Dist
Mexico, Mo July 31, 1861.

SPECIAL ORDERS No. 28.

Capt Jas. E. Calloway, will proceed ~~by~~ at the earliest practicable moment to Springfield Ills., and correct as far as possible
the many errors that have been made in filling Requisitions for
the 21st Ills. Vols. by the Quartermasters Dept. of the State.

He will also transact all public business entrusted to his care,
take charge of such property as may be turned over to him for
transportation to this place, and return and report for duty with
his company & Regt. without unnecessary delay

U. S. GRANT
Col. 21st Regt Inft. U. S. V.

Copy, DNA, RG 94, 21st Ill., Order Book. Capt. James E. Calloway of Tuscola,
Ill., later served as maj. and lt. col. of the 21st Ill.

To Samuel A. Buckmaster

———

Mexico, Mo.
July 31st 1861

S. R. Buckmaster, Esq.
Alton Ill.

Having no acquaintances in Alton and wishing a small favor from some one there I take the liberty of addressing you. I have had a small package of money sent me by express and I understand it is in your city in the hands of the Ex Agt. I wrote a letter several days ago to have it forwarded to this place but it has not yet arrived. The favor I would ask is that you, if it does not put you to too much trouble, would see the Express Agt. and tell him to forward to this place at once as I may be ordered from here shortly.

You will confer a favor on me by attending to this and put me under many obligations.

Your Obt. Svt.
U. S. Grant
Col. 21st Ill. Vols.

ALS, deCoppet Collection, NjP. Samuel A. Buckmaster, an unsuccessful candidate for the Democratic nomination for governor of Ill. in 1860, was elected speaker of the Ill. House of Representatives in 1863. On July 13, 19, 1861, USG had written to his wife that his regt. would be encamped at Alton, Ill.

To Lt. Col. Edward F. W. Ellis

———

Head Quarters Military Dist.
Mexico, Aug. 3d 1861

Lt. Col. Ellis
15th Ill. Vols
Instructions:

Your Command being without bread it will be necessary to procure it on the road. To do this you will get all you can find at Bake houses and any more that may be necessary from private families, giving, in all instances, orders on the Brigade Com.y, who you will also furnish with provision returns covering the issue of the same.

In making the march I would do it mostly by night unless there should be a change of weather making it much more favorable for day marching than for the past few days.

In concecuence of dust the Artillery should go immediately in rear of the Column, the waggon train in rear of the Artillery, and a Rear Guard to bring up the waggons and keep them closed up. An advance Guard should also be thrown out on the march, and where, in your judgement, there might be danger of an ambush, also flank Guards.

Your instructions from Gen. Pope probably point out to you where you are to go and the route, if they do not however you will proceed as expeditiously as possible to Hannibal via New London,[1] at which point you will find Col. Marshall.[2] Should you not meet Col. Marshall at New London however, and find that he has not passed that place, you will await his arrival there.

U. S. GRANT
Col. Comd.g Dist. of Mexico

ALS, IHi. Lt. Col. Edward F. W. Ellis of Rockford, Ill., 15th Ill., was later killed at Shiloh. On Aug. 3, 1861, USG issued Special Orders No. 9. "Lt. Col. E. F. W. Ellis, of the 15th Infty will hold himself in readiness to march from this place by 6 o.clock this afternoon with the entire effective force under his command. One Commissioned Officer, with one Peice of Artillery, fifty rounds of amunition, and the requisite squad of men for manoevering it, will accompany the command under Col. Ellis; also, two companies of the 21st Regt. Ills Infty U. S. V. Capt Davidson of the Artillery will at once report to Col. Ellis. the detail under this order from his Battery. Capt. Ed. Harlan. and Lieut. B. F. Reed with their companies, are detailed from the 21st Infty to accompany the expedition. The command under Col. Ellis will be provided with three days salt meat, and five days of all other rations" Copy, DNA, RG 94, 21st Ill., Order Book.

1. New London, Mo., about eight miles south of Hannibal, Mo.
2. Col. Thomas A. Marshall, 1st Ill. Cav.

To Jesse Root Grant

———

Mexico Mo.
Aug ~~July~~ 3, 1861

DEAR FATHER;

I have written to you once from this place[1] and received no answer, but as Orvil writes to me that you express great anxiety to hear from me often I will try and find time to drop you a line twice a month, and oftener when anything of special interest occurs.

The papers keep you posted as to Army Movements and as you are already in possession of my notions on Secession nothing more is wanted on that point. I find here however a different state of feeling from what I expected existed in any part of the South. The majority in this part of the State are Secessionists, as we would term them, but deplore the present state of affairs. They would make almost any sacrifice to have the Union restored, but regard it as disolved and nothing is left for them but to choose between two evils. Many too seem to be entirely ignorant of the object of present hostilities. You can't convince them but what the ultimate object is to extinguish, by force, slavery. Then too they feel that the Southern Confederacy will never consent to give up their State and as they, the South, are the strong party it is prudent to favor them from the start. There is never a movement of troops made that the Secession journals through the Country do not give a startling account of their almost annihilation at the hands of the States troops, whilst the facts are there are no engagements. My Regt. has been reported cut to pieces once that I know of, and I dont know but oftener, whilst a gun has not been fired at us. These reports go uncontradicted here and give confirmation to the conviction already entertained that one Southron is equal to five Northerners. We believe they are deluded and know that if they are not we are.

Since I have been in Command of this Military District (two weeks) I have received the greatest hospitality and attention from the Citizens about here. I have had every opportunity of conversing with them freely and learning their sentiments and although I have confined myself strictly to the truth as to what has been the result of the different engagements, ~~and~~ the relative strength etc. and the objects of the Administration, and the North Generally, yet they dont believe a word I dont think.

I see from the papers that my name has been sent in for Brigadier Gen.!² This is certainly very complimentary to me particularly as I have never asked a friend to intercede in my behalf. My only acquaintance with men of influence in the State was whilst on duty at Springfield³ and I then saw much pulling and hauling for favors that I determined never to ask for anything, and never have, not even a Colonelcy. I wrote a letter to Washington tendering my services⁴ but then declined ~~Mr. T~~ Gov. Yates' & Mr. Trumbull's endorsement.

My services with the Regt. I am now with have been highly satisfactory to me. I took it in a very disorganized, demoralized and insubordinate condition and have worked it up to a reputation equal to the best, and I believe with the good will of all the officers and all the men. Hearing that I was likely to be promoted the officers, with great unanimity, have requested to be attached to my Command. This I dont want you to read to others for I very much dislike speaking of myself.

We are now breaking up Camp here gradually. In a few days the last of us will be on our way for the Mo. River, at what point cannot be definitely determined, wood & water being a concideration, as well as a healthy fine sigh[t] for a large encampment. A letter addressed to me at Galena will probably find me there. If I get my promotion I shall expect to go there for a few days.

Remember me to all at home and write to me.

Yours Truly
U. S. GRANT

Copy, MoSHi. The last paragraph and closing are reproduced in John H. Gundlach sale, American Art Association, Jan. 5–6, 1927.

1. This letter has not been found.

2. On July 30, 1861, President Abraham Lincoln requested Secretary of War Simon Cameron to send him a nomination as brig. gen. for USG. Lincoln, *Works*, VIII, 593. Cameron replied on July 31, and Lincoln wrote his letter of transmittal the same day. The nomination was received by the Senate on Aug. 1 and referred to the Committee on Military Affairs, reported back on Aug. 3, and confirmed on Aug. 5. *Senate Executive Journal*, XI, 497, 505, 533, 554. The news that USG had been recommended for brig. gen. by the Ill. congressional delegation appeared in the *Illinois State Journal* and *Illinois State Register* on July 31, 1861. Word had reached the 21st Ill. at Mexico, Mo., by Aug. 1. Letter of "Orion," Aug. 1, 1861, in *Missouri Democrat*, Aug. 3, 1861. Chaplain James L. Crane later recalled that he had read of the likely promotion in the *Missouri Democrat* and called it to USG's attention. "Grant as a Colonel," *McClure's Magazine*, VII, 1 (June, 1896), 43. USG said he learned of his promotion through a St. Louis newspaper. *Memoirs*, I, 254.

3. USG believed that Lincoln had requested Ill. congressmen to recommend suitable persons for brig. gen. *Ibid*. USG probably based his belief on a statement made at the end of the Civil War by John A. Logan. *Chicago Times*, May 12, 1865. There is no reliable evidence that Lincoln asked the congressmen of Ill. or any other state to recommend candidates for brig. gen., or even that he considered the appointments a matter for equitable distribution among the states. On the other hand, the Ill. congressmen met once to divide patronage, and then met again to select brig. gens. John Y. Simon, "From Galena to Appomattox: Grant and Washburne," *Journal of the Illinois State Historical Society*, LVIII, 2 (Summer, 1965), 171. Foremost among USG's friends in urging promotion was Republican Elihu B. Washburne. USG knew Democratic Congressman Philip B. Fouke from the days when he lived in St. Louis, and had met Democrats John A. Logan and John A. McClernand when they spoke to his men at Camp Yates. *Memoirs*, I, 238–39, 244–46. Where USG had met Republican Senator Lyman Trumbull is not known, but USG had mustered in the 8th Congressional District Regt. on May 11 at Belleville, Ill., Trumbull's hometown. Republican Senator Orville H. Browning had also favored the promotion of USG. Theodore Calvin Pease and James G. Randall, eds., *The Diary of Orville Hickman Browning* (Springfield, 1925), I, 487–88, 490.

4. See letter of May 24, 1861.

To Julia Dent Grant

———

Mexico, Mo.
J̶u̶ August 3d 1861

DEAR JULIA;

This is the last letter you will get from me from this point. We are now breaking up camp preparitory to moving on to the Missouri river. At what point I cannot yet say. From the accounts ~~of the~~ in the papers I may not go along however.[1] I see some kind friends have been working to get me the Appointment of Brigadier General[2] which, if confirmed may send me any place where there are Ill. troops.

I am glad to get away from here. The people have been remarkably polite if they are seceshers, but the weather is intolerably warm and dry and as there is neither wells nor springs in this country we have drank the whole place dry.[3] People here will be glad to get clear of us ~~here~~ notwithstanding their apparent hospitality. They are great fools in this section of country and will never rest until they bring upon themselvs all the horrors of war in its worst form. The people are inclined to carry on a guerilla Warfare that must eventuate in retaliation and when it does commence it will be hard to controll. I hope from the bottom of my heart I may be mistaken but since the defeat of our troops at Manassas[4] things look more gloomy here.

How long has it been since I wrote to you before? I am kept very busy and time passes off rapidly so that it seems but a day or two. I have received two letters from you since our arrival, one in which you gave me fits for sending Fred. home by himself[5] and one of later date. Fred. will make a good General some day and I think you had better pack his valise and start him on now. I should like very much to see you and the children again.—The weather has been intolerably warm here for the last week.[6]

You need not write to me until you hear from me again. I will write soon and often if I do write short letters. Give my love to all at home. Kiss the children for me. Does Jess. talk about his pa or has he forgotten me. Little rascal I want to see him. Love and kisses for yourself.

U. S. GRANT

ALS, DLC-USG.

1. USG assumed that promotion would mean reassignment.
2. See preceding letter.
3. "There is considerable sickness in camp at present. Water is both inconvenient and impure. A change of rendezvous, where good water can be

procured, will be made as soon as arrangements can be perfected for encampment." Letter of "Orion," Aug. 1, 1861, in *Missouri Democrat*, Aug. 3, 1861.

4. The first battle of Manassas or Bull Run, July 21, 1861.

5. See letter to Jesse Root Grant, July 13, 1861.

6. Four and a half lines crossed out.

To Julia Dent Grant

Mexico Mo.
Aug. 4th 1861

DEAR JULIA;

I wrote you yesterday and now again, wont you get tired hearing from me? The reason I write now is that I have just sent my pay accounts down to St. Louis to C. W. Ford[1] requesting him to draw the money and ~~mail~~ Express it to you. I want you to give each of the children a quarter for their pa, keep fifty dollars and turn the balance over to the store.

I received a letter from Mr. Duncan[2] yesterday and one the day before. You can say to him that as Col. of a Regt. I have no appointments outside of the Regt. and as Brig. Gen. should I get the appointment, none outside the Army. In the latter position however it might be possible to secure him a place either with the Quarter Master or Commissary of the Brigade if either of these officers should have a place to fill. I am not a Brigadier General yet though and cannot build upon what I will do; do not even know where it may carry me.

We will all be away from here by next Thursday.[3] On the line of the Hannibal & St. Jo Railroad seems to be our destination. Soldiers always like to keep moving and are consequently delighted with the change. The weather has been intolerably warm here for the last week, which, with bad water, has made a great many of our men sick. A change always restores a great many.

I expect to go to St. Louis soon after leaving here, for a day or two, but will not be able to go out to see your father. If I knew what day I should be there I would write to him so that if he was visiting the City he might see me.

Remember me to all our relations and friends and to Mother particularly. If you would like to go to Covington and remain for the balance of the War, paying your board, you can do so provided I get the appointment of Brig. Gen.[4] About this you can do just as you please.

Kisses to yourself and the children.

ULYS.

ALS, DLC-USG.

1. Charles W. Ford, whose friendship with USG began at Sackets Harbor, N.Y., was later manager of the United States Express Co. in St. Louis. *PUSG*, 1, *339n*.

2. Probably S. F. Duncan of Galena, twenty-one-year-old stepson of G. W. Brownell. See letter of May 3, 1861, note 5.

3. Aug. 8, 1861.

4. See letter to Julia Dent Grant, Aug. 10, 1861.

General Orders No. 7

Headquarters Ironton Mo

August 8th 1861

GENERAL ORDERS No 7

In pursuance of instructions from Department Hd. Quarters the undersigned hereby assumes command of the Military district of Ironton.

Col: B. Gratz Brown who is relieved by this order will hold himself in readiness to move to St Louis, to-morrow with the portion of his regiment now here, on his arrival at St Louis he will report to Maj: Genl: Fremont for orders.

By order of U. S. Grant,

Brig: Genl: Commanding

To Col: B. Gratz Brown
Commdg: 4th Regt U.S.R.C.   M.S. HASIE[1]

Post Adjutant

Copies, DNA, RG 393, Western Dept., Letters Received; *ibid.*, USG General Orders; *ibid.*, RG 94, 21st Ill., Order Book; DLC-USG, V, 12, 13, 14, VIA, 1. *O.R.*, I, iii, 431. On Aug. 6, 1861, Capt. John C. Kelton, asst. adjt. gen. for Maj. Gen. John C. Frémont, wrote from St. Louis to Brig. Gen. John Pope. "The general directs that you send to this city immediately the Fourteenth, Fifteenth, and Twenty-first Illinois Regiments . . ." *Ibid.*, p. 428. On the same day, Frémont reported to John G. Nicolay, secretary to President Abraham Lincoln. "We are reenforcing and intrenching Ironton, Cape Girardeau, and Bird's Point." *Ibid.*, p. 427.

Before receiving word of USG's transfer, Pope had sent him to St. Louis. On Aug. 5, he wrote to Frémont. "I send down Col Grant of the 21 Ill Vol. to inform you more fully than can be done by letter of the policy I am pursuing here & its effects upon the people—He can also give full information concerning all matters of interest in this region—He bears with him despatches to the Adjt Genl of which I beg your careful perusal—Col Grant is an old army officer thoroughly a gentleman & an officer of intelligence & discretion I receivd a dispatch from Chester Harding Jr asst adjt Genl this morning dated Cairo Aug 3.—It is in cypher & I have not the key. I have directed Col Grant to ask it from you & to return at once by Special Engine." The letter is endorsed "Delivered by Col. Grant." LS, DNA, RG 393, Western Dept., Letters Received. *O.R.*, II, i, 201–2. The following day, Kelton wrote to Maj. Justus McKinstry, q.m. of the Western Dept. "The 14th, 15th and 21st, Illinois Regiments, also Colonel Marshall's Regiment 1st Illinois Cavalry, having been ordered to this city, the General directs that you furnish the necessary transportation. Colonel Marshall, with parts of his regiment and others, will be to day at Hannibal. You may obtain information to aid you in preparing transportation, from Colonel Grant, (of the 21st Illinois,) now at the Planter's House. You will furnish a special engine to be ready to day at Eleven o'clock and Forty five minutes, to convey Colonel Grant to Saint Charles; where an engine will be waiting for him at 1 o/c and 30 minutes." Copy, DNA, RG 393, Western Dept., Letters Sent.

On Aug. 7, when the 21st Ill. reached St. Louis, USG received Special Orders No. 35 from Kelton. "Colonel Grants Regiment, 21st Illinois Volunteers, having arrived in this City, will immediately proceed to Ironton. The Quartermaster Department will furnish the necessary transportation" Copies, *ibid.*, Special Orders; DLC-USG, VIA, 1. *O.R.*, I, liii, 499. About 1:00 P.M., the 21st Ill. boarded the steamer *Jeannie Deans* for transportation to Jefferson Barracks, a few miles below St. Louis, where it encamped. Letter of "Orion," Aug. 8, 1861, in *Missouri Democrat*, Aug. 10, 1861; letter of J. L. C. [James L. Crane?], Aug. 9, 1861, *ibid.*, Aug. 13, 1861; Philip Welshimer to wife, Aug. 9, 1861, *USGA Newsletter*, IV, 1 (Oct., 1966), 6. Also on Aug. 7, Frémont wrote to USG. "It is necessary that your regiment should be ready at an early hour tomorrow, to proceed by Railroad to Ironton An engine will be sent down early in the morning to notify them to be ready for the train. It may be advisable to leave a detachment in charge of the baggage to follow by the train of 11,40." Copy, DNA, RG 393, Western Dept., Letters Sent by Gen. Frémont. The next morning, Kelton sent further orders to USG. "A special train will be sent to take up your regiment at Jefferson Barracks this morning at 9 o'clock. You are directed to proceed to with it to Pilot Knob and take command of the force stationed there under Colonels Brown Hecker and Bland. You will find at the post an officer of Engineers, Major Kraut, engaged in laying out entrenchments which you are requested to push forward with all possible rapidity, employing for this purpose whatever number of men Major Kraut may judge as practicable to use advantageously. It is intended to so strengthen the frontier as to make it tenable against any force likely to be brought against it and to this end additional men and stores will be immediately sent forward. To aid in the works two companies of the Engineer regiments will be sent forward to-day together with four heavy barbett guns. No lighter guns are at this moment disposable. No enemy is reported as advancing with the intention of turning your position and breaking up your communication with St. Louis by destroying the railroads in your rear. You are to scour the country in advance as far as your means will allow, keeping a watchful eye upon the approach by Fredericksburg, and informing yourself immediately of intended movements by employing reliable spies agreeable to the instructions of yesterday's date addressed to Col B. Gratz Brown You are to prepare for the contingency of a sudden movement with the force under your command, holding meanwhile your position until further orders and communicating daily with these Headquarters. A locomotive has been placed at Ironton at the orders of the Commanding officer of the post. Lt. Col. Kalhman is holding the road between Ironton and St. Louis with a sufficient force and you will direct him to withdraw the rolling stock of the road to this place in the event of an attack by a greatly superior force and take such other further measures as your judgment may suggest." Copies, *ibid.*, USG Hd. Qrs. Correspondence; *ibid.*, Western Dept., Letters Sent (Press); *ibid.*, Letters Sent by Gen. Frémont; DLC-USG, V, 7, 8. *O.R.*, I, iii, 430–31.

At Ironton, USG relieved Col. Benjamin Gratz Brown, 4th Regt. U.S. Reserve Corps, a St. Louis lawyer, former member of the Mo. legislature, and unsuccessful candidate for governor in 1857. He was later U.S. Senator from Mo. (1863–67), governor of Mo., and Liberal Republican candidate for vice president in 1872. On Aug. 8, Brown reported to Kelton that the enlistments of his men, three month vols., had expired the previous day, that they insisted on returning to St. Louis, and that "remaining here they would be a positive embarrassment." ALS, DNA, RG 393, Western Dept., Letters Received. When Brown took his regt. to St. Louis, three remained at Ironton: 6th Mo., Col. Peter E. Bland; 24th Ill., Col. Friedrich Hecker; 21st Ill., Lt. Col. John W. S. Alexander. On Aug. 5, 2nd Lt. Montague S. Hasie, post adjt., had reported to Kelton 2,405 men in and near Ironton, 423 of them in Brown's regt. ALS, *ibid.*

On Aug. 8, Edward H. Castle wrote to Frémont. "I arrived here with Genl Grant & Troops at 3. P. M. this day, find all quiet, but badly Scart, they talk of the enemys camps within thirty or forty miles, of this place, but *fighting here* looks to me like gold Hunting in Calafornia—allways Rich leads are a little father on or in some other locality—Genl Grant I am pleasd with. He will do to lead. I find the Iron mountain Rail Road well & expensively built, good Bridges & fair Stock capable of conveying a large number of Troops at any time upon Short notice. Pilot Knob lies several hundred feet above St Louis I should judge after leaving the River Bank the grades ar heavy coming South. I took two Engins and found I had no power to spare—this section of country is Romantic, healthy, good water, & Rather Beautiful fine place for the Troops to spend hot weather, drill & shoot at Target" ALS, *ibid.* Frémont had appointed Castle his superintendent of railroad transportation. *HED*, 37–2–94, p. 11; *HRC*, 37–2–2, part 1, 922–23.

1. See letter to Capt. John C. Kelton, Aug. 9, 1861.

General Orders No. 9

———

Headquarters, Ironton Mo.
Aug. 9th 1861

GENERAL ORDERS No 9

All Regimental and Detachment Commanders will at once report the strength and condition of their respective commands to these Headquarters, also the amount of Amunition on hand, the number and condition of teams, number of public or captured horses, and all other information needful.

All firing must be discontinued by this command in and around camp. The firing of a musket will be the signal of an attack, when the long roll must be beat in every camp and the troops formed on their respective parade grounds, under arms to await orders.

All false alarms must be summarily punished.

Commanders will see that the men of their respective commands are always within the sound of the drum, and to this end there must be at least five roll-calls per day. The Commanding officer from each company must be present at each roll-call and see that all absentees are reported and punished.

When it is necessary to draw the loads of the ~~guns of the~~ old guards, it will be done immediately after guard mounting, and at such place as will hereafter be designated.

Requisitions will at once be made upon the Quartermaster at St. Louis for such Clothing, Camp and Garrison equippage as may be required. Three Dutch Ovens, per company will be included in the requisitions for camp equippage.

The Commander of troops at Pilot Knob[1] will be held responsible for all drunkeness ~~at~~ in and ~~in the vicinity of~~ around that point; and to enable him to preserve sobriety he is authorized to suppress all drinking houses.

Company Officers will read or cause to be read, to their respective commands, the "articles of war" at least twice within the next four days.

Hereafter the strictest discipline is expected to be maintained in this camp and the General Commanding will hold responsible for this all officers, and the degree of responsibility will be in direct ratio ~~to~~ with the rank of the officer.

U. S. Grant
Brig. General

Copies, DLC-USG, V, 12, 13, 14; DNA, RG 393, USG General Orders; *ibid.*, RG 94, 21st Ill., Order Book. On Aug. 9, 1861, Col. Friedrich Hecker sent USG the required reports and also eight pages of "personal observations" on the condition of his regt. ALS, *ibid.*, RG 393, District of Southeast Mo., Letters Received.

1. Pilot Knob, a small elevation about two miles north of Ironton.

To Capt. John C. Kelton

Head Quarters, Ironton Mo.
August 9th 1861

Capt. J. C. Kelton
Asst. Adj. Genl U.S.A.
St. Louis Mo.
Sir:

Enclosed herewith please find consolidated report of the command at this place as near as it can at present be given.[1]

I arrived here yesterday and assumed command in pursuance of directions from Maj. Gen. J. C. Frémont. Since that time I have studied the nature of the ground it may become necessary for me to defend, the character of the troops and other means to do it with &c.

From all that I have yet learned from spies, and loyally disposed citizens, I am led to believe that there is no force within thirty miles of us that entertain the least idea of attacking this position, unless it should be left so weak as to invite an attack.[2] It is fortunate too if this is the case for many of the officers seem to have so little command ~~of~~ over their men, and military duty seems to be done so loosely, that I feel ~~that~~ at present our resistance would be in the inverse ratio of the number of troops to resist with. In two days more however I expect to have a very different state of affairs, and to improve them continuously.

Spies are said to be seen evry day within a few miles of our camp, ~~and~~ maurauding parties are infesting the country, and pillaging union men within ~~within~~ ten miles of here. At present I can spare no force, in fact have not got suitable troops, to drive these people back and afford to ~~the~~ Union ~~people~~ citizens of this neighborhood the protection I feel they should have. Artillery & Cavelry are much needed and the Quarter Master's department is yet quite deficient. The number of teams would scarsely suffice for the use of this as a Military post without making any forward movement, and those we have are many of them barefoot ~~and~~ and without forage. I have taken steps to remedy these latter defects.

> Respectfully
> Your Obt. Svt.
> U. S. GRANT
> Brig. Gen. Comd.g

ALS, DNA, RG 393, Western Dept., Letters Received. *O.R.*, I, iii, 432. Capt. John C. Kelton of Pa., USMA 1851, served as asst. adjt. gen., Western Dept., June 13–Sept. 19, 1861.

1. The report, dated Aug. 9, was prepared by Act. Asst, Adjt. Gen. Montague S. Hasie. "Col: Alexander's, 21st Regt Ill Vol: has an aggregate of 920, Col: Hecker's, 24th Regt Ill Vol: 850, Col Bland's 6th—Mo Vol 825, and a detachment of the 9th Regt Mo—Vol: which arrived here to-day consisting of about 250 men in all making a total aggregate of 2840 men and officers." ALS, DNA, RG 393, Western Dept., Letters Received.

2. C.S.A. Brig. Gen. William Joseph Hardee of Ga., USMA 1838, at Greenville, Mo., was then seeking additional troops for an attack on Ironton. *O.R.*, I, iii, 632–44 *passim*. For Hardee's strength, see letter to Capt. John C. Kelton, Aug. 10, 1861, note 2.

To Capt. John C. Kelton

Headquarters United States Forces
Ironton, Mo., August 9. 1861

Capt. J. C. Kelton
Asst. Adjt. Gen. Western Department
St. Louis, Mo.

Upon taking command here (being without a staff) I detailed Lieutenant M. S. Hasie of the 4th Regiment Reserve Corps as Acting Assistant Adjutant General, and Lieutenant J. H. Holman as Acting Aid-de-Camp

These two officers belong to a regiment whose term of service has now expired, and I would respectfully ask if they can be retained temporarily in the position assigned them and be entitled to pay. Lieutenant Holman is an Engineer, and if he can be attached to my Staff in that capacity, I would esteem it as a favor.

U. S. Grant
Brigadier General Com'dg

Copies, DLC-USG, V, 4, 5, 7, 8; DNA, RG 393, USG Hd. Qrs. Correspondence. 2nd Lt. Montague S. Hasie was later maj. in Bissell's Mo. Engineers, and 2nd Lt. John H. Holman was later lt. col. 26th Mo., and col. 1st U.S. Colored Inf. See letter to Capt. John C. Kelton, Aug. 26, 1861. USG had already arranged for permanent staff officers. *Memoirs*, I, 254–55. These temporary appointments were announced in General Orders No. 11. Copy, DNA, RG 94, 21st Ill., Order Book. On Aug. 14, 1861, USG wrote to Capt. John C. Kelton recommending Hasie for appointment as asst. adjt. gen. *Ibid.*, RG 393, Western Dept., Register of Letters Received.

General Orders No. 12

Headquarters, Ironton, Mo.
August 10th 1861

GENERAL ORDERS No 12

In order to establish and maintain better order and discipline ~~and to secure~~ for the purpose of obtaining a greater efficiency in ~~this~~ your command, ~~there will hereafter be~~ you will have at least three drills per day—by battalion, compan~~y~~ies and squads. All the officers will be present at the battalion ~~Drills~~ and company officers at the company and squad drills.

Any officer found sleeping out of camp will be placed immediately ~~be placed~~ under arrest.

~~Regimental Commanders will at once~~ You will forthwith publish to your command a set of rules for the ~~government of~~ observance of both officers and men.

Each company or part of a company not on duty will have at least one commissioned officer with it at all times.

The command at Pilot Knob will guard the Quartermasters and Commissary stores at that place, and also furnish pickets for the Caledonia, ~~Warrington~~ Farmington and Middlebrook roads.[1]

Col. Blands will station pickets from his command on all the roads, between the Centreville (which runs in a westerly direction from Ironton) and Fredericktown roads. Col. Flecker[2] will guard the Fredericktown road; Col. Alexander will station pickets on the Centreville road.

Capt. Schmitz[3] will place his men every day until further orders on the top of the "Pilot Knob" or any other elevated position from which a view of the surrounding country can be obtained during the day.

A brigade guard will be detailed from the 21st and 24th Regiments alternately, to day it will consist of the following detail; 1 Lieut., 4 corporals, 2 sergeants and 27 privates, to be furnished by the 24th, and mounted this morning at 11 o'clock. The Headquarters for the Brigade guard will be at the Court

House.[4] The Lieut. in command of this guard will report to these Headquarters at 10 30 o'clock for orders; hereafter the Brigade Guard will be mounted every day at 9.30 a.m.

U. S. Grant
Brig. General

Copies, DLC-USG, V, 12, 13, 14; DNA, RG 393, USG General Orders; *ibid.*, RG 94, 21st Ill., Order Book.

1. On Aug. 9, 1861, USG issued special orders for Lt. Col. John W. S. Alexander. "Colonel Alexander of the 21st Illinois Volunteers, will immediately upon receipt of this order, detail one company from his Regiment and send it with one days rations to Pilot Knob to act as pickets on the roads leading from that point. Upon their arrival, Captain Schmitz of the Pilot Knob Home Guards will station the pickets and give them the necessary directions." Copies, DLC-USG, V, 15, 16, 82; DNA, RG 393, USG Special Orders; *ibid.*, RG 94, 21st Ill., Order Book. On Aug. 10, USG again issued special orders for Alexander. "Colonel Alexander commanding 21st Regiment Illinois Volunteers, will immediately detail from his command, one Sergeant and ten privates, who will proceed to Pilot Knob, Mo., and report to the Post Quartermaster, at the Depot, for orders." Copies, *ibid.*

2. Col. Friedrich Karl Franz Hecker, sometimes called Frederick, the leader of an unsuccessful revolt in Baden in 1848, had settled on a farm near Belleville, Ill., and taken a prominent part in Republican politics. *DAB*, VIII, 493–94.

3. Capt. Ferdinand Schmitz commanded the ninety-nine men of the Pilot Knob Home Guards. Robert Sidney Douglass, *History of Southeast Missouri* (New York and Chicago, 1912), p. 342.

4. On Aug. 15, USG issued special orders for Col. Peter E. Bland. "Colonel P. E. Bland, commanding 6th Regiment Missouri Volunteers, will forthwith detail one commissioned Officer, two Sergeants, four corporals and thirty privates, to relieve the Brigade guard at the court house" Copies, DLC-USG, V, 15, 16, 82; DNA, RG 393, USG Special Orders.

To Capt. John C. Kelton

Head Quarters, Ironton Mo.
August 10th 1861

Capt. J. C. Kelton
Asst. Adj. Gen. U. S. A.
St. Louis, Mo.
Sir:

Since my report of yesterday no change has taken place in the strength or position of this command. No information has been received to lead to the supposition that this place is in danger of an immediate attack. The enemy however recconnoiters to within a few miles of our Picket Guards and I would therefore urgently recommend that Cavelry & Field Artillery be sent here as early as they can be spared.

From information received to-day, which I am disposed to think reliable, Gen. Hardee is at Greenville[1] with 2000 men & six or eight field pieces with 1000 more troops[2] thrown forward to Stoney Battery, near Brunot.[3] Of this force one third is represented to be Cavelry, well mounted and equiped.

This being a healthy location I would reccommend that one or two of the newly organized regiments, say Smith's now at Jeff. Bks. and some other one, be sent here for drill & discipline. This would enable me to use the troops now here for scouting parties without calling upon the new volunteers for much service that would take them from their drill.

If equipments complete for one hundred mounted men could be spared, particularly the Carbines & Revolvers, they could be efficiently used here.[4] The twenty-four mounted Home Guards now here are destitute of suitable arms and are almost useless in consequence.

Respectfully
Your Obt. Svt.
U. S. Grant
Brig. Gen. Comd.g

ALS, DNA, RG 393, Western Dept., Letters Received. *O.R.*, I, iii, 432–33.

    1. Greenville, Mo., about thirty-seven miles south of Ironton.
    2. On Aug. 4, 1861, Brig. Gen. William J. Hardee wrote from Greenville to Maj. Gen. Leonidas Polk that his force consisted of 1,000 inf., 250 cav., and a battery of art. He could also put in the field 1,000 to 1,500 Missourians. *Ibid.*, p. 629. Hardee expected 2,000 more men, Mo. state troops commanded by Brig. Gen. M. Jeff Thompson, in order to advance on Ironton, but Thompson was ordered to support Maj. Gen. Gideon Pillow at New Madrid, Mo. *Ibid.*, pp. 631–43; Jay Monaghan, *Swamp Fox of the Confederacy: The Life and Military Services of M. Jeff Thompson* (Tuscaloosa, 1956), pp. 30–32. Problems of C.S.A. command in southeast Mo. are discussed in Nathaniel Cheairs Hughes, Jr., *General William J. Hardee* (Baton Rouge, 1965), pp. 78–79. On Aug. 12, Hardee wrote Polk. "I cannot count on more than 4,000 effective men." *O.R.*, I, iii, 644. See also *ibid.*, I, liii, 725–29.
    3. Brunot, Mo., about twenty-two miles south of Ironton.
    4. See letter to Capt. John C. Kelton, Aug. 14, 1861, note 4.

To Commanding Officer, 15th Illinois

Headquarters Ironton Mo.
August 10 1861

COMD'G. OFFR 15TH ILLINOIS VOLUNTEERS.
IRONTON MO.

    You will place two companies of your regiment on the Iron Mountain Railroad at such points as may be indicated by Lieut Col Kallman[1] and send two Companies to Potosi.[2] The remainder, with the artillery accompanying will come on to Pilot Knob to be disposed of here. The Companies going to Potosi will take with them as many days rations as you have with you for your command, and at least 100 rounds of ammunition. You will report to these Headquarters immediately the number of days issued for, and make a requition upon the commissary at this place in time to insure your men rations

U. S. GRANT.
Brig. Genl.

Copies, DLC-USG, V, 1, 2, 3; DNA, RG 393, USG Letters Sent. The 15th Ill. was commanded by Col. Thomas J. Turner who was probably away at the time USG wrote.

1. Lt. Col. Herman Kallman, 2nd Mo. Reserve Corps. See *O.R.*, I, liii, 498.
2. When Potosi, Mo., about twenty-five miles northwest of Ironton, was attacked by rebels on the evening of Aug. 10, 1861, no cos. of the 15th Ill. were there. See letter to Capt. John C. Kelton, Aug. 11, 1861.

To Julia Dent Grant

Ironton Mo.
August 10th 1861

DEAR JULIA;

Night before last[1] I come down to Jefferson Bks. with my old Regt. leaving my trunk at the Planter's House[2] flattering myself that at 9 O'Clock the next day I would return to St. Louis, get a leave of absence for a few days and pop down upon you taking you by surprize. But my destination was suddenly changed, 9 O'Clock brought me orders, (and cars to carry a regiment) to proceed at once to this place and assume command.[3] My present command here numbers about 3000 and will be increased to 4000 to-morrow[4] and probably much larger the next day. When I come there was great talk of an attack upon this place and it was represented that there was 8000 rebels within a few miles but I am not ready to credit the report.[5]

I have envited Mr. Rollins of Galena to accept a place on my Staff.[6] I wish you would tell Orvil to say to him that I would like to have him come as soon as possible if he accepts the position.

I sent you some money the other day and requested Ford[7] to write to you. Did he do it? The four gold dollars were thrown in extra for the four children. Bless their hearts I wish I could see them.

I certainly feel very greatful to the people of Ill. for the interest they seem to have taken in me and unasked too. Whilst I was about Springfield I certainly never blew my own trumpet and was not aware that I attracted any attention but it seems from what I have heard from there the people, who were perfect strangers to me up to the commencement of our present unhappy national difficulties, were very unanimous in recommending me for my present position. I shall do my very best not to disappoint them and shall hope by dilligence to render good account of some of the Ill. Vols. All my old Regt. expressed great regret at my leaving them and applied to be attached to my Brigade.

I called to see Harry Boggs[8] the other day as I passed through St. Louis. He cursed and went on like a Madman. Told me that I would never be welcom in his hous; that the people of Illinois were a poor misserable set of Black Republicans, Abolition paupers that had to invade their state to get something to eat. Good joke that on something to eat. Harry is such a pittiful insignificant fellow that I could not get mad at him and told him so where upon he set the Army of Flanders far in the shade with his profanity.

Give my love to all the good people of Galena. I hope to be at home a day or two soon but dont you be disappointed if I am. Kiss the children for me.—Dont act upon the permission I gave you to go to Covington to board until you hear from me again on the subject.

ULYS.

ALS, DLC-USG.

1. Actually, Aug. 7, 1861.
2. A downtown St. Louis hotel.
3. See orders of Aug. 8, 1861.
4. The larger figure includes the 15th Ill.
5. See letter to Capt. John C. Kelton, Aug. 10, 1861, note 2.
6. On Aug. 7, USG had written to John A. Rawlins. The letter has not been found. See letter to Julia Dent Grant, Aug. 15, 1861, note 5.
7. See letter of Aug. 4, 1861.
8. Harry Boggs, a cousin of Julia Dent Grant, had been USG's partner in a St. Louis real estate business. *PUSG*, 1, 346n–48n.

To Capt. John C. Kelton

———

Headquarters U. S. Forces,
Ironton Mo August 11 1861.

CAPTAIN J C KELTON
ST LOUIS MO.

Since my report of yesterday, in addition to the ordinary picket guards established, one company has been sent towards Caledonia,[1] two companies to report to Colonel Kallman for the protection of the rail-road, four companies to Potosi, the mounted Home Guards and two spies to ascertain the position, &c, of the Confederate troops.[2] An attack was made on the Home Guards at Potosi last night, resulting in the wounding of five of them and the shooting and taking of six of the other party, shooting three of their horses and getting a number of pistols, shot-guns, rifles, &c.[3] Quite a number of marauders are reported in the Belleville Valley, northwest of Ironton, taking all the horses they can find. The party now moving towards Caledonia may meet them.

The picket guards have brought in four prisoners this evening, well armed. The party of secessionists who attacked the Home Guards at Potosi are estimated to number about 120 men, commanded by Captain White, of Fredericktown. Nothing scarcely can be done towards fortifying this place, for the want of tools to work with. This matter has not been reported before, because two companies of Engineers were expected, and with them all tools required. I neglected in my report of yesterday to notice the arrival of three companies of the 9th Regt Missouri Volunteers,[4] also of two companies 21st Regiment Illinois Volunteers. I have this day appointed 1st Lt Clark B. Lagow, 21st Illinois Volunteers, Aide-de-Camp[5] and 1st Lieut Joseph Vance, of same regiment, to drill and instruct the officers and non-commissioned officers of the 9th Missouri Regiment.[6]

U. S. GRANT.
Brigadier General

Copies, DNA, RG 94, War Records Office, Union Battle Reports; *ibid.*, RG 393, USG Hd. Qrs. Correspondence; DLC-USG, V, 4, 5, 7, 8. *O.R.*, I, iii, 130–31.

1. Caledonia, Mo., about fourteen miles northwest of Ironton.

2. Two USG special orders of Aug. 11, 1861, relate to the deployment of troops. "Colonel Alexander, commanding 21st Illinois Volunteers, will immediately detail and send one company with one days rations, to relieve the company belonging to his Regiment, now on guard at Pilot Knob, as soon as the company now there, has been relieved, it will return to camp at this place. The company sent to Pilot Knob, will report to Captain Schmitz, to be detailed by him as pickets on the roads." Copies, DNA, RG 393, USG Special Orders; dated Aug. 10, 1861, *ibid.*, RG 94, 21st Ill., Order Book; DLC-USG, V, 15, 16, 82. "Major W. E. McMackin, 21st Illinois Volunteers, will forthwith take the detachment of the 9th Missouri Volunteers, consisting of three companies, and one company of his Regiment, with two days rations, and proceed without camp equipage, down the Iron Mountain Railroad as far as Mineral Point, where he will report to Colonel Kallman for further orders. It is absolutely necessary that this order should be promptly complied with and that Major McMackin should have his Battalion on the cars as soon as possible." Copies, *ibid.*

3. On Aug. 11, Maj. Gen. John C. Frémont ordered Col. Frederick Schaefer, 2nd Mo. Vols., to retake Potosi, Mo., and then to report both to him and to USG. Copy, DNA, RG 393, Western Dept., Letters Sent by Gen. Frémont. *O.R.*, I, iii, 436. On Aug. 12, Schaefer wrote to USG from Potosi. "By order by me recieved of Maj Gen Fremont, I hereby Report my self to you. I arrived here, at about, 8. o.clock this morning but did not find any more Rebells here. There where two Co of Col Heckers Regt stationed here, under Comd of Col Kahlman U. S. R. C. The information recd from Capt French of the Home Guards of this place about the fight wich took place here last saturday is as follows. on Staturday Evg at about 6. o clock, the Home Guards where attackted by about 150 Mounted Rebells, at the time of the attack there where only about 20 Home Guards on duty. the rest where out protecting the Bridges on the Road. That brave little Band of Home Guards drove those 150 Mounted Rebells from the Town, taking several of there Horses and wounding five, Rebells, the Home Guards had five of there Men allso wounded but not seriously when I arrived in this Town the two Cos of Heckers Regt U. S A. left to join there Regt. and took (17) seventeen prisoners with them. the Town at present is all quait" LS, DNA, RG 94, War Records Office, Union Battle Reports. *O.R.*, I, iii, 131.

4. The 9th Mo., consisting of cos. raised in Ill., was designated the 59th Ill. on Feb. 12, 1862. Since John C. Kelton was not appointed col. of the 9th Mo. until Sept. 19, 1861, Lt. Col. Charles H. Frederick apparently commanded the regt. at Ironton. *New York Times*, Aug. 21, 1861.

5. By General Orders No. 14, Aug. 11. Copies, DLC-USG, V, 12, 13, 14; DNA, RG 393, USG General Orders. 1st Lt. Clark B. Lagow of Crawford County, Ill., joined the 21st Ill. on May 7. On July 24, Lagow had written to Governor Richard Yates. "If you could get the appointment of 'Aid de Camp from Genl Fremont or Genl Pope for me—you will confer a lasting obligation— The county of Crawford as yet has had nothing in any way. as to our loyalty last fall we need only to refer you to the times—we think that we are entitled to some consideration. Hope you can consider it the same. Would be pleased to hear from you in reffernce to the above" ALS, Yates Papers, IHi. USG stated that he ap-

pointed Lagow because he thought it proper to make one appointment from his own regt. See letter to Julia Dent Grant, Aug. 15, 1861; *Memoirs*, I, 254.

6. USG special orders of Aug. 10 assigned 1st Lt. Joseph W. Vance to instruct the officers of the 9th Mo. Copy, DNA, RG 94, 21st Ill., Order Book.

To Capt. John C. Kelton

Head Quarters Ironton Mo
August 11th 1861.

CAPT J C KELTON
ASST ADJT GEN USA.
ST LOUIS MO;
SIR;

Herewith please find requisition of the 21st Ill Vols. for arms forwarded for the approval of Gen Fremont; The 21st Ill Vols marched from Springfield on the 3d of July with 500 old muskets altered to percussion, expecting to stop at Quincy, where they could be fully equipped Taking the field however immediately upon arrival at Quincy and being kept upon the go ever since there has been no opportunity since of attending to this.

The Regiment is now armed with 500 muskets old patterns altered to perc 84 Harpers Ferry Rifles borrowed from Col Palmer; and the ballance muskets same as first mentioned borrowed from the State of Ill.

I would respectfully request that the Ordnance Department be directed to furnish suitable arms for this Regiment.

Respectfully
Your Obdt Servt
U S GRANT
Brig Gen Vols.

Copy, DLC-USG, VIA, 1.

To George S. Roper

Ironton Mo.
August 11th 1861

G. S. ROPER, ESQ.
SPRINGFIELD ILL.
DEAR SIR:

Yours of the 5th Inst. directed to me at Mexico Mo. has just reached me at this place. In reply I would say that it would afford me much pleasure to have you attached to my Brigade as Com.y. I have reccommended no one for the position nor have I the power to appoint but I can, and do most cheerfully reccommend you as suitable and well qualified for the position.

If this letter can be of any use to you in geting the appointment use it, with the additional assurance that I will be much pleased to have you attached to any Brigade I may have the honor of commanding.

Yours Truly
U. S. GRANT
Brig. Gen. U. S. A.

ALS, Mrs. Walter Love, Flint, Mich. George S. Roper, born in Mass., had a boot and shoe store in Springfield, Ill., from 1859 until the start of the Civil War when he became chief clerk of the Ill. subsistence dept. It was in this office that he met USG. *The United States Biographical Dictionary . . . Illinois Volume* (Chicago, Cincinnati, and New York, 1876), p. 216. On Aug. 20, 1861, President Abraham Lincoln endorsed USG's letter. "Let Mr. Roper be appointed as within recommended by Gen. Grant." On Sept. 9, Roper was appointed capt. in the commissary dept. and ordered to report to Brig. Gen. William T. Sherman at Louisville, Ky. *Ibid*. See letter to Simon Cameron, Sept. 16, 1861.

To Capt. John C. Kelton

———

Head Quarters, Ironton Mo.
August 12th 1861

CAPT. J. C. KELTON, ASST. ADJT. GEN. U. S. A.
ST. LOUIS MO.

Since my report of yesterday my scouts have returned from towards Brunot, having penetrated as far south as where the enemies most advanced Pickets had occupied the night before. All had left and from the best information received two forces are moving, one as if to come in upon the railroad from the West the other from the East.

Magrauding bands are still reported on the road from Potosi to Calidonia, and further South. Tomorrow I shall have a party in pursuit of them.

Yesterday quite a party of horsemen were within seven miles south of here, on a road West of the one leading to Brunot, but could not be found this morning.

Without Cavelry it is impossible to pursue these bands with any prospect of overtaking them, and with the amount of Picket, ~~duty~~ fatigue, Guard and other duty that must necessarily be performed, it is difficult to spare men for these scouts.

To-day my Guards detained the mail coming in and I have stoped the delivery of letters to a few suspected persons, and the forwarding of six packages of letters, as follows: four to points in Arkansas, one to Memphis, via Little Rock, & one to Brunot. These will be detained awaiting the decission of the Department Commander thereon.

I am entirely without orders for my guidance in matters like the above and without recent Acts of Congress which bear upon them.

I would respectfully urge the necessity of forwarding to this point say forty complete teams. About one hundred good & well broken mules, now in use about the furnaces, can be purchased here. Also harness & some good waggons.

> Respectfully
> Your Obt. Svt.
> U. S. Grant
> Brig. Gen. Com

ALS, DNA, RG 393, Western Dept., Letters Received. *O.R.*, I, iii, 438.

To Capt. John C. Kelton

> Head Quarters, Ironton Mo.
> August 12th 1861

Capt. J. C. Kelton
Asst. Adjt. Gen. U.S.A.
St. Louis Mo.
Sir:

I would respectfully request leave to visit St. Louis as soon as the Gen. Comd.g the Department thinks my services can be spared from here for two days.

I left St. Louis unexpectedly and without any preperation hence this request.

> Respectfully
> Your Obt. Svt.
> U. S. Grant
> Brig. Gen. Com.

ALS, DNA, RG 393, Western Dept., Letters Received. This letter was enclosed with the preceding letter.

To Maj. Warren E. McMackin

Headquarters, Ironton Mo
August 12th 1861.

MAJOR W. E. McMACKIN,
COMDG. EXPED to POTOSI MO.

Press into service as many teams as you want, from secessionists, who will be pointed out by Union men of character, and march up by way of Caledonia, to this place. Bring with you as guide Mr. J. O. Sawyer, the bearer of this, and any one of the "home guards" you may choose. They will be sent home by rail. You will do all you can to capture the party of rebels, who are infesting the country through which you pass, but be careful about crediting reports you receive from citizens. When it is necessary to get provisions for your men, you will take them from active secessionists, if practicable, if not practicable, from Union or law abiding citizens, giving an order on the Post Commissary here for the pay.

Compell persons whose teams you press, to send teamsters to take the teams back. You have my private instructions how to conduct this "pressing" business, so as to make it as little offensive as possible.

Order the train taking Mr Sawyer, to return to this place immediately

U. S. GRANT
Brig Genl.

Copies, DLC-USG, V, 1, 2, 3; DNA, RG 393, USG Letters Sent. *O.R.*, I, iii, 438–39. See letter to Julia Dent Grant, June 26, 1861, note 5.

To Mary Grant

Ironton Mo.
August 12th 1861

DEAR SISTER;

Your letter directed to me at Mexico, Mo. come to hand yesterday at this place. A glance at the map will show you where I am. When I come here it was reported that this place was to be attacked by 8,000 secessionests, under Gen. Hardee, within a day or two.[1] Now Hardee's force seems to have reduced and his distance from here to have increased. Scouting parties however are constantly seen within a few miles of our Pickets. I have here about 3000 Vols. nearly all Infantry, but our position being strong and our cause a good one, it would trouble a much larger force of the enemy to dislodge us.—You ask my views about the continuance of the war &c. Well I have changed my mind so much that I dont know what to think. That the Rebels will be so badly whipped by April next that they cannot make a stand anywhere I dont doubt. But they are so dogged that there is no telling when they may be subdued. Send Union troops among them and respect all their rights, pay for evrything you get and they become desperate and reckless because their state sovereignty is invaded. Troops of the opposite side march through and take evrything they want, leaving no pay but script, and they become desperate secession partisans because they have nothing more to loose. Evry change makes them more desperate. I should like to be sent to Western Virginia but my lot seems to be cast in this part of the world. I wanted to remain in St. Louis a day or two to get some books to read that might help me in my profession, and get my uniform &c. made.[2] Mine has been a busy life from the begining and my new made friends in Ill. seem to give me great credit. I hope to deserve it and shall spare no pains on my part to do so.

It is precious little time I shall have for writing letters but I have subscribed for the Daily St. Louis Democrat[3] to be sent to you, through which you may occationally hear from me.

Write to me often even though your letters are not answered. As I told father in my last,[4] I will try and have you hear from me twice a month if I have to write after midnight.

I told Julia she might go to Covington and board whilst I am away but I dont know but she had better stay where she is.[5] The people of Galena have always shown the greatest friendship for me and I would prefer keeping my home there. I would like very much though if you would go and stay with Julia.

If I get a uniform, and get where I can have my Dagueareo-type taken your wish in that respect shall be gratified.

Your Brother
ULYS.

ALS, PPRF.

    1. See letter to Capt. John C. Kelton, Aug. 10, 1861, note 2.
    2. See letter to Capt. John C. Kelton, Aug. 12, 1861.
    3. The *Missouri Democrat* was published in St. Louis. As a result of political shifts in the last decade, the *Missouri Democrat* generally favored the Republican cause while the *Missouri Republican* favored the Democrats. During the past month, the *Missouri Democrat* had carried more news about USG than any other newspaper.
    4. Aug. 3, 1861.
    5. See letter to Julia Dent Grant, Aug. 10, 1861.

To Capt. John C. Kelton

Head Quarters, Ironton Mo.
August 13th 1861

CAPT. J. C. KELTON
ASST. ADJ. GEN. U.S.A.
ST. LOUIS, MO

I have reliable evidence that about 3000 troops,[1] mostly mounted, but badly armed, stayed near ~~Farmington~~ Frederick-town last night and expressed the intention of moving to-day towards Farmington,[2] with the intention of coming in and destroying the railroad. At the same time it is very reliable that

5000 well armed men, under Gen. Hardee, are advancing upon this place.

I express you the facts and leave it to the Gen. Commanding whether in his judgement more troops should not be sent.

I have to report at the same time that the 32 pound iron pieces sent here are not yet mounted and I fear cannot be to-morrow.

Could a Battery of Field Artillery and one Regiment of Infantry be sent here to-morrow I would feel that this point would be secure beyond any present contingency.

My impression, from the facts before me is, that if attacked atal it will be on Thursday, possibly Wednsday.[3]

Respectfully
Your Obt. Svt.
U. S. GRANT
Brig. Gen. Com.

ALS, DNA, RG 393, Western Dept., Letters Received. *O.R.*, I, iii, 440–41. On Aug. 14, 1861, Maj. Gen. John C. Frémont telegraphed to President Abraham Lincoln. "General Grant, commanding at Ironton, attacked yesterday at 6 by a force reported at 13,000. Railroad seized by the enemy at Big River Bridge, on this side of Ironton." *Ibid.*, p. 441. It is possible that USG's report of "3000 troops" was misread as 13,000; in other respects Frémont's telegram is inexplicable.

1. On Aug. 11, Brig. Gen. William J. Hardee wrote to Maj. Gen. Leonidas Polk. "I have ordered the occupation of Fredericktown, 40 miles in advance of this place, with 600 Missourians, under Colonel Lowe, and 250 mounted Arkansians, the whole under command of Colonel Borland." *Ibid.*, p. 642.

2. Fredericktown, Mo., about eighteen miles east of Ironton, is about seventeen miles southeast of Farmington, Mo.

3. Wednesday, Aug. 14.

To Capt. John C. Kelton

Head Quarters, Ironton Mo.
August 13th 1861

SIR:

Since writing the accompanying report the Comd.g Gen.s directions for moving three bodies of troops from this place has been received.[1] You will see from the information contained in it that the movements ordered would not probably have been with these facts known.

I would also report that this Post is not supplied with teams for moving any conciderable body of troops.

	Respectfully
To Capt. J. C. Kelton	Your Obt. Svt.
Asst. Adj. Gen U.S.A.	U. S. GRANT
St. Louis Mo	Brig. Gen. Com

ALS, DNA, RG 393, Western Dept., Letters Received.

1. On Aug. 12, 1861, Maj. Gen. John C. Frémont wrote to USG. "You are hereby directed for the purpose of keeping both your flanks open and retaining control over the whole neighborhood of your position to send one column to Centreville and another to Frederickstown of both which places you will take possession. At the same time you are required to send out with all necessary precautions a moving column on the road to Greenville whose duty it will be to ascertain the enemy's forces, movements, and intentions. A report having reached this department that Potosi had been captured by a force of the enemy's cavalry I yesterday ordered Col. Schaefer with his regiment, strengthened by two companies of Illinois troops and fifty Illinois cavalry to retake and hold that place. After the occupation of Potosi Col. Schaefer is directed to report to you and to make the proper dispositions for the protection of the railroad and bridges. Major Kraut at present in Ironton will be ordered to this city for the purpose of erecting fortifications here. His place will be supplied by First Lieutenant Wm Hoelcke of the Engineer Corps who will be instructed immediately upon his arrival to report himself to you and to carry on and complete the works commenced by Major Kraut." Copies, *ibid.*, USG Hd. Qrs. Correspondence; DLC-USG, V, 7, 8. *O.R.*, I, iii, 437–38.

To Col. Frederick Schaefer

———

Headquarters Ironton, Mo.
August 13th 1861.

COL. SCHAFER COMD'G &c
POTOSI, Mo.

I have reliable information that some 3000 troops, badly armed, are to make a descent upon the railroad tomorrow with the design of cutting off communication with St. Louis. By leaving Potosi in the morning and taking a position on the road you may prevent it.

Since writing the above I have received orders assigning troops at Potosi to my command.[1] You will therefore comply with the above, sending your cavalry to this place.

U. S. GRANT
Brig. Genl

Copies, DNA, RG 393, USG Letters Sent; DLC-USG, V, 1, 2, 3. Col. Frederick Schaefer, 2nd Mo., was born in Germany and named Friedrich Schäfer. He was ordered to Potosi on Aug. 11, 1861, by Maj. Gen. John C. Frémont. *O.R.*, I, iii, 436.

1. See preceding letter.

To Lt. Col. Géza Mihalotzy

Headquarters Ironton Mo.
August 13, 1861.

LIEUT. COL. MIHELOTZY
COMDG DETACHMENT 24TH ILLS. VOLS.

Immediately on receipt of this you will make a forced march for this place, via Zeiglers Pinery, bringing with you all of Col. Schafers command that you may have

U. S. GRANT
Brig Gen'l

Copies, DLC-USG, V, 1, 2, 3; DNA, RG 393, USG Letters Sent. Géza Mihalotzy, born in Hungary, professionally trained as a soldier, served as capt. in the Hungarian Revolution of 1848. Edmund Vasvary, *Lincoln's Hungarian Heroes* (Washington, 1939), p. 67. In Feb., 1861, he organized a co. of Lincoln Riflemen in Chicago, later absorbed in the 24th Ill., of which he became lt. col. Lincoln, *Works*, IV, 184.

To Capt. John C. Kelton

Head Quarters Ironton Mo
August 14th 1861

CAPT. J. C. KELTON
ASST ADJ GEN.L U.S.A.
ST LOUIS MO
SIR.

Since my report of yesterday two spies[1] have come in reporting the position of the enemy about the same as yesterday. Two
companies sent from here yesterday morning travelled north
west to Caledonia meeting there three companies from Potosi.
Found all quiet, as infantry must necissarily do unless they fall
in with an overwhelming party. With the troops from Potosi is
one company of Col Schafers regiment which I have ordered to
St Louis by to-morrows train understanding that Col Schafers
had been ordered there.[2] To-night I have sent out towards
Frederickstown, Col Hecker with all of his regiment not otherwise on duty.

I will call your attention again to the fact that their is no
Field Artillery or Cavelry, at this post. Both are much needed
especially if effective movements are to be made from here. Their
are three 24 pound pieces four 32 pounders and one 6 pounder
Brass piece without a limber. Amunition sufficient for not
exceeding thirty mintes steady fireing. Heavy ordinance can be
of no special service here for their is no point scarcely where
point blank range of a Six pounder can be had., To day supposing
an attack possible, I had eleven teams belonging to the Pilot
Knob Iron Company drawn into service giving a receipt for
same[3]—The command was directed to make storehouses for
their provisions of the wagons, so that in case of a move to the
support of any of the Pickets becoming necissary, supplies could
be moved to them without delay. Evry move of the enemy seems
to evince a determination to fall upon the railroad at some point
North, at the same time an attack is made here. I am not fully

persuaded that an attack will be made here for the present but hold my command ready to make the best resistance possibly with the means at hand—

The engineer ordered here to relieve Maj Kraut has not yet arrived and under the instructions from Genl Fremont, I do not understand that Maj Kraut is to be relieved untill his successor does arrive—

I understand that equipments for one hundred horses are here, but the fact has never been reported to me official.[4]

I should have stated in the proper connection that I have no artillery men nor officer suitable to take command of a company to drill them as such—[5] I would respectfully recomend the appointment of an ordinance Sergeant for this post.

To day I caused the arrest of ten noted secessionest of this place on suspicion that they might comunicate with the rebels.[6] I prefer no special charges against them, but will keep them temporarily, also arrested one man as a spy who has been arrested once before in this camp since I assumed command. Found a pass upon him of yesterdays date to pass the rebels Guards.

Respectfully &c

U. S. GRANT

Brig. Gen. Com

LS, DNA, RG 393, Western Dept., Letters Received. *O.R.*, I, iii, 442–43.

1. On Aug. 13, 1861, USG issued special orders. "Lieutenants Vorhies and Houts, 6th Missouri Volunteers are hereby detailed to go on a recruiting expedition. They will as far as practicable, ascertain the position of the enemy, his strength and all facts possible, and report the same to these Headquarters as soon as possible" Copies, DNA, RG 393, USG Special Orders; DLC-USG, V, 15, 16, 82. It is not certain that these were the "spies" referred to. 1st Lt. Henry C. Houts was killed later in the week while visiting the camp of Brig. Gen. William J. Hardee in disguise. *Illinois State Journal*, Aug. 24, 1861. See letter to Capt. John C. Kelton, Aug. 15, 1861.
2. On Aug. 13, Col. Frederick Schaefer, 2nd Mo., was ordered to Rolla, Mo. *O.R.*, I, iii, 440. On the same day, Maj. Gen. John C. Frémont wrote to USG. "Colonel Schaefer commanding the 2nd Regiment Mo. Vols. at present stationed at Potosi has been ordered to repair at once with his command to this place and report at headquarters. From this place he will proceed to Rolla to reinforce and support Brigadier General Sigel." Copy, DNA, RG 393, Western Dept., Letters Sent (Press).

3. On Oct. 8, W. B. Crane, manager of the Pilot Knob Iron Co., and Sgt. George A. Tryner, 21st Ill., wrote to USG to request the letter by which Frémont had authorized the purchase of mules at Ironton, since the hd. qrs. copy had been lost. ALS, *ibid.*, District of Southeast Mo., Letters Received. Tryner served as clerk for USG at Ironton, and USG wrote to Capt. John C. Kelton on Aug. 26 requesting that Tryner be "ordered to report to him as clerk." *Ibid.*, Western Dept., Register of Letters Received.

4. On Aug. 12, Frémont's hd. qrs. wrote to USG to ask "if 100 sets of Cavalry equipments sent to Ironton, have been received." Copies, *ibid.*, Letters Sent; DLC-USG, VIA, 1. On the same day, Frémont's hd. qrs. requested Capt. Franklin D. Callender to send USG "100 Sabres, and 200 Pistols made as percussion Cal. 54, with ammunition." Copy, DNA, RG 393, Western Dept., Letters Sent.

5. On Aug. 9, USG issued special orders for Col. Peter E. Bland. "Colonel Peter E. Bland, 6th Regiment Missouri Volunteers, will immediately upon receipt of this order, ascertain the number of artillerists in his command and send them to these Headquarters tomorrow morning at 11 O'clock" Copies, DLC-USG, V, 15, 16, 82; DNA, RG 393, USG Special Orders. On Aug. 14, USG issued two special orders detailing portions of the 6th Mo. to service as artillerists. Copies, *ibid.*

6. On Aug. 15, Philip Pipkin and ten others wrote to USG. "Those of us, citizens of the towns of Pilot Knob, Ironton and Arcadia, whose names are signed to this paper, being held as prisoners by you, not, as we are assured, because of any charges to be prefered against us, but to insure greater safety to the Army of the Federal Government under your command and to guard against the possibility of any communication with the enemy, desire to be discharged upon our parole of honor, that we will not, now, nor hereafter, during the present civil war, confer with, nor communicate to, the enemy, any information touching the condition, disposition, or numbers of the Federal forces, which may now be or hereafter come into our possession or knowledge. As an inducement to your favorable consideration of our request, we would say that we have long been residents of this valley, that whatever character we may have, is well known throughout this part of the state, that we are all real estate owners, that our homes and families are here, and that aside from our determination, as honorable men, to observe the binding obligations imposed upon us, we have no inclination to forfeit all these by a wilful violation of the pledges we may make, as a condition to our discharge. We cannot close this communication without expressing our grateful acknowledgments for the courteous and gentlemanly treatment we have received in our imprisonment and the comfortable quarters furnished us at the house of H. N. Tong." DS, *ibid.*, RG 109, Records of the U.S. War Dept. Relating to Confederates, Union Provost Marshal's Citizens File. On an attached sheet, Thomas B. Grigsby submitted a separate statement. "The undersigned Thos B. Grigsby of Madison County, also held as a prisoner with the gentlemen whose names are subscribed to the foregoing communication, desires also to be discharged upon his parol of honor upon the conditions as set forth in said communication—He willingly subscribes to every statement, condition, & pledge therin contained. He desires to state that he is a real estate owner to a considerable extent in this valley as well as in the County of Madison, that he is a resident of the town of Fredericktown, where his family now is, and that he is also sheriff of that county. (Madison)." DS, *ibid.* On the sheet with Grigsby's statement is an-

other, in USG's hand, signed by S. M. Salters. "I, The undersigned, S. M. Salter, do solemnly swear not to take up arms against the Government of the United States, nor to insite others to like offense, nor to give information to the enemies of the Government of the United States to be made use of by them, so help me God." For Grigsby, see letter to Capt. John C. Kelton, Aug. 15, 1861, note 6.

To Capt. John C. Kelton

Head Quarters Ironton Mo
August 15th 1861

SIR:

I have to-day to note the arrival of two regiments of Infantry, Col. Lawlann[1] 7th Iowa Regt, and Col Thayer,[2] 1st Nebraska Regt. I have also ordered the 21st Regt Ill. Vols under Col Alexander, forward upon the Greenville road, and Col Fr Hecker (24th Ill. Vol) upon the Fredericktown road,—taking five days rations—with instructions to form a conjunction at Brunot.[3]

I expect to follow to-morrow,[4] with Artillery should any arrive;—a few companies of infantry, more provisions if means of transportion can be procured, otherwise I shall send teams back from Brunot or Greenville for additional rations.

I purchased to-day sxteen wagons and sixty eight mules, subject to the approval of Maj. Gen. Fremont.

These teams are well adapted for our use; more suitable and more efficient than those which we have heretofore employed or found in the service of this command. I shall to-morrow purchase five more wagons and twenty mules, on the same terms.[5] The teams which I have conditionally purchased ~~five more was~~ have been for some time, in the service of the government without charge, if now purchased, otherwise to receive compensation.

Requisitions were made upon Qr. Master McKinstry, some days since, for camp equipage, &c &c but as yet I have received nothing. At this time I have not a single tent for my headquarters, nor is there any stationery in the Qr. Masters Department. Several prisoners now in my charge, I shall at the earliest convenience, send to the Arsenal for with charges accompanying.[6]

Since writing the above a messenger has come in from a spy I have out, who reports the rebel force much greater than has heretofore been represented—from (25000 to 30000) twenty five to thirty thousand.

The spy mentioned is an officer in disguise. From representations made by the messenger the information which has caused them to retreat was obtained from a preacher of this place, who managed to get out of camp, and is now back again, without a pass. I have ordered his arrest and will have him sent to St Louis, if caught.

I shall move with the detachments of my command viz: the 21st and 24 (Ill Vols) regiments, towards Brunot, subject to any order from your Department, and will report as often as practicable

U. S. GRANT
Brig. Gen. Com

LS, DNA, RG 393, Western Dept., Letters Received. *O.R.*, I, iii, 444.

1. Col. Jacob G. Lauman.
2. Col. John M. Thayer. See *ibid.*, p. 442, for his assignment to USG. Similar orders for Lauman are in DNA, RG 393, Western Dept., Letters Sent by Gen. Frémont.
3. On Aug. 15, 1861, USG issued special orders for Col. Friedrich Hecker. "Colonel F. Hecker, commanding 24th Illinois Volunteers, will as soon as practicable, move with all of his Regiment, towards Brunot, via Fredericktown. At Brunot, he will effect a junction with Colonel Alexander of the 21st Illinois Volunteers and await further orders. Five days rations and as much of the regimental baggage as there is transportation for, will be taken along. Fresh beef will be issued on the route as often as practicable, giving the owners receipts for same. The commanding General does not deem further written instructions necessary for a Commander of Colonel Hecker's Military Experience" Copies, *ibid.*, USG Special Orders; DLC-USG, V, 15, 16, 82.
4. On Aug. 15, USG issued General Orders No. 19. "On the departure of the General commanding Col Bland of the 6th Mo Vol will assume command of this post With the mounted men left with him he will communicate anything that may seem to him of such importance as to require that the Brig Genl. commanding should know it. He will also report daily to Department Head Quarters at Saint

Louis The utmost precaution must be observed to cut of spies from entering camp and all who rest under Sufficient Suspicion to warrant it will be sent to Saint Louis Arsenal for confinement with charges accompanying. The brigade and picket guard duty will be Equalized among the troops, and will be made as Effective as the strength of the command will permit Surgeon   of the 6th Mo Vols assisted by Hospital Steward   of the 24th Ill Vols will have charge of the Brigade Hospital. All of the 21st and 24th Ill Vol and 9th Mo left at this post will be under the treatment of the brigade surgeon All necessary orders for the guidance of the camp will be given by the post commander. No leave of absence ~~will~~ to either officers or soldiers will be granted without first submitting the application to division Head quarters" Copy, DNA, RG 94, 21st Ill., Order Book.

    5. On Aug. 16, Maj. Justus McKinstry wrote to USG. "The General commanding directs that you make the purchase of mules, teams and forage, as expressed in letter of L Bogg, of August 16. 1861, a copy of which is herewith enclosed." Copy, *ibid.*, RG 393, District of Southeast Mo., Letters Received.

    6. On Aug. 16, USG forwarded a list of prisoners with charges against them. John Cole had been arrested on Aug. 14 by Col. Herman Kallman on charges "Of being a spy, & firing a Revolver at Men in the U. S. Service." USG added: "Sheriff of Iron County—Residence Midlebrook. Has once ~~before~~ taken an other." Jerome Nall or Knoll was arrested by pickets as a spy. USG added: "Is represented by a Union man of this place as a bad man but it may not be possible to prove anything against him." J. R. Kuhn was also arrested by pickets as a spy. USG added: "Is probably a soldier in the Southern Army. Has been in this camp now the second time." Thomas B. Grigsby was arrested by USG as a spy. USG added: "Sheriff of Madison County. Was arrested once before ~~since I took com~~ in the last week. ~~Fd~~ Found on him a pass through Rebel Pickets." J. R. Arnold was also arrested by USG as a spy. USG added: "Condemned by Citizens as dangerous." USG had also arrested Fred Smith, Peter Crozat, Ferrier, and Fred Millet in connection with the case of John Cole. AD, *ibid.*, RG 109, Records of the U.S. War Dept. Relating to Confederates, Union Provost Marshal's Citizens File.

To Julia Dent Grant

                                                    Ironton Mo.
                                              August 15th 1861

DEAR JULIA;

    No doubt you will be quite astonished after what the papers have said about the precarious my Brigade has been in for the last few days[1] to learn that to-morrow I move south. This is one of the most delightful places I have ever been in. High enough to

make quite a difference in the atmosphere. Springs of water that
I̶ makes ice cease to be a luxury and scenery equal to anything
you can imagine.

I dont know where to tell you to direct a letter to me. The
safest way is probably St. Louis.—My duties now give me but
precious little. Generally engaged writing until 12 o'clock at
night. I received a letter to-day from Mr. Drum[2] and one from
Collins,[3] the first wanting me to appoint Thad. on my Staff the
second wanting me to give Mr. Thompson some appointment.
Their letters come in since night and I have been busy ever since
until now about 12 o'clock or I would answer them. Tell them
that I have but two appointments and they must be from Lieuts.
of the Army. One I felt it obligatory to make from the Regiment
which I was Col. of[4] and the other I have offered to Mr. Rollins[5]
if he can get the appointment of Lieut. I received one from Mr.
Goodin of St. Louis also wanting a place.[6] I expected to be able
to make a short visit to Galena before this but now it does not
look much like it. I want very much to get back into civilization
for a few days to get me some things that I very much need. I am
without a sword sash or uniform of evry description according to
my grade and see no chance of geting them.—I subscribed for
the Daily Democrat for you because it contains more Army
news than any other paper, and because it has a regular correspondent with one of the regiments of my Brigade.[7] I have
taken Orly[8] into my office. The position will be a pleasant one
giving him a horse to ride but whether I can give him anything to which there is extra pay attached or not I dont know If
I can I will. He is most exemplary in his conduct and is much
thought of by the officers of the Company to which he has been
attached.—From Collins' letter I see Simpson has not yet left.
I hope he is enjoying better health than he could in Covington.
Do the children annoy him any? Does he think Jess a bad boy?
Tell Jess he must be a good boy and learn to read. I hope mother
& Simp will stay with you all Summer and I dont believe but
what he would do better in the Winter there than in Covington.
If I can draw my pay regularly I will supply you liberally. First

however I must send about $300 00 more to the stores to pay Hughletts.[9] Write to me soon & often. Kiss the children for me.

ULYS.

ALS, PPRF.

1. "The rumor is also circulating in camp to-night of an attack from both the east and west by forces from 2,000 to 5,000 on each side." Letter of "Orion," Aug. 13, 1861, in *Missouri Democrat*, Aug. 15, 1861.

2. Philip Drum of Galena, of the firm of P. and S. Drum, chair and cabinet ware manufacturers, located on Main Street close to the J. R. Grant leather store. His son, 1st Lt. Thaddeus G. Drum, 19th Ill., resigned Oct. 20, 1861.

3. E. A. Collins of Galena, former business partner of Jesse R. Grant. *PUSG*, 1, 8*n*; letter of June 17, 1861, note 4.

4. See letter to Capt. John C. Kelton, Aug. 11, 1861.

5. John A. Rawlins, Galena attorney. See letter of April 21, 1861. On Aug. 12, Rawlins wrote to USG. "Your letter bearing date St. Louis, Missouri, August 7th, A. D. 1861, tendering me the position of aid-de-camp on your staff is before me. It is a compliment unexpected; but fully appreciating your kindness and friendship for me, and believing from your long experience in and knowledge of the military service, and its duties, you would not have offered me the position were you not satisfied it is one I could fill, gladly and with pleasure I accept it and whatever the duties and responsibilities devolved upon me by virtue of the same, I will with the help of God discharge them to the best of my ability. Wishing you success in the cause of Constitutional freedom for which you are fighting, I remain . . ." James Harrison Wilson, *The Life of John A. Rawlins* (New York, 1916), p. 53. See letter to Maj. Gen. John C. Frémont, Aug. 21, 1861.

6. In addition to these requests for staff appointments, on Aug. 7, John Belser, clerk in the Ill. AGO when USG had served there, wrote directly to President Abraham Lincoln. "I respectfully request to be appointed Assistant Adjutant General of Illinois Volunteers, to be attached to the staff of Brigadier General Grant" Lincoln endorsed the letter: "I believe the appointment of John Belser, to be Assistent Adjutant General, to Gen. Grant is proper; but, to be sure, send the appointment to Gen. Grant, to be delivered or not, in his discretion." AES, Lincoln Papers, IHi.

7. Letters signed "Orion" in the *Missouri Democrat* were written by a soldier of the 21st Ill., identity unknown.

8. Orlando H. Ross. See letter of June 27, 1861, note 1.

9. Samuel Hughlett of Galena owned the house rented by USG in Galena. See letter of June 17, 1861, note 4.

To Capt. John C. Kelton

Head Quarters, Ironton Mo.
August 16th 1861

S<small>IR</small>:

I have just received a message from one of my spies stating that last night the Rebels returned to the ground retreated from by them the day before. The party returned to Frederickstown number from 1200 to 1500 and will have a column sent out by me upon them by 12 O'Clock, probably, to-day. It is just time for the cars to leave which precludes the possibility of my reporting more fully.

Respectfully &c
U. S. G<small>RANT</small>
Brig. Gen. Com

To Capt J. C. Kelton
Asst. Adj.t Gen U.S.A.
St. Louis Mo

ALS, deCoppet Collection, NjP. *O.R.*, I, iii, 444–45.

To Capt. John C. Kelton

Head Quarters, Ironton Mo.
August 16th 1861

C<small>APT</small>. J. C. K<small>ELTON</small>,
A<small>SST</small>. A<small>DJ</small>. G<small>EN</small>. U. S. A.
S<small>T</small>. L<small>OUIS</small>, M<small>O</small>.

S<small>IR</small>:

I send this evening three Comp.ys 9th Mo. Vols. to St. Louis in accordance with instructions just received. The late hour of receiving the order, and the distance to the railroad Depot precludes the possibility of sending their baggage to-night. That will follow in the morning however.

I have now one regiment of troops twelve miles from here on the Greenville road and eight Comp.y at, or near, Fredericktown. This latter is a key point to the railroad to North from here and should be held.

To-night five companies move from here towards the position occupied on the Greenville road.

Respectfully
Your Obt. Svt.
U. S. Grant
Brig. Gen. Com

ALS, DNA, RG 393, Western Dept., Letters Received. *O.R.*, I, iii, 445.

To Col. Peter E. Bland

Headquarters Ironton Mo.
August 16th 1861.

Col P. E. Bland
6th Missouri Vols

As soon as the wagon train is all up you may move with your command to the first convenient place for halting over night. In the morning move cautiously on to about ten or twelve miles from here and await orders from me.

Permit no pressing of horses, or other property by your command. The policy meets with my decided disapproval and must be suppressed.

U. S. Grant
Brig Genl.

Copies, DLC-USG, V, 1, 2, 3. *O.R.*, I, iii, 445. USG had issued special orders for Col. Peter E. Bland earlier in the day. "Colonel P. E. Bland, 6th Missouri Volunteers, will hold five companies of his regiment ready for marching orders, taking with them six wagons and four days rations. The remaining wagons of his command will move to Pilot Knob and await orders." Copies, DLC-USG, V, 15, 16, 82; DNA, RG 393, USG Special Orders. On Aug. 16, 1861, Bland replied that he was about to start on the expedition with 214 men. *Ibid.*, USG Register of Letters Received; DLC-USG, V, 10.

To Col. Friedrich Hecker

Headquarters. Ironton Mo
August 16th 1861.

Col F. Hecker
24th Ills. Vols

I have information that the rebels have returned to their former position. You will therefore, to avoid the possibility of being cut off at Brunot, by reenforcements from Hardee, take across to Marble creek[1] or some point between Brunont and Ironton, if you can find a practicable road.

If there is no road across, return here

I will direct Col Alexander, not to advance beyond Marble creek until reenforced by you.

U. S. Grant
Brig Genl.

Copies, DLC-USG, V, 1, 2, 3; DNA, RG 393, USG Letters Sent. See General Orders No. 12, Aug. 10, 1861, note 2. On Aug. 17, 1861, Col. Friedrich Hecker sent USG a report of his expedition to Fredericktown, Mo. "To effect the junction with Col. Alexander whom I supposed to be actually in Burton [*Brunot*], I pushed for ward and was determined to be there and have effected the junction to night. I received your dispatch just now half way from fredrictown to Coldwater. I inquired about the roads due west from this road to marble creek. One of them is impracticable for baggage ⅓ mile from the place where I am. The other is the State road who leads direct to Ironton; and a third is six miles from here and six from Coldwater. This latter is said to be a narrow defile largly populated by secessionist, the forth road brings me back to Fredericktown. Now I ascertained partly be eyewittnesses that at Coldwater (Belchers place) is a force of over 2000 secession rebels taking position there infantry and cavalry, most with the exception of 600 poorly armed. I[*f*] Colonel Alexander had been actually at Brunot, or in the neighbourhood I would have sent him word and entered the defile. But as probably besides the road from Coldwater to Brunot, the other road (the narrow defile 6 miles from here and the same distance from Coldwater is occupied by the rebels, and Col. Alexander could not support our forward movement to that defile I rather will hold fredrictown than fall back directly from here to Ironton, on the old State road a mile from here and expect there your further orders P. S. after some reflection I will and can not retire, I shall enter the defile 6 miles above Coldwater and try to come to marble creek." ALS, DNA, RG 393, District of Southeast Mo., Letters Received. Hecker's safe arrival at Marble Creek was reported in a letter from Ironton, Aug. 18, 1861, in *Chicago Tribune*, Aug. 21, 1861.

1. Marble Creek rises about three miles south of Ironton and flows into the St. Francis River about thirteen miles southeast of Ironton.

To Col. John M. Thayer

————

Head Quarters, Ironton Mo.
August 16th 1861

COL.

You will please detail two Compys. from your regiment to relieve two companies of the 24th Ill. Vols. now on the railroad North of here.

Lieut. J. Fritch[1] will accompany them and designate the points they are to guard.

U. S. GRANT
Brig. Gen. Com.

To Col. Thayer
Comd.g 1st Nebrasca Vols.

ALS, IHi. John M. Thayer, born in Mass., a lawyer educated at Brown University, moved to Neb. in 1855. On July 21, 1861, he was appointed col., 1st Neb. For his assignment to Ironton, see letter to Capt. John C. Kelton, Aug. 15, 1861, note 2. See also *Calendar*, [April–Aug.].

1. 1st Lt. Julius Fritsch, 24th Ill.

To Lt. Col. John W. S. Alexander

————

Headquarters Ironton Mo.
August 16 1861

COL. J. W. S. ALEXANDER
21ST ILLINOIS VOLS.

To morrow morning reconnoitre the ground in advance of you as far as Marble Creek. There make a halt for further orders, unless you should have such information as would make it an undoubted good move to depart from these instructions. Since you left I have learned that Hardie has returned to his position at Greenville and is much stronger than has been heretofore supposed. Col Hecker has been instructed to join you at Marble Head[1] if a practicable road is to be found across. Five Companies will leave here to night following you and in case of necessity can reenforce you by a forced march.

U. S. GRANT.
Brig Gen.

Copies, DLC-USG, V, 1, 2, 3; DNA, RG 393, USG Letters Sent. *O.R.*, I, iii, 445. See letter to Julia Dent Grant, June 26, 1861, note 5.

1. Apparently an inadvertent error for Marble Creek.

To Lt. Col. John W. S. Alexander

Headquarters Ironton Mo.
August 17 1861

COL. J. W. S. ALEXANDER
21ST ILLS VOLS.

You will immediately upon receipt of this discharge all your teams but four and order their return to this place. Store the provisions in the remaining wagons, or in a building if a suitable one can be found.

U. S. GRANT
Brig Gen.

Copies, DLC-USG, V, 1, 2, 3; DNA, RG 393, USG Letters Sent.

To Col. Leonard F. Ross

Headquarters Ironton Mo
August 18 1861

Col L. F. Ross.
17th Illinois Vols.

You will hold your regiment in ~~regiment~~ readiness to move upon Fredericktown, which you will occupy until further orders. Quartermaster E. M. Joel[1] will provide necessary transportation

You will make your reports to these Headquarters and receive rations from here. Owing to the scarcity of transportation at this point you will only take with you five days rations and order back as much of your train as can be spared, under a small escort, to get new supplies

Instructions, if not given before, will be sent to you at Fredericktown

You should move as early as Tuesday[2] morning if practicable.

U. S. Grant
Brig Gen.

Copies, DLC-USG, V, 1, 2, 3; DNA, RG 393, USG Letters Sent. *O.R.*, I, iii, 448. Leonard F. Ross of Lewiston, Ill., had served as 1st lt. in the Mexican War, then returned to the practice of law. Active in the Democratic Party, he had served as probate judge of Fulton County before his appointment as col., 17th Ill., on May 25, 1861.

Since USG was no longer in Ironton on Aug. 18, this order may have been prepared earlier. Early in the morning of Aug. 17, Brig. Gen. Benjamin M. Prentiss arrived at Ironton bearing orders from Maj. Gen. John C. Frémont, dated Aug. 15, to take command of U.S. troops stationed near Ironton. *Ibid.*, pp. 443–44; Prentiss to Frémont, Aug. 17, 1861, DNA, RG 393, Western Dept., Letters Received; letters of "Orion," Aug. 17, 18, 1861, in *Missouri Democrat*, Aug. 19, 20, 1861. Prentiss had been a brig. gen. of Ill. troops in May, 1861, when USG held no commission, but was not confirmed as brig. gen. of U.S. vols. until Aug., 1861, when USG was also confirmed, and he stood lower than USG on the list of brig. gens. because USG had prior U.S. army service. Unwilling to serve under an officer junior in rank, USG boarded the train to St. Louis on Aug. 17 to state his case to Frémont. *Memoirs*, I, 257; Capt. John C. Kelton to Frémont, Aug. 19, 1861, DNA, RG 393, Western Dept., Letters Received; letter of "Orion," Aug. 18, 1861, in *Missouri Democrat*, Aug. 20, 1861; "General Grant and General Prentiss," *USGA Newsletter*, III, 2 (Jan., 1966), 8.

The outcome of USG's trip to St. Louis was embodied in two letters addressed to USG on Aug. 19 by Frémont's staff. "The General Commanding directs you to proceed without delay to Jefferson City to assume command of that station and such troops as will be placed at your disposal by the Comd'g General of the district, (Genl Pope,) to whom you will report before leaving." Copy, DNA, RG 393, Western Dept., Letters Sent. Misdated in *O.R.*, I, liii, 499. "The General desires me to say that urgent service requires that your leave be postponed for the present. He will be glad to give you leave to visit Galena, in a short time." Copy, DNA, RG 393, Western Dept., Letters Sent. *O.R.*, I, liii, 501. USG apparently returned to Ironton before proceeding to Jefferson City. See following letter.

On Aug. 10, Brig. Gen. John Pope had written to Capt. John C. Kelton. "I have the honor to request that Colonel (now General) Grant be ordered to report to me to relieve Genl. Hurlbut in the command in North & North East Missouri Genl Grant is a Soldier by education & experience & a discreet prudent man who is eminently needed now for immediate supervision of the disaffected counties north of Hannibal & St Joseph road—I would urge respectfully but earnestly that this change of commanders be made as soon as possible—" LS, DNA, RG 94, Generals' Papers and Books, Stephen A. Hurlbut. This letter helps to explain USG's transfer to a command in the District of North Mo., though USG relieved Col. James A. Mulligan and did not replace Brig. Gen. Stephen A. Hurlbut.

1. Ephraim M. Joel, born in Scotland, later 1st lt. and regt.q.m., 29th Mo.
2. Aug. 20.

To Col. John M. Thayer

———

Headquarters Ironton Mo
August 20 1861

Col. Jno M. Thayer
1st Nebraska Vols.

Lieut Hoelcke reports here this morning that the Lieutenant in command of Company "B" of your regiment, detailed to report to Lieut. Hoelcke of Engineer Department, for fatigue duty, and of course to be under his command, does not keep order in his company and permits utter disregard by his men of the orders of the Lieutenant of Engineers If Lieut Hoelcke or Lieut Avery report them to you again as guilty of the charge, you will forthwith arrest the officer and detail another company.

I would refer the officer in charge of fatigue party to article

39 sec. 888 page 114 Army Regulations,[1] for instructions as to his duties

U. S. GRANT.
Brig Genl.

Copies, DNA, RG 393, USG Letters Sent; DLC-USG, V, 1, 2, 3. See preceding letter. On Aug. 19, 1861, 1st Lt. William Hoelcke sent USG a report of engineer operations in and around Ironton. "Enclosed you will find a report of 2nd Lieutenant Abry of the Engineer Department. I myself found a squad of one of the Regiments, which resembled far more a crowd of Rowdies than soldiers. The officers themselves do not know their duty and ought to be instructed according to army Regulations Article 39 Paragraph 888 Page 114 Edition of 1861. We need the strictest discipline to succeed; if we are not supported in every way by other Officers, it is impossible to finish the works commenced here. I think it would be proper to have with every working party an armed guard of one Sergeant and 10 men, to arrest on the spot every man, who shows disobedience. For to morrow morning 6 o'cl. I want: 1 a fatigue party of one Officer and 40 men without arms to be at the 32 pounder on the road from Pilot Knob to Caledonia, if possible also the above mentioned Guard. 2 a Box waggon with two mules. The driver has to report himself at the Courthouse to morrow morning 5½ o'clock." ALS, DNA, RG 393, District of Southeast Mo., Letters Received.

1. "The officer commanding a working-party will conform to the directions and plans of the engineer or other officer directing the work, without regard to rank." *Revised Regulations for the Army of the United States, 1861* (Philadelphia, 1861), pp. 127–28.

To Maj. Gen. John C. Frémont

Head Quarters, Jefferson City Mo
August 21st 1861

SIR:

Having appointed J. A. Rawlins, of Galena, Ill. Act. Asst. Adj. Gen. I would respectfully request that it may receive the approval of the Gen. Comd.g the Dept. of the West, and be by him forwarded to Washington asking to have Mr. Rawlins appointed in the A. G. Dept.

Respectfully
U. S. GRANT
Brig. Gen. U. S. A.

ALS, Mrs. Walter Love, Flint, Mich. The letter was forwarded to army hd. qrs. on Aug. 23, 1861. DNA, RG 393, Western Dept., Register of Letters Received. It was not received by the AGO until Oct. 4, 1861. *Ibid.*, RG 94, Register of Letters Received. John A. Rawlins was appointed capt. and asst. adjt. gen. on Aug. 30. USG had originally intended to appoint Rawlins an aide-de-camp, but in leaving Ironton had lost the services of Montague S. Hasie, his former adjt. See letter to Julia Dent Grant, Aug. 15, 1861.

To Brig. Gen. John Pope

By Telegraph, From Head Qrs Jeff City [*Aug.*] 21 *1861.*
To Brig Genl Pope
St Louis
Sir,

Send Col. Worthingtons[1] Regiment tents for four companies field & staff & company officers. With these his regiment can be put in camp. The Lieut Colonel is now in St Louis looking after them. I want the building he now occupies for a hospital.

U S Grant
Brig Genl U S A

Telegram received (punctuation added), DNA, RG 393, District of North Mo., Telegrams Received.

1. Col. William H. Worthington, 5th Iowa.

To Brig. Gen. John Pope

By Telegraph, From Hd Quarters Jeff City [*Aug.*] 21 *1861.*
To Genl J Pope

Send ammunition camp & Garrison Equipage as soon as possible I will have requisition made as soon as it can be ascertained what is required. Clothing badly wanted

U S Grant
Brig Genl Comdg

Telegram received, DNA, RG 393, District of North Mo., Telegrams Received. On Aug. 22, 1861, Brig. Gen. John Pope's hd. qrs. replied to USG. "What amount of ammunition and what kind aneeded? also what kind of clothing and who for? Answer." Copy, *ibid.*, Letters Sent. On Aug. 20, Pope's hd. qrs. had written to Col. James A. Mulligan, 23rd Ill. "General Grant will arrive there to-day to take command with an additional force and all the necessary ammunition that will be needed." Copy, *ibid.* On Aug. 21, Pope's hd. qrs. had telegraphed to USG. "The ammunition has been sent up." Copy, *ibid.* See following telegram.

To Capt. Speed Butler

August 22 *1861.*

BY TELEGRAPH, FROM Hd Quarters Jeff City *1861.*
TO CAPT SPEED BUTLER
SIR

Every varity of clothing is required. The Iowa Fifth & Home Guards require it. Blankets & cooking utensils are most required. Can't a depot be established here & issue on requisition approved by me?

U. S. GRANT
Brig Genl Comdg

Telegram received (punctuation added), DNA, RG 393, District of North Mo., Telegrams Received. Capt. Speed Butler was asst. adjt. gen. for Brig. Gen. John Pope. On Aug. 22, 1861, Pope's hd. qrs. replied to USG. "It is impossible even to establish a depot at this place. Please make out a requisition immediately for everything needed, and we will try to have it furnished." Copy, *ibid.*, Letters Sent. On the same day, USG asked Pope's hd. qrs. for "a supply of blanks as soon as they can be furnished." *Ibid.*, Register of Letters Received. On Aug. 24, Pope's hd. qrs. wrote to USG. "The General Commanding requests you to send forward your requisitions for everything needed by you immediately." Copy, *ibid.*, Letters Sent.

To Capt. Speed Butler

Headquarters U. S. Forces
Jefferson City, Mo. August 22, 1861
CAPT SPEED BUTLER A. A. G.
ST. LOUIS, MO.

During yesterday I visited the camps of the different commands about this city and selected locations for troops yet to arrive. I find a great deficiency in everything for the comfort and efficiency of an army. Most of the troops are without clothing, camp and garrison equipage. Ammunition was down to about ten rounds of cartridges and for the artillery none is left. The artillery here consists of four six pounders, without artillerymen, and one twenty four pound howitzer, too heavy for field use. The Post Quartermaster and Commissary have not been here since my arrival, so that I cannot report fully as to these Departments. They are apparently in a bad condition. There are no rations for issue;[1] the mules, sent some time since, are being guarded in a lot, no effort being made to get them into teams; and a general looseness prevailing.

I have fitted out an expedition of three hundred and fifty men to scour the country around where the cars were fired into day before yesterday.[2] Such information has been received here as will probably lead to the arrest of many of the parties engaged: The party in pursuit will subsist off of the community through which they pass. Stringent instructions have been given as to how supplies are to be got. From reports received here the whole of this country is in a state of ferment. They rebels are driving out the union men and appropriating their property. The best force to put this down would be mounted homeguards and I would therefore recommend that as many as possible of this class of troops be put upon horses. Generally, they are able to mount themselves, and when they cannot, horses could be obtained from good secessionists, who have been aiding and abetting the southern cause.

I would further recommend that companies of homeguards be received without any reference to their being organized into regiments. They can be attached to other regiments either by companies or squadrons, and be quite as effective as if in large bodies.[3]

U. S. GRANT
Brig. General

Copies, DLC-USG, V, 4, 5, 7, 8; DNA, RG 393, USG Hd. Qrs. Correspondence. *O.R.*, I, iii, 452.

1. On Aug. 23, 1861, Brig. Gen. John Pope's hd. qrs. wrote to USG. "One hundred thousand rations sent to you this morning." Copy, DNA, RG 393, District of North Mo., Letters Sent.

2. On Aug. 20, Lt. Col. Benjamin W. Grover, Johnson County, Mo., Home Guards, reported to USG. "The P. R. Road train left California at ½ past 8 Oclk A. M. August 20 densely filled with Home Guards 160 belonging to my Command —70 Home Guards from Tipton and 60 from California. When the train got near Lookout Station a concealled body of men opened a brisk fire, on the Cars, the top of the Cars loaded with our men, who returned the fire As soon as the train stoped, Capt Beck, assisted by Capts. Hopkins and Rice, formed our men in line of skirmeshers and cleand the woods in a very short time." Losses were three killed, five wounded. ALS, *ibid.*, RG 94, War Records Office, Union Battle Reports. *O.R.*, I, iii, 140. See also *New-York Tribune*, Aug. 21, 22, 1861; George S. Grover, "Col. Benjamin Whiteman Grover," *Missouri Historical Review*, I, 2 (Jan., 1907), 135–36.

3. USG later explained that rivalry for recruits to fill new regts., with short enlistments offered for inducement, created confusion in Jefferson City which he finally ended. *Memoirs*, I, 258–59.

To Maj. Moore

Head Quarters, Jeff. City, Mo
August 22d 1861

SIR:

You will relieve all guards now at Osage bridge[1] except those belonging to the Irish Brigade[2] and forward them to join their respective commands.

U. S. GRANT
Brig. Gen. Com.

To Maj. Moore
Comd.g Osage Guard

ALS, IHi. Possibly addressed to David Moore, later col., 1st Northeast Mo.

1. Osage Bridge, about eight miles east of Jefferson City at the confluence of the Osage and Missouri rivers.
2. The Irish Brigade was another name for the 23rd Ill., Col. James A. Mulligan.

To Brig. Gen. John Pope

By Telegraph, From Jeff City [*Aug.*] 23 *1861.*

To Genl J. Pope
Sir

Send twenty thousand per C pistol, three thousand (3000) havy havy[1] revolver catridges for Col. Marshall's[2] command. Send today.

U. S. Grant
Brig Genl Comdg

Telegram received (punctuation added), DNA, RG 94, Generals' Papers and Books, Stephen A. Hurlbut. On Aug. 23, 1861, Brig. Gen. John Pope's hd. qrs. replied to USG. "Was not a full supply of pistol cartridges sent to Colonel Marshall's men before leaving this place? So says F. D. Callender, Captain, Ordnance, U. S. A." Copy, *ibid.*, RG 393, District of North Mo., Letters Sent. On Aug. 20, Maj. Gen. John C. Frémont had written to USG. "The Commanders of the 1rst Regiment Illinois Cavalry 465 men, and a battery of artillery—four guns and 91 men—have been ordered to proceed forthwith by railroad with their commands at Jefferson city and there report to you" Copy, *ibid.*, Western Dept., Letters Sent by Gen. Frémont.

1. Apparently a garbled reference to cartridges for Navy Colt revolvers.
2. Col. Thomas A. Marshall, 1st Ill. Cav.

To Capt. Speed Butler

Headquarters U. S. Forces.
Jefferson City Mo, Aug 23 '61

Captain Speed Butler
St Louis Mo.

Since my last report the 25th Illinois Regt Col Coles[1] commanding, and seven companies of the 1st Illinois Cavalry, have reached here.

I telegraphed you yesterday[2] the precarious condition Lexington[3] was in, and of the expedition I was fitting out for the relief of that point. As the gentleman from whom I got my information, (Mr Silver) called upon you, it is not necessary that I should enter into particulars. Col Marshal goes in command of the expedition, taking with him all his own command, about three hundred homeguards and a section of Taylor's Battery,[4] should it arrive in time. They will subsist off the country through which they pass under full instructions.

I am not fortifying here at all. With the picket guard and other duty coming upon the men of this command there is but little time left for drilling. Drill and discipline is more necessary for the men than fortifications. Another difficulty in the way of fortifying is that I have no Engineer officer to direct it, no time to attend to it myself, and very little disposition to gain a "Pillow notoriety"[5] for a branch of service that I have forgotten all about.[6]

I have nothing from west of here since my telegram of yesterday, but shall have today. Will telegraph if any thing of importance should be learned. As soon as possible I will send you a consolidated morning report, and will try and keep this command in such condition, as to enable me to have a report made when called for.

There are no county-maps published for this section of the state, nor any thing to point out the different roads and travelled routes more distinctly than the State-maps you have.[7] I can learn, however, from persons conversant with all the roads, their relative practicability

U. S. GRANT
Brig. General

Copies, DLC-USG, V, 4, 5, 7, 8; DNA, RG 393, USG Hd. Qrs. Correspondence. *O.R.*, I, iii, 452–53.

1. Col. William N. Coler. On Aug. 20, 1861, Brig. Gen. John Pope's hd. qrs. wrote to USG that this force would arrive "this evening or some time tomorrow," and would include a battery of Ill. light art., Maj. Peter Davidson. Copy, DNA, RG 393, District of North Mo., Letters Sent.

2. This telegram has not been located. On Aug. 23, Pope wrote to Maj. Gen. John C. Frémont. "The enclosed dispatch is respectfully submitted for the information of the General comdg the Dept. I would suggest that Genl. Grant be reenforced by several regiments from this place which under his supervision can be rapidly put in condition for efficient service at such points as may be considered advisable—" LS, *ibid.*, Western Dept., Letters Received.

3. Lexington, Mo., about ninety-five miles northwest of Jefferson City.

4. Capt. Ezra Taylor's battery, later Battery B, 2nd Ill. Light Art. See letter to Capt. Speed Butler, Aug. 28, 1861, note 4.

5. See letter of May 6, 1861.

6. On Aug. 26, Frémont ordered Maj. Henry Kraut, formerly engineer at Ironton, to report to USG at Jefferson City. Copy, DNA, RG 393, Western Dept., Letters Sent.

7. On Aug. 27, USG requested "a sectional map of Missouri" from Pope's hd. qrs. *Ibid.*, District of North Mo., Register of Letters Received.

To Brig. Gen. Lorenzo Thomas

Head Quarters Jefferson City Mo.
August 25th 1861

COL. L. THOMAS
ADJT. GEN. USA
WASHINGTON CITY D. C.
SIR:

I would respectfully report that on the 7th day of this month, August, I was assigned to duty as Brigadier General, notice of my confirmation to the office appearing in the Public prints of the country. On the same day I accepted, noting the acceptance on a pay roll. I wish therefore my acceptance to take effect from that date.

No official notice of my appointment has ever reached me, nor of the relative rank of Brigadier;[1] I would therefore respectfully request an official notification, and if it can be furnished, my relative rank with others of the same grade.

Respectfully
Your Obt. Svt.
U S GRANT
Brig. Gen. U. S. A.

ALS, Mrs. Walter Love, Flint, Mich. Received by the AGO on Aug. 30, 1861. DNA, RG 94, Register of Letters Received.

1. An official list of the brig. gens. in order of seniority was embodied in AGO General Orders No. 62, Aug. 20, 1861. In this list, USG stood eighteenth among thirty-five brig. gens. of vols. holding rank from May 17, 1861. See telegram to Maj. Gen. John C. Frémont, Sept. 2, 1861. USG must have known something about relative rank or he would not have left Ironton. See letter to Col. Leonard F. Ross, Aug. 18, 1861.

To Capt. John C. Kelton

Head Quarters, Jeff. City Mo.
August 25th 1861

CAPT.

Evry place I have been thrown in command I have found one abuse which I feel it my duty to report. Commanders of Regts. & in many instances companies, give leavs of absence to their officers and men, in large numbers, to visit their homes and furnish them with free passes going and returning.

For myself I refuse free passes in all instances except where persons are traveling strictly on military duty and allow no leaves of absence without my approval, but I fear that in many instances this is disregarded without my knowledge.

> Respectfully &c
> U. S. GRANT
> Brig. Gen. U. S. A.

To Capt. J. C. Kelton
A. A. Gen U. S. A.
St. Louis Mo

ALS, DNA, RG 393, Dept. of the Mo., Letters Received. On Aug. 22, 1861, USG issued General Orders No. 2. "No passes will be given in future to officers or men to go beyond the limits of this Post without the approval of the General Commanding. In no case will passes be given over the railroad except when persons are travelling on business strictly for the Government. All commanders are required to send in requisitions as soon as possible for such clothing, camp and garrison equipage as they stand in need of." Copies, DLC-USG, V, 12, 13, 14; DNA, RG 393, USG General Orders.

To Capt. John C. Kelton

————

> Head Quarters, Jeff. City Mo.
> August 25th 1861.

SIR.

I would respectfully request that when it can be done without manifest injury to the service, the 21st Reg't Ill Vol's be transfered to my Command. It is the Regiment over which I was Colonel and they having Expressed a unanimous desire to be attached to my Command and regarding it as an efficient and orderly regiment I cannot do less than to make this request.

> Respectfully submitted
> U. S. GRANT.
> Brig Gen U S A

To Capt J. C. Kelton
A A Gen U. S. A.
St Louis Mo.

Copy, DLC-USG, VIA, 1.

To Capt. Speed Butler

Headquarters U. S. Forces
Jefferson City. Mo., Aug 25, 1861

Capt. Speed Butler
St. Louis, Mo.

The instructions of General Fremont, relative to the seizure of the banks at Lexington and Liberty,[1] have been communicated to Colonel Marshall, who was under marching orders at the time the instructions were received.

It is not possible to spare men from here for the expedition to Paris, without leaving this place too much exposed.[2]

With regard to the home-guards, I should like to have some instructions. I have not been able to learn head nor tail about them, notwithstanding all my efforts. I know there are many of them—some mounted, others with teams, and some without arms, teams or saddle-horses.[3] I would recommend that some officer be sent here with special instructions as to how they are to be organized and received, and who will have no other duty to attend to until this is performed.

The party sent out by me to the neighborhood of where the cars were fired into on Tuesday, has returned. The report has not yet been received but may be in time to accompany this. A few persons have been arrested who are suspected of having been engaged in the firing.[4]

I have no reliable information as to the movements of M Cullough's forces,[5] but there is a current rumor here that he is moving towards this point. From a spy who came in yesterday I learn that companies are being organized in all the counties west of here. Some of these bands are acquiring considerable proportions. Many troops have crossed the Missouri river from the north within the last two weeks and are joining the forces on this side. If I had sufficient force here all that could be stopped.

Respectfully &c
U. S. Grant
Brig. Gen. Com

Copies, DLC-USG, V, 4, 5, 7, 8; DNA, RG 393, USG Hd. Qrs. Correspondence. *O.R.*, I, iii, 454; *ibid.*, II, i, 216–17. Facsimile of last three lines and closing in autograph catalogue of Alwin J. Scheuer, 1927, p. 140.

1. On Aug. 20, 1861, Maj. Gen. John C. Frémont wrote to USG. "You are hereby directed to send at once detachments of the forces now stationed at Jefferson city to Lexington Liberty and Paris to take possession of the money of the Farmer's Bank and its branches at those places. The officers commanding the detachments should give proper receipts for the money which is to be forwarded forthwith to this city." Copy, DNA, RG 393, Western Dept., Letters Sent (Press). Paris, Mo., is about 60 miles north of Jefferson City; Liberty, Mo., about 127 miles northwest of Jefferson City and about 14 miles northeast of Kansas City, Mo.
2. On Aug. 25, USG requested the hd. qrs. of Brig. Gen. John Pope to send an art. co. to Paris, Mo. *Ibid.*, District of North Mo., Register of Letters Received. On Aug. 26, Pope wrote to Capt. John C. Kelton transmitting the substance of USG's letter, adding, "I would suggest that orders be sent to Genl Hurlbut at Palmyra to perform that service as Palmyra is barely fifty miles from Paris." LS, *ibid.*, Western Dept., Letters Received. On Aug. 27, Maj. Joseph H. Eaton of Ill., USMA 1835, military secretary to Frémont, wrote to Pope approving this plan. Copy, *ibid.*, Letters Sent (Press). *O.R.*, I, iii, 461.
3. On Aug. 27, Pope's hd. qrs. wrote to USG. "One thousand stand of arms have been sent to you for distribution for Colonel McC[lurg's] Home-Guards." Copy, DNA, RG 393, District of North Mo., Letters Sent.
4. See letter to Capt. Speed Butler, Aug. 27, 1861, note 9.
5. On Aug. 24, Brig. Gen. Benjamin McCulloch, commanding C.S.A. forces in Mo., reported that he had 3,000 men in camp near Springfield, Mo., was "in no condition to advance," and planned to fall back to the Ark. line. *O.R.*, I, iii, 671–72.

To Capt. R. Chitwood

[*August 25, 1861*]

You will march your men through the country in an orderly manner. Allow no indiscriminate plundering—but everything taken must be by your direction, by persons detailed for the particular purpose, keeping an account of what taken, from whom, its value, etc. Arrests will not be made except for good reasons. A few leading and prominent secessionists may be carried along, however, as hostages, and released before arriving here. Property which you may know to have been used for the purpose of aiding the Rebel cause will be taken whether you require it or not. What you require for the subsistence of your

men and horses must be furnished by people of secession sentiments, and accounted for as stated above. No receipts are to be
given unless you find it necessary to get supplies from friends.

Robert K. Black Catalogue No. 78, Jan., 1961. Probably addressed to Capt. R. G.
Chitwood, Osage County Regt., Mo. Home Guards.

To Capt. John C. Kelton

Head Quarters Jeff City Mo.
August 26th 1861

Capt J. C. Kelton
A A Gen U. S. A.
St Louis Mo.
Sir,

When I was in St Louis, Gen Fremont advised me that he
would accept a company of Sharp Shooters (& arm them the best
they could be armed from the ordnance stores on hand at the
time) under the Command of Capt J H Hollman.[1]

Capt H. now informs me that thirty of his discharged three
months men all of the right kind for this service, are now ready
to musterin.

I would respectfully request that they be accepted and the
company filled afterwards. I know Capt Hollman and am satisfied
that he would have a superior company. He is an extra ordinary
shot himself with Sharps rifle, and his object is to have an entire
company of the same sort, and would therefore like to have his
company mustered in and have a little time to pick his men for
filling up.

I hope this will receive the early attention of Gen Fremont,
and his sanction.

Respectfully &c
U S Grant.
Brig Gen USA.

Copy, DLC-USG, VIA, 1. On Aug. 28, 1861, Maj. Joseph H. Eaton replied to
USG. "I am instructed to say in reply to your note through Capt Kelton a a. g.,
that the Company of sharpshooters to be raised by Capt. J. H. Hollman, will be
accepted by Major General Fremont" Copy, DNA, RG 393, Western Dept.,
Letters Sent (Press). On Sept. 5, Eaton wrote to USG. "Capt. Hollman has
gathered together a nucleus of a company of Sharpshooters to the number of
about thirty—They have been mustered into the service of the United States, and
are about receiving Sharps ~~carbines~~ Rifles. Although the Major General commanding objected to mustering in independent companies, he has decided to place
this company under your orders, in the Expectation that it will not only soon be
filled up with accomplished Riflemen, but with a class of men intelligent and
physically fitted to the peculiar duties of light troops. It may also be desireable to
make the company the nucleus of a model rifle Battalion, but of this you will make
report after that company shall be thoroughly armed, drilled & disciplined." Copy,
ibid. On Sept. 23, Eaton wrote to USG. "The General Commanding has ordered
Capt. Halman's Company of sharpshooters, now in this city to be detached for
the present for service in this portion of the State and for special service in the
field." Copy, *ibid.*, Letters Sent by Gen. Frémont.

1. John H. Holman. See letter to Capt. John C. Kelton, Aug. 9, 1861.

To Capt. Speed Butler

———

[*August 26th, 1861*]

I learn that the Springfield army[1] is not moving. The most of
the Mo. troops obtained a twenty days' leave for the purpose of
visiting their respective counties for the purpose of recruiting
and fitting out. They are pressing men into service, getting
wheat ground in many of the mills, and employing tailors, tinners
and other mechanics in preparing an outfit.

Their number, in all their camps, is supposed to be about
3000 men. If I had a sufficient force to send a regiment to Warsaw
and one to Osceola,[2] there is but little doubt their supplies could
be cut off and possibly many men captured. These are the points
at which most of them will cross the Osage River. Wednesday[3]
is the time at which about the last encampment will be broken
up . . .

I am growing prodigiously tired of Home Guards and begin
to despair of learning anything about them. If I could get them

all mounted I would send them to hold some important point away from here. They are orderly and well-behaved and might make fine troops under proper instruction but I have no one to assign to that duty.

Stan V. Henkels Sale No. 1418, Oct. 9, 1928; Thomas F. Madigan, *A Catalogue of Lincolniana* (New York, 1929), No. 127. On Aug. 25, 1861, Brig. Gen. John Pope telegraphed to USG. "A Battery of six pieces artillery goes up tomorrow to Jefferson City. Have you any authentic intelligence of the movements of the enemy South or west of Jefferson City—if so what? General Fremont desires frequent reports of condition of things in your section of country. Report immediately" Copy, DNA, RG 393, District of North Mo., Letters Sent. On Aug. 26, USG informed Pope's hd. qrs. that "Fifteen hundred of Prices command are moving N. E. supposed to be aiming for Jeff. City." *Ibid.*, Register of Letters Received.

1. See letter to Capt. Speed Butler, Aug. 25, 1861, note 5.
2. Osceola, Mo., on the Osage River, about sixty-eight miles southwest of Jefferson City; Warsaw, Mo., also on the Osage River, about twenty-four miles southwest of Osceola.
3. Aug. 28.

To Col. William H. Worthington

Headquarters U S. Forces
Jefferson City Mo Aug 26/61

COL. WORTHINGTON
5TH IOWA VOLS.

See E. B. McPherson, a true Union man, who will show you a copy of the "Booneville Patriot."[1] Bring all the printing material, type &c with you. Arrest J. L. Stevens and bring him with you, and some copies of the paper he edits. Baily is a particularly obnoxious person and should be arrested. B L Wilson and Comp. have been furnishing the rebels with groceries. You may therefore pay him a visit and if you require it, draw two or three days supply for your command, keeping an account of the amount taken, its value &c. Give secessionists to understand what to expect if it becomes necessary to visit them again. Take all canteens you may find from a tinshop which is reported to have been working for the rebels.

It is reported that the proprietor of the ferry boat[2] has observed his part of the engagement entered into as far as practicable but there is no doubt that he is deceived daily as to the character of the parties he is crossing, and now so many will want to cross that his boat will be taken possession of if not given freely

U. S. GRANT.
Brig. Genl.

Copies, DNA, RG 393, USG Letters Sent; DLC-USG, V, 1, 2, 3. *O.R.*, II, i, 217. For the results of the expedition, see letter to Capt. Speed Butler, Aug. 28, 1861, note 2.

1. Boonville, Mo., about thirty-seven miles northwest of Jefferson City.
2. Across the Missouri River.

To Julia Dent Grant

———

Head Quarters, Jefferson City, Mo
August 26th 1861

DEAR JULIA;

The day Orvil[1] arrived here I got a big batch of letters from you the first for a long time. I was surprised to learn that you had not heard from me for so long a time. I have been very particular to write often, and I think a single week has not passed without my writing at least once and generally twice.—Orvil can tell you how busy I have been. Evry night I am kept from 12 O'Clock to 2 in the morning. I stand it first rate however and never enjoyed better health in my life.

I receive a great many letters that I cannot answer and many that I do. Josh Sharp[2] has applied to go on my Staff. He says that he will go on without pay and without position if I will let him go along.

My Staff are, J. A. Rawlins Clark B Lagow & W. S. Hillyer,[3] three of the cleverest men that can be found anywhere. Father's recommendation come too late.[4] I know the father of the young man he recommends and if the son is like him I could not get one that would suit better.

I am sorry that I did not keep Fred with me. He would have enjoyed it very much.

How long we will be here and whether I will get to go home is hard to tell. Gen. Fremont promised that I should but if a forward movement is to take place I fear I shall not.—When I was ordered away from Ironton nearly all the commanders of regiments expressed regret I am told. The fact is my whole career since the begining of present unhappy difficulties has been complimented in a very flattering manner. All my old friends in the Army and out seem to heartily congratulate me. I scarsely ever get to go out of the house and consequently see but little of the people here. There seems to be no stir however except among the troops and they are quiet. There is considerable apprehension of an attack soon but my means of information are certainly better than can be had by most others and my impression is that there is no force sufficiently strong to attempt anything of the kind under a weeks march.

I sent you ten dollars by Orvil to carry you through a few days until I can draw a months pay when I will send $75 or $100 more. I want you to have evrything comfortable and when I get some debts paid will supply you more liberally. My outfit costs $900 00 without being anything extra. This includes three horses saddles & bridles at $600 00.

Give my love to all at home. Remember me to the neighbors around you. I am very much in hopes I shall be able to pay you a short visit but fear I shall not. Kiss the children for me and accept the same for yourself.

Good night.
Ulys.

ALS, DLC-USG.

1. Orvil L. Grant, brother of USG.

2. USG's sister-in-law was Mrs. Alexander Sharp, and Josh Sharp may be a member of that family.

3. William S. Hillyer of St. Louis had been a partner in the law firm of McClellan, Hillyer and Moody, which rented desk space in 1859 to the real estate partnership of Boggs & Grant. Hillyer had witnessed USG's manumission of a slave and had signed the petition for USG's appointment as St. Louis County engineer. *PUSG*, 1, 347–49. For an account of Hillyer's appointment to USG's staff, see *Richardson*, pp. 189–90.

4. See letter to Jesse Root Grant, Aug. 27, 1861.

To Capt. Speed Butler

————

Headquarters U S. Forces.
Jefferson City Mo, Aug. 27 1861

CAPT. S. BUTLER
ST LOUIS MO.

Two spies, one from the neighborhood of Lebanon, and the other from Springfield,[1] have come in this morning. The one from Lebanon reports that the southern army is traveling north in small bodies, and secessionists say, with a view of concentrating about Linn Creek.[2] The citizens of Lebanon expected a body of 10000 men within a few days of the time my informant left.

The one from Springfield reports substantially the same thing, so far as the moving of troops in detachments goes. He says that after the battle of Springfield,[3] the rebels concealed a portion of their artillery and commenced a retreat without burying any considerable portion of their dead Finding however that a retreat had commenced from the other side, they returned to Springfield, after having made a retrograde movement of some five miles.

I sent out on Sunday a detachment of home-guards[4] to arrest two secession captains that I learned had come in. They succeeded in finding them by coming upon them in the night. Their names are J. Johnson of Miller County and B. Barnd[5] of Cole. These men claim to have come in under the proclamation of Governor

Gamble[6] and with the intention of laying down their arms. I have proof however—Wm Mathews, John Hicks and Aaron Bell being the witnesses—that B. Barnd stated that these difficulties had to be settled by the sword, and that he, (Barnd) was going back to Jackson's[7] Army, and that Johnson was also going. The manner and apparent ignorance of these men as to the condition of affairs about Springfield, goes very far against the plausibility of their having come in in good faith.

I have appointed an ordnance sergeant here to take charge of all stores that may arrive. I am getting teams broken in as rapidly as possible.[8] I have to report that the harness sent here is entirely too light and very inferior in quality. The chains are so light and brittle that they snap with the least strain. I have been compelled to order the purchase of new traces here for the teams we are working and shall be compelled to do so as fast as additional ones are hitched up.

The detachment that left here a few days since to arrest parties for firing into the cars west of here, brought in a number of prisoners, but from all the evidence they were the most innocent men in the county.[9] I had them liberated.

I would renew my recommendation of yesterday that a large force be concentrated here; that the road be prepared and possession taken, and protection be given to all the counties bordering on the Missouri.

U. S. GRANT
Brig. General.

Copies, DLC–USG, V, 4, 5, 7, 8; DNA, RG 393, USG Hd. Qrs. Correspondence. *O.R.*, I, iii, 463; *ibid.*, II, i, 220. On Aug. 26, 1861, Brig. Gen. John Pope's hd. qrs. wrote to USG. "The General desires you to inform us of the whereabouts of Colonel Marshall's Cavalry Regiment, and make frequent reports of his movements. The General Commanding the Department requires such information from these Head Quarters, and it is impossible to give it without hearing from you." Copy, DNA, RG 393, District of North Mo., Letters Sent. On Aug. 27, USG sent two telegrams to Pope's hd. qrs. "Reports rebels concentrating at Lynn Creek. Doubts the propriety of continuing colonel Marshall towards Lexington without more force." "Reports that Colonel Marshall made a forced march to capture flour the rebels had at Georgetown." *Ibid.*, Register of Letters Received. See *Calendar*, Aug. 28, 1861.

1. Lebanon, Mo., about 65 miles southwest of Jefferson City, and Springfield, Mo., about 110 miles southwest of Jefferson City.

2. Linn Creek, Mo., about forty-seven miles southwest of Jefferson City.

3. The battle, better known as Wilson's Creek, Aug. 10, had resulted in the defeat of U.S. forces and the death of their commander, Brig. Gen. Nathaniel Lyon. The C.S.A. and Mo. force, led by Brig. Gen. Benjamin McCulloch, was too badly damaged in the hard-fought battle to advance. See letter to Capt. Speed Butler, Aug. 25, 1861, note 5.

4. One co. of the 8th Mo. State Militia Cav., Col. Joseph W. McClurg. Letter of "S.," Jefferson City, Aug. 27, 1861, in *Missouri Republican*, Aug. 28, 1861.

5. A correspondent gave the name as Bond. *Ibid.*

6. Hamilton R. Gamble was named provisional governor of Mo. after Governor Claiborne F. Jackson joined the C.S.A.

7. See note 6.

8. On Aug. 20, Pope's hd. qrs. wrote to USG. "The General Commanding directs me to inform you that fifty wagons, mules and harness were sent to you to-day. You will direct your Quarter Master to send receipts for this property, and also for the twelve wagons, mules and harness sent to you a few days ago. You will at once proceed to organize a wagon train and put it in condition to take the field" Copy, DNA, RG 393, District of North Mo., Letters Sent. On Aug. 22, 1st Lt. A. F. Bond, q. m. District of North Mo., wrote to USG. "I have the honor to inform you that I have shipped on board the Steam Boat 'Sunshine,' Two hundred and ninety (290) Mules, (50) Fifty wagons, part of the Harness required for the Mules, and some other Government property, all of which is consigned to you. The invoices of these supplies I will forward you to-morrow, at which time the remaining Harness, and mules will be shipped. It will be necessary that a detail of men be on hand on arrival of the boat to take care of and receive the property. The boat will leave here to-night at 11 o'clock. The boat will probably arrive at Jefferson City Some time on Saturday next. P. S. Two hundred sixty two (262) mules only were shipped on the Sunshine, Capt. Hillard The boat could not receive any more. Please endorse enclosed Bill of Lading and return it to me." ALS, *ibid.*, District of Southeast Mo., Letters Received.

9. The report of Col. Allen P. Richardson, Cole County, Mo., Home Guards, to USG was probably dated Aug. 25. "I herewith submit my report of the expedition to Marion, Sandy Hook, Jamestown and Lookout. Three hundred infantry, under my command, left at 11 ½ o'clock on the 22d instant, on board the steamer Iatan, while at the same time a battalion of cavalry, (155 men,) under Captain Parker, left for the same places by land. We landed at Marion about 4 o'clock, P.M. On our arrival, I was informed that six of Jackson's men had, upon the approach of the steamer, taken in hot haste to the brush, one of them having swam his horse across to the north bank of the Missouri river. Detailed 40 men in squads of ten each to surround and, if possible, capture the rebels and horses. The details were made from Companies B, Captain Lusk; E, Captain Legg; A, (Boonville company,) under First Lieutenant ———; G, under First Lieutenant Mangel. The Squad under Captain Lusk met the enemy, armed, in the brush, and ordered them to halt, which they refused to do. Capt. Lusk then gave the command to 'fire,' when the rebels retreated in haste, one of them dismounting and leaving two horses, a double-barrel shot gun and a Lieutenant's coat behind, which the Captain took and afterwards delivered at headquarters.

One of the rebels is supposed to have received a slight wound. The other squads which I had detailed returned without having met an enemy. After this, and before the cavalry came up, we visited Eureka, took several persons assembled under suspicious circumstances, examined them and liberated them the next morning, after constituting them a committee of safety for the neighborhood with the following rules for their guidance: Elias Chambers, &c., &c., are appointed a committee of safety for the neighborhood of Eureka to report to me at Jefferson City the names of any person or persons who either raise and drill companies, or in any way disturb the quiet of the neighborhood; also the name or names of any person or persons who may threaten to shoot, or who may raise companies to shoot U. S. soldiers, or to join Jackson's army of invaders. A failure to do so shall work an entire confiscation of all property, which the committee, or any of the committee possess." *Missouri Republican*, Aug. 28, 1861.

To Jesse Root Grant

Jefferson City, Mo.
August 27th 1861

DEAR FATHER;

Your letter requesting me to appoint Mr. Foley on my Staff was only received last Friday night, of course to late to give Mr. F. the appointment even if I could do so. I remember to have been introduced to Mr. F. Sr. several years ago and if the son is anything like the impression I then formed of the father the appointment would be one that I could well congratulate myself upon. I have filled all the places on my Staff and, flatter myself, with deserving men. Mr. J. A. Rawlins of Galena is to be my Adj't. Gen. Mr. Lagow of the Regt. I was formerly Colonel of and Mr. Hillyer of St. Louis, Aides. They are all able men, from five to ten years younger than myself.[1] Without Military experience but very capable of learning. I only have one of them[2] with me yet and having all raw troops, and but little assistance, it keeps me busy from the time I get up in the morning until from 12 to 2 O'Clock at night, or morning.

I subscribed for the Daily Democrat,[3] a staunch Union paper, for you so that you might hear from me often. There is a goodeal of alarm felt by the Citizens of an early attack upon this place and if anything of the kind should take place we are illy prepared. All the troops are very raw and about one half of them Missouri Home Guards without discipline. No Artillery and but little Cavalry here. I do not anticipate an attack here myself, certainly not until we have attacked the enemy first. A defeat might induce the Rebels to follow up their success to this point but that we expect to prevent. My means of information are certainly as good as anyone els has and I cannot learn that there is an organized body of men North of the Osage river or any moving. There are numerous encampments through all the Counties bordering on the Missouri river, but the object seems to be to gather supplies, horses, transportation &c. for a Fall & Winter Campaign.

The country West of here will be left in a starving condition for next Winter. Families are being driven away in great numbers for their Union sentiments, leaving behind farms, crops, stock and all. A sad state of affairs must exist under the most favorable sircumstances that can take place. There will be no money in the country and the entire crop will be carried off, togeth with all stock of any value.

I am interrupted so often while writing that my letters must necessaryly be very meager and disconnected.

I hope you will let Mary go to Galena when Mother returns home. She has never paid us a visit and I would like to have her make a long one. I think it doubtful whether I will go home atal.

U<small>LYSSES</small>.

ALS. PPRF.

1. USG was thirty-nine; John A. Rawlins and William S. Hillyer, thirty; 1st Lt. Clark B. Lagow, thirty-two.
2. Lagow. *Memoirs*, I, 260*n*.
3. See letter to Mary Grant, Aug. 12, 1861.

To Capt. Speed Butler

———

Headquarters U. S. Forces
Jefferson City. Mo. August 28. 1861

CAPT. S. BUTLER
ST. LOUIS, MO.

I have no special information to impart today except the return of Colonel Worthington from Boonville.[1] His report is enclosed herewith.[2] Prisoners taken will be sent to St. Louis to-day, ~~with~~ charges accompanying.

A steamer is now just starting, in compliance with your telegraph of yesterday,[3] to capture all means of crossing the river. I would recommend the stoppage of mails west from here, or at least that they be placed under some regulation which would prevent the indiscriminate transmission of news. Captain Taylor's Battery,[4] four pieces, arrived last night.

A copy of charges against Prisoners[5] is also forwarded to ~~the~~ Commanding Officer at St. Louis Arsenal.

U. S. GRANT
Brig. General

Copies, DNA, RG 393, USG Hd. Qrs. Correspondence; DLC-USG, V, 4, 5, 7, 8. *O.R.*, I, iii, 465.

1. See letter to Col. William H. Worthington, Aug. 26, 1861.
2. This report has not been located. The results of the expedition were communicated to the press. "Col. Worthington, of the Iowa Fifth, who went out to Boonville on Sunday evening with about 150 men of his own regiment and nearly as many more of the Home Guard, returned here yesterday evening. He brought with him five prisoners, who will be taken down to St. Louis to-day. Their names are: J. L. Stephens, Conrad Harness, ——— Houx, ——— Kirton and ——— Andrews. No resistance was offered to him by anybody. Besides the prisoners he brought away $2,000 worth of shoes, which the owners (firm of Curtain & Ritchey) had been selling to the enemy, a large lot of stoves and tinware from the store of Andrews and Houx, who had been engaged in making canteens and camp kettles for the enemy, the types and printing material of the *Patriot* office, also the Boonville ferryboat and eleven skiffs." Letter of "S.," Jefferson City, Aug. 28, 1861, in *Missouri Republican*, Aug. 29, 1861.
3. On Aug. 27, Capt. Speed Butler telegraphed to USG. "Seize all Ferry Boats on Missouri within reach, and take them to Jefferson City. Howell's Ferry,

fifteen miles above Saint Charles, is important to be taken." Copy, DNA, RG 393, District of North Mo., Letters Sent.

4. On Aug. 25, USG had asked Brig. Gen. John Pope's hd. qrs. "whether Taylors artillery has started yet." *Ibid.*, Register of Letters Received. See letter to Capt. Speed Butler, Aug. 23, 1861, note 4.

5. This item has not been located.

To Brig. Gen. Lorenzo Thomas

———

St. Louis, Mo.
August 29th 1861

COL. L. THOMAS
ADJT. GEN. U.S.A.
WASHINGTON D.C.
SIR:

Having appointed John S. Rawlins, of Galena, Ill. Asst. Adj. Gen and W. S. Hillyer of St. Louis, Mo A D. C. I would respectfully request to have their appointments confirmed.

Respectfully
Your Obt. Svt.
U. S. GRANT
Brig. Gen. U.S.A.

ALS, Mrs. Walter Love, Flint, Mich. Endorsed "Approved & respectfully ~~submitted~~ forwarded," by Maj. Gen. John C. Frémont on Aug. 29, 1861. This letter was not received by the AGO until Jan. 3, 1862. DNA, RG 94, Register of Letters Received.

To Julia Dent Grant

———

St. Louis, Mo.
August 29th 1861

DEAR JULIA;

I have a moment to drop you a line in but this time I cannot inform you where I am going. I know that there is a Steamer laying at the Wharf, loaded with troops, ready to start whenever I go aboard. I will have my orders after breakfast. I was taken a goodeal by surprise yesterday about 11 O'Clock to get orders to report at once to Gen. Fremont for Special Orders.[1] I wish I could be kept with one Brigade steadily. But I suppose it is a compliment to be selected so often for what is supposed to be important service.

I will not be able to see any friends this trip. If I have a Brigade assigned to me with any appearance of perminancy I shall try and get Dr. Sharp[2] attached as Brigade Surgeon. I was very glad to learn that the Dr. takes the stand he does.

I am very sorry for the people in West & South Mo. Hundreds & hundreds of families are driven from their homes leaving farm crops stock and evrything behind. Those who are not driven are forced to see their crops, stock and evrything they have to subsist themselvs & families taken.

I should like very much to see Mr. Rawlins on here. I was compelled to leave my Aid[3] behind at Jeff. City for a day to bring up my horse, and to turn over orders &c. to my successor, and I cant find Mr. Hillyer here so that I will leave without any Staff.

Remember me to all in Galena. Kiss the children for me and a hundred for yourself.[4] You should be cheerful and try to encourage me. I have a task before me of no trifling moment and want all the encouragement possible. Remember that my success will depend a greatdeel upon myself and that the safety of the country, to some extent, and my reputation and that of our children greatly depends upon my acts.

I may be able to draw my pay to-day, if so will send you some money.

ULYS.

ALS, DLC-USG.

1. On Aug. 27, 1861, Maj. Gen. John C. Frémont wrote to Col. Jefferson C. Davis, 22nd Ind. "You are hereby directed to assume the command of the forces at Jefferson City relieving Brigadier General Grant who is ordered to report himself to these headquarters for special orders" LS, Robert W. Waitt, Jr., Richmond, Va. On the same day, Frémont wrote to USG. "Colonel Jefferson C. Davis

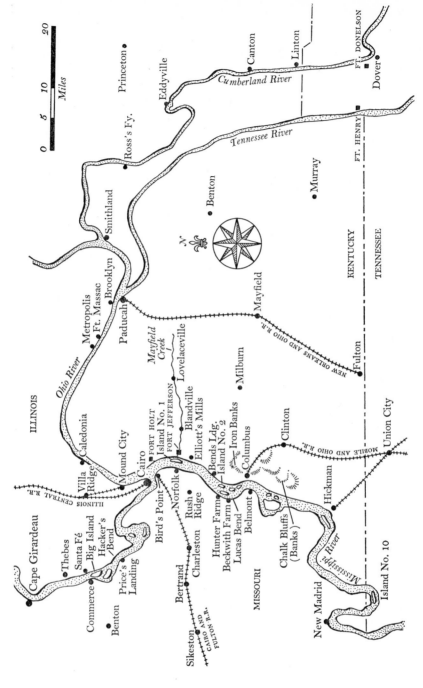

Cairo and Vicinity in 1861

will relieve you in the command of Jefferson City & you are directed to report yourself forthwith at these Head Quarters for special orders" Copies, DNA, RG 393, USG Hd. Qrs. Correspondence; DLC-USG, V, 7, 8, 81.

On Aug. 28, Frémont wrote to USG at St. Louis. "You are instructed to proceed forthwith to Cape Girardeau, and assume command of the forces at that place. A report having reached these headquarters that 4000 rebels are fortifying Benton, Mo. and that 1500 more are encamped behind the hills two miles below Commerce, opposite Big Island; a combined attack by the troops at Ironton and Cape Girardeau has been determined upon to destroy them. Brigadier General Prentiss has therefore been directed to move with all his disposable force to Dallas. From that place he will proceed towards Cape Girardeau, first attacking and destroying the rebels at Jackson should he ascertain that any are stationed at that place. Colonel Smith now in command at Cape Girardeau has been instructed to put himself in communication with General Prentiss at Dallas, and unite the forces at or near Jackson. Upon this junction being effected General Prentiss has been ordered to send information to that effect to Colonel Wallace Commanding at Birds Point, who will thereupon move with two regiments to Charleston, and after occupying that place, make reconnoissances along the railroad and advance as far as possible. Colonel Waagner Chief of Artillery at Cairo left St Louis last night with the regiment of Colonel Pugh by steamboat for Birds Point to exchange the regiment there with Colonel McArthurs, and to undertake an expedition with two gunboats, under Commander Rodgers to Belmont to destroy the fortifications erecting by the rebels, keep possession of that place, and move thence in concert with the two regiments just mentioned towards Charleston with the view of coöperating with the forces from Ironton and Cape Girardeau towards Benton. Brigadier General McClernand of Illinois is moving towards Cairo with two thousand infantry, which he has been instructed to distribute at Centralia and Carbondale on the Illinois Central railroad and at a point opposite Commerce. It is intended in connection with all these movements to occupy Columbus in Kentucky as soon as possible. You will therefore upon assuming the command at Cape Girardeau act in accordance with all the foregoing dispositions, and when the junction with the forces of General Prentiss is effected you will take command of the combined forward movement. Finally I recommend you to do everything to promote the work of fortification, commenced at Cairo, Birds Point, Cape Girardeau and Ironton." Copies, *ibid.*; DNA, RG 393, Western Dept., Letters Sent; *ibid.*, Letters Sent (Press). *O.R.*, I, iii, 141–42.

On the same day, Frémont issued Special Orders No. 101. "The Regiment of Illinois troops at Alton will on the arrival there of transportation, proceed to a point on the Mississippi River opposite Commerce, where they will be stationed. The boat will stop at this City, to take on bord General Grant who will direct its movements. After the troops are landed and General Grant has reac[hed] his Station, the Boat will return to the City. The Quarter Master Captain Turnley will supply the required transportation." Copies, DNA, RG 393, Western Dept., Special Orders; DLC-USG, V, 81, VIA, 1.

Also on Aug. 28, Frémont wrote to Brig. Gen. Benjamin M. Prentiss. "Brig. Genl. Grant has been directed to proceed to Cape Girardeau, assume command of the forces there and cooperate with the troops moving from Ironton When you were ordered to go to Ironton and take the place of General Grant who was transferred to Jefferson city it was under the impression that his appointment was of a later date than your own. By the official list published it appears however that he is your senior in rank. He will therefore upon affecting a conjunction with your troops take command of the whole expedition Brigadier General McClernand of Illinois is moving towards Cairo with 2000 Infantry which he has been instructed to distribute at important points upon the Illinois Central Rail road and on the shore opposite Commerce. It being the intention ultimately to take possession of Columbus and hold it. Colonel Waagner, chief of Artillery at Cairo left St Louis last night with the regiment of Col. Pugh by steamboat for Bird's Point to exchange that regiment there with Colonel McArthur's and to undertake an expedition with the gun boats under Commander Rodgers to Belmont to destroy the fortifications erecting by the rebels. Keep possession of that place and move from there in concert with two regiments from Bird's Point towards Charlestown, with the view of cooperating with the forces from Ironton and Cape Girardeau" Copy, DNA, RG 393, Western Dept., Letters Sent by Gen. Frémont. *O.R.*, I, iii, 142–43.

On Aug. 28, Col. C. Carroll Marsh wrote from Cape Girardeau to Capt. John C. Kelton. "Matters at this post remain much as per last advices—Gen Pillow and Jeff Thompson were both at Benton yesterday, with a force variously reported at from five, to fifteen thousand—Their forces are scattered at short intervals from Benton to a distance ten miles south of that place—Today they broke up camp at Benton and moved south, supposed to be on account of insufficient supply of water—Courriers are constantly passing between Gens Pillow and Hardee: the latter still at, or near Greenville—both, have small parties at the various mills in the adjoining counties and are using the mills constantly to supply their armies Yesterday Com Rogers with the Gun Boats 'Tyler' and 'Lecxington' anchored off this place, brought here by a report at Cairo that this place was to be attacked yesterday: finding all quiet they returned this morning—Work on fortification progressing satisfactorily—It has been found necessary by Capt Flad, Engineer in charge of works to occupy the land on which is the residence of M. Dittlinger—I enclose an appraisel of said property, made by Capt J. O. Pullen selected by me, and John Launsman by M. Dittlinger, said appraisal to be subject to the approval of the General commanding. Work is already commenced on the property mentioned—I beg leave to again call attention to the necessity of cavalry at this post The troops under my command can render much more efficient service if aided by only a small, well equipped, mounted force—" The letter was endorsed by Kelton. "Would it be more advantageous to rent the property which is to be occupied by the fortification at Cape Girardeau than to purchase [it] to be restored after the War." On Aug. 31, Maj. Joseph H. Eaton, military secretary to Frémont, endorsed the letter to USG. "Respectfully referred to Brig'r. Genl Grant, who, instead of adopting the plan herein for the purchase of the land for the U. S. will direct an *appraisal of damages* to the proprietors report himself his approval or disapproval of the amount & forward the same to these Hd. Qrs. for final action." DNA, RG 393, District of Southeast Mo., Letters Received. See letters to Maj. Gen. John C. Frémont, Sept. 20, 1861, and Capt. Chauncey McKeever, Oct. 7, 1861.

While USG received a variety of instructions with his new command, his first duty was to hunt down Brig. Gen. M. Jeff Thompson, 1st Military District, Mo. State Guard, whose irregular and highly mobile forces operated with considerable success in Mo. along the Mississippi River from Cairo to Cape Girardeau. Jay Monaghan, *Swamp Fox of the Confederacy: The Life and Military Services of M. Jeff Thompson* (Tuscaloosa, 1956), pp. 32–36. By coordinating the movements of troops from Ironton to Cape Girardeau, and from Cairo into Mo., USG was to trap Thompson in the middle. *Memoirs*, I, 261.

2. Dr. Alexander Sharp, brother-in-law of USG. See letter to Brig. Gen. Lorenzo Thomas, Aug. 31, 1861.

3. 1st Lt. Clark B. Lagow.

4. Two lines crossed out.

General Orders No. 1

Head Quarters
Cape Girardeau Mo
Aug 30. 1861

GENL ORDERS No 1   EXTRACT

By virtue of instructions dated Head Quarters department of the west Augst 28th 1861,[1] the undersigned herby assumes command of this post. . . . Rations of sugar coffee and Bread will be sent your command. For rations of meat you must depend upon the suplies of the country taking fresh Beef where you can find it.

In getting supplies you will be carefull that your command do not help themselves but evrything must be done by your order making a proper detail to execute it, and all suplies must be accounted for to the Benefit of the United States. The names of persons from whom suplies are taken the amount and cash value will be reported to these Head Quarters. Where the parties are loyal citizens a receipt will also be given to be sent here and payment ordered.

You will proceed to Dallas[2] and their await the arrival of Genl Prentiss reporting as early as practicable after the junction is effected when the undersigned under the same instuctions refered to in Order No 1 will assume command of the combined movement to be made—

To Col. C. C. Marsh[3]   U. S. GRANT
Comdg 20th Regt. Ills Vols   Brig Genl Comdg

P. S. Upon further examination of my instuctions, I find that the junction between Genl Prentiss and troops from this place is to be effected at or near Jackson.[4]

You will therfore make no further forward movement untill joined by Genl Prentiss, unless it may be for a few miles for the better purpose of getting supplies—

To Col. C. C. Marsh   U. S. GRANT
Comdg 20th Regt Ills Vols   Brig. Genl Comdg

Copy, DNA, RG 393, Western Dept., Letters Received.

    1. See letter to Julia Dent Grant, Aug. 29, 1861, note 1.
    2. Dallas, Mo., about twenty-four miles west of Cape Girardeau.
    3. Col. C. Carroll Marsh, 20th Ill., then stationed at Cape Girardeau.
    4. Jackson, Mo., about seven miles northwest of Cape Girardeau. On Aug. 31, 1861, Capt. William S. Hillyer wrote to Marsh. "The remainder of your regiment now at this point will move to join you at Jackson to-morrow morning to-gether with all their camp equipage, transportation and the Bacon rations you request. The detatchment of the 11th Mo will be returnd to this post." Copy, DNA, RG 393, Western Dept., Letters Received.

To Capt. John C. Kelton

Head Quarters, Cape Girardeau, Mo.
August 30th 1861

SIR:

I arrived here at 4 ½ O'Clock this afternoon and assumed command of the Post. Found that Col. Marsh with thirteen companies of Infantry, two pieces of Artillery & about fifty Cavalry, armed with rifles taken from the 9th Regt. Mo. Vols. left here at 10 O'Clock P. M. yesterday. A report is just in from him stating that he was in Jackson. No enemy was found.—This command took with them but two days rations but I have ordered, to leave by daylight to-morrow morning, three days more rations excepting meat. These I have instructed must be supplied by the country, giving special instructions however that it is to be done in a legal way.[1]

Owing to the limited amount of transportation it is impossible to forward much of a supply at one time. Thirteen teams is reported to me as being the extent of transportation at present available. Additional wagons however were received a few days ago and as soon as harness is supplied eight more can be started from captured mules now in our possession.

The fortifications here are in a considerable state of forwardness, and I would judge from visiting them this afternoon are being pushed forward with vigor. I notice that a number of Contrabands, in the shape of negroes,[2] are being employed, apparently much to their satisfaction. I will make enquiries how they come here and if the fact has not been previously reported ask instructions.

A junction with Gen. Prentiss is not reported.

> Respectfully
> U. S. GRANT
> Brig. Gen. Com

To Capt. J. C. Kelton
A. A. Gen. U. S. A.
St Louis Mo.

P. S. No blank muster rolls have ever been received here. I have ordered one copy for each company to be ruled out and the balance to be copied when the blanks are received

> U. S. GRANT
> Brig. Gen. Com.

ALS, DNA, RG 393, Western Dept., Letters Received. *O.R.*, I, iii, 143–44; *ibid.*, II, i, 766.

1. See preceding orders.
2. The use of the term "contraband" in reference to slaves had been popularized by Maj. Gen. Benjamin F. Butler. Richard S. West, Jr., *Lincoln's Scapegoat General: A Life of Benjamin F. Butler* (Boston, 1965), pp. 81–85.

To Brig. Gen. Lorenzo Thomas

———

Head Quarters, Cape Girardeau, Mo
August 31st 1861

Col. L. Thomas
Adj. Gen. U. S. A.
Washington D. C.
Sir:

In pursuance of Gen. Orders No 53 I have the honor of reporting my address at this place.

My Staff are Lieut. Clark B. Lagow, 21st Ill. Vols. and Mr. Hillyer, belonging to no organization, Aides-de-Camp, and John A. Rawlins, Asst. Adj. Gen.

These two latter having been appointed by me their appointments have been forwarded to[1]

AL, DNA, RG 94, Letters Received.

1. The remainder of the letter is torn away.

To Brig. Gen. Lorenzo Thomas

———

Head Quarters U. S. Forces
Cape Girardeau
Aug 31, 1861

Sir

I have to day appointed Dr Alexander Sharp of Missouri Brigade Surgeon to be attached to my staff and would respectfully ask that the appointment be confirmed.

Dr Sharp is my brother in law and I know him to be in every way qualified for the post. He is a citizen of Lincoln County Missouri and is a member of the Home Guard having joined it on its first organization. He is a union man tried and true and will I expect ~~that~~ ~~he~~ ~~would~~ be compelled to leave the county and abandon his buisiness and property He has not applied to me for the appointment. I make it at my own suggestion, having personal knowledge of the facts stated and I ask this confirmation as a special and personal favor knowing that the interests of the service will be at the same time promoted

All of which is respectfully submitted

U. S. GRANT

Brig Gen U. S. A

To L Thomas
Adj Gen U. S. A
Washington D.C.

Copies, DNA, RG 393, USG Hd. Qrs. Correspondence; DLC-USG, V, 4, 5, 7, 8, 78. Dr. Alexander Sharp's appointment was not confirmed, but on Sept. 11, 1861, he signed a contract to serve as surgeon at Cairo at $100 monthly. *HED*, 37-2-101, p. 93.

To Capt. Warren Stewart

Headquarters U. S. Forces.
Cape Girardeau Mo Aug 31/61

CAPT. WARREN STEWART
INDEPENDENT CAVALRY COMPANY.

If you have any extra horses in your command, or horses not yet assigned, I wish you to let the bearer, who is on important business for General Fremont have one of the best.

It will be returned tonight.

U. S. GRANT

Brig. General.

Copies, DNA, RG 393, USG Letters Sent; DLC-USG, V, 1, 2, 3. Capt. Warren Stewart's Independent Cav. Co. later served as Co. A, 15th Ill. Cav., of which Stewart was col.

To Jesse Root Grant

———

Cape Girardeau, Mo.
August 31st 1861

DEAR FATHER;

Your letter of the 26th is just received. As to the relative rank of officers (Brigadiers) you are right but in all the balance you are laboring under an erronious impression. There has been no move made affecting me which has not been complimentary rather than otherwise though calculated to keep me laboriously employed. I was sent to Ironton when the place was weak and threatened with a superior force and as soon as it was rendered secure was ordered to Jefferson City, another point threatened. I was left there but a week when orders were sent me ordering to this point puting me in command of all the forces in S. E. Mo. South Ill. and evrything that can opperate here. All I fear is that too much may be expected of me. My duties will absorb my entire attention and I shall try not disappoint the good people of Ill. who, I learn from evry quarter, express an enthusiasm for me that was wholly unexpected.—Gen. Prentiss is not a particular favorite as you suspect nor is there a prejudice against him. I think all the Brigadiers are acceptable, with the rank assigned them by the President.

The Brigadiers are not all up north as you suspect. I know of but one, Hurlbut, who is there. Gen. McClernand[1] is at Cairo, Prentis at Ironton and I presume Curtis[2] will be with the command under me.

Gen. Hunter[3] is at Chicago but I look upon that as temporary. I have not heard of any command being assigned him as yet and do not know that he has sufficiently recovered from wounds received in the late engagements in Virginia[4] to take the field. Hunter will prove himself a fine officer.

The letters spoken of by you have not all been received. One sent to Galena I got and answered. My promise to write to you evry two weeks has been complied with and however busy I may be I shall continue it if it is but a line. I am now probably done shifting commands so often, this being the fourth in as many weeks.

Your suspicions as to my being neglected are entirely unfounded for I know it was the intention to give me a Brigade if I had not been promoted. Application would have been made to have me assigned, arbitrarily, as senior Colonel from Ill. for the purpose.

I want to hear from you or Mary often. I sent you the Daily Democrat thinking that would keep you better posted in this section than I could do and being a cheap correspondent.

I wrote to you that I would like to have Mary go out to Galena and stay some time. I do not want Julia to leave ~~there~~ Galena being anxious to retain my residence after the many kindnesses received from the people there.

I only arrived at this place last night and can not tell you much about things here. The people however are generally reported to be secessionests.

ULYS.

ALS, PPRF.

    1. See letter to Brig. Gen. John A. McClernand, Sept. 1, 1861.
    2. Brig. Gen. Samuel R. Curtis of Iowa, USMA 1831, was assigned to command the camp of instruction at Benton Barracks, Mo., on Sept. 1, 1861. *O.R.*, I, liii, 502.
    3. Maj. Gen. David Hunter of Ill., USMA 1822, briefly replaced Maj. Gen. John C. Frémont as USG's superior, Nov. 2-9, 1861.
    4. First battle of Bull Run.

To Julia Dent Grant

Cape Girardeau Mo.
August 31st 1861

DEAR JULIA;

Almost evry time I write it is from a new place. I arrived here last evening, looked through the different camps and assumed command. Bayles[1] who lived below the Arsenal commands one of the Regiments here. Another is a Missouri Regiment. My duties are active but I enjoy most excelent health. As I have written several times before I have been expecting soon to get a leave of absence for the purpose of visiting Galena until now all present hope has vanished. My present command is an important one, my being the senior Brigadier General South of St. Louis and all the troops from Ironton to Birds Point & Cairo being in one command. If it should turn up that I could see a week when there would be no necessity for my presence I will still go. That you need not look for for several weeks. This is a most delightful place. Myself & Staff are making Head Quarters at a very quiet nice hotel.[2] If I could have any assurance of remaining here for any time I would have you and the children come down. I know however I shall not remain. Probably by next Wednesday[3] about the day you get this, I shall b[egin] moving. Still however in this section of M[issouri.] There is a greatdeel of marching and counter-marching in this part of our troubled country without coming to blows. They must follow however soon. There is a large rebel force in this section of the state and they are committing all sorts of depridations upon the Union people.

I received a letter from Dr. Sharp[4] this morning and find that he brethes the same sort of Union sentiments I feel myself and I thought wanted an invitation to take Nellie[5] out of the State, to Galena. I at once made out an appointment for him of Brigade Surgeon and sent off the appointment to Washington for confirmation. I wrote to the Dr. at the same time to bring Nelly down to your fathers for the present and him join me until the result is known and I would order payment to be made for the services rendered in case the appointment was not confirmed, that I was almost certain it would be confirmed; ~~however~~ and then to send his family to Galena. I sent him at the same time a free pass for himself and horse to this place. I think the Dr. will come. This will be a good position for him, and I know he will be delighted. Dont you think it would be pleasant to have Nelly with you. Charge Jess that he is not to whip Alexander Jr. I want to see little rascal Jess very much. Did you get some money from Ford?[6] As I passed through St. Louis I left $240 00 with Ford with instructions to pay for my uniform when it arrived and send the balance to you I think there will be something over $100 00 left. One month more and I will be comparitively easy. In fact am so now. By the time what I owe Hewlitt[7] falls due I can have it paid and supply you liberally. Get what you require, keep out of debt and save all you can.

I will send to Dr. Perkett as soon as Hughlett is paid, then to Werner. Bill Barnard I suppose does not hold anything against me. My expenses for horses servants and all are only about $40 pr month and as my pay is a little over $4.000 a year I must save something.

Mr. Hillyer is with me. When I get Dr. Sharp and Mr. Rawlins I will have a clever set about me. If Dr. Sharp had written to me earlyer I would have given him a position about which there would be no doubt about him holding.

Tell Bell that Orlando[8] is with me. His conduct has been as good as can be all the time.

Remember me to all the neighbors and relations. I received a letter from Lank[9] which I will answer. Tell the friends of Mr. Rawlins that I have never had an idea of filling his place with any-one els. I have received four or five letters from different friends of his on the subject.

Kiss the children for me. Same for yourself. Do you have many calls? I suppose mother will be leaving you soon? I wrote to father to let Mary make you a visit.

Good buy.

ULYS.

ALS, DLC-USG.

1. Col. David Bayles, 11th Mo.
2. Probably the St. Charles Hotel, Cape Girardeau. Felix Eugene Snider and Earl Augustus Collins, *Cape Girardeau: Biography of a City* (Cape Girardeau, 1956), p. 227.
3. Sept. 4, 1861.
4. See letter to Brig. Gen. Lorenzo Thomas, Aug. 31, 1861.
5. Mrs. Alexander Sharp, Ellen Dent Sharp.

6. See letter to Charles Ford, Sept. 1, 1861.
7. See letter to Julia Dent Grant, Aug. 15, 1861, note 9.
8. Orlando H. Ross. See letter to Julia Dent Grant, June 27, 1861, note 1.
9. See letter of April 21, 1861, note 5.

General Orders No. 1

———

Head Quarters
Cape Girardeau Mo
Sept 1st 1861

GENL ORDERS NO 1

In persuance of Directions from Head Quarters of the department of the west, the undrsigned herby assumes command of this post.

All orders now in force will remain so untill otherwise ordered—

All the troops at this point will be paraded for muster tomorrow morning at 10. o'clock

Each Regiment or Detatchment commander will act as a mustering officer to his own command.

Five muster rolls must be made out for Each company, in case the Blanks are on hand. Should any of the companies however be without a Blank a roll of the company must be made and the comp.y mustered on that and Blanks filled when recived

U. S. GRANT
Brig. Genl Comdg

Copies, DLC-USG, V, 12, 14, 80; DNA, RG 393, USG General Orders. There is no explanation for USG's use of "General Orders No. 1" on different orders of Aug. 30 and Sept. 1, 1861, except that the earlier communication might have appeared, on reflection, to be more properly a letter to Col. C. Carroll Marsh.

General Orders No. 2

———

Head Quarters
Cape Girardeau Mo Septr 1st 1861
GENERAL ORDERS No 2.

In pursuance of directions from the Department of the west the undersigned hereby assumes command of all the forces in South-East Mo: extending north as far as the line drawn from Pilot Knob to this place, both inclusive.[1]

The commands of the several posts embraced in this district will remain as now constituted until otherwise directed.

The forces now at, or near, Jackson Mo will proceed with as little delay as practicable towards Sikeston Mo :[2] there to receive orders :

The Head Quarters of this command will at once be removed to Birds Point[3] where all reports will be forwarded. If however any information should be received, by commanders of Posts, deemed of importance to the commander of the west, they will forward such information directly there, if it can be done more expeditiously than through the proper channel.

A copy of all such information will also be sent to these Head Quarters.

U. S. GRANT
Brig. Gen. U. S. A.

To Wm H. L. Wallace
Birds Point.

DS, ICHi. Addressed to Col. William H. L. Wallace, 11th Ill. Wallace, a lawyer and Republican politician of Ottawa, Ill., had served as 2nd lt. and regt. adjt. in the Mexican War. He had commanded the 11th Ill. since May 1, 1861. Isabel Wallace, *Life & Letters of General W. H. L. Wallace* (Chicago, 1909).

1. The geographical dimensions of the District of Southeast Mo. were not clearly drawn. Ironton, Mo., though directly south of Pilot Knob, was not included. See letter to Maj. Gen. John C. Frémont, Sept. 17, 1861. All Mo. south and east of Ironton was included, and also all of southern Ill. Later, the district expanded to include all of Ky. in U.S. possession west of the Cumberland River.

2. Sikeston, Mo., about thirty miles south of Cape Girardeau.

3. Bird's Point, Mo., directly opposite Cairo, Ill. On Aug. 31, Maj. Gen. John C. Frémont wrote to USG giving detailed instructions concerning the enlargement and improvement of the camp at Bird's Point. Copies, DNA, RG 393, Western Dept., Letters Sent by Gen. Frémont; *ibid.*, Letters Sent (Press).

To Capt. John C. Kelton

Head Quarters,
Cape Girardeau, Mo.
September 1st / 61

SIR:

Since my report of yesterday[1] reliable information has come in to the effect that the enemy are deserting, or have deserted, all their positions North of the line from Bird's Point to Sikeston, and probably from there. This movement seems to have commenced on the 27th ult.

Not hearing from Gen. Prentiss, and learning the above facts, I have written to Gen. McClernand at Cairo advising that Col. Wallace proceed to Charleston[2] and recconnoitre from there as directed to do after a junction had been formed between this command and the one from Ironton.

Should no instructions be received here different from any I now have, upon hearing of Gen. Prentiss arrival at Jackson I will order the column to move South, under his command, and proceed myself to Bird's Point and take command there.

U. S. GRANT
Brig. Gen. Com.

To Capt. J. C. Kelton
Asst. Adj. Gen. U. S. A.
St. Louis Mo.

ALS, DNA, RG 393, Western Dept., Letters Received. *O.R.*, I, iii, 144. On Sept. 1, 1861, USG telegraphed the substance of this report to Capt. John C. Kelton. "No news of Genl Prentiss. As soon as heard from will order the colum south under his command and go to Birds Point myself and take command there & will wait four hours for answer." Copies, DLC-USG, V, 5, 7, 8, 78; DNA, RG 393, USG Hd. Qrs. Correspondence. On the same day, Maj. Gen. John C. Frémont telegraphed to USG. "Your dispatch of to day not understood. Send telegraphic dispatches to me direct, Keep me minutely and frequently advised." Copies, *ibid.*, Western Dept., Telegrams; DLC-USG, VIA, 1. Also on Sept. 1, Frémont telegraphed to Col. Richard J. Oglesby, 8th Ill. "Say to Gen'l McClernand that Col: Wallace is not to move until Gen'l Prentiss be heard from. Up to noon to day Grant had not heard from Prentiss—" Copies, *ibid.*

1. No letter from USG to Kelton of Aug. 31 has been found. USG may refer to a Sept. 1 letter of Capt. William S. Hillyer to Kelton. "I am directed by Brig Gen Grant Commanding at Cape Girardeau to report to you that on yesterday after noon he received information which he deems reliable that the enemy has abandoned his positions at Benton—near Commerce and Saxton and is rapidly retreating towards New madrid, with the intention of concentrating his force at the last named place—this information is derived from several sources, each corroborating the others—the first information was derived from a union man who had been taken prisoner by the enemy and was released with a pass from 'Jeff Thompson, Comd M. S. G.,' and who brought a proposition from 'Thompson' for the exchange of prisoners. Gen Grant declined to entertain any communication from 'Thompson.' I left Cape Girardeau about 7 o'clock last evening (Aug 31) on board Government Steamer Louisiana. Gen Grant directed me to report further that he would have made this report himself, but the steamer arrived as he was about to write it, and he did not think it necessary to detain her, as the report could be made through me. Up to the time I left Cape Girardeau, no information had been received at Head Quarters of the junction of the forces under Gen Prentiss with the forces under Col Marsh at Jackson, but the information was hourly expected. Gen Grant yesterday ordered the part of Col Marsh 20th Illinois Regiment stationed at Cape Girardea[u] to move this morning and join the detachment under Col Marsh at Jackson, and instruct[ed] Col Marsh upon their arrival to send back the detachment of the 11th Missouri under his command, to Cape Girardeau. The force of the enemy retreating from Benton & Commerce is reported as 6000 men. All which is respectfully submitted." ALS, DNA, RG 393, Western Dept., Letters Received.

2. Charleston, Mo., about twelve miles southwest of Cairo, Ill.

To Capt. John C. Kelton

Head Quarters
Cape Girardeau Mo.
September 1st 1861

SIR:

Gen. Prentiss has just arrived. Will move the column under his command to Sikeston as soon as possible. I will go to Birds Point and take command there and push out from that point.

Gen. P. reports that Hardee left Greenville the day he left Ironton and has fallen back into Arkansas.

The scarsity of transportation here has prevented me having provisions thrown forward to Jackson preparitory for this move and will necessarily cause a delay of at least one day.

U. S. Grant
Brig. Gen. Com.

To Capt. J. C. Kelton
A. A. Gen. U. S. A.
St. Louis Mo

ALS, DNA, RG 393, Western Dept., Letters Received. *O.R.*, I, iii, 145.

To Brig. Gen. John A. McClernand

———

Head Quarters, Cape Girardeau, Mo.
September 1st 1861

Sir.

I learn from information which is reliable that the enemy have left Commerce, Benton[1] and probably Sikeston. They have taken all their Artillery and probably fallen back to New Madrid.[2] I would advise that Col. Wallace push out to Charleston at once and reconoitre as far as possible without waiting to hear from the Colum from Ironton.

As soon as a junction is formed between Gen. Prentiss & Col. Marsh I will be informed of it, and will assume command of all the troops coöperating from this point to Cairo, and will move down the river at once.

If Col. Wagners[3] instructions are not different from mine Belmont[4] should have been taken possession of and held.

U. S. Grant
Brig. Gen. Com.

To Gen. McClernand
Cairo Ill.

ALS, McClernand Papers, IHi. *O.R.*, I, iii, 144–45. Brig. Gen. John A. McClernand of Ill. had just arrived at Cairo with 2,000 new troops. He was also serving his sixth term as U.S. Representative. Born in Ky. in 1812, he lived in Shawneetown, Ill., from 1813 to 1851, where he was a lawyer, newspaper editor, and Democratic politician. He began a second political career after moving to Springfield in 1856. Although his previous military service was limited to three months as a private in the Black Hawk War of 1832, he resigned his seat in Congress on Oct. 28, 1861, to retain his commission as brig. gen. of vols. Victor Hicken, "From Vandalia to Vicksburg: The Political and Military Career of John A. McClernand" (unpublished doctoral dissertation, University of Illinois, 1955). It was intended that McClernand would move his troops to Cairo without superseding the previous commander, Col. Richard J. Oglesby, 8th Ill. Maj. Joseph H. Eaton to McClernand, Sept. 2, 1861. Copy, DNA, RG 393, Western Dept., Letters Sent (Press). *O.R.*, I, iii, 143.

1. Commerce, Mo., about twelve miles southeast of Cape Girardeau on the Mississippi River; Benton, Mo., about fifteen miles south of Cape Girardeau.
2. New Madrid, Mo., on the Mississippi River about thirty-five miles south of Cairo.
3. Col. Gustav Waagner, chief of art. at Cairo, occupied Belmont, Mo., on Sept. 2. Waagner to Maj. Gen. John C. Frémont, Sept. 2, 1861, *ibid.*, pp. 151–52.
4. Belmont, Mo., on the Mississippi River about eighteen miles south of Cairo, opposite Columbus, Ky.

To Col. Morgan L. Smith

Head Quarters
Camp Girardeau Mo
Sept 1st 1861

SIR

The undersigned being instructed from the western Department of the Army to take command of all the troops in South East Missouri, the command of this Post will be relinquished in your favor.

You will therefore take command at once making your reports to Genl Fremont at St Louis from my departure untill otherwise instucted—

It has been enjined upon me to see that the work of fortifying be pushed vigorously forward. You will see therfor that the officers in charge of this work have evry facillity given them that your command affords

U S GRANT
Brig. Genl Comdg

Col M. L. Smith
Comdg 8th Regt Mo Volls

Copies, DLC-USG, V, 1, 2, 3, 78; DNA, RG 393, USG Letters Sent. *O.R.*, I, iii, 144. Col. Morgan L. Smith was appointed to command the 8th Mo. on July 4, 1861.

To Charles Ford

Cape Girardeau, Mo.
Sept. 1st 1861

DEAR FORD,

If my clothing has arrived send it to Cairo to be retained until called for if you should not have an opportunity of sending by private hands.

Hillyer of my Staff is now in St. Louis and will be joining me in a day or two. If he should call give my packages to him and direct him to go to Cairo and await me there should he not find a boat starting when he gets ready to move.

Say to him that I have a horse at Arnott's[1] stable which I want him to bring also.

Yours Truly
U. S. GRANT
Brig.

ALS, USG 3. See letter to Julia Dent Grant, Aug. 4, 1861, note 1.

1. Jesse Arnot kept a livery stable in St. Louis.

To Brig. Gen. Benjamin M. Prentiss

Head Quarters
Cape Girardeau Mo
Sept 2, 1861

SIR

You will proceed to join your command at once, turn it back to Jackson and there take command of the whole expedition and move without delay, to Sikeston or in that direction.

Your orders were deliverd to you in person last night; and their failure to reach your command cannot be placed at the door of any one but your self—

U S GRANT
Brigr Genl Comdg

To Brigr Genl B. M. Prentiss
Present

Copy, DNA, RG 393, Western Dept., Letters Received. "In pursuance of my orders I established my temporary headquarters at Cape Girardeau and sent instructions to the commanding officer at Jackson, to inform me of the approach of General Prentiss from Ironton. Hired wagons were kept moving night and day to take additional rations to Jackson, to supply the troops when they started from there. Neither General Prentiss nor Colonel Marsh, who commanded at Jackson, knew their destination. I drew up all the instructions for the contemplated move, and kept them in my pocket until I should hear of the junction of our troops at Jackson. Two or three days after my arrival at Cape Girardeau, word came that General Prentiss was approaching that place (Jackson). I started at once to meet him there and to give him his orders. As I turned the first corner of a street after starting, I saw a column of cavalry passing the next street in front of me. I turned and rode around the block the other way, so as to meet the head of the column. I found there General Prentiss himself, with a large escort. He had halted his troops at Jackson for the night, and had come on himself to Cape Girardeau, leaving orders for his command to follow him in the morning. I gave the General his orders—which stopped him at Jackson—but he was very much aggrieved at being placed under another brigadier-general, particularly as he believed himself to be the senior. He had been a brigadier, in command at Cairo, while I was mustering officer at Springfield without any rank. But we were nominated at the same time for the United States service, and both our commissions bore date May 17th, 1861. By virtue of my former army rank I was, by law, the senior. General Prentiss failed to get orders to his troops to remain at Jackson, and the next morning early they were reported as approaching Cape Girardeau. I then ordered the General very peremptorily to countermarch his command and take it back to Jackson. He obeyed the order, but bade his command adieu when he got them to Jackson, and went to St. Louis and reported himself. This broke up the expedition. But little harm was done, as Jeff. Thompson moved light and had no fixed place for even nominal headquarters. He was as much at home in Arkansas as he was in Missouri and would keep out of the way of a superior force. Prentiss was sent to another part of the State." *Memoirs*, I, 261–63. See "General Grant and General Prentiss," *USGA Newsletter*, III, 2 (Jan., 1966), 7–11.

On Sept. 1, 1861, Prentiss wrote to Capt. John C. Kelton. "I hereby tender my Resignation as Brigadier General, and ask that it may be received." ALS, DNA, RG 94, Generals' Papers and Books, Benjamin M. Prentiss. On the same day, Prentiss telegraphed to Maj. Gen. John C. Frémont. "I have this day forwarded you my resignation. I see by order from you to Gen Grant that he is to rank me. That makes me Junior when I claim to be Senior Brigadeir Genl from Illinois. I will remain in Service but not as Junior Brig Genl." Telegram received (punctuation added), *ibid.* On Sept. 2, Prentiss wrote to Frémont. "Upon arriving at Cape Girardeau I discovered that so much of your order of 25th August 1861 as placed this expedition under my command had been countermanded and that Brig. Gen. Grant had assumed command. Satisfied this was caused by a misunderstanding of the relative position as to rank of Brig. Gen. U. S. Grant and myself and waiving technical objections going to the validity of the order issued by him, I requested him to allow me three days leave of absence agreeing to join the command at Sikeston, that I might have opportunity to present the facts before you. This request was at once refused. I then proposed to Gen. Grant to join him in a written statement of our relative positions that you might judge between us as to the question of rank by seniority. This was also refused. My third proposition was to leave the question of seniority to the arbitrament of three officers of the regular army of the United States; the arbitrators to be selected by Gen. Grant himself. This being also refused, I further proposed that Gen. Grant should assign the command to the Senior Colonel until I could hear from you. A refusal following upon this proposition I felt bound in honor to tender my resignation to you—as I have done. Having done so I at once preferred to go with the command. This morning, when upon the point of starting back to my command I learned that the column was moving on toward Cape Girardeau, pursuant to orders from me, given in view of the fact that I had received no communication at Jackson. Col. Marshs' regiment was however left at Jackson, no order for his march having been sent to him or transmitted to me. Upon learning this state of facts, Gen. Grant ordered the return of the column to this place. Seeing that there was evident mismanagement and feeling grieved that the laudable ambition which has prompted me heretofore had been curbed by the elevation of a junior officer to the place which I had held as the Senior Brigadier of Illinois: I informed General Grant that while I should place no obstacle in the way of my countrys' cause, but should, to the utmost extent of my ability aid it by my counsel and action with this column: I would wash my hands of such mismanagement and would rather submit to arrest than assume the responsibility of it, whereupon he issued the order, a copy of which I enclose. I at once joined the column and with some anxiety await your instructions." L (signature clipped), *ibid.*, RG 393, Western Dept., Letters Received.

To Brig. Gen. Benjamin M. Prentiss

———

Headquarters U. S. Forces.
Cape Girardeau Mo. Sept 2 1861

BRIG GEN B. M. PRENTISS.

CAPE GIRARDEAU.

My instructions saying that the rebels are fortifying Benton. It may be that they have moved to that point some heavy ordnance which could not be taken away in the hurry of their departure. It would be well therefore to make inquiries in passing through whether such is the case. Should any be found at the point put it under the charge of some secessionist of property, who will be held responsible for its safety until removed by authority.

Should anything come to my knowledge of the enemies movements likely to affect your movement I will communicate with you as early as practicable, either by way of this place or by some point on the river below. Should you learn any thing of importance keep me informed if practicable.

I would recommend the reading of General Fremonts order (Special order No 106) to the troops before leaving Jackson.

U. S. GRANT.
Brig. Genl.

Copies, DNA, RG 393, USG Letters Sent; *ibid.*, Western Dept., Letters Received; DLC-USG, V, 1, 2, 3. *O.R.*, I, iii, 145.

To Col. John Cook

———

Head Quarters
Cape Girardeau Mo
Sept 2d 1861

SIR

Genl Prentiss having placed himself under arrest by his own order the command of the column at Jackson neccissaryly devolves upon the senior Col. with it. The Genl Comdg having no official notice of the relative rank of his officers, will assume that they are arranged according to the numerical order of the regiments which they command. Cols. from different states taking rank according to date of commission—when they have been issued, when they have not according to date of being sworn into the United States Service—

It is assumed therefore that Col Cook 7th Regt Ills Vols is the senior and the command will devolve upon him—

He will at once assume command hold the troops at Jackson for further orders, and make requisitions for one days more rations from this place and get them out to Camp—

The regiment under Col C. C. Marsh 20th Regt Ills Vols is to accompany the Expediton when it moves. He will therfore be directed to send back all his ~~supplies~~ surpulus bagage to this place for shipment by river. Transportation being so limited nothing will be taken not strictly required.

U. S. Grant
Brigr Gen. Comdg

To Col Jno Cook
Comdg 7th Regt Ills Volls
Jackson Mo

Copies, DNA, RG 393, Western Dept., Letters Received (2); *ibid.*, USG Letters Sent; DLC-USG, V, 1, 2, 3. *O.R.*, I, iii, 146. Col. John Cook, 7th Ill., was appointed on April 25, 1861. Because Ill. sent six regts. of vols. to the Mexican War, the first Civil War regt. was numbered the 7th Ill. On Sept. 3, Col. Leonard F. Ross, 17th Ill., wrote to USG. "I came from Jackson late last night to confer with you in regard to the welfare & command of the troops now at that place. Genl Prentiss persists in refusing to take the command unless he is regarded as Senior General Col Cook who is rather young and inexperienced for so important a post has assumed command of the colum. I protest against marching under Col Cook. 1st On account of his inexperience in military affairs. 2d He permits a course to be pursued by his men on the march through the country that will ultimately make of them, but a band of freebooters and robbers. I further protest against marching under any man who will permit theivery and plundering on the march. In conclusion permit me to suggest, 'If it is impossible for you to take command in person, would it not be well to have such a man as Genl Curtis to lead us—I return to day to Camp." ALS, DNA, RG 393, Western Dept., Letters Received. Ross had served as 1st lt. in the Mexican War.

To Maj. Gen. John C. Frémont

Cairo Ills
Sept 2nd 1861

Sir

I left Cape Girardeau at 10 o.clock a.m. Genl Prentiss raised the question of rank and finally refused to obey my orders. Last night he tendered his resignation after being refused a leave of absence, but said he would command as directed untill your deciseon.

To day he positively refused and reported himself in arrest.

I have placed Col Cook in command with directions to remain at Jackson untill further orders.[1] I propose ordering Genl McClernand to that command if not prohibited.—

Thirty thousand Rations were sent to Jackson last night and this morning

I will forward by tomorrows mail[2] a copy of all orders issued to Genl Prentiss to gether with charges

Respectfully
Your obt Servt
U. S. Grant

To Maj Genl J. C. Fremont   Brig Genl Comdg
St Louis Mo

Telegram, copies, DLC-USG, V, 4, 5, 7, 8, 78; DNA, RG 393, USG Hd. Qrs. Correspondence. *O.R.*, I, iii, 145–46. On Sept. 2, 1861, Maj. Gen. John C. Frémont replied to USG's telegram twice by telegraph. "Following is copy of dispatch sent Gen'l Prentiss. 'To Brig. Gen. Prentiss: I would suggest for the interests of the public service that you withdraw your resignation until you can communicate with the War Department for your own satisfaction. General Orders No. 62, and Special Orders No. 141, War Department, both place General Grant above you in the order of precedence, and I had no resource but to restore him to a command from which he had been erroneously removed.' " "General Prentiss is ordered to report to me in person. Forward by Express all telegraphic communications to him" Copies, DLC-USG, V, 4, 5, 7, 8; DNA, RG 393, USG Hd. Qrs. Correspondence; *ibid.*, Western Dept., Telegrams.

1. See letter to Col. John Cook, Sept. 2, 1861.
2. See following letter.

To Maj. Gen. John C. Frémont

Cairo Ill.
September 2d 1861

SIR:

I am under the painful necessity of reporting that Gen. Prentiss positively refused to obey orders from me and has therefore defeated the prompt execution of your instructions. ~~to me.~~

I would have taken command myself and marched upon Sikeston, or Charleston, but before risking the command of Gen. Prentiss in an unknown country it was necessary that an understanding should be had with those who were to coöperate from this end and, if possible, learn the position of the enemy.—Gen. Prentiss did not inform Col. Wallace of his arrival at Jackson as directed but marched on immediately to Cape Girardeau.

I send you herewith a copy of my instructions to Col. Marsh, and also to Gen. Prentiss.[1] It was my intention to meet Gen. Prentiss at Jackson in person, and I had instructions prepared to carry out to him.

Col. Marsh failed to report the approach of Gen. Prentiss to me but I heard of it through another source and had started for Jackson when Gen. Prentiss arrived in Cape Girardeau with an escort of about one hundred & seventy Cavalry, leaving his command to arrive, and go into camp, at Jackson.

I send you herewith a copy of all orders and instructions sent to Col. Marsh and also those given to Gen. Prentiss. I have also enclosed charges against Gen. Prentiss.[2] A copy will ~~also~~ be furnished Gen. Prentiss with instructions ~~for him~~ to ~~place~~ report himself in arrest to you in St. Louis. I telegraphed very fully immediately upon my arrival but have not yet received a reply. This embarasses me very much. I proposed assigning Gen. McClernand to the command from Jackson and commanding the forces from Birds Point and Belmont myself. No answer has yet been received.

The command at Jackson was placed in command of Col.

Cook, 7th Ill. Vols. supposing him to be senior Colonel, with directions to remain at Jackson until otherwise ordered. Rations were forwarded to them for five days and directions for wagons enough to return to Cape Girardeau to take out more for one day.

I have no information here that has not been forwarded by the respective post commanders.

Respectfully
Your Obt. Svt.
U. S. GRANT
Brig. Gen. U. S. A.

To Maj. Gen. J. C. Frémont
Comd.g Dept. of the West
St. Louis Mo.

ALS, DNA, RG 393, Western Dept., Letters Received.

1. These enclosures are printed elsewhere.
2. See following letter.

To Capt. John C. Kelton

Cairo Ill.
September 2d 1861

SIR:

Enclosed herewith please find co charges and specifications prefered against Gen. Prentiss.

In justice to myself I must state that under existing sircumstances I submitted to much more humiliation in trying to concilliate Gen. Prentiss and to induce him to await a time when his services could be better dispensed with before testing the question of rank.

I shall send a copy of the enclosed charges to Gen. Prentiss

and order him to St. Louis in arrest to report to Maj. Gen.
Frémont.

U. S. GRANT
Brig. Gen. U. S. A.

To Capt. J. C. Kelton
Adj. Gen. U. S. A.
St. Louis Mo.

ALS, PHi. The enclosure has not been found.

To Maj. Gen. John C. Frémont

———

Cairo Illinois
September 3d 1861

SIR:

Enclosed I send you a copy of a letter sent to Gen. Prentiss on
receipt of your telegraphic despatch[1] notifying me that he was
ordered to St. Louis.

Respectfully
Your Obt. Svt.
U. S. GRANT
Brig. Gen. U. S. A.

To Maj. Gen. J. C. Frémont
Comd.g Dept. of the West
St. Louis Mo.

ALS, DNA, RG 393, Western Dept., Letters Received. Enclosed is a copy of the
following letter.

1. See letter to Maj. Gen. John C. Frémont, Sept. 2, 1861.

To Brig. Gen. Benjamin M. Prentiss

Cairo Ill.
September 3d 1861

Sir;

Having received from Gen. Frémont orders[1] for you to proceed to St. Louis I of course decline placing you in arrest. Having sent charges to Head Quarters, Department of the West, against you,[2] as in duty bound I send you a copy of them.

In justice to myself I must say that in this matter I have no personal feeling but have acted strictly from a sense of duty and should it be Gen. Frémont's wish am perfectly willing to see the charges quashed and the whole matter buried in oblivion.

A sacrifise of my own feelings is no sacrifise when the good of the service Calls for it.

Some of the despatches sent here for telegraphing, by one of the Newspaper correspondents accompanying were of such a character, and so detrimental to the good of the service that I felt it my duty to suppress them.

Yours &c.
U. S. Grant
Brig. Gen. U. S. A.

To Brig. Gen. B. M. Prentiss
Cape Girardeau Mo.

ALS, PHi. *O.R.*, I, iii, 147. On Sept. 24, 1861, Capt. Chauncey McKeever sent USG a copy of a letter of Sept. 19 from Secretary of War Simon Cameron to Maj. Gen. John C. Frémont. "Your letter in reference to the question of seniority of rank between Generals Grant & Prentiss has been received by this Department. The following is the report of Adjutant General Thomas thereon: 'A. G. O. Sept 10, 1861. Respectfully submitted to the Secretary of War: According to paragraph 5 of the regulations, when two commissions, as in this instance, have the same date, reference must be had to former commissions, and by that rule Genl. Grant should rank. L. Thomas, Adjt. Genl.' The decision of the Adjutant General that Genl. Grant should rank is approved by the Department. You will please communicate this decision to Brigadier General Grant and Brigadier General Prentiss" LS, DNA, RG 393, District of Southeast Mo., Letters Received. Cameron's LS to Frémont is in RG 94, Generals' Papers and Books, Ulysses S. Grant.

1. See letter to Maj. Gen. John C. Frémont, Sept. 2, 1861.
2. See letter to Capt. John C. Kelton, Sept. 2, 1861.

To Col. Gustav Waagner

Cairo Ill
September 3d 1861

Sir

The movements from Jackson having been detained you will retain possession of Belmont until otherwise directed.—The movement upon Charleston being deferred you may make such reconnoisance as is safe and report to me at this place

U. S. Grant
Brig Genl Comdg

To Col Waagner
Chief of Artillery
Belmont Mo

Copies, DLC-USG, V, 1, 2, 3, 77; DNA, RG 393, USG Letters Sent. *O.R.*, I, iii, 147. USG special orders for Col. Gustav Waagner, chief of art. for the District of Southeast Mo., dated earlier on Sept. 3, 1861, have not been found, but after their receipt Waagner wrote to USG. "Your Genl order No 2 dated Cape Girardeau Mo Sept 1st and your special order dated Cairo Ills Sept 3d 1861 I received at 4. o'clock this evening. I shall leave at 3. o'clock tomorrow morning with my command for Charleston leaving the two Gun Boats to watch Columbus and Belmont in fulfillment of my order from the Commander in Chief dated St Louis August 25th 1861 I wish you would be kind enough to inform Col Wallace of this my movement and request him to send an escort of one Company of Cavelry from Charleston to meet me on the half way as I am without Cavelry. I have received no information of any strong force of the enemy in this neighborhood nearer than Benton. W[e] arrested several men but without finding any important information—On the night of Sept 2d and during this day the 3d there was an important movement of cavelry and infantry on the Heights in and near Columbus opposite this point but without any hostile demonstration. A Great many families are moving out from Columbus and the farms in the neighborhood. I have no further news of importance to communcate except to enclose the report of Col McArthur. I hope Col Oglesby, has informed you of the telegraphic dispatch in the Hungarian language received from Brigd Genl Asboth, Head Quarters department of the West. If not I send a translation. I have the honour to enclose a copy of my order from Maj Genl Fremont dated Augst 25th 1861. I send tomorrow

the Gun Smiths boat mentioned in my dispatch of last evening which was attached to the Ferry Boat when she sank this morning. The armorer will take an inventory of the tools found on board.
P. S. ½ past 10. o'clock P. M. The steamer Brown has arrived bringing your order dated Cairo Ills September 3d 1861 which will be carried out. I will make a carefull reconoissance to-morrow morning returned about noon to await your further orders. What shall I do with Kentucky? A new secession flag was hoisted at Columbus this evening and the people about here are very suspicious. I wish you to order the Steamer Brown, down to-morrow to meet the steamer Graham at 12. o'clock half way on the Missuri shore to exchange orders coal & provissions, as I have important reasons for this change in our mode of Communication. I beg you also send the new men of Col McArthurs Regiment in the same way. Col McArthur sends his Quarter Master who will report himself to you to make the neccissary arrangments." ALS, DNA, RG 393, District of Southeast Mo., Letters Received. The report of Col. John McArthur, Sept. 2, to which Waagner referred, was misdated Sept. 25 in docketing, thus erroneously entered *ibid.*, USG Register of Letters Received; DLC-USG, V, 10. The report is in DNA, RG 393, District of Southeast Mo., Letters Received. See also *O.R.*, I, iii, 151–52; *O.R.* (Navy), I, xxii, 310–11.

To Col. William H. L. Wallace

Cairo Ills
September 3d, 1861

SIR

A. Junction being formed between Genl Prentiss and troops from Cape Girardeau Mo. at Jackson you will proceed to carry out the instuctions you received from Head Quarters of the department of the West—

The disposeable force at your command being much smaller than was contemplated by the Genl Commanding department you will proceed with great Caution and avoid if possible rebel forces, getting in between your main column and advance—

Col McArthur[1] moves at 3. o'clock to-day from Belmont upon Charleston—

U. S. GRANT
Brigd Genl Comdg

To Col Wallace
Comdg Birds Point Mo

Copies, DNA, RG 94, War Records Office, Dept. of the Mo.; DLC-USG, VIA, 1.

1. Col. John McArthur, 12th Ill.

To Col. William H. L. Wallace

———

Cairo Ill.
September 3d 1861

Sir:

The column at Jackson being unavoidably detained there the movement of troops from Birds Point and Belmont will be defered until further orders.

They will hold themselvs in readiness for a prompt movement when orders are received.

U. S. Grant
Brig. Gen. Com.

To Col. W. H. L. Wallace
Comd.g Birds Point Mo.

ALS, DNA, RG 393, District of Southeast Mo., Letters Received.

To Julia Dent Grant

———

Cairo Ill.
September 3d 1861

Dear Julia;

Evry time I write it is from a new place. How long I may stay here is impossible to tell but if I am to remain any length of time I want you to come here. Get the children clothed so as to be in readiness to start when I write to you. If you have not got money yet it make no matter for you will have it in a few days. As I told you[1] I left $240 with Mr. Ford to pay express charges on some clothing with directions to send you the balance.

I am now in command of all the troops from Ironton to this

place. For a few days I will be away from here most of the time. I cannot give you the programme of movements but time will tell.

Has Mr. Rawlins got back to Galena?[2] I hear nothing of him.

You and the children can enjoy a few weeks here very well if it should be that I am so fortunate as to remain for that time. I am now stoping at the St. Charles Hotel but shall leave to-morrow, and keep house with my staff.[3] You will not bring Fred I suppose he having been with me before but the balance of the children I want you to bring, Miss[4] & Jess, particularly. Bless their little hearts I want to see them very much. Buck will enjoy a trip down here very much. Fred. can stay at Orvils. I should like to have all of them here but for the expense of the trip. To-day I have had less to do than any time for the last four weeks and feel less like writing. I have so much of it to do, in an official way, that by bed time my hand becomes perfectly cramped. Usually I write to you, and any other private letters I have, after midnight; some official ones too.

All my letters from you come together. I believe it was five I got at once ~~from~~ at Jefferson City and not one since. I know you write somewhat regularly though. As I have told you before I never suffer a week to pass without writing and generally write twice. I want to write to Lank some time but some how I never get time.

Cairo does not appear to be particularly sickly at this time. It is usually considered to be an unhealthy place and looks as if it must be so. The ground is on a level with the river at ordinary stage and much below it at high water.

Remember me to the people of Galena. Kiss the children for me. Write to me at once. Kisses for yourself.

Ulys.

ALS, DLC-USG.

1. See letter of Aug. 31, 1861.
2. Mrs. John A. Rawlins died Aug. 30, 1861, at Goshen, N.Y. James Harrison Wilson, *The Life of John A. Rawlins* (New York, 1916), pp. 53–54.

3. On Sept. 3, Capt. William S. Hillyer wrote to Capt. Reuben B. Hatch, asst. q. m. at Cairo. "I am directed by Genl Grant to request you to provide an office and quarters for the use of the General and his Staff from this date" Copies, DLC-USG, V, 1, 2, 3, 77; DNA, RG 393, USG Letters Sent.

4. Ellen Grant.

To Elihu B. Washburne

Cairo Illinois
September 3d 1861

Hon. E. B. Washburn
Galena Ill.
Dear Sir:

Your very kind letter[1] was received at Jefferson City and would have been answered at once but for the remark that you were about to start for New York City[2] and would not receive it for some days. I should be most pleased to have you pay me the visit here, or where ever els I may be, that you spoke of paying me there.

In regard to the appointment of Mr. Rawlins I never had an idea of withdrawing it so long as he felt disposed to accept no matter how long his absence. Mr. Rawlins was the first one I decided upon for a place with me and I very much regret that family affliction has kept him away so long.[3] The past would have been a good shool of instruction for him in his new duties; the future bids fair to try the back bone of our volunteers. I have been kept actively moving from one command to another, more so perhaps than any other officer. So long as I am of service to the cause of our country I do not object however.

Gen. Frémont has seen fit to entrust me with an important command here, my command embracing all the troops in South East Missouri and at this place.—A little difficulty of an unpleasant nature has occured between Gen. Prentiss and myself relative to rank, he refusing to obey my orders, but it is to be hoped that he will [see] his error and not sacrifice the interest of the cause to his ambition to be Senior Brigadier General of Illinois as he contends he is.

In conclusion Mr. Washburn allow me to thank you for the part you have taken in giving me my present position.[4] I think I see your hand in it and admit that I had no personal claims for your kind office in the matter. I can assure you however my whole heart is in the cause which we are fighting for and I pledge myself that if equal to the task before me you shall never have cause to regret the part you have taken.

Respectfully
Your Obt. Svt.
U. S. GRANT

ALS, IHi. See letter of April 27, 1861, note 2.

1. Not found.
2. Congressman Elihu B. Washburne traveled to New York City to investigate contract irregularities for the Select Committee on Government Contracts.
3. See letter to Julia Dent Grant, Sept. 3, 1861, note 2.
4. See letter to Jesse Root Grant, Aug. 3, 1861, note 3.

General Orders No. 3

Cairo Ills
Sept 4th 1861

GENL ORDER NO 3

By virtue of directions from Head Quarters dept of the west, Cairo will be included in the District of South East Mo. and the undersigned therfore assumes command.

Brigd Genl J. A. McClernand U. S. A being senior officer of this Post will assume command as soon as practicable.

Birds Point and Mound City[1] will be considered as parts of the command at Cairo.

Head Quarters of the Military District of South East Mo.
will be at this place untill otherwise directed.

U. S. GRANT
Brigd Genl U. S. A

To Brigd Genl J. A. McClernand
Cairo Ills

Copies, DLC-USG, V, 12, 13, 14, 80; DNA, RG 393, USG General Orders;
McClernand Papers, IHi. *O.R.*, I, iii, 470. In response to a letter of USG which
has not been found, Brig. Gen. John A. McClernand wrote to USG on Sept. 4,
1861. "Your note of inquiry of this date is received. The communication from
Maj Genl Fremont to which your inquiry related, was an order to assume command of the Post at Cairo &c now in command of Col R J Oglesby. In compliance
with that order, and of your suggestion—I will (consulting Col Oglesby's
Convenience) assume the duties of Post commander, and be happy to co-operate
with you in all things for the good of the service." LS, DNA, RG 94, Generals'
Papers and Books, John A. McClernand; copy, McClernand Papers, IHi. On the
same day, Maj. Gen. John C. Frémont wrote to USG. "General McClernand is
not to be detailed from Cairo on any distant service, but is to remain there or
vicinity, and attend to the rendezvousing of his brigade." Copies, DLC-USG, V,
4, 5, 7, 8; DNA, RG 393, USG Hd. Qrs. Correspondence.

USG stated that his uniform had not yet arrived when he established hd.
qrs. at Cairo on Sept. 4, and Col. Richard J. Oglesby seemed somewhat hesitant
about surrendering his office. *Memoirs*, I, 264. Oglesby confirmed USG's account
in a letter of Sept. 28, 1886, to Thomas Donaldson. *Journal of the Illinois State
Historical Society*, XXXVIII, 2 (June, 1945), 242–44. It seems possible, however, that, since USG had been in Cairo since Sept. 2, the incident remembered by
both had occurred earlier.

1. Mound City, Ill., about six miles north of Cairo on the Ohio River.

To Maj. Gen. John C. Frémont

———

Cairo Ills
September 4th 1861

SIR

The prompt execution of your plan by the troops under my
command having been defeated by Genl Prentiss' withdrawel
from the command at Jackson ~~and~~ delaying the movement of that

colum, and the representations of Commodore Rodgers[1] as to the efficiency of the rebel inland navy, coupled with the impossibility of making a retreat from Belmont except by falling back into the country as far as Charleston and the weakness of the force at Belmont, makes me deem it advisable to withdraw the troops from that point, untill the command assumes shape for concert of action.

From information gathered from the Rebel District I enclose you Reports of Col McArthur and Col Waagner[2] reserving copies

As fast as information is received I will keep you informed by telegraph

Very Respectfully
Your Obt Sevt
U. S. GRANT
Brigd Genl Comdg

To Maj Gen J. C. Fremont
Comdg Dept. of the West
St Louis Mo

Copies, DLC-USG, V, 4, 5, 7, 8, 78, VIA, 1; DNA, RG 393, USG Letters Sent. *O.R.*, I, iii, 148; *O.R.* (Navy), I, xxii, 312. At the same time USG wrote this letter, he telegraphed its substance to Maj. Gen. John C. Frémont. "On advice from Comdr Rodgers I have ordered the withdrawal of troops from Belmont untill such time as the column from Jackson may move. I have no acurate information of the strength of the Rebels at Sikeston but hope to have to day." Copies, DLC-USG, V, 4, 5, 7, 8, 78; DNA, RG 393, USG Hd. Qrs. Correspondence. *O.R.*, I, iii, 148; *O.R.* (Navy), I, xxii, 310.

On the preceding day, Frémont had written to USG. "According to intelligence received by me the enemy has left Benton, but if your own means of information are not more reliable than mine you will still direct the forces at Jackson to move with all ~~possible~~ precaution sending scouts along the road as they advance. Should Benton be still occupied by the enemy, they are to make an attack annihilate him and take possession of the place. With the same precaution you will proceed from Birds Point and cause Col Waagner to advance with his force from Belmont towards Charleston and occupy that place. From Charleston you are ~~strictly~~ immediately to open a direct communication with Benton, and from the information you obtain at both of those places you will determine whether a united attack would prove advantageous to our forces. Should you regard an attack advisable you will leave an adequate reserve on both lines. The united force of the enemy at Sikeston is estimated at sixteen thousand, strongly supported by artillery as well as cavalry the latter being thouroughly experienced in scouting

and having full control over the swampy country around sikeston Before leaving
Birds Point you will see that all the important points on the Illinois Central Rail
Road are guarded by small squads and that the Gun Boats watch all the crossings
on the River between Commerce & Hickman. Should you instead of moving forward make a stand at Benton as well as at Charleston you will throw up without
delay earthworks to strengthen your position and report immediately the disposition of our own forces; and also as far as possible from your Reconnoisances and
the intelligence brought by your scouts the numbers and position of the enemy."
Copies, DLC-USG, V, 7, 8, 81; DNA, RG 393, USG Hd. Qrs. Correspondence.
O.R., I, iii, 146–47.

1. On May 16, Commander John Rodgers was ordered to report to Maj.
Gen. George B. McClellan to organize a naval force for the Ohio and Mississippi
rivers. *O.R.* (Navy), I, xxii, 280. On June 8, he reported the purchase of three
gunboats. *Ibid.*, p. 283. On Sept. 7, he was replaced in command by Capt. Andrew
H. Foote. *Ibid.*, p. 318.
2. See letter to Col. Gustav Waagner, Sept. 3, 1861.

To Maj. Gen. John C. Frémont

————

Cairo Ill.
September 4th 1861

GENERAL;

Information is just in from Sikeston which I am disposed to
credit although the authority is a negro man. He tells a very
strait story. Says that the Rebels left Sikeston last Monday. Had
there four regiments of Tennessee and Mississippi troops, ten
or twelve pieces of Artillery drawn by horses, one large piece
drawn by five yoke of oxen and one mortar drawn by three yoke.
In addition to this Jeff. Thompson[1] had 1500 men. They said
they were going to New Madrid and then to Memphis.

On the strength of reconnoisances made by Col. Waagner I
telegraphed this evening[2] that troops, Artillery Cavalry &
Infantry, can be spared from here, by sending those from
Jackson promptly, to take possession of Columbus heights[3] &
New Madrid will fall within five days after. This should be done
to-morrow night.

Enclosed I send you the report of Commander Rodgers,[4] retaining copy.

> Respectfully
> Your Obt. Svt.
> U. S. GRANT
> Brig. Gen. Com.

To Maj. Gen. J. C. Frémont
Comdg Dept. of the West
St. Louis Mo.

ALS, DNA, RG 393, Western Dept., Letters Received. *O.R.*, I, iii, 149; *O.R.* (Navy), I, xxii, 311–12.

1. Brig. Gen. M. Jeff Thompson, 1st Military District, Mo. State Guard. See letter to Julia Dent Grant, Aug. 29, 1861, note 1.
2. This telegram has not been found. On Sept. 4, 1861, Maj. Gen. John C. Frémont telegraphed to USG. "Your dispatches of today received. Boat leaves tonight with wagons and three thousand guns asked by Col. Oglesby for 8th 9th and 10th Illinois Regiments, five hundred for Gen. McClernand. The guns mentioned by Col. Oglesby to go for the present to General McClernand. Other things will be sent tomorrow. Keep me well advised of your wants." Copies, DLC-USG, V, 4, 5, 7, 8, VIA, 1; DNA, RG 393, USG Hd. Qrs. Correspondence; *ibid.*, Western Dept., Telegrams.
3. Columbus, Ky., on the Mississippi River about eighteen miles south of Cairo.
4. On Sept. 4, Commander John Rodgers wrote to USG. "It was agreed upon this morning upon parting with Col Waagner at Belmont, that the Gun Boats Taylor and Lexington should make a reconnoisance down the river as far as Hickman When we arrived in sight of Hickman we discovered a rebel gun boat with the Confederate flag flying, off that town. The boat fired a shot at us to which we replied. A number of tents extending for a half a mile were upon the shore fronting the river. When three or four shots had been exchanged, a battery on shore fired several guns—then another battery opened upon us. The Lexington and this vessel fired some twenty shots when finding the current fast setting us down upon their batteries, with which we were in no condition to cope, having very little powder on board and only half enough gun tackles for working the battery, we returned I think both Officers and Crew remarkably cool under the fire, it was not indeed so close as to be very dangerous. I intended to wait for this gun boat when away from her batteries—but she ran along side the river bank and made fast Upon passing Columbus and the Chalk Banks, we were fired upon by rebels with muskets. This was returned with muskets principally—but also by two great guns The army at Hickman is considerable." ALS, *ibid.*, RG 94, War Records Office, Union Battle Reports. *O.R.* (Navy), I, xxii, 309. On Sept. 3, Rodgers wrote USG about the "superiority of rebel gunboats over his." DLC-USG, V, 10; DNA, RG 393, USG Register of Letters Received.

To Col. John Cook

―――――

Head Quarters, Dist S. E. Mo
Cairo, Ill. Sept. 4th / 61

SIR;

Yours just received. I have no special instructions for your command only to keep them under restraint. Allow no marauding, insulting of citizens, searching of houses except you may find it necessary, and then let it be done by persons specially detailed for the purpose. Keep four days provisions, at least, on hand and be ready to move the column at any time it may be ordered.

You will not probably leave where you are until Gen. Prentiss has gone to St. Louis, and may be until his return.

Should the Cavalry horses, or mules, require shoeing have it done whilst you are laying still.

Yours &c.
U. S. GRANT
Brig. Gen. Com

To Col. J. Cook
Comd.g Jackson Mo.

ALS, Henry Dwight Scrapbook, OHi. *O.R.*, I, iii, 147–48.

To Lt. S. Ledyard Phelps

―――――

Head Quarters
Cairo Ills Sept 4 / 61

SIR

Heavy cannonading being reported south of here you will proceed with all dispatch and render such assistance as your dispossable means can afford. Should the alarm prove false you will return imediately and report.

U. S. Grant
Brigd Genl Comdg

To Lieut Phelps
Comdg Gun Boat Constago

Copies, DLC-USG, V, 1, 2, 3, 78; DNA, RG 393, USG Letters Sent. *O.R.*, I, iii, 148; *O.R.* (Navy), I, xxii, 310. Lt. S. Ledyard Phelps, in command of the gunboats *Tyler*, *Lexington*, and *Conestoga*, arrived at Cairo on Aug. 12, 1861. *Ibid.*, p. 299. Later he commanded the *Conestoga*.

To *Speaker of the Kentucky House of Representatives*

Cairo Sept 5, 1861

Sir

I regret to inform you that Confederate forces in Considerable numbers have invaded the teritory of Kentucky, and are occupying & fortifying strong positions at Hickman & Chalk Bluffs.[1]

Yours &c
U. S. Grant
Brigd Genl U. S. A

To Speaker House of Representatives[2]
Frankfort Ky

Telegram, copies, DLC-USG, V, 1, 2, 3, 78; DNA, RG 393, USG Letters Sent. *O.R.*, I, iii, 166; *ibid.*, I, lii, part 1, 188. Printed in the *Journal of the House of Representatives of the Commonwealth of Kentucky* (Frankfort, 1861), I, 49, for Sept. 5, 1861, as addressed "To Speaker of House and President of Senate." On Sept. 6, 1861, Maj. Joseph H. Eaton wrote to USG. "I am directed by Major General Fremont to inform you that Brigade and other Commanders are not to correspond with State or other high authorities, in matters pertaining to any branch of the public service, either in initiating such correspondence or in replying thereto. All such subjects are to be submitted to the Major General Commanding the Department for his information and action, by telegraph if of immediate importance, otherwise by regular course of mail." Copies, DLC-USG, V, 4, 5, 7, 8, 81; DNA, RG 393, Western Dept., Letters Sent (Press); *ibid.*, Letters Sent by Gen. Frémont; *ibid.*, USG Hd. Qrs. Correspondence. *O.R.*, I, lii, part 1, 189.

Also on Sept. 5, USG issued special orders to all post commanders through Capt. William S. Hillyer. "The people of South-West Kentucky, having permitted large bodies of armed men in rebellion to the government, to assemble upon her soil, to erect Batteries and fire upon the Federal Flag, are guilty of an offence which must be resisted and punished. All commanders therefore, on the Kentucky borders, within this military District, are directed to embarass their communications with Rebels in every way possible. To this end all ferry's, yawls, flats and other boats within the reach of these troops, will be seized and taken in charge. Such orders as may be necessary for carrying into execution this order, will be promulgated at once by Post Commanders" Copies, DNA, RG 393, USG Special Orders; DLC-USG, V, 15, 16, 82. *O.R.*, I, iii, 150.

1. Hickman, Ky., on the Mississippi River about twenty-eight miles south of Cairo. C.S.A. Maj. Gen. Leonidas Polk explained that his forces landed at Hickman to avoid U.S. art. placed at Belmont, Mo., opposite Columbus, Ky. *Ibid.*, I, iv, 180. Chalk Bluffs refers to the area of Columbus.
2. Richard A. Buckner.

To Maj. Gen. John C. Frémont

Head Quarters
Cairo, Ills, Sept 5, 1861

GENERAL,

Enclosed I send you plans and estimates of the works proposed opposite this place and Birds Point. A party have been on the Kentucky shore most of the day making the preliminary arrangements for prosecuting the work with larger details hereafter. The labor of clearing will have to be done by the troops exclusively and probably a great portion of the digging.

All information to day has been telegraphed fully.[1] I am now nearly ready for Paducah (should not a telegraph arrive preventing the movement) on the strength of the information telegraphed.

On the subject of fortifications I scarcely feel myself sufficiently conversant to make recommendation but it appears to me that the fortifications here needs much more labor expended in that way and heavier armament before labor is expended on the opposite shore

The works ordered by you will be prosecuted however with
all the force available for that service

Very Respectfully

U. S. GRANT

Brig Gen Com'g

To Gen John C. Fremont
Comg Dept of West
St Louis Mo.

Copies, DLC-USG, V, 4, 5, 7, 8, 78; DNA, RG 393, USG Hd. Qrs. Correspondence. *O.R.*, I, iii, 150. On Sept. 5, 1861, Maj. Gen. John C. Frémont wrote to
USG. "You will commence and prosecute with the utmost speed all the preperation of the place selected for the Fort and Entrenched Camp on the Kentucky
Shore forming a triangle with Cairo & Birds Point. Which fortifications we will
call Fort Holt. The Point if not determined now should be defined by Colonels
Waagner and Webster and Lieutenant Freeman who was specially intrusted with
the selection of the spot. To protect the place and the work to be done there you
will order a sufficient force of Infantry Cavalry and Artillery selecting the troops
according to your own judgment from Cape Girardeau, Cairo & Birds Point and
replacing them from our forces concentrated at Jackson. The Force employed
on the Kentucky Shore should number at least six Regiments of Infantry two
squadrons of Cavalry and a Battery of Artillery and only after the force is there
and the place secured against attack will you plant the four heavy Guns to be
brought by Captain Schwartz. Beside one of the two Artillery Companies
organized by Colonel Waagner you will detach all the Artillerists of Col Smiths
Regiment of Zouaves to Fort Holt and using the Sand Bags at Cairo and the
gabions going with the Guns, and employing day and night the largest force of
workmen obtainable you will put the place in a state of Defense in the shortest
possible time. The Ammunition called for by Requisition of Captain Brinck acting
ordnance officer at Cairo will be sent tomorrow. If you feel strong enough you
will take possession of Paducah but if not then opposite that place on the Illinois
side of the River, which you will do without delay with the view of planting a
Battery which shall command the Ohio and the mouth of the Tennessee River.
In a few days I will send an adequate force with sufficient artillery to hold that
position. If in your power it would be well to make preperations for building a
Bridge to connect the Illinois shore with Paducah. While conducting these operations on the Kentucky and Illinois shore you will not abandon your operations in
Missouri and taking Charlestown and Sikeston as well as holding Belmont you
will follow the retreating Rebels to New Madrid; this however must depend
upon your disposable force and the truth of the report that the enemys troops from
Greenville have retreaded to Arkansas" Copies, DLC-USG, V, 4, 5, 7, 8, 81;
DNA, RG 393, USG Hd. Qrs. Correspondence. *O.R.*, I, iii, 149–50.

The substance of Frémont's letter was telegraphed in Hungarian to USG on
the same day. "The Kentucky shore opposite Cairo should be fortified and the
necessary preparations should be taken immediately. The Cape Girardeau
regiment of infantry supported properly by artillery and cavalry should be sent

there from Cairo and Birds Point. Ammunition urgently requested by Captain Brink will be sent tomorrow. Paducah should be occupied if it is possible; if not, the mouth of the Tennessee River should be guarded safely from the opposite side. I will send four regiments to assist within a few days. In addition be careful about the towns of Belmont, Charleston, Sickestown, and New Madrid." Copy (Hungarian), DNA, RG 393, Western Dept., Telegrams. USG later recalled that he had received no answer to his telegram on Sept. 5, and had not received Frémont's letter authorizing the seizure of Paducah until after he had seized it. *Memoirs*, I, 265, 267. Frémont clearly had replied by telegraph to USG's telegram of Sept. 5; it is not clear, however, that the telegram had been sent to Cairo, received in intelligible form, and translated into English before USG left for Paducah, and USG's statement indicates that it probably was not available. Further, since this was the first telegram sent to USG in Hungarian, he may not have known what to do with it.

On Sept. 4, Alexander Asboth at Frémont's hd. qrs. telegraphed in Hungarian to Lt. Raphael Guido Rombauer, adjt. for Col. Gustav Waagner. "Two thirty-two and two twenty-two pounders are ready to depart immediately under the command of Capt. Schwarz to be positioned on the Kentucky shore opposite Cairo and Birds Point. Lieutenant Freeman was put in charge of staking out the place on the twenty-ninth. The sandbags will be kept in readiness. 200 gabions will go with the guns. If the number and the power of the ironclads is overwhelming, Waagner should not enter in battle but should withdraw to Cairo to cooperate with the forts. Inform Gen. Grant about this immediately." Copy (Hungarian), DNA, RG 393, Western Dept., Telegrams.

On Sept. 9, Frémont wrote to USG. "Your report dated September 5th 1861, together with that of Major Webster has been forwarded and the suggestions therein contained have received consideration. In my order of the 5th of September directions are given for detaching a sufficient force of Infantry, Cavalry and Artillery for the protection of the place about Fort Holt. That the work should be ready for immediate use is of far greater importance than that it should be permanent. Both the telegrams to which Major Webster alludes & the order to you of the 4th day of September, directed the use of sand bags & gabions, as the time at present at our command, does not permit the erection of a work capable of resisting an overflow of the river. Too much stress cannot be laid on the importance of the utmost dispatch. You will therefore prosecute the work day and night with a large force of workmen and as many sand bags & gabions as can be procured. After the guns are mounted, the camp around it can be entrenched and if necessary measures can be taken for the erection of such a work as is suggested in your report." Copies, *ibid.*, Letters Sent (Press); *ibid.*, USG Hd. Qrs. Correspondence; DLC-USG, V, 7, 8.

1. Telegrams from USG to Frémont of this date have not been found, with the exception of the telegram concerning Paducah which obviously was sent later than the letter. On Sept. 5, Frémont telegraphed to USG. "How are the different forces under your command disposed at the present moment. Answer in Hungarian" Copies, DNA, RG 393, Western Dept., Telegrams; DLC-USG, VIA, 1.

To Maj. Gen. John C. Frémont

Cairo, Sept. 5, 1861

MAJ. GEN. JNO. C. FREMONT
ST LOUIS, MO.

On information telegraphed you, brought by Charles de Arnaud I am getting ready to go to Paducah. Will start at 6½ o'clock

U. S. GRANT
Brig. General

Telegram, copies, DLC-USG, V, 4, 5, 7, 8; DNA, RG 393, USG Hd. Qrs. Correspondence. Charles de Arnaud, a former officer of the Russian army, was employed as a spy by Maj. Gen. John C. Frémont. Bruce Catton, *Grant Moves South* (Boston and Toronto, 1960), p. 494; John C. Frémont, "In Command in Missouri," *Battles and Leaders of the Civil War*, eds., Robert Underwood Johnson and Clarence Clough Buel (New York, 1887), I, 285; Charles A. de Arnaud, *The Union, and its Ally, Russia* (Washington, 1890), pp. 9–11, 30–31; *HRC*, 49–2–4171. On Sept. 5, 1861, de Arnaud telegraphed to Frémont. "Just arrived from Memphis and Union City, Tenn. The enemy is marching in large force to take Paducah, on the Ohio River, to invade Southern Illinois. Our occupation of Paducah will frustrate the enemy's plans and secure for us the Tennessee River. Have communicated this to General Grant. He will move at once. No time to lose." *Ibid.*, Part 1, p. 3. See letter to Charles de Arnaud, Nov. 30, 1861.

To Brig. Gen. John A. McClernand

Brigade Head Quarters
Cairo Ills Sept 5 1861

GEN.

Please order, by my direction, Smiths Regt. to come to Cairo by first Boat. Send order by Land tomorrow morning.

U. S. GRANT
Brig Comg.

To Gen. McClernand

Copy, McClernand Papers, IHi. On the same sheet, Brig. Gen. John A. McClernand copied his letter to Col. Morgan L. Smith, 8th Mo. Vols., at Cape Girardeau. "Please comply with the above order at the earliest minuit."

When USG left Cairo for Paducah, he placed McClernand in command at Cairo and McClernand issued General Orders No. 1. "By order of Major General John C. Fremont, Commanding the Western Military Department, and a supplemental order of Brigadier General U. S. Grant, Commanding the District of Southeast Missouri, this Military Post, with its dependencies, including the floating defenses, has been placed under my command." Printed copy, *ibid.* Later the same day, Capt. William S. Hillyer wrote to McClernand for USG. "You will please detail two Regts of Infantry a Battery of Light artillery and two Gun boats to proceed without delay to Paducah Ky They will be instructed in the object of the expedition after leaving Cairo by the Com'r of the District who will accompany them" Copies, DLC-USG, V, 1, 2, 3, 77; DNA, RG 393, USG Letters Sent. At midnight, McClernand reported to Maj. Gen. John C. Frémont. LS, *ibid.*, Western Dept., Letters Received. *O.R.*, I, iv, 196.

Proclamation

———

PROCLAMATION,
TO THE CITIZENS OF
PADUCAH!

I have come among you, not as an enemy, but as your friend and fellow-citizen, not to injure or annoy you, but to respect the rights, and to defend and enforce the rights of all loyal citizens. An enemy, in rebellion against our common Government, has taken possession of, and planted its guns upon the soil of Kentucky and fired upon our flag. Hickman and Columbus are in his hands. He is moving upon your city. I am here to defend you against this enemy and to assert and maintain the authority and sovereignty of your Government and mine. I have nothing to do with opinions. I shall deal only with armed rebellion and its aiders and abetors. You can pursue your usual avocations without fear or hindrance. The strong arm of the Government is here to protect its friends, and to punish only its enemies. Whenever it is manifest that you are able to defend yourselves, to maintain the authority of your Government and protect the rights of all its

loyal citizens, I shall withdraw the forces under my command
from your city.

U. S. GRANT,
Brig. Gen. U. S. A., Commanding.

Paducah, Sept 6th. 1861.

Printed document, Morristown National Military Park, Morristown, N.J. *O.R.*,
I, lii, Part 1, 189; *ibid.*, II, ii, 55.

To Brig. Gen. Eleazer A. Paine

Headquarters Dist. S. E. Mo.
Paducah, Sept. 6, 1861

BRIG. GEN. E. A. PAINE COMDG.
9TH ILLS. VOLS.

Upon my departure you will assume command of the troops
at this post and make such disposal of the forces as will best
enable you to retain possession and control of the city. A portion
of the troops can be quartered at the Marine Hospital

You are charged to take special care and precaution that no
harm is done to inoffensive citizens. That the soldiers shall not
enter any private dwelling nor make any searches unless by your
orders and then a detail shall be made for that purpose. Exercise
the strictest discipline against any soldier who shall insult
citizens, or engage in plundering private property.

Make frequent reports to me at District Headquarters[1] and
also to the Department of the West at St. Louis, sending me
copies of such reports

By order of Brig. Gen. Grant
WM S. HILLYER.
Captain & A. D. C.

Copies, DNA, RG 94, War Records Office, Union Battle Reports; *ibid.*, RG 393,
USG Letters Sent; DLC-USG, V, 1, 2, 3, 77. *O.R.*, I, iv, 198. Brig. Gen. Eleazer

A. Paine of Ohio, USMA 1839, resigned as 2nd lt., 1st Inf., on Oct. 11, 1840, then resumed army service as col., 9th Ill., on July 26, 1861. His promotion to brig. gen., dated from Sept. 3, 1861, was so recent that he commanded only a regt. on Sept. 6.

1. Cairo.

To Maj. Gen. John C. Frémont

Headquarters Dist. S. E. Mo.
Cairo, Ills., Sept. 6, 1861.

MAJ. GEN. J. C. FREMONT
ST. LOUIS, MO.

I left Cairo at half past ten o'clock last night taking two gunboats and three steamboats,[1] with the 9th Illinois under General E. Paine; the 12th Illinois, under Col. J. McArthur, and Smith's battery—four pieces light artillery under Lieutenant Willard.[2]

I met with some detention at Mound City, owing to an accident to one of the steamers, creating a necessity for a transfer of troops. During the detention I was joined by Captain Foote,[3] U. S. Navy, who accompanied the expedition.

Arrived at Paducah at half past eight this morning. Found numerous secession flags flying over the city, and the citizens in anticipation of the approach of the rebel army, who was reliably reported thirty eight hundred strong sixteen miles distant.[4] As we neared the city Brigadier General Tilghman[5] and staff, of the rebel army, and a recruiting Major with a company raised in Paducah, left the city by the railroad, taking with them all the rolling stock. I landed the troops and took possession of the city without firing a gun. Before I landed the secession flags had disappeared, and I ordered our flags to replace them. I found at the railroad depot a large number of complete rations and about two tons of leather marked for the confederate army. Took possession of these and ordered the rations to be distributed to the troops. I also took possession of the telegraph office, and seized some letters and dispatches, which I herewith transmit.[6] I further took possession of the railroad. The enemy was reported as coming down the Tennessee river in large force, but this I do not credit. I distributed the troops so as best to command the city and least annoy peaceable citizens, and published a proclamation to the citizens,[7] a copy of which will be handed you by Captain Foote. I left the two gunboats and one of the steamboats at Paducah, placed the post under command of General E. Paine, and left Paducah at 12 o'clock, arriving at this post at four this afternoon.

Last night I ordered the 8th Missouri Vols. Colonel M. L. Smith, stationed at Cape Girardeau, to report here immediately.[8] I will send them to reinforce General Paine at Paducah to-night. I would respectfully recommend that two additional pieces be added to the excellent battery of Captain Smith, commanded by Lieutenant Willard, making it a complete battery of six pieces. He has men sufficient for six pieces, but will require horses and harness.

Colonel Waagner accompanied me and manifested great zeal and precaution.

I must acknowledge my obligations to General McClernand, commanding this force, for the active and efficient cooperation exhibited by him in fitting out the expedition.

U S GRANT
Brig. Gen.

Copies, DLC-USG, V, 4, 5, 7, 8, 77; DNA, RG 94, War Records Office, Union Battle Reports; *ibid.*, RG 393, USG Hd. Qrs. Correspondence. *O.R.*, I, iv, 197; *O.R.* (Navy), I, xxii, 317. On the same day, USG telegraphed the substance of his letter to Maj. Gen. John C. Frémont. "Have just returned from Paducah. Found secession flags flying in different parts of the city in expectation of greeting the arrival of southern army, said to be sixteen miles off, thirty eight hundred strong. Took quiet possession of telegraph office, railroad depot, and marine hospital. Found a large number of complete rations, and leather for the southern army. I will go to Cape Girardeau to night and give necessary directions for movement of troops from there, and return tomorrow. Left two gunboats for the present." Copies, DLC-USG, V, 4, 5, 7, 8; DNA, RG 94, War Records Office, Union Battle Reports; *ibid.*, RG 393, USG Hd. Qrs. Correspondence. *O.R.*, I, iv, 196–97. On Sept. 6, 1861, Frémont telegraphed to USG. "We will reinforce you from here." Copies, DLC-USG, V, 4, 5, 7, 8, VIA, 1; DNA, RG 393, Western Dept., Telegrams; *ibid.*, USG Hd. Qrs. Correspondence.

Also on Sept. 6, Frémont wrote to USG. "To Enable you to continue personally in command of our ~~command~~ forces at Cairo Birds Point, Cape Girardeau and Ironton, I have directed Brigadier Genl Smith to repair to Paducah and assume command of the forces now at that place and on the Kentucky side of the Mississippi and Ohio Rivers. The order of the 5th instant informs you as to the nature of the operations to be carried on, on both sides of the Mississippi River." Copies, DLC-USG, V, 7, 8, 81; DNA, RG 393, USG Hd. Qrs. Correspondence. *O.R.*, I, iii, 471. Brig. Gen. Charles F. Smith of Pa., USMA 1825, had served as commandant of cadets at USMA during the first two years USG was there. Whether or not his appointment to command at Paducah was intended as a rebuke to USG has been disputed by USG's biographers.

1. Gunboats *Tyler* and *Conestoga*; steamboats *Graham, Terry,* and *Platte Valley.* Due to the breakdown of the *Terry,* troops were transferred to the *W. H. B.* at Mound City before proceeding to Paducah. Letter of "S. H. E.," Sept. 6, 1861, in *Chicago Tribune,* Sept. 11, 1861.

2. Capt. James Smith and 1st Lt. Charles M. Willard, later of Battery A, 1st Ill. Light Art.

3. On Aug. 30, Capt. Andrew H. Foote was assigned "to take command of the naval operations upon the Western waters." *O.R.* (Navy), I, xxii, 307. See James M. Hoppin, *Life of Andrew Hull Foote* (New York, 1874).

4. The extent of C.S.A. forces near Paducah is not known. Maj. Gen. Leonidas Polk had thirteen regts. at Columbus. *O.R.*, I, iii, 699.

5. C.S.A. Brig. Gen. Lloyd Tilghman of Md., USMA 1836.

6. These have not been located.

7. See proclamation of Sept. 6, 1861.

8. See letter to Brig. Gen. John A. McClernand, Sept. 5, 1861.

To Brig. Gen. John A. McClernand

Head Quarters Dist. of S. E. Mo.
Cairo, Sept. 6th 1861

GEN.

Please have all the Camp and Garrison equipage and rations already issued to the 8th Ill Vols and Smith Battery sent to the river for shipment as soon as possible.

The Steamer B[1] has already gone to Birds Point for the

baggage of the 12th Ill. Vols. and will take the whole to Paducah at once.

U. S. GRANT
Brig. Gen. Com.

To Gen. McClernand
Comd.g Post
Cairo Ill.

ALS, McClernand Papers. IHi.

1. Also known as *Bee*.

To Brig. Gen. Eleazer A. Paine

———

Head Quarters Dist. S. E. Mo
Cairo Sept 6, 1861

GENL

Take possession of the wharf boats at the landing and make use of them for store houses ~~immediately~~

I would recommend that you have your captured stores and all others sent to these boats immediately to guard against losing them.

I send you five companies of Col Oglesby's Regt.[1] without baggage and I want them returned by the same boat that takes Smith's regiment

I can send you one or two companies of Cavalry in a day or two and am in hopes 2 more pieces of artillery will be added to the battery you now have—

U S. GRANT
Brig Gen Comg

To Gen Paine
Comg Post Paducah Ky.—

Copies, DLC-USG, V, 1, 2, 3, 77; DNA, RG 94, War Records Office, Union Battle Reports; *ibid.*, RG 393, USG Letters Sent. *O.R.*, I, iv, 198. On Sept. 6,

1861, Capt. William S. Hillyer wrote to Brig. Gen. Eleazer A. Paine. "I am instructed by Gen Grant who has left for Cape Girardeau to add to the foregoing the additional instruction that should you apprehend an attack from the enemy, you will ~~take~~ seize all the money in the banks, assuring the citizens that it is done for the purpose of of securing the deposits of the Union men as well as to guard against its falling into the hands of the enemy—You will then place it on one of the gun boats for safe keeping—" Copies, DLC-USG, V, 1, 2, 3, 77; DNA, RG 94, War Records Office, Union Battle Reports; *ibid.*, RG 393, USG Letters Sent. *O.R.*, I, iv, 198.

1. Richard J. Oglesby, a lawyer of Decatur, Ill., had served as 1st lt. in the Mexican War. In 1860, he was elected to the state Senate, but resigned to command the 8th Ill.

To Col. Morgan L. Smith

———

Head Quarters Dist S. E. Mo
Cairo Sept 6th 1861

Sir—

Without leaving the steamer you are now on, you will proceed at once to Paducah Ky and there report to Brig Gen Paine now in comman[d] at that place for duty

I have selected your regiment and yourself for that ~~purpose~~ post deeming it of the utmost importance to have troops and commander that can be ~~relied~~ expected to do good service

U. S. Grant
Brig Gen Com'g

To Col M. L. Smith
Comg 8th Regt Mo Vol

Copies, DLC-USG, V, 1, 2, 3, 77; DNA, RG 94, War Records Office, Union Battle Reports; *ibid.*, RG 393, USG Letters Sent. *O.R.*, I, iv, 198.

To Col. John Cook

———

Cape Girardeau Mo
September 7th 1861.

SPECIAL ORDER

All the troops now encamped at Jackson Mo. excepting the 7th & 20th Ills Regts, will march into Cape Girardeau as speedily as possible.

After the departure of such troops as will be ordered from Cape Girardeau, Col. Cook will march his Regiment in and take command of the Post.

Col Marsh will continue to hold Jackson with his regiment and one half of Capt Stewart's Company of Cavalry.

Reports will be made to Head Quarters Cairo until further orders.

U. S. GRANT
Brig. Gen Com.

To Col. J. Cook
Comdg Jackson Mo.

Cape Girardeau Mo.
Sept. 7th 1861

COL.

I want the troops under your command to be in the City to take boats as fast as they can be provided, but it is not absolutely necessary that they should all march into town to-day. I would like however the Artillery, Cavalry and Col.s Ross & Heckers commands to come to-day and the balance, to-morrow specified in orders, to-morrow.

U. S. GRANT

Copies, DLC-USG, V, 15, 16, 77, 82; DNA, RG 393, Western Dept., Letters Received; *ibid.*, USG Special Orders. The accompanying note is an ALS, IHi. Also on Sept. 7, 1861, USG issued special orders for Col. John Cook. "The three Companies of Cavalry now at Jackson Mo. will proceed by land to Cairo, crossing over to the Ill shore at this point. The Baggage of the Command will be sent by boat, excepting so much as can be easily carried in the wagons belonging to the

Companies. One man to each Company may remain with the Baggage. It is expected the Cavalry will reach Cairo tomorrow evening" Copies, DLC-USG, V, 15, 16, 77, 82; DNA, RG 393, USG Special Orders. On the same day, Cook replied to USG. "Orders bearing date September 7th 1861 have been received and in compliance therewith orders have been issued upon Col. Hecker 24th Ills. Lt Col Wood Comdg 17th Ills Buels Battery and Cavalry unde[r] Com.d Capt Delano and Major Nemett to proceed without delay under instructions to report to the Genl. Comdg Cape Girardeau. The remaining Regiments under my command are also in pursuance to your orders held in readiness to march tomorrow morning 8th inst at 7 o.clock. Col Marsh has been put in possession of copy of order, and awaits the arrival of the half compy of Cavalry Capt. Stewart. The troops are greatly delighted at the prospect of moving, and especially under your command. We are badly off for transportation especially for the sick however all shall be done within the bounds of possibilities—hoping soon to join your command" ALS, *ibid.*, District of Southeast Mo., Letters Received.

On Sept. 8, USG issued special orders relating to the troop transfer. "The steamer Illinois will proceed imediately to Cape Girardeau and bring the Bagage of the 17th & 24th Regt Ills Volls including their teams, and such troops as she is able to bring in addition" Copies, DLC-USG, V, 15, 16, 77, 82; DNA, RG 393, USG Special Orders. On the same day, 1st Lt. Clark B. Lagow wrote to Cook. "I am directed by the Genl Commdg to say to you that the troops at Cape Girardeau that are moving from there will bring all their transportation with them" Copies, DLC-USG, V, 2, 77; DNA, RG 393, USG Letters Sent.

To Maj. Gen. John C. Frémont

Cairo Ills Sept 7th 61

To MAJ GENL FREMONT
St LOUIS MO.

I have just returnd from Cape Girardeau where I have been making arrangement to have the troops move expeditiously to this point to be disposed of—The 7th Ills & 11th Mo are left at Cape Girardeau, Ills 20th at 20th at Jackson for the present with one company of Cavelry.

U. S. GRANT
Brigd Genl Comdg

Telegram, copies, DLC-USG, V, 4, 5, 7, 8, 78, VIA, 1; DNA, RG 393, USG Hd. Qrs. Correspondence; *ibid.*, Western Dept., Telegrams. See letters to Col. John Cook, Sept. 7, 1861.

To Maj. Gen. John C. Frémont

Cairo, Sept 7, 1861.

Maj. Gen. J. C. Fremont,

I sent Col Webster[1] to Paducah to night to direct the beginning of fortifications there—have been pushing the work of fort Holt[2] for three or four days.

U. S. Grant
Brig. Gen. Comdg.

Telegram, copies, DNA, RG 393, Western Dept., Telegrams; DLC-USG, VIA, 1. USG sent his telegram in response to a Sept. 7, 1861, telegram from Maj. Gen. John C. Frémont. "Six eight inch Columbiads and ten thirty two pounder guns with barbette carriages left Pittsburg for Cairo in two special trains. The first last night the second at noon today. One regiment from this place should arrive at eight to morrow. A boat sent to take regiment from opposite Commerce to Cairo. Other reinforcements will follow to morrow. Gen Smith must throw up earth works and plant guns at Paducah, but make no advance. He should occupy Smithland with four companies if they can be spared. At least one gun boat should be kept at Paducah. The works at fort Holt should be immediately commenced with all the laborers at Cairo & Birds Point. The place should be strongly guarded an advance guard pushed across Cane Creek and the heights Commanding Fort Jefferson and Blandville should be occupied. Crossings of Norfolk and Belmont, watched." Copies, *ibid.*, V, 4, 5, 7, 8, VIA, 1; DNA, RG 393, Western Dept., Telegrams; *ibid.*, USG Hd. Qrs. Correspondence. *O.R.*, I, iii, 476. Frémont's telegram arrived at Cairo before USG returned from Cape Girardeau, and Capt. William S. Hillyer sent appropriate instructions to Brig. Gen. John A. McClernand at Cairo, Brig. Gen. Charles F. Smith at Paducah, Brig. Gen. Eleazer A. Paine at Paducah, Commander John Rodgers at Paducah, and Lt. Henry C. Freeman at Fort Holt. Copies, DLC-USG, V, 1, 2, 3, 77; DNA, RG 393, USG Letters Sent. *O.R.*, I, iv, 256–57.

On Sept. 7, Paine reported to USG. "If one fourth the reports are true that I hear I shall need three Regiments more of troop more field pieces and at least two companies of cavalry. I beg of you to send two Regiments at least; I do not wish to be compelled to give way an inch. I will follow your instructions to the letter. Major Phillips went out seven miles and destroyed a Rail Road Bridge. Gen. Pillow has come from Missouri and will be here in two days with 4000 or 5,000 troops. Gen Tilghman has 2000 armed with Enfield Rifles twenty miles from here. Col Rhoades with his command arrived safe. We shall have a struggle here within a few days and I am not going to be beaten. Send all of my camp equipage, tents &c our men are on the ground to night. Send all of Col. Rhodes equipage. I will send by next Boat copies of invoices of property siezed. I wish the Post Master of Cairo to send all of the Paducah Mail including my own and the Rigiments here. If Gen Grant is not at Cairo, I wish Gen McClernand would see that ~~this~~ the requests herein asked are promptly sent. I would not ask it as I do if it was not absolutely necessary. Send Col. Pugh's Regiment from Birds Point if others are not ordered I had a meeting of the principal citizens here and they will do all the can to keep quiet, but in fact there are very few Union men here I want for Hospital the Mattresses on the Steam Boat Terry" ALS, McClernand Papers, IHi. An undated letter from Paine, addressed to "Genl. Grant or Genl. McClernand," was probably written the same day. "It is of the utmost importance that I have five Regiments more, all of the Artillery and Cavalry you can send me. Gen. Pillow is marching on the place, with a force reported, undoubtedly, three times as large as it is, but, secessionists here say that if Paducah is held by us that it is the worst thing for them and that we must be driven off. I shall hold this place even at an immense sacrifice—I could do it better, and assume the offensive if the least opportunity offers,—If I could be armed with sufficient force I would hold three or four counties south and west by moving forward twenty miles. With what men I now have I can only defend in position. An accidental discharge of one of the 64s, on the Gun Boats gave the people an idea of a Gun Boat, and its efficiency. Send me if possible twenty loads of bread. A Blacksmith refused to shoe a horse for me. I arrested him and gave him five minutes to shoe the Horse or be shot, he immediately went to work. I am compelled to be severe for nearly every man here is a rank secessionists, I have taken 1,000 BBLs flour a large amount of bacon, candles, Leather &c" ALS, *ibid.* See also *O.R.*, I, iii, 475, 480.

On Sept. 7, Frémont sent another telegram to USG. "Let detachment of 8th Illinois, as well as 8th Missouri remain at Paducah, until replaced in a few days from St. Louis." Copies, DNA, RG 393, USG Hd. Qrs. Correspondence; DLC-USG, V, 4, 5, 7, 8. On Sept. 7, USG telegraphed to Frémont. "They have not yet arrived, the steamer with them stopped to take on troops at Cape Girardeau." Copies, DNA, RG 393, Western Dept., Telegrams; DLC-USG, VIA, 1.

1. Joseph D. Webster of N. H. resigned as capt. of topographical engineers on April 7, 1854, then went into business in Chicago. On June 1, 1861, he was appointed maj. as an additional paymaster of vols., but was assigned to engineering duty at Cairo. *DAB*, XIX, 593–94.

2. For instructions concerning Fort Holt, Ky., opposite Cairo and Bird's Point, Mo., see letter to Maj. Gen. John C. Frémont, Sept. 5, 1861. On Sept. 8, Hillyer wrote to the capt. of the Cairo and Bird's Point Ferry. "In making your regular trips from Cairo to Birds Point (except when detailed on special service) you will both going and coming land at Fort Holt" Copies, DLC-USG, V, 1, 2, 3, 77; DNA, RG 393, USG Letters Sent. On Sept. 11, USG telegraphed to Frémont. "I am pleased to report that the last gun at Fort Holt is in our possession" Copy, DLC-USG, VIA, 1. This text is apparently garbled, for, on Sept. 11, Frémont telegraphed to Col. Edward D. Townsend. "Gen Grant telegraphs from Cairo that the first gun is in position at Fort Holt Kentucky." Copy, DNA, RG 393, Western Dept., Telegrams.

Capt. John A. Rawlins

This and the following photographs were taken at Cairo, Illinois
in October, 1861. *Courtesy Library of Congress.*

1st Lieutenant Clark B. Lagow

Capt. William S. Hillyer

Maj. James Simons

To Brig. Gen. Charles F. Smith

Head Quarters Dist S. E. Mo
Cairo Sept 7, 1861

GENERAL

I have received the following telegram from Maj Gen Fremont

"Gen Smith[1] must throw up earth works and plant guns at Paducah, but make no advance. He should occupy Smithland[2] with four companies if they can be spared"

I expect several guns here to morrow and next day. You will please inform me how many you require not exceeding six and I will send them to you immediately

Respectfully
Your Obt Svt
U S. GRANT
Brig Gen Com

To Brig Gen C. F. Smith
Comg Post Paducah

Copies, DLC-USG, V, 1, 2, 3, 77; DNA, RG 393, USG Letters Sent. See preceding telegram. The instructions from Maj. Gen. John C. Frémont had already been sent to Brig. Gen. Charles F. Smith by Capt. William S. Hillyer. On Sept. 9, 1861, Smith replied to USG. "I recvd last night your letter of the 7th inst, conveying the telegram of Genl. Fremont in relation to throwing up earth-works here. I accept your proposition most readily to receive the six heavy Guns, with their carriages, ammunition &c. I should be very glad to have the remainder of Co. B Chicago Lt. Artillery: that is to say the remaining two guns and 2 twelve Pdr Howitzers, which I am told is at Birds Point, with the teams and train complete—Spades, Shovels, Barrows &c. We want means of transportation exceedingly—say thirty wagons, with teams complete. Rations for 5000 men for such no of days as you can spare them, are also needed as one of our first wants. Do not forget, if you please, your offer of Cavalry—a description of force much needed. P. S. Please meet my wishes, as far as you can, at the earliest moment." LS, DNA, RG 393, District of Southeast Mo., Letters Received. On the same day, Smith wrote to Frémont. "I recvd (through Genl Grant at Cairo) last evening the Major General's telegram directing the erection of earthworks. Genl Grant in transmitting this says he will furnish me with some heavy guns, not exceeding six. The works will be commenced as soon as possible. I rode around the town, and in advance of it yesterday, in company with Genl Paine and Col Webster (Engineer) and made a general disposition of the Troops. Col Webster is now out making, with a loyal person well acquainted with the vicinity, a reconnoissance and plan for the commencement of the works. I will enclose before finishing this a sketch of the roads and position of the troops. A bridge to Brooklyn of boats or other material, however desirable, will be exceedingly difficult of accomplishment, if at all, in any reasonable time. Brooklyn is some three miles below this. The river is from ⅜ to ¾ of a mile wide. The Quarter Master is now trying to purchase or seize, if need be, the proper working tools—spades, picks &c" LS, *ibid.*, Western Dept., Letters Received.

1. Instructions for Smith were sent through USG because there was no telegraphic link between Paducah and St. Louis; Smith's command was intended to be independent. See letter to Maj. Gen. John C. Frémont, Sept. 6, 1861. On Sept. 7, Smith telegraphed to USG. "I am about Leaving here for Cairo by Special train and have despatch for you Please Let Staff officer meet me on the arrival of train" Telegram received, DNA, RG 393, Dept. of the Mo., Telegrams Received (unarranged).
2. Smithland, Ky., at the mouth of the Cumberland River.

General Orders No. 4

Headquarters District S. E. Missouri
Cairo, September 8, 1861

GENERAL ORDER NO. 4.

1st. The following staff officers having been duly appointed will be obeyed and respected as such, to wit:

Capt. John A. Rawlins,[1] Assistant Adjutant Gen'l

Capt. Clark B. Lagow, Aid-de-Camp

Capt. Wm. S. Hillyer, Aid-de-Camp

Surgeon James Simmons,[2] U. S. A., Medical Director.

2nd. All Post Commanders within this District will, immediately upon the receipt of this order, send to these Headquarters a consolidated morning report, and whenever the strength of their command is changed by the addition of new forces or by the ordering away of any under them, they will report it.

3d. These Headquarters being remote from Ironton, Cape Girardeau and Jackson, Mo., the commanders of those posts will make their regular weekly reports direct to General Fremont and will also report all valuable information they may receive of the movements of the rebels there sending at the same time copies here.

4th. A list of names of all commissioned officers with their rank and arm of service to which they belong will be furnished these Headquarters at once and also report all new arrivals of commissioned officers that may take place at any time hereafter.

U. S. GRANT

Brig. Gen'l Comdg.

Copies, DLC-USG, V, 12, 13, 14, 80; DNA, RG 393, USG General Orders.

1. This order apparently coincides with the arrival in Cairo of Capt. John A. Rawlins. See letter to Brig. Gen. Lorenzo Thomas, Aug. 29, 1861.

2. Maj. James Simons of S.C., surgeon, had been in the U.S. Army since 1839 and had been asst. surgeon attached to the 4th Inf. in 1843 when USG began U.S. Army service. On July 1, 1861, Brig. Gen. Benjamin M. Prentiss issued orders appointing Simons medical director at Cairo. Copy, Wallace-Dickey Papers, IHi.

General Orders No. 5

———

Head Quarters Dist S. E. Mo

Cairo Sept 8th 1861

GENERAL ORDER No 5

It is with regret the Genl Comdg sees and learns that the closest intimacy exists between many of the officers and soldiers of his command; that they visit together the lowest drinking and dancing saloons; quarrel, curse, drink and carouse generally on the lowest level of equality, and neglect generally the interests of the Government they are sworn to serve

Such conduct is totally subversive of good ~~conduct~~ order and Military Disipline and must be discontinued.

In future it will be the duty of every Commanding officer of a Regiment or detachment to at once arrest any one of their commands guilty of such conduct and prefer charges against them, and the duty of all officers who have a decent respect for themselves and the service they have entered ~~into~~ to report everything of the kind.

Disipline cannot be maintained where the officers do not command respect and such conduct cannot insure it.

In this military District Disipline shall be maintained even if it is at the expense of the commission of all officers who stand in the way of attaining that end

U. S. GRANT
Brig Genl Comdg

Copies, McClernand Papers, IHi; DLC-USG, V, 12, 13, 14, 80; DNA, RG 393, USG General Orders.

To Maj. Gen. John C. Frémont

Cairo, Sept 8 1861.

MAJ GEN. FREMONT,
HEADQUARTERS,

Two 2 regiments & Buels battery[1] just arrived from Cape Girardeau The big guns & infantry landed at Fort Holt by the battery at Birds Point.

U. S. GRANT.
Brig. Gen. Comdg:

Telegram, copies, DNA, RG 393, Western Dept., Telegrams; DLC-USG, VIA, 1.

1. Capt. James T. Buel led an independent Mo. battery, later Battery I, 2nd Mo. Light Art.

To Maj. Gen. John C. Frémont

————

Cairo, Sept 8 1861.

GENL J. C. FREMONT,
ST. LOUIS,

Information received from a spy & also from Kentukians who have fled from their houses report the rebels strength at Columbus to day at eighteen (18) regiments of infantry a considerable number of artillery & cavalry They have two batteries of heavy pieces & two 2 gun boats—one of their gunboats has been up to within three 3 miles of Cairo this evening[.] no troops from St. Louis to day.

U. S. GRANT.

Telegram, copies, DNA, RG 393, Western Dept., Telegrams; DLC-USG, VIA, 1. *O.R.*, I, iii, 479.

To Maj. Gen. John C. Frémont

————

Head Quarters Dist S. E. Mo.
Cairo, Sept. 8th 1861

MAJ. GEN. J. C. FREMONT
ST. LOUIS MO.
SIR:

I telegraphed to you this [*evening*] the substance of news received to-day. I have however information that five hundred Cavalry are picketed seven miles from Fort Holt, unsupported by Artillery or Infantry and that Jeff. Thompson is marching upon Norfolk.[1] If so the latter will be received by a regiment of Infantry and two Howitzers sent for the purpose.

I enclose you a printed order of yesterdays date by Maj. Gen. Polk.[2]

The following Steamers are laying at Columbus; to wit: Prince, Prince of Wales, Ingomar, Wm Morrison, Jno. Walsh, W. H. R. Hill, Charmer and Equality. Also the Gun Boat Yankee, two guns 84 & 64 pounders. The latter is Iron Clad and fast. There is not two gun boats as reported by me this evening by telegraph.[3]

> Respectfully
> Your Obt. Svt.
> U. S. GRANT
> Brig. Gen. Com.

ALS, DNA, RG 393, Western Dept., Letters Received.

1. Norfolk, Mo., on the Mississippi River about eight miles south of Cairo.
2. Leonidas Polk of N.C., USMA 1827, resigned as bvt. 2nd lt. on Dec. 1, 1827, to study for the ministry. At the start of the Civil War, he left his post as Episcopal Bishop of La. to serve as C.S.A. maj. gen. On Sept. 7, 1861, by General Orders No. 19, Polk organized his force at Columbus, Ky., into field brigades. *O.R.*, I, iii, 699. According to a letter from Cairo, Sept. 9, a scout from Columbus brought in a printed copy of this order late the previous evening. *Chicago Tribune*, Sept. 11, 1861.
3. See preceding telegram.

To Brig. Gen. John A. McClernand

> Head Quarters, Dist. S. E. Mo.
> Cairo Sept. 8th 1861

GEN.

I enclose you letter[1] directed to Gen Frémont and refered to me relating to the drinking shops in this community.

I would recommend the appointment of a Provost Marshall, or officer by another name of necessary, who would have this whole matter in charge and entirely suppress drinking saloons or put them under wholsome regulations.

> Yours
> U. S. GRANT
> Brig. Gen. U. S. A.
> Comd.g Dist.

To Brig. Gen. J. A. McClernand
Comd.g Post
Cairo Ill.

ALS, McClernand Papers, IHi. On Sept. 8, 1861, Brig. Gen. John A. McClernand replied to USG. "Your's of this date is received this morning, enclosing and referring to me a communication from Henry B. Smith of Cairo, to Major Genl. John C. Fremont, concerning the drinking saloons and other sources of disorder and crime in this city. I have to acknowledge the receipt, also, this afternoon, of your General Order No 5, of this date likewise, advising me of your knowledge, 'that the closest intimacy exists between many of the officers and soldiers of his (your) command, that they visit together the lowest drinking and dancing saloons, quarrel, curse, drink and carouse generally on the lowest level of equality; and neglect generally the interests of the Government they are sworn to serve,' which you properly denounce as 'totally subversive of good conduct and military discipline,' and to be repressed. You will reeollect that I had selected an encampment for the new Brigade organizing under my command, in another portion of the State, desiring to prepare my men for the field, as far removed as possible, from influences of the character mentioned in your order; and my reluctance to remove them to this vicinity, would have been increased, had I been fully aware of the grave disorders you have noticed. The necessity, either of establishing martial law, or of placing at the control of the civil authorities of the city, an adequate military force, was apparent to me on my arrival with my Brigade. You will recollect a suggestion made by myself to you to that effect, which failed to meet your views. I was placed by you in command of this post on the fourth instant, and before three hours had elapsed, I was engaged in organizing the expedition to Paducah:—on the two succeeding days, three several detatch-ments, with artillery, have been forwarded to the same point—a lodgement made upon the Kentucky shore at Fort Holt—and engineering and working parties, covered by guards detailed for that purpose. To-day, the sabbath, I am devoting to an inspection of the defences at Bird's Point, and other urgent duties growing out of these complicated operations and the critical condition of affairs here. In the meantime, I have been receiving, encamping, organizing and equipping my Brigade, which is still incomplete, and being filled up by daily arrivals. To what-ever point of aggravation the disorders referred to by yourself, may have reached before my arrival, (of which those previously in command, can better judge than myself,) I trust that the men whom I have brought here, have not, during the few days since their arrival, furnished occasion for so grave a censure. I should be extremely mortified to find it so. While making these explanations to avert the inf[e]rence that such disorders had originated under my command, and which I had failed to repress, I have to assure you of my concurrence in your views of discipline and duty, and that it is my determination, while in command, to enforce, if necessary, with a strong hand, the observance of both, as essential to the individual welfare of the officers and men, and indispensable to honorable, and successful service. To this end, I am now preparing and shall publish today, general orders, sufficient to the demand of the occasion, and shall endeavor to *enforce* them. And I will also add, I have observed no elements of insubordination in the army, or of public disorder, to discourage the hope that your utmost wishes may, in a few days, be attained." LS, DNA, RG 393, District of Southeast Mo., Letters Received; ADfS and ADf (incomplete), McClernand Papers, IHi.

On the same day, McClernand drafted a similar explanation for Maj. Gen. John C. Frémont. ADf, *ibid*.

    1. Not found.

To Col. Friedrich Hecker

Head Quarters Dist S. E. Mo
Cairo Sept 8th 1861

C<small>OL</small>

I have reliable information that a guard of 500 Cavalry unsupported by Infantry or Artillery are now seven miles from you on the Cairo and Columbus Road.

By leaving at 11 o.clock or later I think you will be able to take them.

Be exceedingly cautious not to be led to far and surprise them if you can.

I am at the same time fitting out an expedition to try and surprise Jeff Thompson who is on the Missouri side of the River about the same distance off.

Keep these matters to yourself for tonight

U. S. G<small>RANT</small>
Brig Genl Comdg

To Col Hecker
Comdg 24th Regt Ill Vol

Copies, DLC-USG, V, 1, 2, 3, 77; DNA, RG 393, USG Letters Sent. *O.R.*, I, iii, 479.

To Col. John B. Turchin

—————

Head Quarters Dist S. E. Mo
Cairo Sept 8th 1861

COL

I am informed that Col Hecker has got to the rear of some Rebel forces while Col Ross Regiment is in their front.

You will proceed at once with six companies of your command to their releif ~~at once~~.

Capt Schwartz[1] of the artillery who is at Fort Holt will give you the necessary directions.

U. S. GRANT
Brig Genl Comdg

To Col Turchin Comd
19th Regt Ill Vol Inftry
Fort Holt Ky

Copies, DLC-USG, V, 1, 2, 3, 77; DNA, RG 393, USG Letters Sent. *O.R.*, I, iii, 480. John B. Turchin, born Ivan Vasilevitch Turchinoff in Russia, was a graduate of the Imperial Military School at St. Petersburg and a veteran of the Crimean War. At the outbreak of the Civil War, he was living in Chicago and employed as an engineer for the Illinois Central Railroad. On June 17, 1861, he was appointed col., 19th Ill. See telegram of July 12, 1861.

1. Capt. Adolph Schwartz, later maj., 2nd Ill. Light Art. On Sept. 25, Capt. John A. Rawlins for USG issued special orders assigning Schwartz "as Acting Chief of Artillery for this command." Copies, DLC-USG, V, 15, 16, 77, 82; DNA, RG 393, USG Special Orders.

To Julia Dent Grant

—————

Cairo Illinois
Sept. 8th 1861

DEAR JULIA;

Mr. Cook[1] of Galena is just here and although I am very busy I will write you a few lines to send by him. I will enclose with them my Commission as Brigadier General[2] knowing that you will take better care of it than I will.—I suppose you have seen from the papers that I have quite an extensive and important command. It is third in importance in the country and Gen. Frémont seems desirous of retaining me in it. There are so many officers of higher rank, with less commands however that I do not see how I am to retain it long.

You have seen my move upon Paducah Ky! It was of much greater importance than is probably generally known. I had just learned through a Spy that Pillow was moving there to get possession of that point and cut us off on the Ohio river. Secession flags were flying through the city in anticipation of the arrival of Southern troops. ~~and~~ Our arrival therefore put quite a damper upon their hopes.

We are likely to have lively times here.

The Rebels are in great force on the opposite side of the river at different points and an attack somewhere cannot be postponed many days.

I am very well. Send kisses to yourself and the children.

ULYS.

ALS, DLC-USG.

1. Probably John Cook of the produce firm of Cook, Pendleton, and Co., Galena. See letter to Julia Dent Grant, Sept. 29, 1861.
2. USG's commission as brig. gen., dated Aug. 9, 1861, now in The Smithsonian Institution, is shown in Lawrence A. Frost, *U. S. Grant Album* (Seattle, 1966), p. 64.

To Maj. Gen. John C. Frémont

———

Cairo, Sept 9, 1861.

MAJ. GENL. J. C. FREMONT

Col Hecker has got in rear of five hundred cavalry, Kentucky side, Col Ross regiment is in front & six 6 companies of Turchins will go their assistance. We occupy Norfolk.

U. S. GRANT,
Brig. Genl.

Telegram, copies, DLC-USG, VIA, 1; DNA, RG 393, Western Dept., Telegrams. *O.R.*, I, iii, 480. For the reply, see following telegram, note 1. Also on Sept. 9, 1861, Capt. William S. Hillyer for USG sent special orders to Col. Friedrich Hecker. "The Command at Fort Holt Kentucky for the present will be held as a part of the Cairo command and will make their reports accordingly. For the present the Senior Officer will assume direction as far as designating the number of Guards location of Pickets, and having a General supervision over the details of a post or command." Copies, DLC-USG, V, 15, 16, 77, 82; DNA, RG 393, USG Special Orders.

To Maj. Gen. John C. Frémont

Cairo Sept 9th 1861

SIR

Your two dispatches received[1] I will start copy of them to Gen Smith at Paducah at once.

Col Hecker has been no further in Kentucky than you directed Pickets to be thrown

No Troops from St Louis yet.

I do not know if Gen. Smith has been reinforced or not. He returned here the Battallion of Oglesbys Regt which he was ordered to retain untill reinforcements did arrive.

Pillow had not started yesterday for Paducah.

~~Should he move in that direction allow me to move on Columbus.~~[2]

I telegraph to you every reinforcement that arrives at this place[3]

U. S. GRANT

To Maj Genl J. C. Fremont
St Louis Mo

Telegram, copies, DLC-USG, V, 4, 5, 7, 8, 78; DNA, RG 393, USG Hd. Qrs. Correspondence; *ibid.*, Western Dept., Telegrams. *O.R.*, I, iii, 481–82.

1. On Sept. 9, 1861, Maj. Gen. John C. Frémont telegraphed to USG. "Has Gen Smith gone to Paducah. I am credibly informed from Louisville that Pillow with 7,000 men & artillery is marching on Paducah also that the Tennesseens

are going to make a forward movement to night or to morrow to Kentucky. Has the reinforcement from St. Louis reached Cairo; inform Gen Smith at Paducah that I direct him to place a battery at the Marine hospital immediately, and the other on the heights near cross creek & prepare for forward movements towards Mayfield as soon as reinforcements arrive." Copies, DLC-USG, V, 4, 5, 7, 8, VIA, 1; DNA, RG 393, USG Hd. Qrs. Correspondence; *ibid.*, Western Dept., Telegrams. *O.R.*, I, iii, 480. Frémont sent another telegram to USG on the same day. "Second dispatch about Hecker not understood, Keep strictly within your orders in reference to the Kentucky movements. After Norfolk is occupied take a position at or near Belmont, out of reach of gun boats, so as to prevent any communication between Belmont & Charleston, with the object to surround & annihilate Thompson who is reported yet to be at or near Commerce Say to Gen Smith that it is most important that Smithland should be occupied by four companies immediately to control the Cumberland river." Copies, DLC-USG, V, 4, 5, 7, 8, VIA, 1; DNA, RG 393, USG Hd. Qrs. Correspondence; *ibid.*, Western Dept., Telegrams. *O.R.*, I, iii, 481.

2. This request, deleted here, was included in a letter to Frémont, Sept. 10, 1861.

3. Accordingly, USG sent three additional telegrams to Frémont on Sept. 9. "The second Iowa, nineteenth Ills: & three companies of cavalry from Cape Girardeau arrived today." "The seventh Iowa Volunteers have just arrived." "The twenty third 23 Indiana bound for Paducah & the twenty eight 28 Illinois regts: for this place, have just arrived." Copies, DNA, RG 393, Western Dept., Telegrams; DLC-USG, VIA, 1.

To Maj. Gen. John C. Frémont

Cairo Sept 9th 1861

MAJ. GEN. J. C. FREMONT
ST. LOUIS, MO.

It is necessary that I should have control of cash to pay for secret service rendered. Orders on Quartermasters will not pay.

U. S. GRANT
Brig. General

Telegram, copies, DLC-USG, V, 4, 5, 7, 8, VIA, 1; DNA, RG 393, USG Hd. Qrs. Correspondence; *ibid.*, Western Dept., Telegrams.

To Maj. Gen. John C. Frémont

———

Cairo, Sept 9, 1861.

GENL. FREMONT,

Gun boat "Conestoga" has arrived with three prisoners, one from Tennessee river one from Cumberland river, & one from Paducah; trial must be had before condemnation, have put a guard over officers & crew until proper steps are pointed out—secure as witness.

U. S. GRANT
Brig. Genl.

Telegram, copies, DLC-USG, VIA, 1; DNA, RG 393, Western Dept., Telegrams. See following letter. In two letters to USG, both dated Sept. 9, 1861, Lt. S. Ledyard Phelps, commanding the gunboat *Conestoga*, reported the seizure of the steamer *Jefferson* on the Tennessee River and the steamer *Tradewater Belle* on the Cumberland River. LS, DNA, RG 393, District of Southeast Mo., Letters Received.

To Maj. Gen. John C. Frémont

———

Head Quarters Dist S. E. Mo
Cairo Illinois
Sept 9th 1861

MAJ GENL J. C. FREMONT
COMDG DEPT OF THE WEST
ST LOUIS MO
SIR

Enclosed I send you evidence of the character of steamers captured and brought into this Port this morning.[1]

The steamers with Cargoes have been turned over to the collector of Customs for this place who will keep them in his charge until a decision is made in their case.

The officers and crew I have directed should be detained as witnesses at least detained for your orders in the matter

> Respectfully
> Your obt Servant
> U. S. GRANT
> Brig Genl Comdg

Copies, DLC-USG, V, 4, 5, 7, 8, 78; DNA, RG 393, USG Hd. Qrs. Correspondence.

1. Not found. See letter to Maj. Gen. John C. Frémont, Sept. 18, 1861.

To Brig. Gen. John A. McClernand

> Head Quarters, Dist. S. E. Mo.
> Cairo Sept. 9th 1861

GEN.

The Steamers John Galt, ~~Baldwin~~ Jefferson and Treawater Bell, prizes just brought in to this Port by Gun Boat to gether with their cargoes will be turned over to the Collector of Customs for this Port.

The officers and crew will be detained as prisoners until instructions are received from St. Louis what disposition to make of them.

I would also recommend the appointment of two or more Army officers to examine their books and safe and make a report of contents.

> Respectfully
> Your Obt. Svt.
> U. S. GRANT
> Brig. Gen. Com.

To Gen. J. A. McClernand
Comd.g Post
Cairo Ill.

ALS, McClernand Papers, IHi. See preceding letter.

To Col. John Cook

Head Quarters Dist S. E. Mo
Cairo Sept 9th 1861

SIR

You will please send an express to Jackson immediately upon the receipt of this and direct Col Marsh to move into Cape Girardeau with all his command at once.

He will then proceed by first conveyance to this place bringing all his baggage with him.

Col Stewart with his Cavalry company will cross the River at Cape Girardeau and march to this place as soon as joined by the detachment at Jackson sending his baggage by River.

Push the works of fortifying as rapidly as possible to completion. With them completed your Garrison will be sufficient to hold the place against any force that can be suddenly brought against it.

By order of
U. S. GRANT
Brig Genl Comdg

To Col J. Cook
7th Ill Vols
Comdg Cape Girardeau Mo

Copies, DLC-USG, V, 1, 2, 3, 77; DNA, RG 393, USG Letters Sent. *O.R.*, I, iii, 481. Col. John Cook, commanding at Cape Girardeau, was apparently away on Sept. 9, 1861, for Col. David Bayles, 11th Mo., "Comdg Post," wrote to USG that day. "Enclosed is a synopsis of business transacted under your instructions. Col. Hecker arrived about five oclock P. M. Sept 7th and imediately departed on the Steamer Desmoins. Squadron of horse under Major Nemeth arrived at 5 ½ oclock and imediately proceeded across the river. All got over by 8 oclock P. M. and took up their line of march for Cairo. Capt Buells artillery arrived at 6 oclock P. M. Went on board the Steamer Ills all aboard by 7 ½ oclock same day. At 8 oclock the 17th Ills arrived and embarked on the Steamer Illinois. A part of their baggage was put on board the Ferry Boat Luella, & three companies of Col. Smiths Regt. detached Did'nt all get aboard until three oclock next morning, departed, soon after. The 7th Ills 19th Ills 2nd Iowa and 7th Iowa, arrived at 11 oclock A. M. 8th inst. The 2nd Iowa went on board the Steamer Wisconsin and departed about 11 oclock same night. The 19th Illinois went aboard the Steamer

Arizana and Barge attached and departed about 12 oclock at night. The 7th Iowa marched on board the Louisiana ~~and~~ at 12 M ~~9 inst~~ to day and sailed imediately. The several trains belonging to the different Regiments that have gone forth are being loaded on the Illinois and will start as soon as loaded. The Brigade train twenty two waggons in all are crossing the river into Ills and will go down by land, you having in your order ~~having~~ said nothing about them. Also the train of the 17th Ills will go there being no room for them on board the Illinois and they prefering it. I hope all will meet with your approbation." ALS, DNA, RG 393, District of Southeast Mo., Letters Received. On Sept. 11, Cook replied to USG. "In pursuance with your order I have called in from Jackson the 20th Reg Ills. Vols. Col. C. C. Marsh and half of Capt Stewarts Cavalry and have issued orders upon Gov. Transport S. B. Illinois for transportation to Cairo. Have ordered Capt Stewarts Cavalry to take transportation on board with 20th Reg there being an abundance of room and a very severe rain storm commencing at midnight. (the hour your order was received) and lasting until 10 oclock to day flooding every thing and in the opinion of old citizens in this region rendering the roads and bridges by land to Cairo unsafe for troops. This order which is contrary to your order has been given believing it under the circumstances the most speedy and for the best interests of the service and hope the same may meet your approval. Upon assuming the command of this post I find nothing of record whatever to govern me in the proper discharge of my duty, and have by communication to Gen Fremont stated the same fact and have asked for such instructions as he may deem necessary, and hope you will have the goodness to place me in possession of such instructions as you in your judgment may deem necessary, and every exertion shall be made upon my part to execute all orders and carry out all such instructions. The S. B. 'Meteor' on yesterday ran the Blockade without 'coming to,' simply showing her colors. is she Loyal? Rumor says your troops are enjoying a little passtime with the Rebels below Cairo hope it may be true and that you have given them before this their just deserts and regret exceedingly having been denied the privilege of participating. For Picket duty at this Post we greatly need at least one full Compy of Cavalry. The command is greatly reduced numerically in consequence of sickness principally measels. In the absense of more troops I have called the Fremont Rangers (25 head horses) and such of the Home Guard as are willing to serve on duty to Police & Patrol the city & find the Home Guard decidedly disobliging even around their *own* homes. An order for their disbandment has been issued but as yet has not been complied with. Should they persist in not serving had their arms better not be surrendered? hope you will fully instruct me. The work on the fortifications has been considerably damaged by the heavy rain of last night, but as soon as the ground dries sufficiently will put upon the work an increased force & complete earth works as soon as possible." ALS, *ibid.* Cook's letter to Maj. Gen. John C. Frémont, Sept. 11, 1861, is in Western Dept., Letters Received.

To Col. Michael K. Lawler

———

                                    Head Quarters Dist S. E. Mo
                                        Cairo Sept 9th 1861
Col

It is of the last importance that the Gun Boats now being built at Mound City[1] should be well protected. To attain that end at least one company must be specially detailed each night as a Guard exclusively for those Boats.

The officers of the company so detailed will be a part of the Guard and must stay with it

This detail will only be for night duty
                                    By Order
                                    U. S. Grant
                                    Brig Genl Comdg
To Col Lawler
Comdg 18th Ill Vol

Copies, DLC-USG, V, 1, 2, 3, 77; DNA, RG 393, USG Letters Sent. Col. Michael K. Lawler, 18th Ill. See letters of May 21, 22, 1861.

1. Three of the seven gunboats which James B. Eads of St. Louis was building for the War Dept. were under construction at Mound City: the *Cairo*, *Cincinnati*, and *Mound City*. A. T. Mahan, *The Gulf and Inland Waters* (New York, 1883), pp. 12–15; *O.R.* (Navy), I, xxii, 386–87.

To Lt. S. Ledyard Phelps

———

                                    Head Quarters Dist S. E. Mo
                                        Cairo Sept 9th 1861
Sir

I understand Norfolk is being marched upon by troops on the Mo side also that the Gun Boat Lexington will likely be attacked you will therefore proceed to her assistance as soon as practicable.

By order of

U. S. GRANT

Brig Genl Comdg

To Commander
Gun Boat Conestoga

Copies, DLC-USG, V, 1, 2, 3, 77; DNA, RG 393, USG Letters Sent. *O.R.*, I, iii, 481; *O.R.* (Navy), I, xxii, 322.

On Sept. 8, 1861, Col. Gustav Waagner wrote to USG. "In consequence of your order received yesterday.—I started this morning at 5 o'c on the gun boat Lexington Commanded by Captain Stembell for a reconoiter to Columbus, at about 7 o'c A M. we passed Islands No 3 & 4 where we discovered the camp fires, a few miles above Columbus on the Kentucky Shore, exactly in the centre of the two natural platform bluffs, commanding the river and Belmont, in attempting to pass the foot of Lucas Bend near Columbus two batteries opened fire on us one consisting of 3 the other of 4 Guns, but notwithstanding the high elevation given to their pieces their Shot all fell short. We did not answer as they were out of range and we could not do them any damage. The calibre of the guns being two 24 pound Howitzers and 24 and 32 pounders on Barbette carriages, the direction of their guns was good, the powder weak, and the fuzes entirely to long. I was quite well satisfied with the reconoiter, but having some suspicion of gun boats laying in Lucas bend, I requested Capt Stembell to throw some shell in the bend, this was done,—and caused the appearance of two gun boats, one of them followed us.— as it was not our intention to enter into an engagement we retreated and arrived at Cairo this day at 10 o'c A M. It is beyond doubt that on the bluffs at Columbus there is a camp of at least 2000 Men with two Batteries of Haevy guns about Six pieces in all, and opposite between Belmont and Lucas Bend there are about 1000 Men and some field pieces. It affords me pleasure to report the cool, calculating and energetic behavior of Capt Stembell his officers and men" Copy, DNA, RG 94, War Records Office, Union Battle Reports. *O.R.*, I, iii, 167–68; *O.R.* (Navy), I, xxii, 327–28.

On Sept. 9, Capt. William S. Hillyer wrote to Waagner. "I am directed by Genl Grant to acknowledge the receipt of your dispathes from 'Camp near Norfolk' and to inform you that he has issued orders to Col Wallace to send you four additional companies of Infantry and two days Rations for your whole command.— you will hold your position as long as you think it prudent to do so." Copies, DLC-USG, V, 1, 2, 3, 77; DNA, RG 393, USG Letters Sent. *O.R.*, I, iii, 480–81. On the same day, Hillyer wrote to Col. William H. L. Wallace. "You will send two days Rations to the troops at Norfolk and four additional companies without delay." Copies, DLC-USG, V, 1, 2, 3, 77; DNA, RG 393, USG Letters Sent.

To Maj. James Simons

—————

Head Quarters Dist S. E. Mo
Cairo Sept 9th 1861

Sir

You will proceed as early as practicable to Springfield Ills, and see his excellency the Governor of the State of Illinois and urge upon him the necessity of filling immediately the vacancies of Surgeons & Assistant Surgeons at least of the Ill Regts now stationed here

By order of
U. S. Grant
Brig Genl. Comdg

To Surgeon James Simmons
Medical Director of Dist
Cairo Ills

Copies, DLC-USG, V, 1, 2, 3, 77; DNA, RG 393, USG Letters Sent. See General Orders No. 4, Sept. 8, 1861, note 2.

To Maj. Gen. John C. Frémont

—————

Cairo, Sept 10, 1861.

Maj. Gen Fremont,

Commander Stoebel & Lieut. Phelps command Gun boat Lexington & Conestoga the two boats here the Lexington must lay up to repair machinery the Tyler is at Paducah.

U. S. Grant.

Telegram, copies, DNA, RG 393, Western Dept., Telegrams; DLC-USG, VIA, 1. On the same day, Maj. Gen. John C. Frémont had telegraphed to USG. "Who commands the gun boats." Copies, *ibid*. Frémont apparently wanted the information to incorporate in a telegram to Brig. Gen. Lorenzo Thomas. Copies, *ibid*. The *Lexington* was commanded by Commander Roger N. Stembel, the *Conestoga* by Lt. S. Ledyard Phelps.

To Maj. Gen. John C. Frémont

Cairo Ills Sept 10th 1861

To Maj Genl Fremont St Louis Mo

Our Troops from Norfolk have reconnoitred as far as Beckwith Farm[1] to day without finding an enemy.

They were supported by Gun Boats Conestoga & Lexington which have been engaged at long shot all day with two Rebel Boats. I fear they have gone beyond a masked Battery

A scout sent out yesterday reports the enemy as occupying the same position as the day before. They Received two Boat loads of reinforcements yesterday and a train load last night

Our works at Fort Holt are progressing finely

U. S. Grant
Brig Genl Comdg

Telegram, copies, DLC-USG, V, 4, 5, 7, 8, 78, VIA, 1; DNA, RG 393, USG Hd. Qrs. Correspondence; *ibid.*, Western Dept., Telegrams. On Sept. 10, 1861, Maj. Gen. John C. Frémont telegraphed to USG. "Dispatch received. Push forward actively on the Mo. side. Move the Gunboats cautiously, in concert with the troops on shore, and confine yourself to holding the positions we have taken in Kentucky. Gratified to know that Fort Holt is progressing well. Inform General Smith that the 11th Regiment Indiana Volunteers with three companies of regular cavalry and one company of volunteer cavalry left for Paducah this morning at four o'clock." Copies, DLC-USG, V, 4, 5, 7, 8, VIA, 1; DNA, RG 393, USG Hd. Qrs. Correspondence; *ibid.*, Western Dept., Telegrams. *O.R.*, I, iii, 484.

1. On the Mississippi River in Mo., about twelve miles south of Cairo.

To Maj. Gen. John C. Frémont

Head Quarters Dist. S. E. Mo
Cairo Sept 10th 1861

General

This morning Col Waagner started from Norfolk with all the force that could be spared from that point to reconnoitre towards Belmont supported by the Gun Boats Conestoga &

Lexington ~~They~~ He went as far as beckwith farm about five miles below Norfolk.—Found no regular force but had one man wounded and lost one Horse by shots from the Pickets of the Rebels.—The Gun Boats however penetrated further & found large numbers of Cavalry on the Missouri shore and as near as they could ascertain fifteen pieces of artillery on wheels and one large piece in position. Some of the pieces were ascertained to be 24 pounder rifled guns.

The Rebel Gun Boat Yankee could not be induced to come far from a Battery on the Ky shore. Capt Stembal however succeeded in bursting a shell in her wheel house disabling her so much that she retired working but one engine.

The Batteries on shore were silenced and the officers commanding Gun Boats think with considerable loss to the enemy on two occasions they saw shell explode in the midst of their batteries after which they could see by the aid of their Glasses men being ~~sent~~ carried to the rear. One man was wounded dangerously by a musket ball fired from the shore. Further than this no damage was sustained by either of the Boats.

The machinery of the Lexington is out of order and I have permitted her to go to mound city for repairs. All the forces show great alacrity in preparing for any movement that looks ~~as if it was to~~ meeting ~~an~~ the enemy and if disipline and drill was equal to their zeal I should feel great confidence even against large odds.

The enemy were seen to cross and recross the river with what design I am at a loss to tell—my impression is they want time to prepare either for defense of their present position or for an advance on one of our positions likely Paducah.

If it was discretionary with me with a little addition to my present force I would take Columbus Your order however will be executed

> Respectfully
> Your obt Servant
> U. S. GRANT
> Brig Genl Comdg

To Major Genl J. C. Fremont
Com Dep of the West
Saint Louis Mo

Copies, DLC-USG, V, 4, 5, 7, 8, 78; DNA, RG 94, War Records Office, Union
Battle Reports; *ibid.*, RG 393, USG Hd. Qrs. Correspondence. *O.R.*, I, iii, 168–
69; *O.R.* (Navy), I, xxii, 328. Much of the information was transmitted by
USG to Maj. Gen. John C. Frémont by telegram on the same date. "Gun Boats
returned. Engaged Batteries at Lucas Bend all day. Found sixteen guns on Mo
shore. Rebel Batteries all silenced. One man on Conestogo wounded. The Gun
Boat Yankee was disabled and would have been taken but for land battery near
Columbus. The Rebels must have suffered severely. Discovered large bodies of
Cavalry on Mo side Saw no troops on Kentucky side" Copies, DLC-USG, V, 4,
5, 7, 8, 78; DNA, RG 94, War Records Office, Union Battle Reports; *ibid.*, RG
393, USG Hd. Qrs. Correspondence; *ibid.*, Western Dept., Telegrams. *O.R.*, I,
iii, 168; *O.R.* (Navy), I, xxii, 329.
    Also on Sept. 10, 1861, Lt. S. Ledyard Phelps reported to Capt. Andrew
H. Foote. LS, DNA, RG 45, Area 5. *O.R.* (Navy), I, xxii, 324–25. On Sept. 13,
Commander Roger N. Stembel reported to Foote. *Ibid.*, pp. 326–27.

To Brig. Gen. John A. McClernand

Head Quarters Dist. S. E. Mo.
Cairo Sept. 10th 1861

GEN.

    In addition to the information called for in orders No 4[1] I
would like to have information of the amount of land transportation at this post. I want to know the number of teams in ~~the~~
possession of each regiment and also the number in the hands of
Post Quarter Master.

Respectfully
Your Obt. Svt.
U. S. GRANT
Brig. Gen. Com.

To Brig. Gen. J. A. McClernand
Comd.g Post
Cairo Illinois

ALS, McClernand Papers, IHi. On Sept. 10, 1861, Capt. Reuben B. Hatch, asst. q. m., wrote to USG. "I have the honor to report that I have in my possession at this time ready for service in the field the following means of land transportation viz

17—	6	mule teams complete
24—	4	" " "
2—	2	Horse " "

Col Wallace has transportation consisting of 20— 4 horse teams complete which have been turned over to him by this Dept. Of the condition of the other Regiments I cannot write as they have not been supplied in this Dept. All the above teams cannot be sent into the field as they comprise all I have and none would be left for local service." ALS, DNA, RG 393, District of Southeast Mo., Letters Received.

1. See General Orders No. 4, Sept. 8, 1861.

To Brig. Gen. Charles F. Smith

———

Cairo Illinois
September 10th 1861

GEN

The heavy ordnance I proposed sending you has not yet arrived. As soon as it reaches here it will be forwarded.

I am sending you today 50000 Rations.[1]

The Artillery you ask for cannot be spared from here I have however applied to Genl Fremont for two additional peices to be added to Lieut Willards Battery.

I regret to say also that it will be impossible to send you Cavalry from this Post for the present.

There are but three companies, only one of them fully armed, at all three posts, and Gen Fremont has directed me to send not less than two Companies to Fort Holt.

Please inform me if you have received information from up the Ohio.

The information I get here have rather indicated that the Rebels have withdrawn their forces from towards Paducah and are organizing at Columbus Ky where they now have not less than sixteen Regiments of Infantry, Thirteen seige Guns, four

Batteries of Field artillery and two Battallions of eight companies each of cavalry. In addition to this they have a column of two to three thousand on the Mo side opposite.

I get my information from an official of Maj Genl Polk, Brigading this command.

On the return of the Steamer Graham I will send her to Saint Louis and put some other Boat in her place

	Respectfully
To Gen C. F. Smith	Your Obt Servt
Comdg U. S. Forces	U. S. GRANT
Paducah Ky	Brig Genl Comdg

Copies, DLC-USG, V, 1, 2, 3, 78; DNA, RG 393, USG Letters Sent. *O.R.*, I, iii, 484–85.

1. On Sept. 10, 1861, USG wrote to Capt. Reuben C. Rutherford, post commissary. "You will please send aboard the Steamer Graham 50.000 rations to be shipped to the command at Paducah Ky as soon as possible. Report to me the amount of stores on hand. I do not want the exact amount but wish to know for about how many days" Copies, DLC-USG, V, 1, 2, 3, 77; DNA, RG 393, USG Letters Sent.

To Col. John Cook

———

Head Quarters Dist S. E. Mo
Cairo Sept 10th 1861

SIR

Pickets should be thrown out so as to guard every approach of the enemy to your Camp and also if practicable to watch his movements.

A Cavalry Picket should occupy the heights commanding Blandville & Fort Jefferson.[1]

Be careful to give such directions that your Pickets shall not be surprised but collect information as remote from your camp as possible

By order of
Brig Genl U. S. GRANT

Copies, DLC-USG, V, 1, 2, 3, 77; DNA, RG 393, USG Letters Sent.

1. Blandville, Ky., about ten miles southeast of Cairo on Mayfield Creek; Fort Jefferson, Ky., about five miles south of Fort Holt on the Mississippi River.

To Col. Friedrich Hecker

———

Head Quarters Dist S. E. Mo
Cairo Sept 10th 1861

SIR

Sergeant Jas. B. Mason and twenty men are sent to Fort Holt as Artillerymen to be attached to the command there

They will draw Rations on sperate provision Returns approved by the officer in charge of the Artillery at the Fort under whose command they will be

They are a Detachment of the 8th Mo Vols.

U. S. GRANT

To Col Hecker   Brig Genl Comdg
Comdg
Fort Holt Ky

Copies, DLC-USG, V, 1, 2, 3, 77; DNA, RG 393, USG Letters Sent.

To Col. Gustav Waagner

———

Head Quarters Dist S. E. Mo
Cairo Sept 10th 1861

SIR

You made the reconnoisance upon which the expedition to Norfolk was based and I directed therefore that you should have the direction of it.

Directions however does not necessarily imply command. A Senior should never knowingly be subjected to the orders of a junior, but may be directed by him.

In this case it is the order of the commanding officer communicated through the officer having direction that is being obeyed.

If therefore Col Oglesby has been longer in commission as a Col than yourself he will command whilst you may direct the position to be occupied by these troops

U. S. GRANT
Brig Genl Comdg

To Col Waagner
Chief of Artillery

Copies, DLC-USG, V, 1, 2, 3, 78; DNA, RG 393, USG Letters Sent.

To Capt. Reuben B. Hatch

Head Quarters Dist S. E. Mo
Cairo Sept 10th 1861

MAJ

In view of number of Steamers necessarily kept at this post and the importance of having them always ready for any service and in order I would suggest the propriety of employing a commandore for the fleet.

None but an energetic experienced Steamboatman should be employed, and such a one would add materially to our inland navy.

U. S. GRANT
Brig Genl Comdg

To Maj Hatch
Brig Q. M.
Cairo Ills

Copies, DLC-USG, V, 1, 2, 3, 78; DNA, RG 393, USG Letters Sent. See letter to Maj. Gen. John C. Frémont, Sept. 18, 1861. Reuben B. Hatch served as 1st lt., 8th Ill., before his appointment as capt. and asst. q. m., post of Cairo, on Aug. 3, 1861. Early letters addressed to Hatch as maj. and brigade q. m. reflect uncertainty about his status and duties.

To Capt. Reuben B. Hatch

Head Quarters Dist S. E. Mo
Cairo Sept 10th 1861

SIR

You will please engage the Steamer Swallow as a Hospital for the use of troops at Fort Holt and have her towed there at once.

I understand the steamer can be had for twenty five Dollars per day. More should not be paid

U. S. GRANT
Brig Genl Comdg

To Major Hatch
Brig Q. M.
Cairo Ills

Copies, DLC-USG, V, 1, 2, 3, 77; DNA, RG 393, USG Letters Sent.

To Maj. Gen. John C. Frémont

Head Quarters Dist S. E. Mo
Cairo Sept 11th 1861

MAJ GENL J. C. FREMONT
COMMANDING DEPT OF THE WEST
SAINT LOUIS MO

SIR

since my report of last night nothing has transpired of note except the information that reinforcements to the number of about 5000 men arrived at Columbus last night. About that number crossed to the Missouri shore.

The Rebels have not shown themselves as far up the River to day as yesterday.

To day a Soldier[1] representing himself as a member of Col Bowens[2] Regiment deserted and succeeded in reaching our Gun

Boat. He states that he is from Wisconsin, emigrated to southern Missouri last year and when our difficulties broke out was pressed into service. He says that Jeff. Thompson with about 2600 men, 700 of them Cavalry, occupy ground opposite Columbus. They are badly armed and clothed. Last night 5000 men from Louisiana Mississippi and Tennessee arrived and about an equal amount· crossed to Mo shore. These troops are represented as well clothed and armed. Provision Blankets, Clothing, Ammunition, and arms, are plenty in their camp. Thinks most of their Pork is obtained from Ohio. Hears the officers talk of attacking Birds Point and Cairo at times then again of awaiting an attack where they are. Are throwing up Breastworks along the whole front of Columbus. They are represented as to havinge from thirty five or forty peices of Field Artillery, a portion Rifled, and six or seven seige peices in position and more on the ground ready to put up.—In Col Bowens Regiment there are quite a number of northern men who are not there from choice, but only await an action to turn on their officers and leave the Southern Confederacy forever.

I would respectfully urge the necessity of having clothing of almost every discription particularly shoes, Blankets, and shirts forwarded here as soon as possible. Tents also are required.

Cavalry is much needed also. Cavalry equipments for the troops here, and more Batteries of light Artillery.

All the reinforcements that can be spared for this post, of every arm of service would be welcome.

There are Two Companies of the 7th Iowa Vols now stationed at Potosi Mo the balance of the Regt here. I would recomend that they be releived and sent to their Regiment

Respectfully
Yours Obt Servant
U. S. GRANT
Brig Genl Comdg

Copies, DLC-USG, V, 4, 5, 7, 8, 78; DNA, RG 393, USG Hd. Qrs. Correspondence. *O.R.*, I, iii, 486.

1. John L. Mann, formerly of Racine, Wis. Letter of "B.," Sept. 11, 1861, in *Chicago Tribune*, Sept. 13, 1861.

2. C.S.A. Col. John S. Bowen of Ga., USMA 1853, who had been captured at Camp Jackson while serving as chief of staff for Brig. Gen. Daniel M. Frost, was given command of the 1st Mo. after his release. Bowen, who had resigned as 2nd lt. in the Mounted Rifles on May 1, 1856, and had been an architect in St. Louis on the eve of the Civil War, was an acquaintance of USG. See letter to Julia Dent Grant, Oct. 1, 1861.

To Brig. Gen. John A. McClernand

Head Quarters, Dist. S. E. Mo.

Cairo September 11th 1861

GENERAL,

One of the three Gun Boats is at Paducah, one laid up for repairs and I think it would be imprudent to detach the third[1] to go so far as you propose.

The boat now undergoing repairs will be for service in a day or two if that will answer the purpose.

Yours &c

U. S. GRANT

Brig. Gen. Com Dist.

To Gen. J. A. McClernand
Comd.g Post
Cairo Ill.

ALS, McClernand Papers, IHi. Although the letter to which USG replied has not been found, Brig. Gen. John A. McClernand wrote a note concerning its contents. "Advise Genl Grant that I want one of the Gun boats to convoy a cargo of Hay from Smithland to this place—the boat to leave Smithland for here abt. daylight next Saturday" AD, *ibid*. On Sept. 11, 1861, McClernand replied to USG. "The Gun Boat, to be used, temporarily, as a convoy, will not be needed at Smithland before next Saturday morning, hence the Gun Boat at Paducah, if repaired, in time, will answer the purpose. If not, I will not expect one." Copy, *ibid*.

Also on Sept. 11, McClernand wrote to USG. "Col. Oglesby desires me to send a Steam Boat to Norfolk, to open a communication, by water, with that place, and to transport to & from that place, whatsoever may be needful. Before complying with the above request, I deem it proper to ask to be advised by you, whether one or more of the gun boats are below Norfolk and in a position to protect any boat I might send there." DfS, *ibid*.; LS, DNA, RG 393, District of Southeast Mo.,

Letters Received. On the same day, Capt. William S. Hillyer replied for USG. "I am instructed by Gen Grant to inform you that the Gun boat Connestoga is reconnoitring in the neighborhood of Cairo, and a steamboat should be put in communication between this post and Norfolk" ALS, McClernand Papers, IHi. McClernand then replied to USG. "I have the honor to inform you, that I caused the Steamer 'W. H. B' to lie to at 'Birds Point' last night, subject to the order of Col. Wallace for the purpose of communicating with these Head Quarters—also, the Steamer 'Rob Roy' Capt. Brown, to lie to, at 'Fort Holt' for the purpose of enabling Col. Ross to do the same." ALS, *ibid.* USG wrote across the bottom of McClernand's letter. "I think the same order should be observed evry night."

On Sept. 12, McClernand wrote to USG. "As the security of the Federal forces encamped at Norfolk, Missouri, will depend more or less upon the continuance of the Gun Boat now below that point, near there, I beg to be advised, in advance, of any order that may be made recalling her from that vicinity." ADfS, *ibid.* On the same day, Hillyer wrote to Capt. Reuben B. Hatch. "If you have a Steamboat that can be spared, a steamboat should be stationed at Norfolk for the use of the forces stationed there. The boat should not remain there at night except when protected by a Gun Boat" Copies, DLC-USG, V, 1, 2, 3, 77; DNA, RG 393, USG Letters Sent.

1. The *Tyler* was at Paducah, the *Lexington* under repair at Mound City, and the *Conestoga* ready for action.

To Brig. Gen. Charles F. Smith

———

Cairo Sept 11th 1861

Genl

I have just learned that a number of Minnie Rifles belonging to the Paducah City Guards are concealed on Capt McConnells place in the edge of the City.

A Negro Barber keeping shop on the cor of Court & Market Streets can point out to you a slave named Butch who concealed them or knows where they are.

Constable Dan Fourshee of Paducah is a man that I am told you can place reliance in to ferret out this matter

Respectfully
Yours Obt Servt

To Gen C. F Smith   U. S. Grant
Comdg Paducah Ky   Brig Genl Comdg

Copies, DLC-USG, V, 1, 2, 3, 78; DNA, RG 393, USG Letters Sent.

To Col. Richard J. Oglesby

————

Head Quarters Dist S. E. Mo
Cairo Sept 11th 1861

Col

Throw forward under the direction of Col Waagner as large a force as can be spared from Norfolk to reconnoitre down the River in conjunction with the Gun Boat Conestoga.

Norfolk must be held. Send back to your post for Rations. The forces from Cairo will be relieved as soon as another Regiment arrives to take their place

U. S. Grant
Brig Genl Comdg

To Col Oglesby Comdg
Norfolk Mo

Copies, DLC-USG, V, 1, 2, 3, 77; DNA, RG 393, USG Letters Sent. *O.R.*, I, iii, 487; *O.R.* (Navy), I, xxii, 329. On Sept. 11, 1861, Col. Richard J. Oglesby wrote to USG. "I have just received your order of this date through Col Wallace Yesterday I made a full recognoisance for 6 miles below this point. On the river road; full particulars of which were reported to Brig Gen John A McClernand— Twenty men in one day can ~~report~~ repair the road for Artillery, for Eight miles down the river to the Hunter farm, where the Rush Ridge road from Birds point is intersected. I have established pickets today, with the assistance of Col Dougherty, which will effectually protect this point. I would give you a detached statement of my position here, were it of importance enough. Should the enemy remain in force on this side of the river it may become necessary to send reinforcements here—As at present situated I am strong enough, excepting in Cavalry—You would greatly favor us by sending down one full Company of the latter well armed. We have none, except what we can borrow from Col Wallace at Birds Point—Yesterday Col Wagner accompanied me, with two pieces of Light Artillery, about three miles. I did not safe in taking my Regiment but one mile further on towards the enemy—Leaving Major Post in Command. I went on with the Cavalry squad some two miles, and had a fair view of their Camp, and witnessed the engagement between the Gun Boats and the Land and River forces of the enemy. They are several thousand strong, but I regret I cannot state more definitely their force. The Conestoga had left before I received your order, besides Col Wagner has not been here today to convey it, and I therefore have sent out no force. Will you allow the Tents of the 11th 22d and my own Regiments to be sent down, since we are to remain here for some time—I would be very glad to have my Company at Big Muddy relieved immediately, as I shall need my whole force here. I will communicate all material facts—The forces here are as follows

11th Regt 200—22d 496, 8th Regt 626—and 4 Guns of Capt Taylors Battery Will you allow us to be supplied with Ice daily as the water is miserable—"
ALS, DNA, RG 393, District of Southeast Mo., Letters Received. Reports of action near Norfolk, Mo., Sept. 10 and 11, 1861, from Brig. Gen. John A. McClernand to Maj. Gen. John C. Frémont are in *O.R.*, I, iii, 169. See also *ibid.*, p. 488.

To Col. Gustav Waagner

Head Quarters Dist S. E. Mo
Cairo Sept 11th 1861

COL

You will renew your reconnoisance of yesterday pushing as far down the River as practicable and annoying the enemy in every way possible.

Col Oglesby is instructed to give you all the force that can be spared from Norfolk and the Gun Boat Conestoga will act in conjunction with you.

Should you make any important discoveries inform me as early as possible.

U. S. GRANT
Brig Genl Comdg

To Col Waagner
Chief of Artillery
Norfolk Mo

Copies, DLC-USG, V, 1, 2, 3, 77; DNA, RG 393, USG Letters Sent. *O.R.*, I, iii, 487; *O.R.* (Navy), I, xxii, 329.

To Charles Ford

Cairo, September 11th 1861

DEAR FORD:

My clothing has come at last but no bill with it. Please send the bill and inform me how much money you had to send to my wife.

Things down here begin to look like work. Whether there will be any regular engagement soon or not is hard to foresee. Either party could bring such a thing about very easily.

The papers keep you advised of all the facts and a greatdeel more so that it will not be necessary for me, as busy as I am kept, to write more on the subject.

Yours Truly
U. S. Grant

ALS, USG 3.

To Mary Grant

Cairo,
September 11th, 1861.

Dear Sister:

Your letter with a short one from Father was received yesterday, and having a little time I answer it.

The troops under me and the rebel forces are getting so close together however that I have to watch all points. Since taking command I have taken possession of the Kentucky bank opposite here, fortified it and placed four large pieces in position. Have occupied Norfolk, Missouri, and taken possession of Paducah. My troops are so close to the enemy as to occasionally exchange shots with the pickets. To day, or rather last night, sixty or seventy rebels came upon seventeen of our men and were repulsed with a loss of two men killed on their side, none hurt on ours. Yesterday there was skirmishing all day. We had but two wounded however, whilst the loss must have been considerable on the other.

What future operations will be, of course I don't know. I could not write about it in advance if I did. The rebel force numerically is much stronger than ours, but the difference is more than made up by having truth and justice on our side, whilst on the other they are cheered on by falsehood and deception. This war however is formidable and I regret to say cannot end so soon as I anticipated at first.

Father asks for a position for Albert Griffith.[1] I have no place to give and at best could use only my influence. I receive letters from all over the country for such places, but do not answer them. I never asked for my present position, but now that I have it I intend to perform the duties as rigidly as I know how without looking out for places for others. I should be very glad if I had a position within my own gift for Al. but I have not.

My duties are very laborious and have been from the start. It is a rare thing that I get to bed before two or three o'clock in the morning and am usually wakened in the morning before getting awake in a natural way. Now, however, my staff are getting a little in the way of this kind of business and can help me.

I have been stopped so often already in writing this that I have forgotten what I was going to write about.

Are you talking of paying Julia a visit? I wrote to you and father about it several times but have failed to elicit an answer on that point. I intended to have Julia, Miss[2] and Jess come down here to pay me a visit but I hardly think it would be prudent at this time. Hearing artillery within a few miles it might embarrass my movements to have them about. I am afraid they would make poor soldiers.

Write to me again soon.

Good night.
ULYS.

J. G. Cramer, pp. *56–58.*

1. Albert Griffith was probably a son of Mary Simpson Griffith, a sister of USG's mother.
2. Ellen Grant.

To Richardsen, Spence & Thompson

Cairo, Ill.

Sept. 11th 1861

MESSRS RICHARDSEN, SPENCE & THOMPSON
NEW [*York*] CITY N. Y.
SIRS:

The clothing ordered from you has all arrived with the exception of sword belts. I wish you would send me, to be paid on delivery one sword belt for Brigadier General, and one for Aid to Brigadier.

I would be pleased if you will send these immediately upon receipt of this. Send by Express to this place to collect on delivery.

If you do not keep these articles please turn the order over to Mr. Hosseman and advise me if the articles will be sent.

U. S. GRANT
Brig. Gen. U. S. A.

Copy, NN. An undated fragment, apparently a portion of the original order sent in Aug., 1861, gave USG's measurements.

"Round the Breast under the Coat	35½
" " Waist " " "	31
From Middle Back Seam to Elbow	20½
" Elbow to rist for length of sleeves	12½
From Collar Seam to hip button	19
Hip Buttons to bottom of skirt for length of Coat	16
Round the rist	8
" " Elbow	12
For pants	
Round the Waist	29
From top of Waistband to bottom outside	49

Please send in addition to the above one set of buttons and shoulder straps. The pants I would like full in the legs and quite long." ADS, Joseph L. Eisendrath, Jr., Highland Park, Ill.

To Maj. Gen. John C. Frémont

Cairo, Sept 12, 1861.

GEN J. C. FREMONT

Cannot the troops moved from this place to Paducah or a part of them be returned; more troops are needed here.

U. S. GRANT,
Brig. Gen.

Telegram, copies, DNA, RG 393, Western Dept., Telegrams; DLC-USG, VIA, 1. *O.R.*, I, iii, 488. On Sept. 12, 1861, Maj. Gen. John C. Frémont replied to USG. "I will send you more troops. Keep me informed minutely." Copies, DNA, RG 393, Western Dept., Telegrams; *ibid.*, USG Hd. Qrs. Correspondence; DLC-USG, V, 4, 5, 7, 8, VIA, 1. *O.R.*, I, iii, 489. It was probably in response to this telegram that USG telegraphed to Frémont on the same day. "Twentieth Ills. vol. & Capt Stewarts cavalry have just arrived from Cape Girardeau." Copies, DNA, RG 393, Western Dept., Telegrams; DLC-USG, VIA, 1.

To Maj. Gen. John C. Frémont

Cairo, Sept 12, 1861.

GEN. J. C. FREMONT,

None of the guns from Pittsburg have yet arrived. I have informed Gen Smith that I would send him six.

U. S. GRANT.

Telegram, copies, DNA, RG 393, Western Dept., Telegrams; DLC-USG, VIA, 1. On Sept. 12, 1861, Maj. Gen. John C. Frémont had telegraphed to USG. "How many of the sixteen guns from Pittsburg went to Paducah? Were they complete with carriages and had they an ample supply of ordnance stores? Is Captain Foote at Cairo?" Copies, *ibid.*, V, 4, 5, 7, 8, VIA, 1; DNA, RG 393, USG Hd. Qrs. Correspondence; *ibid.*, Western Dept., Telegrams. After receiving USG's reply, Frémont telegraphed. "When the guns arrive from Pittsburg, send six of them to Paducah as you propose and complete with ordnance stores. Telegraph me extent of supply of ammunition received with guns. Large re-enforcements of cavalry will be sent you at once" Copies, *ibid.* On the same day, Frémont again telegraphed to USG. "I will send tomorrow for Paducah three twenty four pound guns, with siege carriages, and one hundred and twenty five solid shot; one hundred and fifty spherical case shot and one hundred shells. Also a battery of light artillery with ammunition." Copies, *ibid.*, USG Hd. Qrs. Correspondence; DLC-USG, V, 4, 5, 7, 8. See letter to Maj. Gen. John C. Frémont, Sept. 13, 1861.

To Maj. Gen. John C. Frémont

Cairo, Sept 12, 1861.

Maj. Gen Fremont,

Can Gen Smith have authority to have a telegraph put up from here to Paducah.

U. S. Grant

Telegram, copies, DNA, RG 393, Western Dept., Telegrams; DLC-USG, VIA, 1. On Sept. 13, 1861, Maj. Gen. John C. Frémont replied to USG. "I will order a telegraph line from Cairo to Paducah." Copy, DNA, RG 393, Western Dept., Telegrams. Also on Sept. 13, Alexander Asboth telegraphed to USG. "Paducah should be immediately connected with Cairo & St. Louis by telegraph, in accordance with Gen Smiths proposal—The funds required by Gen. Smith will be sent at once." Copies, *ibid.*; *ibid.*, USG Hd. Qrs. Correspondence; DLC-USG, VIA, 1.

To Maj. Gen. John C. Frémont

Head Quarters Dist S. E. Mo
Cairo Sept 12th 1861

To Maj Genl Jno C Fremont
Comdg Dep of the West
Saint Louis Mo
Sir

To day our scouts have not been able to discover any thing of the enemy. A reconnoisance has been made of the Roads around Fort Jefferson and I shall take possission of it day after tomorrow with most of the force at Fort Holt. A Battery at fort Jefferson will not command down the River but very little but commands up to the mouth of the Ohio completely.

I am told that a paper picked up below here today gives the

Rebels loss in the little engagement with our Gun Boats yesterday at 68 killed three Guns and Gun Boat Yankee disabled and a large number wounded. Of course the Federal loss is reported very large.

McCulloch is reported to have been in Columbus within the last few days. He is such an ubiquitous character that I place no great reliance in it.

I would earnestly repeat my recomendation that a complete assortment of clothing be sent here ~~immediately~~ at once, also accoutrements arms & Tents.

I am very glad to hear that Cavalry is to come here immediately and would also be pleased to hear of the expected arrival of more Artillery.

I am of opinion that if a demonstration was made from Paducah towards Union City[1] supported by two columns on the Kentucky side from here. The Gun Boats and a force moving upon Belmont the enemy would be forced to leave Columbus leaving behind their heavy ordnance.

I submit this to your consideration and will hold myself in readiness to execute this or any plan you may adopt.

I enclose you a map[2] giving a sketch of the proposed field of operations.

I telegraphed to day requesting that six Telescopes be sent here.[3] They were suggested by Col Waagner and I think are much needed.

A Large map of Kentucky is much needed. The Austrian musket[4] now in the hands of some of our men are reported to be entirely unreliable. The difficulty seems to be more in the Cap than in the arm itself.

> Respectfully
> Your Obt Servant
> U. S. GRANT
> Brig Genl Comdg

Copies, DLC-USG, V, 4, 5, 7, 8, 78; DNA, RG 393, USG Hd. Qrs. Correspondence. *O.R.*, I, iii, 488–89. On Sept. 12, 1861, USG telegraphed the substance of his letter to Maj. Gen. John C. Frémont. "Fort Jefferson does not command the river. I had a reconnaisance made to day the enemy have not moved today I am informed that the rebels report sixty eight (68) Killed three (3) pieces on the gun boat Yankee disabled yesterday. McColloch is reported to have been in Columbus in consultation." Copy, DNA, RG 393, Western Dept., Telegrams.

On Sept. 11, Frémont had telegraphed in Hungarian to USG and Brig. Gen. Charles F. Smith. "Fort Jefferson desires one battery, but you should prepare the road for both advance and retreat, properly utilizing our natural advantages along the line of Mayfield Creek from the Mississippi to Lovelaceville. If the enemy cannot be prevented from crossing at Belmont, their advance to Charleston should be prevented. Inform me about our present strength on the Kentucky shore and the Missouri shore." Copy (Hungarian), *ibid.* Another translation of this telegram in the USG letterbooks, misdated Sept. 12, is in *O.R.*, I, iii, 489. On Sept. 11, USG telegraphed in Hungarian to Frémont. "Fort Jefferson is the top of the hill opposite the First Island four miles below Fort Holt and it controls the roads to Blandville and Mellborn, the line of Mayfield Creek, the river and the branch of the river. . . . Belmont doesn't control it." Copy (Hungarian), DNA, RG 393, Western Dept., Telegrams.

1. Union City, Tenn., about forty miles south of Cairo, and about twenty miles south of Columbus, Ky.

2. The map has not been found.

3. On Sept. 12, USG telegraphed to Frémont. "We are in want of six (6) field telescopes for the use of this point." Copies, *ibid.*; DLC-USG, VIA, 1.

4. See letter to Maj. Gen. John C. Frémont, Sept. 15, 1861, and Testimony, Oct. 31, 1861.

To Col. John Cook

Head Quarters Dist S. E. Mo
Cairo Sept 12th 1861

Sir

All Boats passing your Post not recognized as in the employ of the Government will be hailed and brought to, papers examined and if necessary cargo.

Every thing must be done to prevent the Enemy receiving supplies.

The works on the fortifications should be pushed forward as rapidly as possible. Protect all loyal Citizens in all their right but carry out the proclamation of Genl Fremont upon all subjects known to come under it.¹ Keep out Pickets & scouts so that you cannot be surprised.

I have no information about the Home Guards under your command but so long as they carry U. S. arms and government rations they are entirely subject to the orders of the commanding officer.

Should they refuse to obey you arrest the officers disarm the soldiers and report the matter at once to Genl. Fremont and also to me.

If you are strong enough to give protection to points distant from you it may be done, but be cautious to have always the post protected.

I approve of your course sending Capt Stewarts Cavalry by boat. I should not have ordered them by land after the storm of yesterday.

See that your Post is constantly kept supplied with rations at least ten days ahead and that a full supply of ammunition of all kinds is constantly on hand

U. S. Grant
Brig Genl Comdg

To Col Jno Cook Comdg
Cape Girardeau Mo

Copies, DLC-USG, V, 1, 2, 3, 77; DNA, RG 393, USG Letters Sent. *O.R.*, I, iii, 490. On Sept. 14, 1861, Col. John Cook wrote to USG. "In conformity with your order I have commenced work in earnest on the fortifications at this Post, and owing to the insufficiency of citizen labor have issued a genl order for detail of fifty privates 1. Lt. 1 Sergt. & 2 corporals daily (Sunday excepted) from the 7th Ills. & 11 Mo. the only regiments here, and this detail together with detail Genl. & Camp Guard very materially weakens our means of defense leaving in my own Regt. less than two Hundred men for drill (which is greatly needed) and other purposes, and if you will allow me the privilege I would earnestly recommend the stationing of at least one more regiment at this Post, with a similar detail from one more Regt. the work could be soon completed. Small bands of armed rebels who have followed at a distance in the wake of our column are now collecting at different points in the neighborhood & are doing considerable damage to the property of Union citizens threatning lives &c but from the limited force especially the absense of Cavalry little or nothing can be done to afford the protection they ask and really seem to need Every thing is being used to protect and hold the Post, and hope soon to receive permission to report at your Head Quarters and report such facts as may more fully inform you in relation to matters here. I have in my charge several prisners of war recieved from Col. Marsh and one arrested by & recieved from Genl. Prentiss with indeffinite and untenible charges as I am not able (knowing as little as I do of the whereabouts of or names of witnesses against them to proceed with much certainty. Among the number is Major Beatty of Jackson & a rebel capt Woods the latter arrested by order of Genl. Prentiss and detained without trial until now, with your permission I would like to bring them before you for investigation, but if you direct I can examine them and if they return to their allegiance under the proclamation discharge them. I am told the most if not all already desire to do so. I am gratified to communicate the fact that all is peacefull & quiet here and secession sentiment in this immediate vicinity is decreasing. I should be greatly pleased to have you at your leisure visit the Post and receive instructions from you—You would greatly oblige me by the issue of an order upon my Reg. the 7th Ills to the commandants of companies to fill their companies within a certain time or compel them to give way to full companies that are and have been waiting to join the Regt. all have had an abundance of time allowed them for this purpose and a non compliance has not only rendered the Regt. inefficient, but the order for equalization of companies taking from active officers men for even temporary use of Lazy ones is tending to a demoralization of the whole. Your early attention to this matter which is for the best interests of the service is earnistly desired." LS, DNA, RG 393, District of Southeast Mo., Letters Received.

1. In a proclamation of Aug. 30, Maj. Gen. John C. Frémont established martial law in Mo. and declared that property of actively disloyal persons would be confiscated. Slaves of such persons were "hereby declared freemen." *O.R.*, I, iii, 466–67. Because Frémont's proclamation involved emancipation, it had widespread political repercussions, and contributed to his eventual removal from command of the Western Dept.

To Col. Richard J. Oglesby

Head Quarters Dist S. E. Mo
Cairo Sept 12th 1861

COL

You will continue to occupy Norfolk. Throw out Pickets to keep you constantly informed of the movements of the enemy but make no movements with the main body of your command without further instructions unless it should be necessary for protection.

Your whole command should have their baggage with them and I gave directions to that effect yesterday.

Have delivered to Col Waagner the accompanying orders I direct him to come here and report to me for other service

U. S. GRANT
Brig Genl Comdg

To Col Oglesby
Comdg
Norfolk Mo

Copies, DLC-USG, V, 1, 2, 3, 77; DNA, RG 393, USG Letters Sent. *O.R.*, I, iii, 489. *O.R.* identifies the letter to Col. John Cook of Sept. 12, 1861, as an enclosure in the letter to Col. Richard J. Oglesby, but gives no explanation. On Sept. 12, Oglesby wrote to USG. "I have just returned from a march of four miles inland from Norfolk, in the direction of the enemy. I find the country thickly wooded but cut by several fit for artillery to approach for the marshes are substantially dry, not affected by the late rain to impede the march of an army. The two bridges destroyed some days ago are of no consequence, as the sloughs are passable at several points near there. Lieut—Tuffts was directed to approach the lines of the enemies pickets of this side of the Hunter farm. He has about 25 Cavalry men with him. Will be in tonight if anything important is reported will inform you" ALS, DNA, RG 393, District of Southeast Mo., Letters Received.

To Julia Dent Grant

————

Cairo, Sept. 12th 1861

DEAR JULIA,

I have been intending to send for you to come here but now things begin to look so much like a fight that I hardly think it would be prudent. The Rebels are in large force and we are near enough to have little brushes occationally with our Gun Boats and scouting parties.

Yesterday we had quite a little brush all day, resulting however in only two wounded on our side.[1] To-day some of our scouts picked up a paper printed in New Madrid in which they acknowledge 68 killed, their Gun Boat and three pieces of Artillery disabled, and many men wounded.

To-day they have not come out. I should like very much to have you here but I am afraid that it might embarass my movements.

Has Ford sent you the money yet I left with him? and how much? I will send you $100 each month hereafter and want you to save all you can. I can spare that and pay up my debts besides. When they are paid I can spare $250 pr month. Dr. Sharp is with me. I received a letter from Emma yesterday and will answer it soon.

Jim Casey is a Union man very much to your fathers disgust. The Dr. went out to see him and says that he considers us all against him. With all that however he is very much elated at the idea of my being a Brigadier.

My labor is excessive but I never enjoyed better health in my life. I have a large command and have to look out for all points and it keeps me very busy.

How I should like to see you all in Galena.

When I was in St. Louis I had some business at the Arsenal geting arms for some of my troops. As I passed by I stoped in at the Lynches for a few minuets. They all enquired very particularly for you. Rose has written me a letter since and said she was going to write to you.

I have not answered her letter yet and as I have so little time do not know that I shall. If you write to her however you might mention that I received it.

I have the Regt. that young Drum[2] is in, in my command and had the one Col. Chetlain[3] is in also a few days ago. I sent them to Paducah. Remember me to all our friends and our neighbors. I am still in hopes that it will not be a great while before I will see you all.

It is after 12 o'clock, at night, and I must close to get my letter in to-night. Good buy. Kisses to all the children, & yourself from me. Tell Buck to kiss Susy Felt for me.

ULYS.

ALS, DLC-USG.

1. See letter to Mary Grant, Sept. 11, 1861.
2. See letter to Julia Dent Grant, Aug. 15, 1861, note 2.
3. Lt. Col. Augustus L. Chetlain, 12th Ill.

To Maj. Gen. John C. Frémont

Head Quarters Dist S. E. Mo
Cairo Sept 13th 1861

MAJ GENL FREMONT SAINT LOUIS

Ten thirty two pounder Guns with barbette and chaise Carriages—six eight inch columbiads with Carriages—560—8 inch shells, 770—32 pounder cannon Balls 30 Boxes ordnance stores and ten Bundles wood for eight inch circular Platforms arrived from Pittsburg

U. S. GRANT

Telegram, copies, DLC-USG, V, 4, 5, 7, 8, 78, VIA, 1; DNA, RG 393, USG Hd. Qrs. Correspondence; *ibid.*, Western Dept., Telegrams. On Sept. 13, 1861, Maj. Gen. John C. Frémont telegraphed to USG. "Telegram about guns from Pittsburg has been received." Copies, DLC-USG, V, 4, 5, 7, 8, VIA, 1; DNA, RG 393, USG Hd. Qrs. Correspondence; *ibid.*, Western Dept., Telegrams. On Sept. 13, Capt. William S. Hillyer wrote to Capt. William F. Brinck. "You will have 4 Peices of the Cannon which arrived this morning from Pittsburg delivered at the Wharf Boat for shipment to Paducah on tomorrow mornings boat, also a proportionate amount of the ammunition" Copies, DLC-USG, V, 1, 2, 3, 77; DNA, RG 393, USG Letters Sent.

To Maj. Gen. John C. Frémont

Head Quarters, Dist. S. E. Mo.
Cairo, September 13th 1861

GENERAL:

Your telegraph enquiring "by what authority I had telegraphed Major Montgomery[1] of Indianapolis Ia. for wagons" is received. I replied by telegraph that I had not telegraphed Maj. Montgomery nor anyone els in Indianapolis for supplies of any kind. I had sent no place but St. Louis for supplies

This statement may explain however. The 23d Indiana regiment come here with a class of arms that had been supplied them by their state and such as we have not got at this post, consequently had no ammunition suitable for them. On their arrival at Paducah Lieut. Col. Anthony[2] of said regiment was sent back to Indianapolis, not by my order, after ammunition.

Col. A. stated that Gov. Morton[3] had agreed to supply his regiment with transportation and requested a letter from me to the Governor urging it to be furnished speedily. He was informed that I could not hold official communication with Governor Morton.—I gave Col. Anthony a letter[4] however stating my inability to furnish him with the kind of ammunition he required immediately and that if the Gov. of Indiana furnished it he would be doing the Government a service

This was entirely unofficial and could not have been made use of before to-day. Any telegraph sent has certainly been without my concent or knowledge.

My letter to Col. Anthony not being official I did not save a copy of it, but the purport is, as near as I can recollect, as given above.

> Respectfully
> Your Obt. Svt.
> U. S. GRANT
> Brig. Gen.

To Gen. J. C. Fremont
Comd.g Dept. of the West
St. Louis Mo.

ALS, DNA, RG 393, Western Dept., Letters Received. On Sept. 13, 1861, Maj. Gen. John C. Frémont had telegraphed to USG. "By what authority have you acted in telegraphing to Maj. Montgomery at Indianapolis for wagons and teams?" Copy, *ibid.*, Letters Sent (Press). On the same day, USG replied by telegraph. "I have sent no telegraph to Maj. Montgomery or no one else at Indianapolis have sent no place for anything wanted here except St. Louis." Copies, *ibid.*, Telegrams; DLC-USG, VIA, 1. On Sept. 15, Frémont again telegraphed to USG. "Your reply of 13th received—Telegram from Major Montgomery at Indianapolis was received stating that that Genl. Grant had telegraphed to him for wagons & teams, hence my inquiry by what authority you had acted. I have telegraphed to Major M. to Explain." Copies, *ibid.* On Sept. 16, Maj. Alexander Montgomery wrote to Frémont. "I enclose herewith a letter from Gov Morton and a copy of a letter from Genl Grant to Lt Col D C. Anthony 23d Regt Ind Vols. asking the latter to call on his Excellency the Governor for ammunition and transportation. I was under the impression that the call was made by telegram, and hence my telegram to Maj McKinstry." ALS, DNA, RG 393, Western Dept., Letters Received. The enclosures are missing.

1. Maj. Alexander Montgomery of Pa., USMA 1834, asst. q.m. stationed at Indianapolis, Ind.
2. Lt. Col. DeWitt C. Anthony, 23rd Ind.
3. Oliver Perry Morton, governor of Ind., 1861–67.
4. This letter has not been found.

To Brig. Gen. John A. McClernand

Head Quarters, Dist. S. E. Mo
Cairo, Sept. 13th 1861

GEN.

Whilst on the Mo. side of the river to-day I planned a reconnoisance from Birds Point towards Charleston and from Norfolk towards Belmont, and gave the necessary orders at the latter place whilst there.[1]

To-night I gave orders for the expedition from Birds Point and directed a copy of the order to be sent to you. Maj. Brayman[2] informs me that it was not sent however. ~~and~~ I will furnish it to-morrow.

Respectfully
Your Obt. Svt.
U. S. GRANT
Brig. Gen. Com Dist.

To Brig. Gen. J. A. McClernand
Comd.g U. S Forces
Cairo Ill.

ALS, McClernand Papers, IHi.

1. See letters to Cols. Richard J. Oglesby and William H. L. Wallace, Sept. 13, 1861.
2. Maj. Mason Brayman of Springfield, Ill., served on the staff of Brig. Gen. John A. McClernand while holding rank in the 29th Ill.

To Brig. Gen. John A. McClernand

—————

Head Quarters Dist S. E. Mo
Cairo Sept 13th 1861

SPECIAL ORDERS

The Troops now at Fort Holt Ky, with the exception of the 24th Ill Vol Col Hecker commanding, the detachment of artillery and Capt Delano's[1] company of Cavalry will march tomorrow and take position at Fort Jefferson Ky.

Colonel Ross will select the position for the camp establish guards and make all needful regulations for the new camp

The movement will be protected from the water by Gun Boat Taylor[2]

By Order of Brig Genl Grant
WM. S. HILLYER
Capt & Aid de Camp

To Brig Genl McClernand
Comd.g Post
Cairo Ills

DS, McClernand Papers, IHi.

1. Capt. Sterling P. Delano, 2nd Ill. Cav.
2. When Commander John Rodgers purchased the steamer *A. O. Tyler* for conversion to a gunboat, he suggested that a change of name to "Taylor" might be auspicious. *O.R.* (Navy), I, xxii, 283. He based his recommendation on the decision of former President John Tyler to support the Confederacy. The gunboat was known officially as *Tyler*, but Rodger's recommendation was not entirely ignored: there are frequent references to the gunboat as "Taylor" in military records.

To Col. Richard J. Oglesby

————

Head Quarters Dist. S. E. Mo
Cairo Sept 13th 1861

COL

Tomorrow I would like to have a reconnoisance down the River as far as you can safely go.

Take all the force that can be spared. At the same time an expedition will be sent out from Birds Point towards Charleston and one from Fort Holt.

It is important to find the position of the enemy if possible.

U. S. GRANT
Brig Genl Comdg

To Col R. J. Oglesby
Comdg U. S. Forces
at Norfolk Mo

Copies, DLC-USG, V, 1, 2, 3, 77; DNA, RG 393, USG Letters Sent. *O.R.*, I, iii, 491. On Sept. 16, 1861, Col. Richard J. Oglesby wrote to USG. "Under the order of the General, Commanding in South East Mo, I moved with my entire command on Saturday morning 14th inst to observe the position of the enemy, in the direction of Belmont—At 10 a. m. the advance guard left camp under Command of Colonel Dougherty, at 11 ½ o'clock I followed with the 8th Reg't At four o'clock I joined the forces under Col Dougherty at the junction of the Charleston and Norfolk Roads, six miles above Belmont Col Dougherty had advanced one mile further down the river and returned to meet me at the point indicated; We saw nothing of the enemy excepting a Company of Cavalry, some two miles below the junction of the Roads; They disappeared as soon as the Gun Boat moved in that direction. I am satisfied the enemy has no ~~enemy~~ encampment this side of Belmont—nor do I think they intend any movement against us from that place. I could not correctly learn the enimies strength, but think it not over Three Thousand, and and about nine pieces of Artillery; We found the road entirely accessible to Artillery. We were between nine and Ten miles below Norfolk; The day was excessively hot, and the men suffered a good deal going down. I returned to Camp at 10 o'clock P. M.—I have been so unwell since my return, that it has been impossible to make any report of my actions. The Officers and men behaved well, and Col Dougherty aided me most heartily in everything pertaining to the expedition" ALS, DNA, RG 393, District of Southeast Mo., Letters Received.

To Col. William H. L. Wallace

———

Head Quarters, Dist. S. E. Mo
Cairo, September 13th 1861

COL.

You will please detach one Company of your command, (Cavalry) to report to Col. Oglesby to-morrow for special service.

U. S. GRANT
Brig. Gen. Com.

To Col. Wallace
Comd.g Forces
Paducah[1] Mo.

ALS, MoSHi.

1. An error for Bird's Point.

To Col. William H. L. Wallace

———

Head Quarters Dist S. E. Mo
Cairo Sept 13th 1861

SIR

You will please direct a reconnoisance towards Charleston with as large a force as can be spared from your command tomorrow.

It is important to find out the position of the enemy and I wish it conducted with a view of ascertaining if he has taken up a position in that direction

Col Oglesby has been directed to make a similar movement toward Belmont

U. S. GRANT
Brig Genl Comdg

To Col W. H. L. Wallace
Comdg U. S. Forces
Birds Point Ky.

Copies, DLC-USG, V, 1, 2, 3, 77; DNA, RG 393, USG Letters Sent; McClernand
Papers, IHi. *O.R.*, I, iii, 491. On Sept. 14, 1861, Col. William H. L. Wallace
wrote to USG. "In obedience to an order recieved from you late last night, I sent
a detachment of 85 cavalry, at 6 ½ o'clock this morning, and a detachment of
infantry amount to 240 men at 7 ½ o'clock by the rail road train, with directions
to meet at Charleston at 10 o'clock & reconnoitre that vicinity to ascertain
whether the enemy have any position in that neighborhood—The cavalry force
consisted of 20 men of Capt. Nolemans company—45 men of Capt. Pfaffs company 20 men of Capt. Burrills company and the infantry, and of 50 of Co. K. 11th
Regt. Ill. Capt. Carter—110 of companies E & G. 20th Ill—80 of companies C &
G 2nd Iowa. The Cavalry force is under the direction of Lieut. Tufts of Capt.
Nolemans cavalry—Col. Tuttle of the 2nd Iowa has command of the infantry &
general direction of the whole force. I have also ordered Capt Stewarts cavalry
company to move to Norfolk & report to Col. Oglesby. They left at about 7 o'clock
this morning. I also sent Capt Noleman with 30 of his men to Norfolk at 6 ½ o'clk
to report to Col. Oglesby for special duty for today. The cavalry force at Col
Oglesbys disposal today amounts to something over 100 strong. I trust the commanding General will excuse me for referring to a matter which I fear may lead
to confusion & misunderstanding Brig. Genl. McClernand has assumed command
of the forces at Cairo, Birds point & Mound city & has directed me to make
consolidated reports of the forces at this point to him. The same order gives Col.
Waagner command of the artillery forces & directs all artillery companies to
report to him. It thus seems that the forces under my command & which I am
directed to report, are subject to be removed from my command without any notice
to me. As an instance of this, I learned incidentally this morning that Capt. Buel
of the artillery recieved an order from Col. Waagner direct & not through me to
have a section of his battery in readiness to move at a moments notice with six
days rations. I mention this matter at this time & in this manner not that I am
disposed to complain on my own account, but lest the interest of the service may
suffer by orders being given by the different commanders without a perfect understanding as to what the other commanders have ordered or intend to order. As I
understand the state of the command here, you have the general command of all
the forces in South Eastern Missouri & at Cairo, and now those at Fort Holt &
Paducah. Genl. McClernand in subordination to your general command and in
accordance with directions from Maj. Genl. Fremont assumes the immediate
command of the forces at Cairo, Birds point & Mound city. According to my
understanding of military law I would be justified in disregarding any orders
except those given me through or by my immediatel commander. But I do not
make this point practically, but have obeyed orders directly from yourself, & I
only allude to the subject from the fear that confusion may arise from this departure
from military law." ALS, DNA, RG 393, District of Southeast Mo., Letters
Received; LS, McClernand Papers, IHi. On Sept. 14, Capt. William S. Hillyer
replied to Wallace. "I am directed by Genl Grant to reply to your communication
and state to you that your views as to the proper method of transmitting orders
are correct as a general rule. But the order of a senior officer must always be
obeyed whatever may be the channel of communication Emergencies frequently
arise where the delay of communicating orders through an intermediate authority
cannot be suffered. When Genl Grant published the order last night it was at two
late an hour to send it through Genl McClernand and have you get in time. You
would probably not have received it before morning.—He therefore sent the

order direct to you and a copy of it to Genl McClernand that he might have early information of the movement. In reference to Col Waagners position, he is chief of all the artillery at this Post including Cairo Birds Point Fort Holt & Norfolk and his authority over it is similar to that of a Colonel over his Regiment. The portion of the artillery at any point is under the command of the commanding officer at such point and all orders should be communicated through him. The order given by Col Waagner was certainly irregular but was done in consequence of his knowledge that the order was about to be made by General Grant" Copies, DLC-USG, V, 1, 2, 3, 77; DNA, RG 393, USG Letters Sent.

To John A. Kasson

Head Quarters, Cairo Ill.
September 13th 1861

HON J. A. KASSON
1ST ASST. P. M. GEN.
WASHINGTON D. C.
SIR;

Permit me to recommend to you for the position of Mail Agent between Evansville Indiana and this place the name of O. H. Ross.[1]

Mr. Ross is entirely capable and will no doubt give entire satisfaction to the Department should he be appointed. He is now performing the services from here to Paducah Ky.[2] and probably without a prospect of any compensation.

Respectfully
Your Obt. Svt.
U. S. GRANT
Brig. Gen. Com.

ALS, PHi. John A. Kasson, Iowa Republican politician, had been appointed 1st asst. postmaster-general by President Abraham Lincoln.

1. Orlando H. Ross. See letter to Julia Dent Grant, June 27, 1861, note 1.
2. On Sept. 13, 1861, USG appointed Ross by order. "O. H. Ross is hereby appointed mail agent between Cairo and Paducah until such time as Government may establish a regular mail on said route, or during the continuance of the service being performed by Government boats under military authority, unless removed by proper authority." *O.R.*, I, lii, Part 1, 190.

General Orders No. 6

Head Quarters Dist S. E. Mo
Cairo Sept 14th 1861

GENERAL ORDER No 6

Hereafter no furloughs to soldiers or leave of absence to officers will be considered valid unless first receiving the approval of the commanding officer of the Post where the applicant is stationed

Furloughs or leaves of absence will in no case entitle the Soldier or officer to a free Pass by any conveyance at the expense of Government.

The system of granting leaves of absence and free passes having been so much abused hereafter no passes will be received by Steam Boats Rail Roads or other public conveyance except by order of the commanding officer of the Post where granted, and each pass must state that the officer or soldier is traveling on public service.

Quarter Masters will only provide transportation for Government stores, and troops on an order from the commanding officer having authority to give such order

By order Brig Genl U S Grant Comdg Dist
WM. S. HILLYER
Aid de Camp
A. A. Adjt Genl

Copies, DLC–USG, V, 12, 13, 14, 80; DNA, RG 393, USG General Orders. A printed version of this order is dated Sept. 16, 1861, and signed by Capt. John A. Rawlins. McClernand Papers, IHi. On Sept. 13, Capt. William S. Hillyer had written to Brig. Gen. John A. McClernand. "You will please order the commanding officers of the different regiments under your command that no fuloughs will be considered valid unless approved by you—and that no free passes will be given to officers or privates to travel on furlough" ALS, *ibid*. On Sept. 17, 1st Lt. Clark B. Lagow wrote to McClernand. "I am directed by Genl Grant to say to you that you as commander of the Post, issue passes in complyance with Genl order No 6. I send you Blank Pass Book & Transportation—" ALS, *ibid*. On Sept. 19, Rawlins wrote to Col. Peter E. Bland. "The number of names of officers registered at the Hotels in Saint Louis Mo. show an alarming degree of laxity on the part of the commanding officer of your Post, in granting Furloughs and leaves of absence. Hereafter you will ~~issue~~ grant no furloughs or leaves of absence except in cases of the most extreme necessity and free passes in no cases whatever. Your attention is directed to General order No 6 a printed copy of which is herewith enclosed, and you are respectfully requested to cause its strict observance and enforcement at your Head Quarters'' Copies, DLC-USG, V, 1, 2, 3, 78; DNA, RG 393, USG Letters Sent. See letter to Capt. John C. Kelton, Aug. 25, 1861.

To Brig. Gen. Lorenzo Thomas

Head Quarters, Cairo Ill.
September 14th 1861

Gen. L. Thomas
Adj. Gen. U.S.A.
Washington D. C.
Sir:

In accordance with your instructions of the 22d of August,[1] received but a few days ago, I have taken the prescribed oath and enclose it herewith properly authenticated.

Under the same instructions I also have the honor to inform you that my age is Thirty-nine years & four months, was born in Ohio, residence Galena Ill.

I am Sir, very respectfully
Your Obt. Svt.
U. S. Grant
Brig. Gen. U. S. A.

ALS, Mrs. Walter Love, Flint, Mich. The oath was attested to at Cairo, Sept. 14, 1861. DS, DNA, RG 94, Letters Received.

1. Not found.

To Maj. Gen. John C. Frémont

————

Cairo Sept 14th 1861

To MAJ GENL JOHN C. FREMONT
SAINT LOUIS MO

Reconnoisance to day show no enemy between Charleston & Two miles above Belmont in Missouri nor on the Kentucky shore within Two miles. Our Troops occupy Fort Jefferson

U. S. GRANT

Telegram, copies, DLC-USG, V, 4, 5, 7, 8, 78; DNA, RG 393, USG Hd. Qrs. Correspondence. Misdated Sept. 16, 1861, *ibid.*, Western Dept., Telegrams; DLC-USG, VIA, 1. *O.R.*, I, iii, 497.

To Brig. Gen. John A. McClernand

————

Head Quarters, Dist. S. E. Mo.
Cairo, September 14th 1861

GEN.

You will please have a section of Col. Buells Battery[1] detached from his command to report to Col. Ross for temporary duty on the Ky. shore.

Col. Waagner, chief of artillery will direct the location of the pieces detached.

Respectfully
Your Obt. Svt.
U. S. GRANT
Brig. Gen. Com Dist.

To Brig. Gen. J. A. McClernand
Comd.g U. S. Forces
Cairo & Birds Point

ALS, McClernand Papers, IHi.

1. See telegram to Maj. Gen. John C. Frémont, Sept. 8, 1861, note 1.

To Brig. Gen. John A. McClernand

Head Quarters, Dist. S. E. Mo.
Cairo, Sept. 14th 1861

Gen.

The steamer John Galt[1] being necessary for the use of this post I would advise that the prisoners aboard of her be disposed of on shore and the steamer chartered for our use.

Respectfully
Your Obt. Svt.
U. S. Grant
Brig. Gen. Com. Dist.

To Brig. Gen. J. A. McClernand
Comd.g Cairo & Birds Point.

ALS, McClernand Papers, IHi.

1. See letter to Maj. Gen. John C. Frémont, Sept. 18, 1861.

To Maj. Gen. John C. Frémont

Head Quarters Dist S. E. Mo
Cairo Ills Sept 15, 1861

To Maj Genl John C. Fremont
St Louis Mo

Your dispatch just recd, the 24th Ills Regt is at Fort Holt, the 19th Regt Ills at Fort Jefferson.

They will be dispatched at once

U S Grant
Brigr Genl Comdg

Telegram, copies, DLC-USG, V, 4, 5, 7, 8, 78, VIA, 1; DNA, RG 393, USG Hd. Qrs. Correspondence; *ibid.*, Western Dept., Telegrams. On Sept. 15, 1861, Maj. Gen. John C. Frémont telegraphed to USG. "Embark with as little delay as possible on the Illinois Railroad at Cairo for Sandoval the regiment of Col Hecker (24th Illinois) and Col. Turchin's (19th Illinois) Transportation will await them there, by orders of the President. Answer on receipt of this. Telegraph when they will be there." Copies, DLC-USG, V, 4, 5, 7, 8, VIA, 1; DNA, RG 393, USG Hd. Qrs. Correspondence; *ibid.*, Western Dept., Telegrams. *O.R.*, I, iii, 494. Later the same day, USG telegraphed to Frémont. "The 24th Regt Ill Vol will leave here at 12 o.clock. The 19th Regt at 4 a.m." Copies, DLC-USG, V, 4, 5, 7, 8, 78; DNA, RG 393, USG Hd. Qrs. Correspondence. Frémont then telegraphed to USG. "Dispatch received. Order the two regiments provided with three days cooked rations." Copies, *ibid.*, Western Dept., Telegrams; misdated Sept. 16, DLC-USG, V, 4, 5, 7, 8, VIA, 1; DNA, RG 393, USG Hd. Qrs. Correspondence.

On Sept. 15, Capt. William S. Hillyer wrote to Col. Friedrich Hecker. "You will without delay march your Regiment to this place with all their Camp equipage and Baggage without transportation to be transported North by Rail." Copies, DLC-USG, V, 1, 2, 3, 77; DNA, RG 393, USG Letters Sent. On the same day, Hillyer wrote to Capt. Reuben B. Hatch. "You will furnish railroad transportation for 1500 men from Cairo to Odin or Sandoval as directed to leave as soon as possible" Copies, *ibid.* Frémont's Special Orders No. 194, Sept. 15, stated that "the 19th and 24th Illinois Regiments Cols Turchin and Hecker will proceed to Washington City D. C." Copy, DLC-USG, V, 81.

On Sept. 16, USG telegraphed to Frémont. "Shall I send the trains belonging to the nineteenth & twenty fourth after them, nineteenth not got off." Copies, *ibid.*, VIA, 1; DNA, RG 393, Western Dept., Telegrams. On Sept. 16, Frémont replied to USG. "Dispatch received. Send no transportation with the regiments going." Copies, DLC-USG, V, 4, 5, 7, 8, VIA, 1; DNA, RG 393, USG Hd. Qrs. Correspondence; *ibid.*, Western Dept., Telegrams. Also on Sept. 16, 1st Lt. Clark B. Lagow wrote to Col. John B. Turchin. "I am directed by Genl Grant to say to you to provide your Regiment with three days cooked rations at once P. S. In place of cooking Rations here draw them and stop long enough at the Ohio & Missisppi R. R. to prepare them" Copies, DLC-USG, V, 1, 2, 3, 77; DNA, RG 393, USG Letters Sent. On Sept. 17, Frémont reported the two regts. were at Cincinnati. From there they were sent to Ky. *O.R.*, I, iii, 498, 552; *Ill. AG Report*, II, 143, 323.

To Maj. Gen. John C. Frémont

Head Quarters Dist S.E.Mo
Cairo Sept 15th 1861

To MAJ GENL FREMONT

Mr J. W. Pruett sergeant at arms Ky Senate who is endorsed by the union members of the Legislature Genl Leslie Combs, Mr Richard T Jacobs[1] & other prominent union men of Kentucky

is here praying the release of his Brother James L. Pruett. The
Papers will be forwarded to you in the morning
    I would earnestly reccomend his release

U. S. Grant

Telegram, copies, DLC-USG, V, 4, 5, 7, 8, 78, VIA, 1; DNA, RG 393, USG Hd.
Qrs. Correspondence; *ibid.*, Western Dept., Telegrams. *O.R.*, II, ii, 749. On
Sept. 15, 1861, USG wrote to Maj. Gen. John C. Frémont. "Enclosed I send you
letters and petition pertaining to the prisoner Jas. L. Pruett sentenced to ninety
days hard labor at this place." ALS, DNA, RG 393, Western Dept., Letters
Received. The docket noted five enclosures, probably those printed in *O.R.*, II,
ii, 747–49.
    On Sept. 13, Capt. William S. Hillyer wrote to Brig. Gen. John A. McCler-
nand. "You are directed to remand the prisoners James L. Pruett, Charles Dolson
and Angus McKinney under a suitable escort to the prison from which they were
taken this evening and they will be held in my custody until further orders" ALS,
McClernand Papers, IHi. Misdated Sept. 14 in *O.R.*, II, ii, 749.
    On Sept. 18, John W. Pruett telegraphed to Frémont. "Please examine &
decide upon papers &c sent you in case of Jas L. Prewitt through kindness of Gen
Grant to me & let me hear by telegraph today square work & true." Copy, DNA,
RG 393, Western Dept., Telegrams. On the same day, Frémont telegraphed to
USG. "Release James L Pruett & the prisoner Dalson who was sentenced with
him to ninety (90) days at Cairo" Telegram received, McClernand Papers, IHi.
USG wrote his reply on the back of Frémont's telegram. "I released Pruett this
morning in time to go with his brother in the 4 O'Clock train. Dolson not yet
released." ADS, *ibid.* USG had earlier written to the officer of the day. "The
Officer of the day, will in pursuance of instructions just received from Headquarters Department of the West, ~~release~~ have Mr. James Pruett released from
confinement. ~~and bring him~~ He will be brought to these Headquarters." Copies,
DLC-USG, V, 15, 16, 77, 82; DNA, RG 393, USG Letters Sent. *O.R.*, II, ii,
749.
    On Sept. 5, James L. Pruett had written to Maj. Justus McKinstry. "It is now
3 weeks since the unfortunate affair on olive st. and my release by the civil
authorities. I regret as much as any man can the fact that fire arms were found
upon me, but you will permit me to assure you, that they were carried only and
specially to preserve my life against the attack that *was* made upon me, and which
I knew would be made I am willing to, and do give you my word of honor as a
gentleman, that I will, at all times hereafter, hold myself in readiness to answer
to all charges made against me by all persons whomsoever." ALS, DNA, RG 109,
Records of the U.S. War Dept. Relating to Confederates, Union Provost Marshal's
Citizens File.

    1. Gen. Leslie Coombs and Richard T. Jacob were prominent Ky. Unionists;
Jacob was later col., 9th Ky. Cav.

To Maj. Gen. John C. Frémont

Head Quarters, Dist. S. E. Mo
Cairo, Sept. 15th 1861

GEN. J. C. FREMONT,
COMD.G DEPT. OF THE WEST,
ST. LOUIS, MO.
SIR:

Reconnoisances which I had made yesterday disclose the fact that the enemy have broken up their Camp above Belmont, also that they have no force from there to some distance ~~beyond~~ beyond Charleston. ~~for some distance.~~

As telegraphed by me to-day I believe they are leaving Columbus. Whether marching upon Paducah or leaving Kentucky altogether I will try and determine to-morrow.

I have ordered the 10th Ill. Vols. Col. Morgan[1] Comd.g to Fort Holt to take the place of the 24th leaving to-night, and the 7th Iowa to Elliotts Mills,[2] near Fort Jefferson, to take the place of the 19th Ill.

I would call your attention to the fact that there are many troops here without arms, and some armed with the Austrian musket[3] which, ~~the~~ with the caps now furnished, are unreliable. Also that Clothing Camp & Garrison equipage and accoutrements are deficient. Requisitions I am told are before the proper departments for all these articles.

Money is much required here to pay for secret services. It is highly necessary to get information which cannot be obtained from our own reconnoitering parties, and, without money to pay, the services of citizens cannot much longer be obtained.

I am Sir, Very respectfully,
Your Obt. Svt.
U. S. GRANT
Brig. Gen. Com.

ALS, DNA, RG 393, Western Dept., Letters Received. *O.R.*, I, iii, 494. On

Sept. 15, 1861, USG telegraphed to Maj. Gen. John C. Frémont. "I have reasons to believe that the rebels are retreating from Columbus." Copies, DNA, RG 393, Western Dept., Telegrams; DLC-USG, VIA, 1.

1. Col. James D. Morgan.
2. Elliott's Mills, Ky., about ten miles south of Cairo, near Fort Jefferson.
3. See letter to Maj. Gen. John C. Frémont, Sept. 12, 1861.

To Brig. Gen. John A. McClernand

Head Quarters, Dist. S. E. Mo.
Cairo Sept. 15th 1861

GEN.

You will please direct Col. Morgan to move his regiment to Fort Holt this evening to relieve Col. Hecker who is under marching orders. Also direct the 2d Iowa to move with all despatch to Col. Ross' command at Elliott's Mills.

Respectfully
Your Obt. Svt.
U. S. GRANT
Brig. Gen. Com

To Gen. J. A. McClernand
Comd.g Post

ALS, McClernand Papers, IHi. *O.R.*, I, iii, 494–95. See telegram to Maj. Gen. John C. Frémont, Sept. 15, 1861.

To Brig. Gen. John A. McClernand

———

Head Quarters, Dist. S. E. Mo.
Cairo, Sept. 15th 1861

GEN.

Enclosed I send you note of Capt. Hatch. Will you please order the necessary detail. It may be important that we get these troops off to night.

Respectfully
Your Obt. Svt.
U. S. GRANT
Brig. Gen.

To Gen. J. A. McClernand
Comd.g Post
Cairo Ill.

ALS, McClernand Papers, IHi. See telegram to Maj. Gen. John C. Frémont, Sept. 15, 1861.

To Brig. Gen. John A. McClernand

———

Head Quarters, Dist. S. E. Mo.
Cairo, Sept. 15th 1861

GEN.

Col. Wilson[1] having orders from Gen. Fremont to build a telegraph from here to Paducah it is necessary to afford him evry facility in our power. I would suggest therefore that two companies be detailed from the 18th Ill. Vols. Col. Lawler commanding, to assist in this service until the line is put up. Col. Wilson could then call upon these companies for such men as he might want should he require less than the whole force.

Respectfully
Your Obt. Svt.
U. S. GRANT
Brig. Gen. Com

To Brig. Gen J. A. McClernand
Comd.g Post

ALS, McClernand Papers, IHi.

1. Col. John James Speed Wilson of Ill. acted as superintendent of the military telegraph in that part of the Western Dept. east of the Mississippi River. William R. Plum, *The Military Telegraph During the Civil War in the United States* (Chicago, 1882), I, 117–20.

To Brig. Gen. John A. McClernand

Head Quarters Dist S. E. Mo
Cairo Sept 15th 1861

GENERAL

To settle the difficulties under which Capt Hopkins is laboring and the necessities of service requiring it, I wish him to move with his company on the steamer scott tomorrow to report for duty there.

I am sending five heavy Guns on the same steamer

Respectfully
Your obt. Servant
U. S. GRANT
Brig Genl Comdg

To Gen J. C. McClernand
Comdg Post
Cairo Ills

Copies, DLC-USG, V, 1, 2, 3, 77; DNA, RG 393, USG Letters Sent. This letter apparently concerns Capt. Caleb Hopkins, Battery C, 2nd Ill. Light Art. See letter to Maj. Gen. John C. Frémont, Sept. 18, 1861, note 2.

To Brig. Gen. John A. McClernand

Head Quarters, Dist. S. E. Mo.
Cairo, September 15th 1861

GENERAL;

A Mr. Avery[1] representing himself as a correspondent of the Chicago Times is reported to me by officers of the Army as having made remarks, publicly, whilst in Cape Girardeau that makes him at least a suspicious person.—I would direct therefore that if found in the city after the train leaves here to-morrow morning he be confined and further investigation had.

I would suggest that no pass be given him.

Respectfully
Your Obt. Svt.

To Gen. J. A. McClernand   U. S. GRANT
Comd.g Post.   Brig. Gen. Com. Dist.

ALS, McClernand Papers, IHi. On Sept. 15, 1861, Brig. Gen. John A. McClernand wrote to R. B. Avery. "By order of Genl. U. S. Grant, Com'g the district of South East Missouri, you are hereby notified that if found here after the departure of the Central Rail Road train in the morning you will be arrested." ALS, *ibid*. McClernand may have opened the matter by writing to USG on Sept. 15. "A sergeant from Col. Hecker's regiment brings a man whose answers to my interrigatories promt me to refer him to you" LS, *ibid*.

1. R. B. Avery is listed as a correspondent for the *Chicago Times* in J. Cutler Andrews, *The North Reports the Civil War* (Pittsburgh, 1955), p. 751.

To Col. Leonard F. Ross

Head Quarters Dist S. E. Mo
Cairo Sept 15th 1861

COL

You will please detach as much cavalry as you can spare from your command to make a Reconnoisance in the direction of Blandville under the directions of Col Waagner

You will be Reinforced by one Regiment tomorrow should they not arrive to night

                    Yours &c
                    U. S. GRANT
                    Brig Genl Comdg

To Col Ross
Comdg U. S. Forces
Elliotts Mills Ky

Copies, DLC-USG, V, 1, 2, 3, 77; DNA, RG 393, USG Letters Sent. *O.R.*, I, iii, 495.

To Capt. Reuben B. Hatch

                    Head Quarters Dist S. E. Mo.
                    Cairo Sept. 15th 1861

CAPT.

You will please furnish transportation for one Regiment from Fort Holt to Cairo, one from Fort Jefferson to same place, also as soon as it can be done one Regiment is to be sent from here and one from Birds Point to take their places.

                    U. S. GRANT
                    Brig. Gen. Com.

To Capt Hatch
Qr. M. of the Post
Cairo Ill.

Copies, DLC-USG, V, 1, 2, 3, 77; DNA, RG 393, USG Letters Sent. See telegram to Maj. Gen. John C. Frémont and letter to Brig. Gen. John A. McClernand, Sept. 15, 1861.

To Simon Cameron

Cairo September 16th 1861

Hon S. Cameron
Sec of War
Washington D. C.
Sir

I take great pleasure in recomending to you for the appointment of commissary of subsistence in the Volunteer service, the name of Geo. S. Roper[1] of Springfield Illinois

I have not yet had assigned to me an officer of the subsistence Department and would be much pleased to have Mr Roper.

He has had considerable experience in the Department as a clerk and from his general intelligence and business habits his appointment could not fail to give universal satisfaction

Very Respfully
Your obt Servant
U. S. Grant
Brig Genl Com

Copies, DLC-USG, V, 4, 5, 7, 8, 78; DNA, RG 393, USG Hd. Qrs. Correspondence. Simon Cameron, Pa. Republican, served as secretary of war March 5, 1861—Jan. 14, 1862.

1. See letter to George S. Roper, Aug. 11, 1861.

To Maj. Gen. John C. Frémont

Head Quarters, Dist. S. E. Mo.
Cairo, September 16th 1861

Maj. Gen. J. C. Frémont
Comd.g Dept. of the West
St. Louis Mo.
Sir:

I have no news of the movements of the enemy to-day to communicate that has not been telegraphed.[1] If not moving from, he is keeping close to Columbus.

The most important point learned, if true, is that Gen. A. S. Johnson[2] was to take command and on Friday last was to have moved with 10.000 men upon Paducah.

I do not think this movement has been made however or I should have heard of it.

The ordering away of the 19th & 24th Ill. Vols.[3] will prevent extensive reconnoisance until their places are supplied. I feel that the place of Col. Hecker's regiment cannot be supplied by any one ordinary regiment.

I am sir, Very respectfully
Your Obt. Svt.
U. S. Grant
Brig. Gen. Com.

ALS, ICarbS. On Sept. 19, 1861, Capt. John R. Howard replied to USG. "The Commanding General instructs me to acknowledge receipt of your despatch of Sep. 16th, and to inform you that one regiment will be forwarded to Cairo today, to replace to that extent those ordered away from your Command." ALS, DNA, RG 393, District of Southeast Mo., Letters Received.

1. On Sept. 16, USG telegraphed to Maj. Gen. John C. Frémont. "A deserter just in reports that the rebels ten thousand strong under Gen Johnson were to leave Columbus last Friday to attack Paducah he left Thursday evening went to New Madrid thence to Charleston Jeff Thompson was at Belmont." Copies, DLC-USG, VIA, 1; DNA, RG 393, Western Dept., Telegrams. On Sept. 16, Frémont replied to USG. "Despatch received, where have you reason to suppose the rebels are going" Copies, DLC-USG, V, 4, 5, 7, 8, VIA, 1; DNA, RG 393, Western Dept., Telegrams; *ibid.*, USG Hd. Qrs. Correspondence. On Sept. 16, USG tele-

graphed again to Frémont. "Gen'l Smith sends same accounts as telegraphed by
me in Hungarian." Copies, *ibid.*, Western Dept., Telegrams; DLC-USG, VIA, 1.
USG then telegraphed in Hungarian to Frémont. "According to a certain message
which I just received there are six thousand 6000 enemy troops in Mayfield. There
will be more and the total number will be 15000. They intend to overrun Paducah.
They signal the enemy with candles. The enemy has 12 guns and seven hundred
well armed cavalry commanded by General Johnson at Columbus. I will send the
battalion with a battery immediately." Copies (Hungarian), *ibid.* On Sept. 16,
Brig. Gen. Charles F. Smith wrote to USG. "The Steamer (Gun boat) Conestoga
returned last night from a trip up the Cumberland some 50 miles bringing as
prizes two Steamers. The information Capt. Phelps brought from different persons
where he landed goes to confirm the report of your agent Mr. *L.* in reference to
the force gathering and to be gathered at *Mayfield*, only increasing the force to be
there to 20.000.—If you send me a field battery, as promised, I trust the artillerists
will accompany it, for I have none outside of the present batteries. I can get
assistance from Capt. Phelps to work the heavy guns. My impression is the
enemy will be upon us before anything arrives and can be made useful. Our food
is running short. Have you any to spare?" ALS, DNA, RG 393, District of Southeast Mo., Letters Received.
    2. C.S.A. Gen. Albert Sidney Johnston of La., USMA 1826, was assigned to
command Dept. No. 2 on Sept. 10, 1861. *O.R.*, I, iv, 405. After assuming command at Nashville, Tenn., on Sept. 15, his first move was to occupy Bowling
Green in central Ky. *Ibid.*, pp. 407–15.
    3. See telegram to Maj. Gen. John C. Frémont, Sept. 15, 1861.

To Brig. Gen. John A. McClernand

Head Quarters, Dist. of S. E. Mo.
Cairo Sept. 16th 1861

Gᴇɴ.

    Capt. Buell's Artillery[1] is wanted at Paducah as soon as it can
possibly be got there. Will you send an order for them to move
to the river at once.

Respectfully
U. S. Gʀᴀɴᴛ
Brig. Gen.

To Gen. J. C. McClernand
Comd.g Post

ALS, McClernand Papers, IHi. On Sept. 16, 1861, Capt. John A. Rawlins wrote
to Capt. Reuben B. Hatch. "You will please have a Steam Boat got in readiness to

take Capt Buels company of artillery to Paducah to night from Birds Point"
Copies, DLC-USG, V, 1, 2, 3, 77; DNA, RG 393, USG Letters Sent.

1. See letter to Brig. Gen. John A. McClernand, Sept. 14, 1861.

To Brig. Gen. John A. McClernand

Head Quarters, Dist. S. E. Mo.
Cairo, Sept. 16th 1861

GEN.

The prisoners belonging to Col. Heckers Regiment can follow the regiment to day in charge of the officer left by Col.
Hecker in charge of his baggage.

Respectfully
Your Obt. Svt.
U. S. GRANT
Brig. Gen. Com

To Gen. J. A. McClernand
Comd.g Post
Cairo Ill.

ALS, McClernand Papers, IHi.
There was further correspondence concerning the prisoners of the other regt.
which left the District of Southeast Mo. On Sept. 17, 1861, Capt. John A. Rawlins
wrote to Brig. Gen. John A. McClernand. "Your note of this date relating to the
Prisoners W. H. Rice and Walter G. Adams said to be deserters from the 19th
Regiment Co. G. Ill Vol Col Turchin comdg were duly received were duly
received and I am instructed to say to you to forward them by the most direct
and usual Rail Road route to Washington City D.C. where their Regt was
ordered. where as the witnesses (if any) of their desertion are most likely to be.
You will place Tickets for their transportation in the hands of the Officer of the
Guard with instructions with instructions to take them from the Guard House
tomorrow and put them on the Cars for Washington City D.C. to join their Regt
and furnished with three days rations" Copy, DLC-USG, V, 77, marked "This
order has been countermanded by order of Brig Genl Grant." On Sept. 17, 1st
Lt. Clark B. Lagow wrote to McClernand. "I am directed by Genl Commanding
to say to you that the men left by the 19th Regt Ill Vol as prisoners or through
negligence on their part will be assigned to other Regiments have those that were
detained by good and sufficient reasons will be detailed as Hospital nurses untill

opportunity occurs for them to rejoin their Regiments" ALS, McClernand
Papers, IHi. On Sept. 17, McClernand wrote to USG. "W. H. Rice and Walter
G. Adams are prisoners in the Guard House on charge of desertion six weeks since,
having been ~~recaptured~~ arrested at Norfolk. They await your orders for trail."
Copy, *ibid.* On Sept. 18, Rawlins wrote to Col. John B. Turchin. "I am instructed
by Brig Genl U. S. Grant comdg to inform you that four Privates belonging to
your Regiment are her viz ~~as follows~~ James Atherton Co "C," Isaac Binister Co
"B," W. H. Rice and Walter Adams, the former two have been detailed for
'Hospital Service' and the latter two have been attached to an artillery company
in Col Waagners ~~Regiment~~ Command, untill an opportunity is offered to forward
them to their Regt under your command" Copies, DLC-USG, V, 1, 2, 3, 77;
DNA, RG 393, USG Letters Sent.

To Col. Michael K. Lawler

Head Quarters Dist S. E. Mo
Cairo Sept 16th 1861

SPECIAL ORDER

Adjutant Fondy[1] of the 18th Ill Vol is hereby authorized and
appointed to swear into the service of the United States Capt
U. M. Lawrence[2] and company whenever it may number twenty-
five men.

After being sworn in the comy of subsistence at Mound City
will issue Rations on returns signed by Capt Lawrence and approved by the comdg officer of the Post.

Morning Reports must accompany and compare with the
Provision Returns

U. S. GRANT
Brig Genl Com

To Col M. K. Lawler
Comdg 18th Ill Vols
Mound City Ills

Copies, DLC-USG, V, 15, 16, 77, 82; DNA, RG 393, USG Special Orders.

1. William B. Fondey of Springfield, Ill.
2. Lawrence was apparently unsuccessful. He may be Uriah M. Lawrence,
later capt., 107th Ill.

To Maj. Gen. John C. Frémont

———

Cairo, Sept 17, 1861.

MAJ. GEN. FREMONT,

The taking of two regts : from this command makes me deem it prudent to withdraw troops from vicinity of Fort Jefferson to Fort Holt. The order is given.[1]

U. S. GRANT, Brig. Gen

Telegram, copies, DNA, RG 393, Western Dept., Telegrams; DLC-USG, VIA, 1.

1. See letter to Col. Leonard F. Ross, Sept. 17, 1861.

To Maj. Gen. John C. Frémont

———

Cairo, Sept 17, 1861.

MAJ. GEN. J. C. FREMONT

The big guns went to Paducah.[1] We have one hundred 100 shells for each gun but only ten 10 barrels of gunpowder. We asked for more gunpowder by telegraph. The present position of my command is : the tenth 10 and the seventeenth (17) Illinois, the second (2) and the seventh (7) Iowa, the battery of Schwartz and three (3) companies of cavalry—three thousand (3000) men—in Fort Holt and in Fort Jefferson Ky; the eleventh (11) and the twentieth (20) Illinois and three (3) companies of cavalry—seventeen hundred (1700) men in Birds Point; the twenty-seventh (27), twenty-ninth (29) thirtieth (30) thirty-first (31) and one company of cavalry—thirty-three hundred (3300) men—in Cairo, among the last some unarmed . . . brand new soldiers; the eighteenth (18) Illinois—nine hundred thirty (930) men—in Mound City; the eighth (8) and the twenty-second (22) Illinois, Taylor's battery, four (4) guns, two (2) are in Paducah,—eighteen fifty (1850) men—in Norfolk. One sixth of the whole command is ill.

U. S. GRANT.

Telegram, copy (Hungarian), DNA, RG 393, Western Dept., Telegrams. On Sept. 16, 1861, Maj. Gen. John C. Frémont telegraphed to USG. "Are the six (6) heavy guns which you sent to Paducah well supplied with ammunition. Send Buells battery to Paducah, answer immediately as far as you can statement of your force and its disposition, send in Hungarian" Copies, DLC-USG, V, 4, 5, 7, 8, VIA, 1; DNA, RG 393, USG Hd. Qrs. Correspondence; *ibid.*, Western Dept., Telegrams. In a telegram to Secretary of War Simon Cameron, Sept. 15, Frémont had listed for USG's command "Cape Girardeau, 650; Bird's Point and Norfolk, 3,510; Cairo, including McClernand's brigade, 4,826; Fort Holt, opposite Cairo, Kentucky shore, 3,595 . . ." *O.R.*, I, iii, 493. Since then USG had sent two regts. out of his district.

USG prepared an estimate of forces under his command as of Sept. 30, 1861, which showed a total of 13,105 officers and men present and absent, divided into 11,963 inf., 747 cav., 395 art. Of the total, 9,509 were ready for duty, 1,888 were sick, and 1,707 were absent (including those on detached service). DS, DNA, RG 393, Western Dept., Letters Received; copy, DLC-USG, VIA, 1. A statement of U.S. forces in the Western Dept. as of Oct. 10 listed 13,608 men under USG's command. *SED*, 37–2–1, II, 55.

On Sept. 28, Capt. Chauncey McKeever wrote to Col. William P. Carlin at Ironton. "Your post is not in General Grant's district." Copy, DNA, RG 393, Western Dept., Letters Sent. On Sept. 29, McKeever wrote to USG. "The Posts of Ironton and Rolla will not be included in your district. No consolidated reports of your command have been received for some time. You will please hereafter furnish this office with one on Monday of every week." LS, *ibid.*, District of Southeast Mo., Letters Received. There is no clear evidence that Ironton had ever been in USG's district, but see letter to Maj. Gen. John C. Frémont, Sept. 6, 1861, and General Orders No. 4, Sept. 8, 1861.

1. On Sept. 17, Frémont telegraphed to USG. "Where are the Batteries stationed of Captain Buell and Captain Schwartz." Copies, DLC-USG, V, 4, 5, 7, 8, VIA, 1; DNA, RG 393, USG Hd. Qrs. Correspondence; *ibid.*, Western Dept., Telegrams. On the same day, USG replied to Frémont. "I order'd Buels battery to Paducah last night & telegraphed the fact to you, he must have reached there about noon today." Copies, DLC-USG, VIA, 1; DNA, RG 393, Western Dept., Telegrams. On Sept. 18, Frémont telegraphed to USG. "Your second despatch about Buells battery to Paducah received, first one not to hand." Copies, DLC-USG, V, 4, 5, 7, 8, VIA, 1; DNA, RG 393, USG Hd. Qrs. Correspondence; *ibid.*, Western Dept., Telegrams.

To Brig. Gen. Charles F. Smith

Head Quarters Dist S. E. Mo
Cairo Sept 17th 1861

Genl

I regret exceedingly that I am not able to spare you any troops in the present emergency.

A most extriordinary movement took place here yesterday which will compel me to contract my present limits particularly on the Ky shore[1]

I have received orders and have sent off two of the best regiments under my command, where can only be surmised. My orders read to the O & M.[2] R R where transports would await them

I send you a Battery of Artillery which may be of material service The substance of your communication was dispatched last night[3]

Very Respt.
Your obt Servant
U. S. Grant
Brig Genl Com

To Brig Genl C. F. Smith
Comdg Forces
Paducah Ky

Copies, DLC-USG, V, 1, 2, 3, 77; DNA, RG 393, USG Letters Sent. *O.R.*, I, iii, 497.

1. See telegram to Maj. Gen. John C. Frémont, Sept. 15, 1861.
2. Ohio and Mississippi.
3. See letter to Maj. Gen. John C. Frémont, Sept. 16, 1861, note 1.

To Col. Leonard F. Ross

———

Hd Qrs Dist S. E. Mo.
Cairo Sept 17 1861

COL. L. F. ROSS, COM'G &c
ELLIOTTS MILLS KY.

Our forces having been so much reduced by the withdrawal of two regiments I deem it prudent to withdraw your camp from its present position. You will therefore return with all your command to Fort Holt. Upon your return ~~there~~ to Fort Holt Ky Col Morgan's regiment will be relieved from duty at that point and return to their old quarters.

U. S. GRANT
Brigadier General Comd'g

Copies, DLC-USG, V, 1, 2, 3, 77; DNA, RG 393, USG Letters Sent. *O.R.*, I, iii, 497.

To Maj. Gen. John C. Frémont

———

Head Quarters Dist S. E. Mo
Cairo Sept 18th 1861

GEN

Enclosed I send you—result of investigation into cause of detention of Steamers "John Gualt" and "Jefferson."[1] I have not yet ordered their release having submitted the matter to you and the collector of Customs of this Port ~~having~~ I have also submitted the same matter to the District Attorney for the Suothern District of Illinois

I also enclose you a statement from Gen McClernand of the condition of his Brigade as respects arms.[2]

I am Very Respectfully
Your Obedient Servant
U. S. GRANT
Brig Gen Com

Maj Gen J C Fremont

Copies, DLC-USG, V, 4, 5, 7, 8, 78, VIA, 1; DNA, RG 393, USG Hd. Qrs. Correspondence.

1. On Sept. 8, 1861, Commander John Rodgers wrote to USG. "The 'John Gault,' a Louisville Packet, left Louisville on last Thursday night for Cairo. She proceeded down the Ohio stopping at various landings until she arrived at Smithland, at the mouth of the Cumberland, to which point most of her freight was consigned. The wharf boat at Smithland refused to receive her freight, whereupon she ran up the Cumberland river to Ross's Ferry about 25 miles from the mouth where she discharged the greater part of her cargo into the J. H. Baldwin—a Nashville packet This last act is, I judge contrary to the proclamation of the President of the U S. and enough to condemn her I turn her over to the proper authorities for trial, some of the Officers should be detained as witnesses" LS, *ibid.*, Western Dept., Letters Received. On Sept. 17, Brig. Gen. John A. McClernand wrote to USG concerning the *John Gault* and *Jefferson.* LS, McClernand Papers, IHi; copy, DLC-USG, VIA, 1. *O.R.*, II, i, 130. On Sept. 19, McClernand wrote to USG concerning further investigation of the *Jefferson.* LS, DNA, Western Dept., Letters Received; Df, McClernand Papers, IHi. On Sept. 20, Maj. Gen. John C. Frémont telegraphed to USG. "The Steamer 'John Gault' may be released as suggested by General McClernand." Copies, DLC-USG, V, 4, 5, 7, 8, VIA, 1; DNA, RG 393, USG Hd. Qrs. Correspondence; *ibid.*, Western Dept., Telegrams; *ibid.*, Letters Sent by Gen. Frémont. See letters to Brig. Gen. John A. McClernand, Sept. 14, 24, 1861.

2. On Sept. 17, McClernand wrote to USG. "The unarmed condition of the troops remaining at this place is such as to demand earnest attention. Of the 3,068 effective men in my Brigade in camp here, not more than 2,000 are armed. These are supplied with the old altered U. S., and English Four muskets, fit, perhaps, for *drill*, but *not* for service. The cartridges, sent for the English muskets, being manufactured for another kind, are too small, and can not be used. Capt. Carmichael's cavalry company of 65 effective men are without arms or uniforms and cannot even drill in this condition; and, therefore, are becoming much disheartened. Capt. Dollin's company of 96 men and horses are in the same condition. Capt. Burrell's cavalry company, now at Bird's Point, has been employed on dangerous service, encountered enemies, made captures and suffered losses—all without arms or the proper equipments. Capt. Hopkins' Artillery company are without guns. Three days ago, Col J. D. Morgan represented his regiment as being armed with muskets, so unservicable that he should reproach himself as the *murderer* of his men, should he lead them to battle in this condition. These facts call for earnest consideration. Military spirit and discipline can not well be preserved in a camp of unarmed men. A sufficient supply of good arms with suitable ammunitions, equipments and clothing for at least 4,000 infantry and 500 cavalry, are necessary for efficient service of this Brigade. These facts are actually discouraging enlistments, and the manifest necessary of the case demands that I should thus bring it to your notice. I desire that you will represent this matter to Genl. Fremont in a strong light, and have, as soon as possible, an addition to our now meager means of defence." LS, DNA, RG 393, Western Dept., Letters Received. On the same day, McClernand wrote a similar letter to Frémont. LS, *ibid.*

To Maj. Gen. John C. Frémont

Head Quarters Dist S. E. Mo
Cairo Sept 18th 1861

GEN

The necessity for running Boats in various directions and having them always ready at a moments notice has made the duties of the Quartermaster of this post so onerous that I deem it advisable to employ an experienced Steamboat man who shall have special care of all the Government Boats at this and adjacent points

I have therefore ordered the employment of such a person and the Quartermaster has employed Capt G. W Graham

This is subject to your approval which is respectfully asked

I am sir Very Respectfully
Your obt servant
U. S. GRANT
Brig Gen Com

To Major General Jno. C. Fremont
Comdg Dept of the West
St Louis Mo

Copies, DLC-USG, V, 4, 5, 7, 8, 78; DNA, RG 393, USG Hd. Qrs. Correspondence. No reply from Maj. Gen. John C. Frémont has been found, but George Washington Graham continued his services to USG. On Sept. 11, 1861, Capt. Reuben B. Hatch wrote to USG. "I have the honor to report to you that G. W. Graham has been appointed Commodore of the fleet of boats plying from this port in the U. S. Service. He has the sole control of them and will be under the orders of this Dep't to which all orders for transportation will be addressd. A time table will be issued and sent you tomorrow morning stating the service and route of the boats" ALS, *ibid.*, Dept. of Tenn., Miscellaneous Letters Received 1862–63. See letter to Capt. Reuben B. Hatch, Sept. 10, 1861. Graham was listed in the 1860 U.S. Census as a twenty-eight-year-old merchant of Cairo. He was a partner in "Graham, Halliday & Co., Forwarding Merchants and Wharf-Boat Proprietors . . . Special Shipping Agents of Illinois Central Railroad Company." *Cairo Gazette*, Sept. 12, 1861. He is variously mentioned as capt. and commodore in military correspondence, and his official position seems anomalous. In 1888, his widow's application for a pension was rejected on the grounds that he was a civilian employee of the Q. M. Dept. Rebecca Graham Application, DNA, RG 15. Unfavorable comments on his character and relations with USG are in William Henry

Perrin, ed., *History of Alexander, Union and Pulaski Counties, Illinois* (Chicago, 1883), pp. 60, 64–65; Benjamin P. Thomas, ed., *Three Years with Grant as Recalled by War Correspondent Sylvanus Cadwallader* (New York, 1955), pp. 106–7.

To Col. John Cook

Head Quarters Dist S. E. Mo
Cairo Sept 18th 1861

COL

Enclosed you will find charges against a prisoner who I wish you to take with you to Cape Girardeu and there held untill such time as you can send him with those now in your charge to Saint Louis Arsenal for trial.

Report at these Head Quarters the hour you will leave and the name of the Boat and the Prisoners will be sent to you there

Yours &c

U. S. GRANT

Brig Genl Com

To Col Jno Cook
Comdg U. S. Forces
Cape Girardeau Mo

Copies, DLC-USG, V, 1, 2, 3, 77; DNA, RG 393, USG Letters Sent. On Sept. 18, 1861, Capt. John A. Rawlins for USG wrote to Col. John Cook. "You will send G. M. Beattie T. B. Turnbaugh and J. Wood to Saint Louis. A copy of charges must accompany them together with the names of the witnesses and where to be found. They will be sent under charge of an officer an such other Prisoners as ~~may~~ in your judgment should be sent there for trial will accompany them" Copies, *ibid.*

On Sept. 20, Cook wrote to the commanding officer, St. Louis Arsenal. "In pursuance to orders from Head Quarters S. E. Mo. Brig. Genl. U. S. Grant Comdg, I have this day forwd. to St. Louis Arsenal certain Prisoners of War together with Charges &c accompaning, which I hope may prove satisfactory—" ALS, *ibid.*, RG 109, Records of the U.S. War Dept. Relating to Confederates, Union Provost Marshal's Citizens File. The names of the prisoners are given as Joseph Hunter, George M. Beattie, Thomas B. Turnbold, and James Woods. On Sept. 25, Cook wrote to USG transmitting "Statements in reference to Major Beattie who was arrested, tried, and discharged." DLC-USG, V, 10; DNA, RG 393, USG Register of Letters Received. See letter to Col. John Cook, Sept. 12, 1861.

To Col. Leonard F. Ross

———

Head Quarters Dist S E. Mo
Cairo Sept 18th 1861

SPECIAL ORDERS

It is reported that Col Oglesbys Pickets have been driven in
Hold your command in readiness for any emergency that may arise either to resist an attack or to move to their assistance

U. S. GRANT
Brig Genl Com

To Col Ross
Comdg Fort Jefferson Ky

Copies, DLC-USG, V, 15, 16, 77, 82; DNA, RG 393, USG Special Orders.

To Col. *William H. L. Wallace*

———

Head Quarters Dist S. E. Mo
Cairo Sept 18th 1861

COL

I understand Col Oglesbys Pickets have been driven in
Hold your command in readiness to afford all the assistance you can

Respt &c
U. S. GRANT
Brig Genl Com

To Col Wallace
Comdg Troops
Birds Point Mo

Copies, DLC-USG, V, 1, 2, 3, 77; DNA, RG 393, USG Letters Sent. *O.R.*, I, iii, 501.

Pass for Col. John J. S. Wilson

————

Head Quarters Dist S. E. Mo
Cairo Sept 18th 1861

To COMDRS GOVERNMENT STEAMERS

Col J. J. S. Wilson has permission to pass free on any Government Steamer plying between Cairo and Paducah or to pass such men as he may wish from place to place between these two points

Boats will land the Col or his party at such points as they may designate and take them on board whenever signalled to do so. —This to hold good untill the Telegraph between this place and Paducah is completed

U. S. GRANT
Brig Genl Com

Copies, DLC-USG, V, 1, 2, 16, 77, 82; DNA, RG 393, USG Letters Sent. See letter to Brig. Gen. John A. McClernand, Sept. 15, 1861.

To Capt. Reuben B. Hatch

————

Head Quarters Dist S. E. Mo
Cairo Sept 18th 1861

SIR

You will proceed as soon as practicable to Saint Louis Mo for the purpose of obtaining funds for the use of the Quartermasters Department at this Post and such other duty as you may have to perform there

U. S. GRANT
Brig Genl Com

To Capt R. B. Hatch
Brig Q. M.
Cairo Ills

Copies, DLC-USG, V, 1, 2, 3, 77; DNA, RG 393, USG Letters Sent.

To Capt. Reuben B. Hatch

Head Quarters Dist S. E. Mo
Cairo Sept 18th 1861

S<small>IR</small>

You will please provide transportation for Lieut D. F. Bremner 19th Ill Vols and fifteen men of the 19th and 24th Regts Ill Vols to Washington D C to join their respective commands

U. S. G<small>RANT</small>
Brig Genl Com

To Cap Hatch
Brigade Q. M.
Cairo Ills

Copies, DLC-USG, V, 1, 2, 3, 77; DNA, RG 393, USG Letters Sent. On Sept. 18, 1861, Capt. John A. Rawlins for USG wrote to 1st Lt. David F. Bremner, 19th Ill. "You are hereby ordered to take charge of the following list of men belonging to the 19th and 24th Regt Ill Vols . . . and proceed with them to Washington City D. C. and deliver them up to their respective Regts where they will rejoin the same. You will take with you three days prepared rations for each man." Copies, *ibid*. On the same day, USG wrote to Capt. Reuben C. Rutherford. "You are directed to issue three days rations for fifteen men under the charge of Lieut D F Bremner 19th Ill Vols" Copy, DLC-USG, V, 77.

To Capt. Parmenas T. Turnley

Head Quarters Dist S. E. Mo
Cairo Sept 18th 1861

C<small>APT</small>

I have this day drawn upon you for twelve Hundred (1.200) dollars, funds to be used in the secret service of the United States.

Please have recepts made out and send to me and I will sign and return them at once.

I would make out sign and send you the recipts at once but I am not posted as to the exact form you may require for funds for this particular service

                                        Respectfully &c
                                        U. S. GRANT
                                        Brig Genl Com

To Capt P. T. Turnley
Asst Q. M. U. S. A
Saint Louis Mo

Copies, DLC-USG, V, 1, 2, 3, 7, 78; DNA, RG 393, USG Letters Sent; *ibid.*, USG Hd. Qrs. Correspondence. On Sept. 18, 1861, Capt. Parmenas T. Turnley of Tenn., USMA 1846, chief q. m., St. Louis Depot, replied to USG. "Your request for funds for secret service is approved and ordered. How can I get it to you. If you can get the money near you on drafts on me I will honor the same if accompanied by your receipts." Copies, DLC-USG, V, 4, 5, 7, 8; DNA, RG 393, USG Hd. Qrs. Correspondence.

To 1st Lt. James F. Langley

                                        Head Quarters Dist S. E. Mo
                                        Cairo Sept 18th 1861
SPECIAL ORDER

1st Lieut J. F. Longly 10th Ill Vol will proceed to St Louis Arsenal in charge of a guard and thirty five prisoners

After turning over the Prisoners to the Commanding Officers at the Arsenal he will return ~~he will return~~ with the ~~command~~ Guard by the first Government Boat bound for this place

                                        U. S. GRANT
                                        Brig Genl Com

Copies, DLC-USG, V, 15, 16, 77, 82; DNA, RG 393, USG Special Orders. 1st Lt. James F. Langley, 10th Ill., was promoted to capt. on June 13, 1862. On Sept. 18, 1861, Capt. John A. Rawlins for USG wrote to Capt. Reuben B. Hatch. "The Quartermaster of the Post will ~~provide peure~~ procure transportation for one Officer, four men and thirty four prisoners of war, to St Louis Mo. Also return passage for the guard of one commissioned officer and four men" Copies, *ibid.* On the same day, Rawlins wrote to Capt. Reuben C. Rutherford. "You are directed to issue two days prepared rations for thirty four Prisoners and guard consisting of four men immediately" Copies, DLC-USG, V, 1, 2, 3, 77; DNA, RG 393, USG Letters Sent.

On an undated "List of Prisoners of War Confined at Camp Cairo," a list of thirty-four names was followed by a comment. "All of these prisoners were in the fight at Charleston the night of the 19th August & morning of the 20th between a detachment of troops from Bird's point and the rebels and were found in arms when taken—The Federal detachment consisted of infantry under command of Col Dougherty 22d Regt Ill Vols & Cavalry under Capt Noleman.—The Official Report of the affair at Charleston will doubtless be found at Head Quarters at St Louis—communicated by Col. R. J. Oglesby, 8th Regt. Ill Vols, Commdg forces at Cairo at that date." DS, *ibid.*, RG 109, Records of Union Provost Marshals Relating to Prisoners, Station Rolls, Ill.

The man originally intended to be the thirty-fifth prisoner is described on the front of the document. "Richard Cranshaw—Arrested as a 'Spy' by Col W H L. Wallace Commdg Birds Point is accused by A. W. Nims (who was employ[ed] in Federal secret service) as being one of t[hose] who arrested him near Charleston—This m[an] came into Birds Point under pretence of [be]ing after a runaway negro—" Across this is noted, "Not with these Prisoners."

To Capt. Adolph Schwartz

Head Quarters Dist S. E. Mo
Cairo Sept 19th 1861

CAPT

The senior officer at a post is necessarily the Commander of it. And Col Morgan being ordered to Cairo necessarily leaves you in the position of commanding officer of Fort Holt Ky.

Col Morgan has been directed by me[1] to furnish one company for a guard to your command untill such time as I may be able to spare a Regiment or part of a Regiment for that Post. And you as commander can post the Guard

I will inform Col Morgan to that effect

U. S. GRANT
Brig Genl Com

To Capt Schwartz
Comdg Fort Holt Ky

Copies, DLC-USG, V, 1, 2, 3, 77; DNA, RG 393, USG Letters Sent. See letter to Col. John B. Turchin, Sept. 8, 1861, note 1.

1. By letter of Sept. 19, 1861, from Capt. John A. Rawlins to Col. James D. Morgan. Copies, DLC-USG, V, 1, 2, 3, 77; DNA, RG 393, USG Letters Sent.

To 1st Asst. Surgeon Charles B. Tompkins

Head Quarters Dist S. E. Mo
Cairo Sept 19th 1861

SPECIAL ORDER

Asst Surgeon C. B. Tompkins will proceed by first Government Steamer to Cape Girardeau and there detain the Boat sufficient time to get aboard the sick of the 17th Ill Vols whom he will report with to the medical Director or purveyor St Louis

From Saint Louis he will visit Ironton and there collect the sick of same Regt and dispose of them in the same manner

Having collected the sick of said Regt in Hospital at St Louis Asst Surgeon Tompkins will rejoin his proper command without delay

U. S. GRANT
Brig Genl Com

To Asst Surgeon Tompkins
17th Ill Vols

Copies, DLC-USG, V, 15, 16, 77, 82; DNA, RG 393, USG Special Orders. 1st Asst. Surgeon Charles B. Tompkins of Lewiston, Ill., 17th Ill., was promoted to surgeon on July 1, 1863.

To Capt. George H. Walser

Head Quarters Dist S. E. Mo
Cairo Sept 19th 1861

SPECIAL ORDER

Leave of absence for twenty days for the benefit of his health is hereby granted Capt Walsen 20th Ill Vols at the expiration of which time he will ~~rejoin~~ return to his Company for duty.

U. S. GRANT
Brig Gen Com

Copies, DLC-USG, V, 15, 16, 77, 82; DNA, RG 393, USG Special Orders. USG endorsed a letter of Sept. 13, 1861, from Col. C. Carroll Marsh to Maj. Gen. John C. Frémont requesting that Capts. John A. Hoskins and George H. Walser, 20th Ill., be removed without trial. "I am aware that ordinarially the within request could not be granted but believing that the exigency of the service demand such an assumption of authority and that the good of the service will be promoted by it, I have no hesitation in reccommending the removal of Capts. Hoskins & Walser." Copy, *ibid.*, Western Dept., Register of Letters Received. Walser resigned on Nov. 3, and Hoskins on Dec. 2, 1861.

To Maj. Gen. John C. Frémont

Cairo, Sept 20/61.

MAJ. GEN. FREMONT
    Genl. Smith reports arrival of Barges at Paducah.
                                        U. S. GRANT,

Telegram, copies, DNA, RG 393, Western Dept., Telegrams; DLC-USG, VIA, 1. These barges were part of the pontoon bridge constructed across the Ohio River. See Philip M. Thienel, "The Longest Floating Bridge," *The Military Engineer*, XLIX, 328 (March–April, 1957), 120–21; *HED*, 37–2–94, p. 21. On Sept. 13, 1861, Maj. Gen. John C. Frémont telegraphed to USG and Brig. Gen. Charles F. Smith. "The pontoon bridge will reach Paducah to morrow or Sunday from Cincinnati. It can be put up in a few hours. Infantry & artillery will be needed for its protection." Telegram, copies (English and Hungarian), DNA, RG 393, Western Dept., Telegrams; DLC-USG, VIA, 1.

To Maj. Gen. John C. Frémont

Head Quarters Dist S. E. Mo
Cairo Sept 20th 1861

MAJ GENL J. C. FREMONT
COMDG DEPT OF THE WEST
SAINT LOUIS MO
SIR
    There has been nothing in the movements of the enemy for the last few days, that I could learn worthy of note. They now

seem to be falling back from Mayfield[1] upon Columbus, Ky. I have received no confirmation of the rumor that Gen A. S. Johnson was to take command.[2]

I would respectfully call your attention to the fact that the 10th Ill ~~Vols~~ Regiment Col Morgan commanding has but seven companies in it, and the 11th Ills has but nine companies.

These two Regiments are commanded Colonels[3] of experience and who have profitted by their experience. I would therefore urgently recomend that the Governor of Illinois be requested to assign companies to these Regiments to fill them up as soon as possible.

I left here after 1 o.clock this morning for Cape Girardeau and returned arriving at 2 o.clock P. M. My visit was in reference to the Bittinger Property[4] which has been taken possession of for purposes of Fortifications. I appointed a Board of three officers to assess the damages done the property[5] and wanted to make an agreement myself for the monthly rent to be paid whilst held for the use of the Government. Mr Bittinger was absent however and I left this part of the contract to be agreed upon hereafter.

I find the fortifications progressing fairly considering the large sick report at this post.

> I am Sir Very Respectfully
> Your obt Servant
> U. S. GRANT
> Brig Gen Com

Copies, DLC-USG, V, 4, 5, 7, 8, 78, VIA, 1; DNA, RG 393, USG Hd. Qrs. Correspondence. *O.R.*, I, iii, 501.

1. Mayfield, Ky., about twenty-three miles south of Paducah.
2. C.S.A. Gen. Albert Sidney Johnston had hd. qrs. at Columbus, Ky., from some time between Sept. 17 and Sept. 19 to Oct. 12, 1861. *Ibid.*, I, iv, 412–44 *passim*.
3. Col. James D. Morgan, 10th Ill., and Col. William H. L. Wallace, 11th Ill.
4. Dittlinger property. See letters to Julia Dent Grant, Aug. 29, 1861, note 1, and Capt. Chauncey McKeever, Oct. 7, 1861.
5. By special orders of Sept. 20, 1861. Copies, DLC-USG. V, 15, 16, 77, 82; DNA, RG 393, USG Special Orders.

To Brig. Gen. Charles F. Smith

Head Quarters Dist S. E. Mo
Cairo Sept 20th 1861

Genl

Orders by telegraph have just reached me from Head Quarters Western Department for the Gun Boat Conestoga to proceed at once to Saint Louis[1]

Will you please communicate the order

I will send you one of the two left here tomorrow evening. One of them is now undergoing repairs and cannot be got off the stocks before that time.

I have just returned from Cape Girardeau and consequently did not get your note[2] inquiring of the position occupied by Col Waagner in time to answer by to days boat. The Col has been appointed by Genl Fremont as Chief of Artillery as I understand, and is addressed from Head Quarters as such. The position I do not know that I understand the full effect of, but I have ordered here that all ~~the~~ reports from Artillery companies shall come through Col Waagner

I had no plan to submit to you for action, but Col Waagner having been very active in the reconnoisances which I have ordered from time to time some of them extending near Columbus, I have talked to him of the plan I would approve or recommend if we were in a situation to advance. At present however the force is scarcely more than a week garrison. Two of the most efficient Rigiments were ordered to Washington[3] two days ago and I sent you one half the field artillery left me.

I am Sir Very Respectfully
Your obt Servant
U. S. Grant Brig Gen

To Brig Genl C. F. Smith
Paducah Ky

Copies, DLC-USG, V, 1, 2, 3, 78; DNA, RG 393, USG Letters Sent. *O.R.*, I, iii, 501–2.

1. On Sept. 20, 1861, Maj. Gen. John C. Frémont telegraphed to USG in Hungarian. "The 'Conestoga' shall be ordered here immediately. If she is still in Paducah another boat shall be sent in her place." Copies (English), DLC-USG, V, 4, 5, 7, 8; DNA, RG 393, USG Hd. Qrs. Correspondence. Copies (Hungarian), *ibid.*, Western Dept., Telegrams; DLC-USG, VIA, 1. On Sept. 20, USG replied by telegraph to Frémont in Hungarian that the *Conestoga* was at Paducah and would be ordered to St. Louis as soon as possible. General Smith would have no gunboat for three days. Copies (Hungarian), *ibid.* Later the same day, Frémont sent two additional telegrams to USG. "Depth of water insufficient. Order for 'Conestoga' countermanded." "Dispatch received. Keep the 'Conestoga' at Paducah, we do not need her." Copies, DNA, RG 393, Western Dept., Telegrams; DLC-USG, V, 4, 5, 7, 8.

2. Not found.

3. See telegram to Maj. Gen. John C. Frémont, Sept. 15, 1861.

To Julia Dent Grant

Cairo, Sept. 20th 1861

DEAR JULIA,

I believe I have written to you that Dr. Sharp is with me. Casey was also here yesterday and day before. He says Emma was very anxious to come down and see us and probably will be down soon.

I dont know what to say about your coming. I should like to have you here and at the same time I feel that I may have to leave any day. I am in most excelent health, work all the time scarsely ever geting a half hour to take a ride out on horseback.—Evrything looks quiet here now but it may be simply a quiet before a storm.—I believe I have gone longer without writing this time than any time previous since commencing soldiering. Your last letter informed me of poor Simp's death.[1] It did not take me much by surprise but it was right sad that he should die away from home. Did you hear whether he was consious of his approaching end or did he think all the time he would be better again?—In the matter of mourning you can do as you like. I send you $20 00 by express and will send you $100 00 at the end of the month. I want to pay old man Hughlett as fast as possible after which I can supply you liberally enough. I will be able to send $250 00 per month to pay debts and support you and this saving I want to have the best care taken of. I want something after the War, if I am alive, and for you if I am not. How much I should like to see you and the children. It will cost at least $50 00 for you to come down and then you might not be able to stay with me more than one day.

Capt. Rawlins is now with me and Hillyer I have been compelled to give a leave of absence to. His wife is with her mother and her father dying sudden a few days ago, and one of her brothers also, he was obliged to go there to fix up their estate for settlement. He will be back in about ten days.

How did Buck happen to get a whiping? I thought he was too good a boy ever to require anything of the kind. Little Jess must talk now like a book, dont he? Do you think Jess would know me? I wish you would write more about the children, what they say and do. Fred. was a great favorite with the regiment whilst he was with it and I regret now that I did not keep him till this time.

Cairo is not half so unpleasant a place as I supposed it would be. I have a nice office and live with the members of my staff immediately back of it. I did stay about one week at the St. Charles but got very tired of it. Kisses for yourself and the children. Love to all our friends. Did Buck kiss Susy Felt for me?

ULYS.

ALS, DLC-USG.

1. Samuel Simpson Grant, USG's brother, died near St. Paul, Minn., on Sept. 13, 1861.

To Brig. Gen. Lorenzo Thomas

———

Head Quarters Dist S. E. Mo
Cairo Sept 21st 1861

GENERAL L. THOMAS
ADJT GENL U. S. A.
WASHINGTON D. C.
SIR

Complaint has just been lodged with me by a Mr Wm. W. Howell of Jackson Missouri that on or about the 8th day of the present month he lost a negro Boy, said to have been carried off by some of the members of the 19th Regiment of Illinois Volunteers

The 19th is now in or about Washington City and I respectfully refer the matter ~~there~~ for investigation

The Boy is discribed as being 21 years ~~of age~~ old full 6 feet high, of dark copper color, foot remarkably large, and he answers to the name of Will.

Respectfully
Your obt Servant
U. S. GRANT
Brig Gen Com

Copies, DLC-USG, V, 4, 5, 7, 8, 78; DNA, RG 393, USG Hd. Qrs. Correspondence. Although the fugitive slave laws remained in force during the early part of the Civil War, the House of Representatives, on July 9, 1861, resolved "That in the judgment of this House it is no part of the duty of the soldiers of the United States to capture and return fugitive slaves." *O.R.*, II, i, 759. Amid considerable uncertainty, army officers adopted a variety of methods for dealing with fugitive slaves. *Ibid.*, pp. 750–818 *passim*.

On Sept. 28, 1st Lt. Clark B. Lagow wrote to Col. C. Carroll Marsh. "You will deliver at once to J D McFarland a Negro Boy named 'John' brought from Jackson Mo" Copies, DLC-USG, V, 2, 77; DNA, RG 393, USG Letters Sent. On Oct. 26, James D. McFarland of Cape Girardeau wrote to USG transmitting "statements and depositions in relation to a negro boy taken from him by 20th Ill. Inf. Vols." DLC-USG, V, 10; DNA, RG 393, USG Register of Letters Received.

To Maj. Gen. John C. Frémont

Cairo, Sept 21, 61.

GEN FREMONT

Made reconnoissance today in force to within five miles of Columbus Kentucky shore by Gun boats. No enemy nearer than Columbus. From Gunboats their encampments look large.

U. S. GRANT.

Telegram (punctuation added), copies, DNA, RG 393, Western Dept., Telegrams; DLC-USG, VIA, 1.

To Col. Jacob G. Lauman

Head Quarters Dist S. E. Mo
Cairo Sept 21st 1861

COL

I want a reconnoisance made in force from your command from Elliotts Mills towards the River at Bends landing above Island No 2.[1]

You will be supported by two Gun Boats and Col Oglesby will be instructed to cross the River and follow in your rear.[2]

Let this expedition start as early as possible. Four companies of Infantry will be sufficient to retain possession of Fort Jefferson[3]

U. S. GRANT
Brig Genl Com

To Col Lawman
Com Fort Jefferson

Copies, DLC-USG, V, 1, 2, 3, 77; DNA, RG 393, USG Letters Sent. *O.R.*, I, iii, 502. Jacob G. Lauman, born in Md., moved to Iowa in 1844. On July 11, 1861, he was appointed col., 7th Iowa.

1. Island No. 2 in the Mississippi River about twelve miles below Cairo.

2. On Sept. 21, Capt. John A. Rawlins wrote to George W. Graham. "You will have three Steam Boats got in readiness for moving and have the Captains of them report to these Head Quarters one of them immediately" Copies, DLC-USG, V, 1, 2, 3, 77; DNA, RG 393, USG Letters Sent.

3. On Sept. 21, Rawlins wrote to Capt. Edward McAllister, Battery D, 1st Ill. Light Art. "Captain McAllister of the Artillery, will as soon as practicable, place one of his guns at Fort Jefferson, Ky., with sufficient number of men and rounds of ammunition at Ft Jefferson Ky." Copies, DLC-USG, V, 15, 16, 77, 82; DNA, RG 393, USG Special Orders.

To Col. C. Carroll Marsh

Head Quarters Dist S. E. Mo
Cairo Sept 21st 1861

Col

Drs McFarland & Cannon Mess Howill & Flinn all having been honorably discharged from the custody of the United States are entitled to recover their private property. You are instructed therefore (and the same instructions are to apply to all commanders who may hold any of their property) to afford them every facility to find any of their property that may be in the possession of your Regiment and to return to them whatever may belong to them.

Yours &c
U. S. GRANT
Brig Genl Com

To Col C. C. Marsh
Comdg 20th Ills Vols
Birds Point Mo

Copies, DLC-USG, V, 1, 2, 3, 78; DNA, RG 393, USG Letters Sent. On Sept. 22, 1861, 1st Lt. Clark B. Lagow wrote to Col. C. Carroll Marsh conveying the same information. Copies, DLC-USG, V, 2, 77; DNA, RG 393, USG Letters Sent.

To Col. Richard J. Oglesby

———

Head Quarters Dist S. E. Mo
Cairo Sept 21st 1861

Col

I have directed a reconnoisance in force on the Ky shore, to be made to day. You will please cross over about one half of your command to Fort Jefferson and follow up the expedition.

Instruct the steamer that crosses you over that it is to run down the river this evening to take you aboard at a landing below Island No 1[1]

U. S. Grant
Brig Genl Com

To Col Oglesby
Comdg Norfolk Mo

Copies, DLC-USG, V, 1, 2, 3, 77; DNA, RG 393, USG Letters Sent. *O.R.*, I, iii, 502. See letter to Col. Jacob G. Lauman, Sept. 21, 1861.

1. Island No. 1 in the Mississippi River about six miles below Cairo.

To Maj. Gen. John C. Frémont

———

Cairo, Sept 22/1861.

Maj. Gen. Fremont,

Your telegraph rec'd, will send the guns to Genl. Smith at once,[1] Noble's Cavalry here.[2]

U. S. Grant, Brig. Gen.

Telegram, copies, DNA, RG 393, Western Dept., Telegrams; DLC-USG, VIA, 1. On Sept. 22, 1861, Maj. Gen. John C. Frémont telegraphed to USG. "Your dispatch received. I am informed by the President that the rebels have seized Owensboro. Direct Captain Foote to use gunboats to drive rebels from there and to protect the Ohio river. Have Noble's cavalry yet reached Fort Massac. Direct him to report for orders to General Smith. Send forward three heavy guns to Gen. Smith to be placed at Smithland." Copies, *ibid.*, V, 4, 5, 7, 8, VIA, 1; DNA, RG 393, USG Hd. Qrs. Correspondence; *ibid.*, Western Dept., Telegrams. See letter to Capt. Andrew H. Foote, Sept. 22, 1861. See President Abraham Lincoln to Frémont, Sept. 22, 1861, in Lincoln, *Works*, IV, 533.

1. See letter to Brig. Gen. Charles F. Smith, Sept. 22, 1861.
2. On Sept. 22, USG wrote to Capt. Silas Noble, 2nd Ill. Cav., at Fort Massac, Ill. "A Telegraphic dispatch has just reached me from Head Quarters, Western Department—directing that you shall report to Brigd Genl C. F. Smith at Paducah Ky for duty with your command" Copies, DLC-USG, V, 1, 2, 3, 78; DNA, RG 393, USG Letters Sent.

To Maj. Gen. John C. Frémont

Head Quarters, Dist. S. E. Mo.
Cairo, September 22d 1861

GENERAL:

Yesterday I directed a reconnoisance, in force, to discover the position of the enemy. The main part of the troops from Norfolk and Fort Jefferson were landed below Island No 1 and marched from there down the beach road, supported by the Gunboats Tyler & Lexington. The result proved the Confederates to be in and around Columbus. No outposts are occupied by them nearer to us.

Mayfield has been deserted by the rebels. Col. Waagner, Chief of Ordnance, left here this evening in pursuance of orders telegraphed to him. His energy and ability have been of great service to me, particularly in directing reconnoisances, and his loss from this post will be felt.

To-day the advanced sentinels of one of our pickets fired into a scouting party of about one hundred rebels killing one horse and unhorsing five or six men. This took place about one mile from Elliotts Mills on the Columbus road.[1]

The general health of this command is improving but the number of sick is still very large.

I am Sir, very Respectfully
Your Obt. Svt.

To Maj. Gen. J. C. Frémont
Comd.g Western Dept.
St. Louis, Mo.

U. S. GRANT
Brig. Gen. Com

ALS, DNA, RG 393, Western Dept., Letters Received. *O.R.*, I, iv, 199–200.

1. On Sept. 22, 1861, Col. Jacob G. Lauman wrote to USG. "My outposts consisting of a detachment of eight or ten men infantry stationed on the road beyond Elliotts Mills was attacked this afternoon by the enemys Cavalry, about one hundred in number, and were repulsed with the loss of four known to be either killed or wounded as they tumbled out of their saddles and were carried off in their precipitate retreat—One Horse was killed, and the Horse furniture remains in the hands of my picket as a trophy—If possible send us some addition to our Cavalry force and I pledge you they wont approach our pickets again with impunity—" ALS, DNA, RG 94, War Records Office, Union Battle Reports. *O.R.*, I, iv, 200.

To Brig. Gen. John A. McClernand

Head Quarters, Dist. S. E. Mo
Cairo, Sept. 22d 1861

GEN.

Will you please direct a detail of forty men under an officer, to be made to report to Capt. Brink.[1]

I have just received a telegraph[2] ~~that~~ to send three big guns to Smithland at once.

Yours &c.
U. S. GRANT
Brig. Gen. Com.

P. S. It will probably require a second detail of the same number of men to relieve the first to-night.

GRANT

ALS, IaHA.

1. Capt. William F. Brinck, ordnance officer at Cairo.
2. See telegram to Maj. Gen. John C. Frémont, Sept. 22, 1861.

To Brig. Gen. John A. McClernand

———

Head Quarters Dist S. E Mo
Cairo Sept 22d 1861

General

Your communication of this date[1] in relation to Capt Hawley[2] is just received. I have made enquiries and find that he shows no authority for being here. He has no company, has not been sworn into service and I cannot see that he is entitled to any consideration other than as a citizen.

Capt Hawley should be compelled to show his authority for raising a company, and that he has complied with his instuctions in raising it. When this is done by reporting to Col Waagner Chief of ordinance and act. chief of artillery for instuction he will be assigned to duty.

There can be no independent command within this command and no conditions made to suit the whims of disatisfied persons.

Respectfully
Your Obt Sevt
U S Grant
Brigr Genl Comdg

To Brigd Genl J. A. McClernand
Comdg Post
Cairo Ills

Copies, DLC–USG, V, 1, 2, 3, 78; DNA, RG 393, USG Letters Sent.

1. Not found.
2. "Captain Hawley, of the Lockport Artillery, formerly commandant of Fort Prentiss, arrived here tonight. He has organized a company of siege artillery, which will be accepted for the three years service." Letter of "N.," from Cairo, Sept. 12, 1861, in *Illinois State Journal*, Sept. 16, 1861. Hawley was apparently unsuccessful in assembling a co.

To Brig. Gen. Charles F. Smith

———

Head Quarters Dist S E Mo
Cairo Sept 22 1861

GENL

In persuance of instuctions just received from Head Quarters Dept of the west,[1] I send you three Heavy Guns to be put in position at Smithland Ky.

I am also directed to notify Capt Noble of the Cavelry to report to you. He should be at Fort Massic[2] and orders accompanny this[3] to that affect

Very Respectfully
Your Obt Servt
U S GRANT
Brig Genl Com

To Brigd Genl C. F. Smith
Comdg U S troops
Paducah Ky

Copies, DLC-USG, V, 1, 2, 3, 78; DNA, RG 393, USG Letters Sent.

1. See telegram to Maj. Gen. John C. Frémont, Sept. 22, 1861.
2. Fort Massac, on the Ill. shore of the Ohio River about ten miles below Paducah, Ky.
3. See telegram to Maj. Gen. John C. Frémont, Sept. 22, 1861, note 2.

To Capt. Andrew H. Foote

———

Head Quarters Dist S. E. Mo
Cairo Sept 22d 1861

CAPT

In pursuance of Telegraphic instructions received from Head Quarters ~~Dept of the~~ Western Dept.[1] you will proceed with the Gun Boat Lexington from here and Conestoga from Paducah, to

Owensboro Ky where the Confederates are said to have taken possession, and dislodge them.

Genl Fremonts instructions are that the Ohio River is to be kept open.

U. S. GRANT
Brig Genl Com

To Capt A. H. Foote
Comdg Naval Forces
Western Waters

Copies, DLC-USG, V, 1, 2, 3, 77; DNA, RG 393, USG Letters Sent. *O.R.*, I, iv, 266; *O.R.* (Navy), I, xxii, 345. On Sept. 22, 1861, Maj. Gen. John C. Frémont telegraphed to Capt. Andrew H. Foote. "The President has ordered me to seize Owensboro now in the hands of the rebels, you will receive order through Gen Grant to send gunboat at once to dislodge them." Copy, DNA, RG 393, Western Dept., Telegrams. On Sept. 23, Foote wrote to USG. "As the Ohio River is low and falling, and opinions among Pilots being divided about there being sufficient water for the Gun Boats, I have detained the 'Bee' for the purpose of accompanying us th up the [Riv]er to haul us off in case we should get aground. I regret to inform you that the 'Conestoga' is not here, but has gone up the Cumberland probably. I shall however proceed without her unless I find her soon after the 'Lexington' arrives. Neither of the Boats are available yet. I only wait for them, even one of them, to execute promptly my orders." ALS, *ibid.*, District of Southeast Mo., Letters Received. *O.R.* (Navy), I, xxii, 346. On Sept. 25, Foote sent a fuller report to Frémont. ALS, DNA, RG 45, Area 5. *O.R.*, I, iv, 273–74; *O.R.* (Navy), I, xxii, 348–49. No C.S.A. forces were found at Owensboro, Ky. *O.R.*, I, iv, 275, 279; *O.R.* (Navy), I, xxii, 345–47.

1. See telegram to Maj. Gen. John C. Frémont, Sept. 22, 1861.

To Julia Dent Grant

———

Head Quarters, Dist. S. E. Mo.
Cairo, Sept. 22d 1861

DEAR JULIA;

I sent you to-day $20 00 for yourself and one dollar for the children, also your watch. Father wrote to me that I was to have Simps and as it is very important for me to have the time I would like to have it expressed to me at once.

I have very little news to write and but little time. Evry thing is quiet with us. To-day however our Pickets had a little skirmish with some rebels killing three or four probably.[1] These things are so common that they are hardly noticed.

Fathers letter giving an account of Simps last moments made me sad. I have felt sad all day long. Why did not Mary go out with father? I regret exceedingly that my force here has been, from necessity, kept too much reduced to admit of an advance upon Columbus. Taking possession of Paducah has necessarily taken off a large force and to advance a Garrison must be left to occupy the positions around Cairo. I would like to have the honor of commanding the ~~honor~~ Army that makes the advance down the river, but unless I am able to do it soon cannot expect it. There are to many Generals who rank me that have ~~a~~ commands inferior to mine for me to retain it.

Kiss all the children for me. Jess is to have two bits to spend for himself and Martha Rebecca[2] the same. One at a time however is enough for them to spend their money.

Father speaks of coming by here on his way home. I should like to see him very much.

Give my love to all our friends. Write to me often.

ULYS.

ALS, DLC-USG.

1. See telegram to Maj. Gen. John C. Frémont, Sept. 22, 1861.
2. Ellen Grant.

To Maj. Gen. John C. Frémont

————

Sept 23 1861.
Cairo 1861.

MAJ. GEN. FREMONT

Information from Columbus indicate the rebels are crossing to Belmont, taking away two gun boats. The third is laid up &

weakening my force as has been done may force me to abandon Norfolk & Fort Jefferson. I will hold on to them as long as it is prudent. Our pickets had a passage at arms last night one & half miles below Hunters, three men & horses missing.[1]

U. S. Grant

Brig. Genl.

Telegram (punctuation added), copies, DNA, RG 393, Western Dept., Telegrams; DLC-USG, VIA, 1. The information in this telegram was probably included in a letter to Maj. Gen. John C. Frémont of the same date which has not been found. On Sept. 26, 1861, Capt. Chauncey McKeever, adjt. for Frémont, wrote to USG. "Your report of the 23rd inst. is received. I will order arms to be furnished for the regiments under command of Brig. Gen. McClernand and reinforce you with two new regiments as soon as possible. By this means you will be enabled in concert with Brig. Gen. Smith to control the rebel forces on both the Kentucky and Missouri shores. Should the enemy expose a weak point on either side of the river you may inflict upon him a combined blow, but at present I am not in favor of incurring any hazard of defeat. It is not impossible that the enemy may cross at Belmont and attempt to march upon Cape Girardeau by way of Charleston. Should you be unable with your limited force to prevent this by the occupation of Charleston, you will do so by frequent demonstrations and strong reconnoisances in that direction." LS, DNA, RG 393, District of Southeast Mo., Letters Received. *O.R.*, I, iii, 507.

1. On Sept. 22, Col. Richard J. Oglesby wrote to USG. "About dark this evening a portion of my cavalry, near Hunters, met a number of the Enemy's cavalry, in a skirt of woods—and in the fight that ensued some two or three of our men, were wounded, or lost—and some four or five horses. Upon their return to Camp I signalled the Gun Boats, and they were in the act of moving towards Cairo and did not heed me. I wish to send two or three companies of Infantry down on one of them, to recover the men and horses, will you be good enough to send one down—as I wish the Infantry to go down and return before day light—Some of the enemys Infantry were two miles below Hunters today—" ALS, DNA, RG 393, District of Southeast Mo., Letters Received.

To Brig. Gen. John A. McClernand

Head Quarters, Dist. S. E. Mo.
Cairo, Sept. 23d 1861

GENERAL:

The prisoner refered to in your note of this evening[1] will have to be kept in confinement until some authority can be found for trying him. I confess myself at a loss to know how jurisdiction can be found, but I believe, under the circumstances, he can be tried by a Military Commission.

Respectfully
Your Obt. Svt.
U. S. GRANT
Brig. Gen.

To Brig. Gen. J. A. McClernand
Commanding Post
Cairo Ill.

ALS, McClernand Papers, IHi.

1. On Sept. 23, 1861, Maj. Mason Brayman wrote to USG. "Enclosed find letter letter from Col. R J Oglesby, 8th Regt. at Norfolk, which explains itself. The prisoner was last night committed to custody and ironed, and awaits your order." ALS, *ibid.* On Sept. 22, Brayman had written to Col. Richard J. Oglesby. "I am instructed by Brig. Genl. McClernand to advise you of the delivery into his custody of the prisoner, Peter O'Brien, by your Sergeant Howell. The list of witnesses, however, does not accompany your letter. P[lease] f[or]ward th[eir na]mes as they will be required in presenting his case to Genl. Grant." ALS, Oglesby Papers, *ibid.* On Sept. 24, Brig. Gen. John A. McClernand wrote to USG. "Enclosed are the names of witnesses against Peter O'Brien, charged with murder, a statement of which, by Col Oglesby, is in your hands. The prisoner is in Jail." Copy, McClernand Papers, *ibid.* On Sept. 20, Oglesby had written to USG "in reference to the case of the man O'Brien 8th. Ill. Inf. Vols charged with willful murder." DLC-USG, V, 10; DNA, RG 393, USG Register of Letters Received. See letter to Capt. Chauncey McKeever, Sept. 29, 1861. On Oct. 4, Capt. John A. Rawlins for USG issued special orders appointing a military commission to try Peter O'Brien, 8th Ill. Copies, DLC-USG, V, 15, 16, 77, 82; DNA, RG 393, USG Special Orders; (Printed) McClernand Papers, IHi. Private Peter O'Brien deserted on Dec. 2, 1861.

To Col. Jacob G. Lauman

————

Head Quarters Dist S. E. Mo
Cairo Sept 23d 1861

Col

Move two regiments and all your Cavalry but one company to Norfolk, as soon as possible. The balance must be held in readiness for a move

Put your Baggage aboard of a Steamboat to be taken to Birds Point where it will have to be discharged.

U. S. Grant
Brig Genl Com

To Col Lawman
Comdg Fort Jefferson Ky

Copies, DLC-USG, V, 1, 2, 3, 77; DNA, RG 393, USG Letters Sent. *O.R.*, I, iii, 503. This order was probably enclosed in a letter of the same date from Capt. John A. Rawlins to George W. Graham. "You will send two good sized Steam Boats to Fort Jefferson and the accompanying order to commander of Post at that Place" Copies, DLC-USG, V, 1, 2, 3, 77; DNA, RG 393, USG Letters Sent. Earlier on Sept. 23, 1861, Rawlins wrote to Col. Jacob G. Lauman. "Information having reached these Head Quarters that the enemy are crossing the River, you are directed to ascertain the fact, and should it be so hold yourself in readiness to be thrown across the River to Norfolk with your entire command abandoning Fort Jefferson entirely if it should be necessary" Copies, *ibid*. On the same day, 1st Lt. Clark B. Lagow wrote to Brig. Gen. John A. McClernand. "You will order one Company of Cavelry and their Baggage to report themselves to Col Lawmann Comdg 7th Regt Iowa Volls—at once—at Fort Jefferson Ky" LS, McClernand Papers, IHi. Misdated Sept. 22 in DLC-USG, V, 1, 2, 3, 77; DNA, RG 393, USG Letters Sent.

To Col. Richard J. Oglesby

Head Quarters Dist S. E. Mo
Cairo Sept 23d 1861

Sir

Information having reached me that the confederates are crossing the River at Columbus you are directed to watch their movements observing however proper Caution.

Should there be indications of a formidable attack upon your Post try and inform me in time to reinfoce you.

If it should become necessary the whole force from Fort Jefferson and Elliotts Mills could be sent to you

U. S Grant
Brig Genl Com

To Col Oglesby
Comdg Post
Norfolk

Copies, DLC-USG, V, 1, 2, 3, 77; DNA, RG 393, USG Letters Sent. *O.R.*, I, iii, 503. On Sept. 24, 1861, Col. Richard J. Oglesby wrote twice to USG. "Yesterday evening the 2d Iowa, 7th Iowa and Capt Langs, Cavalry—arrived at this point and were immediately posted for the night, under your order to send their baggage to Birds Point The 2d Iowa were without tents. I have ordered the Col of the 2d Iowa, this morning—to move with his Regiment by land to Birds Point. I still hold at the place, the 7th Iowa and Cavalry Company—on the Steamer Louisiana, ready to move to Bird's Pt—when I shall obtain the position of the Enemy—this I shall know by 4 o'clock. P. M. today—I think the Louisiana will get to the Point to day night—Unless specially and strongly threatened, I will not leave here immediately, unless you shall otherwise direct The night was quiet. Pickets observed nothing unusual" "I am satisfied that the enemy contemplate no attack upon this point. at present my scouts are all In from my front and from below as far as the Hunter Farm—Captain Noleman encountered at the Lower line of the Beckwith farm about 40 of the enemies cavalry who fled back of the corn field towards the woods and soon disappeared—I have increased my Pickets for to night and have ordered the 7th Iowa Regt Col Lauman to report on Board Steamer Louisiana at Birds Point Mo—one of the cavary companies Just in from the old Rushes Ridge road three miles In my front and across the Lake—report that on Sunday morning at 8 oclock a company of the enemies cavaly 120 strong visited the church there—It Looks a little as though they may have a camp on the road from Belmont to Charleston—this can be easily assertained from Birds Point—" LS and ALS, DNA, RG 393, District of Southeast Mo., Letters Received.

To Col. William H. L. Wallace

———

> Head Quarters Dist S. E. Mo
> Cairo Sept 23d 1861

Col

Move the portion of your Regiment now at Birds Point to the support of Col Oglesby at Norfolk. I want a reconnoisance made to night and if it appears that the Rebels are crossing the River in force I want the whole command moved to Birds Point in the morning.

> U. S. Grant
> Brig Gnl Com

To Col W. H. L. Wallace
Comdg Bird Point Mo

Copies, DLC-USG, V, 1, 2, 3, 77; DNA, RG 393, USG Letters Sent. *O.R.*, I, iii, 503.

General Orders No. 9

———

> Head Quarters Dist S. E. Mo
> Cairo Sept 24th, 1861

General Orders No 9

The President of the United States having appointed Thursday the 26th inst as a day of Humiliation, Prayer and ~~Thanksgiving~~ Fasting for all the people of the nation and reccomend that if be observed and kept in all humility and with all religious solemnity to the end that the united prayer of the nation might ascend to the Throne of Grace and bring down plentiful blessings upon our own country;

It is therefore ordered, That the day be properly observed by the several commands of this district that all military duty be suspended except such as may be forced upon us by unavoidable necessity, and that the officers non commissioned officers and Privates according to their several creeds and modes of worship, unite in the offering of fervent supplications to almighty God for his blessings upon our beloved country

By order of Brig Genl U. S. Grant
Jno. A. Rawlins
Asst Adjt Genl

Copies, DLC-USG, V, 12, 13, 14, 80; DNA, RG 393, USG General Orders. On Sept. 24, 1861, 1st Lt. Clark B. Lagow wrote to Capt. Reuben B. Hatch. "You will have 50 copies of Genl Order No 9 printed immediately" Copies, DLC-USG, V, 2, 77; DNA, RG 393, USG Letters Sent. See Lincoln, *Works*, IV, 482–83.

To Maj. Gen. John C. Frémont

Head Quarters Dist S. E. Mo
Cairo Sept 24th 1861

Genl J. C. Fremont
Comdg Dept of the West
Saint Louis Mo.
Sir

I have no new move of the enemy to report. I still continue active reconnoisances, and have I believe driven the enemy back to Columbus and Belmont.

Every day our advance scouts come in sight of parties of Rebels but they allways retreat upon sight of our troops.

I have withdrawn all the troops from Fort Jefferson and strengthened the command at Norfolk.[1] Should reinforcements be sent here however I will retake that position. It was only abandoned this morning.

The three men reported missing by me day before yesterday[2] have all returned with the ~~exception~~ loss of one Horse.

It is reported to me by Capt Walker[3] of Gun Boat Tyler that his men cannot receive pay short of Cincinnati. As it would be attended with much injury to the service to grant leaves of absence to his men to go there for their pay and with great expense either to the men or to ~~the~~ Government to send them, I would respectfully reccomend that some arrangement be made by which they may be paid here.

The numbers of applications for discharge on surgeon certificate of disability has become so great and as appears to me granted on such trivial grounds that I have felt it my duty to throw such restrictions in the way that certificates cannot be obtained in the future when not really deserved.[4]

I would ask whether it is necessary that the final discharge should come from Department Head Quarters or whether they may not be given here

> Respectfully
> Your Obt Servant
> U. S. GRANT
> Brig Genl ~~Genl~~ Com

Copies, DLC-USG, V, 4, 5, 7, 8, 78; DNA, RG 393, USG Hd. Qrs. Correspondence. *O.R.*, I, iii, 504–5.

1. See letters to Cols. Jacob G. Lauman and William H. L. Wallace, Sept. 23, 1861.

2. See telegram to Maj. Gen. John C. Frémont, Sept. 23, 1861.

3. Commander Henry Walke was assigned to command the gunboat *Tyler* on Sept. 12, 1861. *O.R.* (Navy), I, xxii, 333. See H. Walke, *Naval Scenes and Reminiscences of the Civil War . . .* (New York, 1877).

4. On Sept. 13, Brig. Gen. John A. McClernand wrote to USG. "Herewith you find four certificates of disability for discharges, which I have enclosed to you for consideration, believeing that I have no authority to act upon in view of the 139th paragraph of the 19th article of Army Regulations 1857" DfS, McClernand Papers, IHi. On Sept. 17, McClernand again wrote to USG. "Capt James Monroe, company B. 7th Ill. commanded by Col John Cook has brought to me a number of Surgeon's certificates of disability, for the purpose of getting my approval thereto in order to give them the effect of Soldier's discharges. Upon examination of the 159th paragraph of Art. 19 of Army regulations, 1861, I find it is only 'the commander of the department or of an army in the field,' who can grant a discharge 'on a certificate of disability.' Considering that Maj. Genl. Freemont is the commander of the Department and that you are commander in the field in this district, I have hitherto abstained from signing such certificates. If I am in error I ask to be corrected." ADfS, *ibid.* On Sept. 20, USG issued General Orders No. 8. "The number of certificates of Disability coming up for action is becoming so alarming that the General commanding has decided that in each case hereafter, besides being signed by the Surgeon of the Regiment ~~to which~~ or detachment to which the

applicant belongs, they must be approved by a board of at least two Surgeons, appointed for the purpose. Discharged Soldiers being entitled to mileage to the places of their enlistment no free passes will be granted to them in future" Copies, DLC-USG, V, 12, 13, 14, 80; DNA, RG 393, USG General Orders; (Printed) McClernand Papers, IHi. On Sept. 21, Capt. John A. Rawlins for USG issued special orders appointing a board of three surgeons to examine applicants for discharge. Copies, DLC-USG, V, 15, 16, 77, 82; DNA, RG 393, USG Special Orders; (Printed) McClernand Papers, IHi.

To Brig. Gen. John A. McClernand

[*Sept. 24, 1861*]

I received a despatch from the Western Dept. Head Quarters several days ago to rlease the Steamer John Gault. I accordingly directed the Surveyor of the Port to release her and think he must have received my note.

Yours &c.

U. S. GRANT

Brig. Gen. Com

AES, McClernand Papers, IHi. At the bottom of a Sept. 24, 1861, letter from Brig. Gen. John A. McClernand. "Are you prepared to render your decision in the case of the Steamer John Gault. ? I have received a telegraphic despatch from the captain of the boat wishing to know" LS, *ibid.* On Sept. 23, USG had written to Charles D. Arter, surveyor of the port of Cairo. "In pursuance of instructions from Head Quarters 'Department of the West' dated Sept 20th 1861, the Steamer Jno Gault is relieved from custody. My understanding is that this also releases her cargo" Copies, DLC-USG, V, 1, 2, 3, 77; DNA, RG 393, USG Letters Sent. See letter to Maj. Gen. John C. Frémont, Sept. 18, 1861.

To Charles D. Arter

————

                              Head Quarters Dist S. E. Mo
                                 Cairo Sept 24th 1861

Mr Arter
Surveyor of Port
Cairo Ills
Sir
  Untill otherwise directed by competent authority you will be authorized to pass to Paducah Ky and any other Point in said state that may be Garrisoned by Federal Forces all goods, arms &co upon being fully satisfied that they are for the use only of Federal Troops or persons in the employ of the Government

                              Yours &co
                              U. S. Grant
                              Brig Genl Com

Copies, DLC-USG, V, 1, 2, 3, 77; DNA, RG 393, USG Letters Sent. Charles D. Arter is listed in the 1860 U.S. Census as a thirty-year-old merchant of Cairo, born in Ohio.

To Brig. Gen. John A. McClernand

————

                              Head Quarters, Dist. S. E. Mo.
                                 Cairo, Sept. 25th 1861

Gen.
  The Company of Col. Oglesby's Regt. now on duty guarding the bridge over Big Muddy[1] having been on duty there, detached from the main part of the Command, for a long time I would suggest that it be relieved by a Company from the 10th Ill.
  The Company forming this Guard should take one weeks

rations with them and at that time, and weekly hereafter, be relieved.

Yours &c.

U. S. GRANT

Brig. Gen. Com.

To Gen. J. A. McClernand
Comd.g Post
Cairo Ill.

ALS, McClernand Papers, IHi.

1. The Illinois Central Railroad bridge over the Big Muddy River just north of Carbondale, Ill., about sixty miles north of Cairo, had been guarded against destruction by Confederate sympathizers continually since April 22, 1861, when the first Ill. troops were sent to Cairo. *Ill. AG Report*, I, 8.

To Charles D. Arter

Head Quarters Dist S. E. Mo
Cairo Sept 25th 1861

SIR

Boats leaving this point to go up the Ohio are forbid carrying all venders of papers or other articles, for sale without express permission from the surveyor of the Port to do so.

Such permits must state the exact priveledge extended and under what restrictions a copy of which the vender or agent must furnish to the commander of the Boat upon which he travels. It will be the duty of such commander to report all violations of priveleges granted under these instructions

U. S. GRANT

Brig Gnl Com

C. Arter
Surveyor of Port
Cairo Ills

Copies, DLC-USG, V, 1, 2, 3, 77; DNA, RG 393, USG Letters Sent.

To Julia Dent Grant

Cairo, September 25th/61

DEAR JULIA;

I received three letters from you to-day all written last month and two of them a month or more ago. You complain ~~bitterly~~ of my not writing. It may be that you have not received all my letters but I do not think that I have ever gone a whole week without writing and generally not more than three or four days.[1]

All is quiet here now. How long it will remain so is impossible to tell. If I had troops enough not long. My force I look upon as sufficient to hold this place but not sufficient to make an aggressive movement against the large force now occupying Columbus. I see from father's letter that he expects to come by here. I shall be very glad to see him.

The news from Lexington to-day is bad but is conciderably relieved by the report that the rebels are about to be taken and Lexington retaken.[2] I have reduced the duties of my office very much from what they were by being a little more exclusive than I was at first so that now I can take a ride evry evening after 4 O'Clock. At night however I am busy. Our mails come in at such an hour that from 12 at night until 1 or 2 in the morning I am always busy, Sunday night excepted.

To-morrow is Thanksgiving Day and will be a Sunday with us. I send you a copy of my order for the occation.[3] I see some of the papers get hold of all my orders by some means or other and publish them. I do not know how it is. I do not let newspaper correspondents come about me. I see they are not published in the Democrat[4] however.

Dr. Sharp lives with me. He has received two or three letters from Nellie. They are all well. Broady Hull[5] is a Lieut. Col. and has lately distinguished himself by stealing a lot of mules and horses from citizens of Missouri who have been guilty of the henious crime of loyalty although they had not taken up arms in defence of their country.

Give my love to all at home. Kiss the children for me. Did you get the watch I sent you and $21 00 in money ?[6] I want the other sent to me. It is important that I should have a correct time piece and the one I had gets sometimes an hour out of the way in a single day. Do you see much of our neighbors ? How much I should like to be back in Galena for a day or two.

Remember me to the Felts, Haynes and the Brownels.[7] Tell Buck to kiss Miss Mary[8] for me and all the children kiss their Ma for the same old boy. I will try and send you all something to buy a nice present in a week. I will also get the photograph of myself and staff.

ULYS.

ALS, DLC-USG.

1. Letters printed in this volume support this statement. Since there are none dated between Aug. 10 and Aug. 26, or between Sept. 12 and Sept. 20, 1861, some may have miscarried.
2. The siege of Lexington, Mo., by Maj. Gen. Sterling Price, Mo. State Guard, ended on Sept. 20 with the surrender of some 3,000 U.S. troops. The news did not appear in the *Chicago Tribune* until Sept. 24, 1861. Rumors of the recapture of Lexington were unfounded.
3. See General Orders No. 9, Sept. 24, 1861. It was actually a day of "public humiliation, prayer and fasting . . ." Lincoln, *Works,* IV, 482.
4. *Missouri Democrat.*
5. Lt. Col. Edward B. Hull, 2nd Div. (Cav.), Mo. State Guard.
6. See letter to Julia Dent Grant, Sept. 22, 1861.
7. For the Felt and Brownell families, see letters of May 3, June 1, 1861. A. M. Haines, wholesale dealer in dry goods, lived near USG in Galena.
8. Mary Duncan. See letter of May 3, 1861.

To Mary Grant

———

Cairo,
September 25th, 1861.

DEAR SISTER:

I have just received your last letter, also another written by you about one month ago, which has followed me around until at length it reached this place. I am very well, but have no news to communicate.

I had extended my lines nearly half way to Columbus and made reconnoissances frequently to within sight of the rebel camps, but my force has to be so reduced that it would be imprudent to make an attack now until I am reinforced.

I hope some day, if I am allowed to retain this command, to give a good account of ourselves. Simpson's death, though looked for for the last two years, causes me a great deal of sadness. The day I heard of it, I received a number of letters from Galena. In two or three of them his arrival at St. Paul was noted, and it was stated that he was no better. Our family has been peculiarly blessed up to this time. But few families of the same number have gone so many years without the loss of a single member.

I expect Father here as soon as Orvil returns to Galena.

BROTHER ULYS.

J. G. Cramer, pp. 59–60.

To Capt. Chauncey McKeever

Head Quarters, Dist. S. E. Mo.
Cairo, September 26th 1861

CAPT. C. McKEEVER
ASST. ADJ. GEN. U.S.A.
ST. LOUIS, MO.
SIR:

Yours of the 24th inst.[1] calling my attention to a Circular from Head Quarters Western Department dated August 31st is just received.—In reply I have to state that long before the circular refered to was promulgated I knew the proper channel through which to approach a senior officer, and always adopted the proper approach until directed by Maj. Gen. Fremont, over his own signature, to communicate with him direct.[2]

In future I will address all official communications to the Commanding General through the Adjt. Gen.

> Very Respectfully
> Your Obt. Svt.
> U. S. GRANT
> Brig. Gen. Com

ALS, DNA, RG 393, Western Dept., Letters Received. Capt. Chauncey Mc-Keever of Md., USMA 1849, was asst. adjt. gen. for Maj. Gen. John C. Frémont.

1. On Sept. 24, 1861, McKeever wrote to USG. "The Major General Commanding directs that your attention be called to the Circular from these Head Quarters, dated Aug. 31st 1861, and that in future all official Communications sent by mail, will be directed to the Assistant Adjutant General at these Head Quarters." LS, *ibid.*, District of Southeast Mo., Letters Received.

2. See letter to Capt. John C. Kelton, Sept. 1, 1861.

To Capt. Chauncey McKeever

———

> Head Quarters, Dist. S. E. Mo.
> Cairo, September 26th 1861

CAPT. C. MCKEEVER;
ASST. ADJ. GEN. U. S. A.
WESTERN DEPARTMENT
ST LOUIS MO.
SIR;

For the information of the Gen. Comd.g the Western Department I have to report that reconnoisances which I have directed for the last two days show the enemy to have abandoned their position near Hunters farm. They are now confined to their encampments at Columbus and Belmont.—A party of Cavalry sent out by my order this morning succeeded in surprising a detachment of about forty of Jeff. Thompsons command to-day. I enclose herewith Col. Oglesby's report of the result.[1] I have to report the loss of two good soldiers by the culpable conduct of

Lieut. J. W. Campion 20th Ill. Vols. on yesterday.—Col. Marsh's report of the circumstances are enclosed herewith.[2]

There are two companies of the 7th Iowa regiment stationed at Potosi Mo. which I would respectfully ~~might~~ request to be relieved and sent here to join their regiment.

Yesterday a party of Cavalry from Columbus come up to the neighborhood of Elliotts Mills and arrested a farmer there for the crime of loyalty to his country. To-day I directed in retaliation the arrest of two noted secessionests who were informed that they would be released on the safe return of the union man sent to Columbus.[3] The party making the arrest went into Blandville and brought from there also a ~~Dr~~. Mr. Blake[4] who is charged with recruiting a company for the Southern Army. He will be sent to St. Louis for trial.

Respectfully
Your Obt. Svt
U. S. Grant
Brig. Gen Com

ALS, DNA, RG 94, War Records Office, Union Battle Reports. *O.R.*, I, iii, 197; *ibid.*, II, ii, 79.

1. On Sept. 26, 1861, Col. Richard J. Oglesby wrote to USG. "Captain Stewart in command of the Squadron of Cavalry that left here this morning consisting of a small detachment of this own company Captain Langes Compny and Captain Pfaffs Company returned at five Oclock P M with four Prisoners and four horses and riging He met the Cavalry of the enemy at the Hunter farm near the edge of the timber and by a skillful maneuver Surround and captured a portion of them Capt. Steward reports some ten or twelve killed and several wounded, one Horse lost I send the Prisoners by the 'January' this evening will retain the horses for the use of the Cavalry until otherwise ordered you will Learn from the Prisoners that the position of the enemy is unchanged at Belmont Jeff Thompson Still has only 2,500—800 Cavalry included I will give no detailed statement as you will learn all from the prisoners We are not threatened by them But the Steamer Jeff Davis is still below us waiting to be taken I have sent the German Cavalry back to the point to night" ALS, DNA, RG 94, War Records Office, Union Battle Reports. *O.R.*, I, iii, 197–98. On Sept. 28, Oglesby wrote to USG. "Yesterday I sent down 200 Infantry of Col Dougherty's Reg't (Capt Challenor) to sustain the Cavalry if repulsed. At the Beckwith farm five miles below here, Capt Challenor met the Enemy ~~sustained~~ stationed to surprise our Cavalry, by drawing it into an ambuscade—Upon the first fire from Capt McAdam's Co, the whole force fled in confusion—The enemy were about 400, besides a small body

of Cavalry. They have never been so near us before. It means nothing more than an effort to catch our Cavalry Companies scouting the country about Hunters farm. We were not troubled by the Jeff Davis last night, although she was in two miles of us apart of the time" ALS, DNA, RG 94, War Records Office, Union Battle Reports. *O.R.*, I, iii, 198.

2. On Sept. 25, Col. C. Carroll Marsh wrote to Capt. John A. Rawlins. "I have to report that 1st Lieutenant J W. Campion of Company 'B' 20th Reg Ill Vols. also was sent in charge of his company to protect the 'Burnt Bridge' on the Charleston R. R. did in excess of his orders leave his company at the Bridge, and with privates Albert H. Rowan and Henry C Manker go to Charleston where he remained for some two hours or more ~~was~~ spending most of the time (as I am informed) in conversation with a lady, and until he was overhauled by some thirty of the rebel cavalry and with the privates above mentioned taken prisoners. His conduct in leaving his Post is so unwarrantable that I feel authorized to request that his name be dropped from the roll of commissioned officers. Should an opportunity soon occur for an exchange of prisoners, I reccommend to your attention privates Rowan and Manker who are both good soldiers—" Copy, DLC-USG, VIA, 1. 1st Lt. John W. Champion, Co. C, 20th Ill., was released on Oct. 23, and resigned on Nov. 10, 1861. *O.R.*, II, i, 513.

3. On Sept. 25, Rawlins wrote to Lt. Col. Enos P. Wood, 17th Ill. "You will make a reconnoisance tomorrow towards Elliotts Mills and beyon if found practicable. Learn all you can of the movements and position of the enemy but avoid being led into ambush. Take two leading secessionists from the neighborhood of Elliotts Mills prisoners to be held as hostages for the safety of Wm Mercer a union man and Kentuckyian taken by the invaders of his state and carried to Columbus or elsewhere as a prisoner." Copies, DLC-USG, V, 1, 2, 3, 77; DNA, RG 393, USG Letters Sent. *O.R.*, I, iii, 506–7; *ibid.*, II, i, 511.

4. See following letter.

To Brig. Gen. John A. McClernand

———

Head Quarters, Dist. S. E. Mo.
Cairo, Sept. 26th 1861

GEN.

I have caused the arrest, and confinement, of three citizens of Blandville by the names of Blak, Corbett and Vaughan. The two latter are held as hostages for the safety and return of a Mr. Mercer, a Union man and citizen of Ky. who was arrested by the rebels and carried into Columbus a few days since.

The former I propose sending to St. Louis charged with recruiting a company for the southern army. Witnesses, Sergeant

John Caton Capt. Delano's Comp.y of Cavalry and Mr. Ed. Mercer now living at Fort Holt.

Respectfully &c.

U. S. GRANT

Brig. Gen. Com

To Gen. J. C. Frémont[1]
Comd.g Post
Cairo Ill.

ALS, McClernand Papers, IHi. See preceding letter.

1. This is obviously an error.

To Capt. Reuben B. Hatch

Head Quarters Dist S. E. Mo.
Cairo Sept 26th 1861

CAPT

You are directed to proceed to Saint Louis as soon as practicable for the purpose of procuring fund pertaining to the Quartermaster Department for the use of this post.

This Post having been built and carried along on the strength of the Government credit now for five months without any funds much to the inconvenience of creditors and embarrassment of the service you will urge upon the proper authorities the importance of your mission

U. S. GRANT

Brig Genl Com

To Capt R. B. Hatch
Brigade Q. M.
Cairo Ills

Copies, DLC-USG, V, 1, 2, 3, 77; DNA, RG 393, USG Letters Sent.

To Brig. Gen. John A. McClernand

Hd Qrs. Dist. S. E. Mo.
Cairo, Sept 27th 1861

The proceedings of the Court Martial refered to are just in and I am now reviewing them. In the case of Ewing the Court have found him guilty as charged and sentence him to be drumed out of service.

U. S. GRANT
Brig. Gen. Com.

AES, McClernand Papers, IHi. On reverse of Brig. Gen. John A. McClernand to USG, Sept. 26, 1861. "Will you please inform me what sentence was passed upon Andrew J. Ewing, of the 7th Regiment, Iowa Volunteers, by the General Court Martial. He is confined in the Guard house and I have not been notified of any sentence having been passed against him." LS, *ibid.* On Oct. 7, Capt. John A. Rawlins for USG issued special orders that Private Andrew J. Ewing, 7th Iowa, be drummed out of service in the presence of his regt. Copies, DLC-USG, V, 15, 16, 77, 82; DNA, RG 393, USG Special Orders.

To Lt. Col. Marcellus M. Crocker

Head Quarters Dist S. E. Mo
Cairo Sept 27th 1861

SPECIAL ORDER

Lt Col M. M. Crocker of the 2nd Regiment of Iowa Vols, will proceed immediately to Saint Louis Mo, and collect together there the sick of his Regiment and forward to this place by River such as are likely to be soon fit for duty. This done he will proceed to Ironton Mo, and there get all the sick of his Regiment, left at that place and bring them to St Louis where those unfit for duty will be left in Hospital the remainder will be forwarded to their Regiment.

Upon his return Col Crocker will detain the Boat upon which he may return at Cape Girardeau sufficient time to get the sick of that point. All who are able to rejoin their regiment will be brought to it

Sufficient ~~well~~ may men will be left with the sick to take proper care of them.

U. S. GRANT
Brig Genl. Com

Copies, DLC-USG, V, 15, 16, 77, 82; DNA, RG 393, USG Special Orders. Lt. Col. Marcellus M. Crocker of Iowa, a nongraduate of USMA 1851, was appointed capt. in the 2nd Iowa on May 27, 1861, and rose to brig. gen. on Nov. 29, 1862.

To Brig. Gen. John A. McClernand

Head Quarters, Dist. S E. Mo.
Cairo, Sept. 28th 1861

GENERAL:

Will you please direct the prisoner Blake to be sent before me as soon as practicable.

Yours &c.
U. S. GRANT
Brig. Gen. Com.

To Gen. J. A. McClernand
Comd.g Post
Cairo, Ill.

ALS, McClernand Papers, IHi. See letter to Capt. Chauncey McKeever, Sept. 26, 1861.

To Col. John Cook

Head Quarters Dist S E Mo
Cairo Sept 28 1861

SIR

You will please direct the Quartermaster at Cape Girardeau to enter into a contract for the hire of the stmr "Luella" said contract to take date from the time said steamer was seized by Col Marshs order. Place your endorsement upon the contract and forward to me for action.

U S GRANT
Brg Genl Comdg

To Col John Cook
Comdg U S Forces
Cape Girardeau

Copies, DLC-USG, V, 1, 2, 3, 77; DNA, RG 393, USG Letters Sent. On Sept. 26, 1861, Capt. John A. Rawlins had written to Col. John Cook. "You are hereby authorized to employ A. S Lightner as Pilot and to command 'Ferry Transport Luella' at Cape Girardeau Subject to appoval of Major General John. C. Fremont Commanding Dept of the West" Copies, DLC-USG, V, 2, 77; DNA, RG 393, USG Letters Sent. On Oct. 1, Col. Joseph B. Plummer wrote to USG. "I have the honor to acknowledge the receipt of your communication of the 28th Ultimo, Addressed to Col John Cook, my predecessor in Command, and turned over by him to me, directing a contract to be made for hire of Steamer 'Luella' I sent for the owner of the Boat, and directed my Quartermaster to make a contract with him. I herewith enclose a communication of the former in regard to his action in the matter which I have approved I would remark that I consider the demmand of Mr Vancil Exhorbitant and that eight or ten dollars a day is ample remuneration for the use of this Boat I have given Mr Vancil permission to visit Cairo to see you upon the subject" Copy, *ibid.*, Post of Cape Girardeau, Letters Sent. See letter to Capt. Chauncey McKeever, Oct. 4, 1861.

To Col. John T. Fiala

Cairo Sept 29th/1861

JNO T FIALA,
       I have not got a company of sappers & Miners here.

U. S. GRANT.
Brig Gen.

Telegram, copies, DNA, RG 393, Western Dept., Telegrams; DLC-USG, VIA, 1. John T. Fiala, born in Hungary, served as lt. col., 2nd Mo. Reserve Corps, May 7—Aug. 16, 1861, and on Sept. 20 was appointed topographical engineer with the rank of col. on the staff of Maj. Gen. John C. Frémont. As Frémont left

St. Louis for the field on Sept 24, Capt. Chauncey McKeever was informed by Col. Joseph H. Eaton, Frémont's military secretary, that he was to act in concert with Fiala in forwarding information to Frémont and in sending any necessary reinforcements to USG and Brig. Gen. Charles F. Smith. Copy, DNA, RG 393, Western Dept., Letters Sent by Gen. Frémont. On Sept. 28, Fiala telegraphed to USG. "Can you send a company of pioneers to Paducah, to guard bridge? Reply immediately." Copies, *ibid.*, Telegrams; DLC-USG, VIA, 1; dated Sept. 29, *ibid.*, V, 4, 5, 7, 8; DNA, RG 393, USG Hd. Qrs. Correspondence.

To Capt. Chauncey McKeever

Head Quarters, Dist. S. E. Mo.
Cairo, Sept. 29th 1861

SIR;

Evry thing here is quiet and no rumors to disturb it. I have heard this evening that Hardee has arrived at New Madrid, from Bloomfield, probably to reinforce Johnson at Columbus. I scarsely credit the rumor but it may be true.

There are quite a number of troops at this place, doing service, that have never been sworn in. I would respectfully ask that a mustering officer be sent, or some one already here be duly authorized to act as such.[1]

I have in confinement here a soldier charged with willful and malicious murder, committed upon a fellow soldier.[2] The crime was perpetrated in Missouri where it is impossible to bring the criminal to justice by usual process; by law he cannot be tried in any court out of the state where the offence was committed. I would therefore ask if he cannot be tried by a Military commission.

The cold Season is now so nearly at hand that it is time to think of providing winter Quarters for the garrison that must necessarily occupy this place. Log huts could be cheaply built but even they would call for the outlay of some money. Credit will not do at this place longer. I understand that the credit of the Government has been already used to the extent of several hundred thousand dollars and no money ever paid out. This causes much murmering among the citizens and unless a Paymaster is soon sent to pay off the troops the same may be expected from the soldiers. I would respectfully urge therefore that funds be ordered here for the Quartermaster's Department and also that the troops be paid as soon as practicable.

> I am Sir, Very respectfully
> Your Obt. Svt.
> U. S. GRANT
> Brig. Gen. Com

To Capt. Chauncy McKeever
Asst. A. Gen Western Dept.
St. Louis Mo.

ALS, DNA, RG 393, Western Dept., Letters Received. *O.R.*, I, iii, 509. At the same time, USG telegraphed to Capt. Chauncey McKeever. "It is reported here that Hardee has arrived at New Madrid from Bloomfield to reinforce Jnoson the information is derived from furloughed troops from Columbus tell me if you have reliable information from Hardee" Copies, DNA, RG 393, Western Dept., Telegrams; DLC-USG, VIA, 1. On Sept. 29, 1861, McKeever telegraphed to USG. "We have reliable information that Hardee with nine regiments & twenty six pieces of artillery was moving on Columbus or rather Belmont—2000 muskets have been shipped for McClernands brigade." Copies, *ibid*.
    On Sept. 29, Col. C. Carroll Marsh wrote to Capt. John A. Rawlins. "Information just received by an agent whom Col Wallace has employed, to the effect that day before yesterday Gen Hardee was at West-Prairie near the termination of the plank road from W-Praire to Point Pleasant: two days March from New Madrid—He brings no information of the strength of Gen Hardees forces" ALS, DNA, RG 393, District of Southeast Mo., Letters Received. On Sept. 28, McKeever had written to USG. "Col. Carlin reports from his headquarters at Ironton, Mo, under date of Sept 26th, that there is no rebel force nearer that point than Pittmans Ferry Arkansas, except small marauding bands near Bloomfield. On the 23d inst. Hardee was at Pittmans Ferry & Pocahontas with 7000 men. Three of his regiments left that day for Columbus, Ky, via Point Pleasant, Mo; for the latter place the balance of the force were to leave about next week. The whole command was composed of nine regiments and 26 pieces artillery." LS, *ibid*. *O.R.*, I, iii, 508. On Sept. 17, Hardee had received orders from Maj. Gen. Leonidas Polk to move his command of about 4,000 men from Pitman's Ferry, Ark., to Point Pleasant, Mo., about forty miles southwest of Cairo and about ten miles southwest of New Madrid, Mo. *Ibid*., pp. 702–3. Hardee found the road so poor that the last detachment of his command did not leave until Sept. 25. *Ibid*., pp. 705–7.
    At the same time, C.S.A. Gen. Albert Sidney Johnston was planning another movement. On Sept. 28, Maj. Gen. John C. Frémont wrote to USG. "It is reported

that the rebels have evacuated Columbus and crossed over to Belmont to attack Cape Girardeau or Ironton. Should that be the case the troops now stationed at Fort Jefferson, Elliot's Mills and at Norfolk should be immediately ordered to Birds Point. One battalion of infantry and a small detachment of cavalry should be left at Fort Holt for the protection of the siege battery, and the two gunboats stationed near Island No. 1, to protect Fort Holt and control Norfolk. As soon as the concentration of troops at Birds Point is completed a demonstration against Charleston should be made. Paducah is, under all circumstances, to be held and Smithland well protected for the control of the junction of the Ohio and Cumberland rivers." Copies, DLC-USG, V, 7, 8; DNA, RG 393, USG Hd. Qrs. Correspondence; *ibid.*, District of Southeast Mo., Letters Received. *O.R.*, I, iii, 507–8. On Sept. 29, Frémont wrote a similar letter to Brig. Gen. Charles F. Smith, and Smith sent a copy to USG. Copies, DLC-USG, V, 7, 8; DNA, RG 393, USG Hd. Qrs. Correspondence. *O.R.*, I, iii, 508–9. For Smith's reply, see *ibid.*, p. 510. On Sept. 29, C.S.A. Brig. Gen. M. Jeff Thompson was ordered to advance to Farmington, Mo. On Sept. 30, Thompson wrote that he would attack either Ironton or Cape Girardeau. *Ibid.*, pp. 709, 712.

1. On Oct. 2, McKeever replied to USG. "In reply to your communication of the 29th ult. I have the honor to state that you are authorized by the Major Genl. commanding to appoint a mustering Officer for your District. Please forward me a list of Officers for the Military Commission, also name a Judge Advocate. There is no money in the Quartermaster's Department. The Deputy Paymaster General will be ordered to pay off the troops at the earliest possible moment." Copies, DLC-USG, V, 4, 5, 7, 8, 81, VIA, 1; DNA, RG 393, USG Hd. Qrs. Correspondence; *ibid.*, Western Dept., Letters Sent. On Oct. 4, Rawlins issued special orders appointing Capt. William S. Hillyer mustering officer for the district. Copies, DLC-USG, V, 15, 16, 77, 82; DNA, RG 393, USG Special Orders.

2. See letter to Brig. Gen. John A. McClernand, Sept. 23, 1861.

To Capt. Chauncey McKeever

Head Quarters Dist S. E. Mo
Cairo Sept 29th 1861

ASSISTANT ADJUTANT GENERAL
SAINT LOUIS MO
SIR

We are greatly in need of some kinds of Blanks and would respectfully request you to send as soon as possible the following kinds Viz: Weekly and Monthly Division Reports and such other kinds as are needed at Division Head Quarters also some Blank Steamboat and Rail Road Passes

By forwarding the above immediately you will greatly oblige

Your obt Servant
U. S. GRANT
Brig Genl Com

Copies, DLC-USG, V, 4, 5, 7, 8, 78; DNA, RG 393, USG Hd. Qrs. Correspondence.

To Col. C. Carroll Marsh

Head Quarters Dist S. E. Mo
Cairo Sept 29th 1861

COL

I have just received information that the Steamer J. H. Dickey landed on her trip down yesterday seven Boxs mdse at a point between Birds Point and Commerce. The Goods were marked Charleston Mo and a wagon and twenty men were waiting there to recieve them.

If you have control of the cars I wish you to take or send the effective portion of infantry Regiment out and secure the goods if possible.

Should the cars not be in your possession send all the cavalry you can spare and let the infantry march out part way to support them should they be forced to retreat

U. S. GRANT
Brig Genl Com

To Col C. C. Marsh
Comdg U. S. Forces
Birds Point Mo

Copies, DLC-USG, V, 1, 2, 3, 77; DNA, RG 393, USG Letters Sent. On Sept. 29, 1861, USG telegraphed to Capt. Chauncey McKeever. "Capt Harding seventeenth Illinois volunteers, a passenger on the Dickey yesterday reports her leaving seven boxes Merchandise on Missouri side marked Charleston a wagon and guard of twenty men there to receive them." Copies, *ibid.*, Western Dept., Telegrams; DLC-USG, VIA, 1. On Sept. 30, USG again telegraphed to McKeever. "I sent yesterday to Charleston & apprehended the goods reported as landed by steamer Platte Valley yesterday." Copies, *ibid.* On Sept. 30, Col. C. Carroll Marsh wrote to Capt. John A. Rawlins. "Maj Goodwin of the 20th Ill Vols reached camp at 2 Oclock this morning with his command, having in possession the goods ordered to be taken at Charleston together with a lot landed yesterday at Prices Landing by the Steamer Platte Valley—The goods are in the hands of the Q Mr Agent at this post who holds them subject to the order of the General Commanding" ALS, DNA, RG 393, District of Southeast Mo., Letters Received. An inventory of the items seized at Charleston, Mo., prepared by Maj. John W. Goodwin, contains a long list of miscellaneous goods. Copies, *ibid.*, Western Dept., Letters Received; DLC-USG, VIA, 1. On Oct. 22, Rawlins wrote to Col. William H. L. Wallace. "You will cause to be shipped to the address of B. G. & T Slevins Main Street St Louis Mo. The remainder of the Goods seized by order Col Marsh at charleston Mo. on or about the 29th day of Sept A. D. 1861. on the first Gov't Steamer said Goods claimed by K Gorman" Copies, *ibid.*, V, 1, 2, 3, 77; DNA, RG 393, USG Letters Sent. See letter to Capt. Chauncey McKeever, Oct. 1, 1861.

To Capt. Samuel R. Black

Head Quarters, Dist. S. E. Mo.
Cairo, Sept. 29th 1861

SPECIAL ORDER

Capt. S. R. Black, 7th Regt. Iowa Vols. will proceed to Keocuck Co. Iowa and establish a recruiting depot for his regiment.

All recruits made will be forwarded, by boat, to this place as fast as ten, or any larger number, can be got together, giving a certificate of the number transported, and that they actually are recruits for the U.S. Army.

U. S. GRANT
Brig. Gen. Com.

ALS, IHi. Capt. Samuel R. Black, 7th Iowa, resigned on July 22, 1863.

To Capt. Reuben B. Hatch

Head Quarters Dist S. E. Mo
Cairo Sept 29th 1861

CAPT R. B. HATCH
BRIGADE Q. M.
CAIRO ILLS
SIR

you will deliver on board the Steamer Chancellor invoiced to the Quartermaster at Paducah tomorrow one hundred (100) Axes and (50) fifty Picks with receipt for the same to be signed and returned.

U. S. GRANT
Brig Genl Com

Copies, DLC-USG, V, 1, 2, 3, 77; DNA, RG 393, USG Letters Sent. On Sept. 29, 1861, Brig. Gen. Charles F. Smith telegraphed to USG. "I need at once one hundred axes and fifty Picks please send as many as you can" Telegram received, *ibid.*, Dept. of the Mo., Telegrams Received (unarranged).

To Telegraph Officer

Head Quarters Dist S. E. Mo
Cairo Sept 29th 1861

TO THE PROPER OFFICER
OF THE ILL & MISS TEL CO

You will establish and maintain Telegraph offices at Mound City Caledonia and Fort Massac or Metropolis[1] untill further orders

You will also extend Telegraphic communication from this point to Fort Holt Ky by repairing the present Cable across the Ohio River and the wire along the River to that point and placing

thereon the necessary Batteries Instruments operaters &c
U. S. Grant
Brig Genl Com

Copies, DLC-USG, V, 1, 2, 3, 16, 77, 82; DNA, RG 393, USG Letters Sent.

1. All along the Ill. shore of the Ohio River.

To Julia Dent Grant

Cairo, Sept. 29th 1861

Dear Julia;

I get but very few letters from you yet I know you must write. I see from fathers letter that mine to you are far apart also. There was five or six days at one time when I was kept so absorbed with my duties that the time passed almost like so many hours and nothing scarsely crossed my mind but movements of troops and preparation for any imergency. At that time I did not write for six days. That is the longest that I remember to have gone at any one time since I left.[1]

There is one letter of mine which you have not acknowledged the receipt of which I think you would have noticed.—I enclosed you my commission as Brigadier General. Did you get it? I sent it by Mr. Cook, of the firm of Cook Pendleton & Co.[2] If you have never received it send to Mr. Cook for it. I do not want my Commission lost.

All is very quiet here now. Evry day or two I have reconnoisances made down near the enemy and occationally we surprise a scouting party of the enemy. A day or two ago some of my Cavalry got into a nest of them and killed ten or twelve, took four prisoners and four horses, and a lot of shot guns and rifles.[3] I will send Fred one of the rifles the first opportunity. By the way I would like to take Fred. with me the balance of the Campaign.

Wont you let him come? If you will send him down when father comes, I will take good care of him. Gen. McClernand has his son, about the same age, with him and so have several other officers.

I think we will have a paymaster here in a few days. I will then send you $100 00 and send $200 00 towards paying my debt to Hughlett. My board, horsefeed, servant hire & wash bill amounts to about $55 00 a month, $5 00 for tobacco and other expenses is about what it costs me to live. This is pretty cheap for a Brigadier. I will send you $100 as regularly as I draw my pay and hope you will be able to save something out of it. From the balance I will pay my debts and save $100 00 more per month.

Have you sent Simps. watch? I need one very much. I think you had better remain in Galena. It woud be very pleasant living in Covington, but your prejudice against Clara,[4] and her incorigable persiverance in practicing her rigid economy upon evrybody but herself would make it insupportable. I could not live there with her in peace and you probably would be further from it than me. Kiss all the children for me. Kisses for yourself. Write me a long letter dear Julia and tell me more about the children.

ULYS.

ALS, DLC-USG.

1. See letter to Julia Dent Grant, Sept. 25, 1861, note 1.
2. See letter to Julia Dent Grant, Sept. 8, 1861, note 1.
3. See letter to Capt. Chauncey McKeever, Sept. 26, 1861, note 1.
4. Clara Grant, oldest sister of USG.

To Capt. Chauncey McKeever

By Telegraph from Cairo Sept 30 *1861*
To Capt C McKeever
AAG

Our pickets were attacked today below Norfolk. A Rebel mortally wounded reports Pillow Twenty Thousand moving on Mayfield. We are threatened toards Charleston.

U. S. Grant
Brig Gen

Telegram received (punctuation added), DNA, RG 94, War Records Office, Dept. of the Mo.; copies, *ibid.*, RG 393, Western Dept., Telegrams; DLC-USG, VIA, 1. *O.R.*, I, iii, 510. On Sept. 30, 1861, Capt. Chauncey McKeever telegraphed to USG. "The 10th Iowa leaves here this evening for Cape Girardeau." Copies, DNA, RG 393, Western Dept., Telegrams; *ibid.*, USG Hd. Qrs. Correspondence; DLC-USG, V, 4, 5, 7, 8, VIA, 1. On Oct. 1, Col. John T. Fiala telegraphed to Maj. Gen. John C. Frémont. "Gen Grant reports under yesterdays date that Gen Smith is threatened from Maysville—Have telegraphed Smith & Grant to report immediately the extent of danger. No reply yet. Cape Girardeau is reinforced. Two regts. more are ready for Cairo if necessary. Two gun boats are between Cairo & Paducah a third one is on the way. I think the movement against Norfolk a mere demonstration. If Grant & Smith support each other, neither need be to much exposed." Copy, DNA, RG 393, Western Dept., Telegrams. See telegram to Brig. Gen. Charles F. Smith, Sept. 30, 1861.

To Brig. Gen. John A. McClernand

Head Quarters, Dist. S. E. Mo.
Cairo, Sept. 30th 1861

Gen.

Myself and Staff purpose going to Paducah to-day and closing the office entirely during our absence. I notify you that you may take entire charge of this post, and the enemy around.

Should any troops arrive during the day will you be kind

enough to direct them to Norfolk to report to Col. Oglesby for position.

I am Sir, Very respectfully
Your Obt. Svt.
U. S. GRANT
Brig. Gen. Com.

To Brig. Gen. J. A. McClernand
Comd Post
Cairo, Ill.

ALS, McClernand Papers, IHi.

To Brig. Gen. Charles F. Smith

BY TELEGRAPH FROM Cairo [*Sept.*] 30th *1861*
To GEN SMITH

A prisoner mortally wounded & brought into Norfolk confirms the report that Pillow 20 000 strong is marching ~~on~~ upon Mayfield—Our pickets have been engaged with the enemy to-day, in two directions—

U. S. GRANT
Brig Gen

Telegram received, DNA, RG 94, War Records Office, Dept. of the Mo. On Sept. 30, 1861, Col. John J. S. Wilson telegraphed to USG. "Col Ross informs me that wounded Rebel who is dying at Norfolk reports that twenty thousand under Gen Pillow left Columbus yesterday supposed destination to attack Paducah—" Telegram received, *ibid.* On the same day, Brig. Gen. Charles F. Smith telegraphed to USG. "Can you send in the direction of Blandville and learn something of the reported movement of Pillow and his twenty thousand and let me know." Telegram received, *ibid.*, RG 393, Dept. of the Mo., Telegrams Received (unarranged).

To Col. Joseph B. Plummer

Head Quarters Dist S. E. Mo
Cairo Sept 30th 1861

COL
SIR

I am directed by the Genl comdg to say to you to keep at work as much of your force as can be employed in the Ditches and finish Fortifications as quick as possible.

Also that he ordered a board a short time since to examine into and assess the damages to property known as the Dittinge Property from which no report has yet been had.[1] If they have convened please cause a report of their proceedings to be forwarded in pursuance of said order to these Head Quarters if not order it to do so immediately substituting Col Cook for Col Bayles[2]

And that you will keep yourself well posted as to the movements of the enemy around you, and in case of any threatened attack report here and to Saint Louis by Telegraph by sending a Messenger to Jonesboro Ills the nearest Telegraph Station.

Yours Respectfully
JNO. A. RAWLINS
Asst. Adjt. Genl

To Col Plummer
Comdg Post
Cape Girardeau Mo

Copies, DLC-USG, V, 1, 2, 3, 77; DNA, RG 393, USG Letters Sent. Joseph B. Plummer of Mass., USMA 1841, who held the rank of capt., 1st Inf., was appointed col. of the 11th Mo. on Sept. 24, 1861, and sent to take command at Cape Girardeau, Mo. *O.R.*, I, iii, 505. On Sept. 28, Col. John Cook wrote to USG concerning his displacement as commander at Cape Girardeau by Plummer, and the letter was received on Sept. 30. DLC-USG, V, 10; DNA, RG 393, USG Register of Letters Received.

1. See letter to Maj. Gen. John C. Frémont, Sept. 20, 1861. On Sept. 27, Capt. John A. Rawlins wrote to Cook. "I am directed by Brig Genl U. S. Grant

to make inquiry of you if the board ordered by you to assess damages to property taken for Fortifications &c at your Post has convened, and if so request that you send report of their proceedings to these Head Quarters as soon as practicable."
Copies, DLC-USG, V, 1, 2, 3, 77; DNA, RG 393, USG Letters Sent.

2. Col. David Bayles had been replaced by Plummer as commander of the 11th Mo.

Calendar

━━

1861, [APRIL–AUG.].   To President Abraham Lincoln or Secretary of War Simon Cameron, alleged in a statement by Postmaster General Montgomery Blair recorded by John M. Thayer. "One day in cabinet meeting Lincoln turned to the Secretary of War and said: 'Did we not receive a communication some time last spring from a man by the name of Grant, out at Springfield, Illinois, forwarded by Governor Yates, laying out a plan of campaign down the Mississippi?' The Secretary replied that he believed that such a paper was received. The President requested him to have it looked up, which was done, and it was read in cabinet meeting. It made a strong impression on all the members, Lincoln remarking that at the time it was received it had impressed him favorably; but in the multiplicity of cares it had been forgotten till now, when he had just received a communication from Representative Washburn of Illinois, calling his attention to General Grant and suggesting that he be sent to Cairo. Lincoln then said, 'Mr. Secretary, send an order to General Frémont to put Grant in command of the District of Southeast Missouri.' "—John M. Thayer, "Grant at Pilot Knob," *McClure's Magazine*, V, 5 (Oct., 1895), 437. An earlier account by Thayer appeared in the *St. Louis Globe-Democrat*, Aug. 8, 1885. No support for this statement has been found in the reminiscences of USG, Yates, or Frémont; no communications of the sort described exist from Washburne to Lincoln or Lincoln to Frémont; no verification has been located in any other source; and Thayer is frequently inaccurate about other matters. The statement is rejected by Kenneth P. Williams in *Lincoln Finds a General* (New York, 1949–59), III, 453–54.

John W. Emerson discussed in detail strategic planning by USG at Ironton, Mo., in Aug., 1861, and quoted 1st Lt. Charles B. Steele. "I copied a great plan of campaign which General Grant sent to Congressman Washburne to lay before the President."—"Grant's Life in the West and his Mississippi Valley Campaigns," *Midland Monthly*, IX, 2 (Feb., 1898), 115–18. Emerson then quoted Thayer's account and concluded that "Governor Thayer's high standing places the truth of this corroborative statement above all cavil or doubt."— *Ibid.*, p. 119. Thayer apparently referred to an earlier letter; there is no other instance known of Steele performing secretarial duties for USG, and several objections to the Thayer account apply to Emerson as well. In the following issue of the *Midland Monthly*, pp. 219–21, Emerson provided corroborating statements from Francis P. Blair, Jr., and Elihu B. Washburne which did not counteract the basic implausibility of the account.

1861, MAY 16.   To Col. Thomas S. Mather.—*ABPC* 1913, p. 774.

1861, JUNE 26.   USG Orders No. 12 promoting Privates Isaiah S. Taylor to sgt. maj., Robert H. Jones to q. m. sgt., Alonzo L. Mills to commissary sgt., and Lorenzo L. Hollister to hospital steward.—Copy, DNA, RG 94, 21st Ill., Order Book.

1861, JUNE 27.   USG Orders No. 15 appointing a board of survey to inspect commissary stores.—Copy, DNA, RG 94, 21st Ill., Order Book.

1861, JUNE 29.   To Secretary of War Simon Cameron "in relation to the appointment of two addl Lieutenants to fill places of those appt Adjt and Rt. QMr."—DNA, RG 107, Register of Letters Received.

1861, JULY 1.   USG Orders No. 20 arranging co. transfers of fourteen privates of the 21st Ill.—Copy, DNA, RG 94, 21st Ill., Order Book.

1861, JULY 2.   USG Orders No. 21 assigning 1st Lt. Thomas E. Dawson, 2nd Ill. Light Art., to assume the duty of act. asst. q. m. and act. asst. commissary for the troops remaining in Camp Yates.—Copy, DNA, RG 94, 21st Ill., Order Book. Another copy, headed "Order No. 1" and with different wording, ICHi.

1861, JULY 26.   USG Orders No. 26.   "Company Commanders are expected to use proper diligence in having their Company Books made out at this time of the Regiment being encamped; and it is hereby ordered that the Same be done immediately and the same reported to the Adjutants Office"—Copy, DNA, RG 94, 21st Ill., Order Book. The same order appears later in the same book as an unnumbered special order marked "Void."

1861, JULY 28.   USG Special Orders No. 6. "Capt.   Commanding Co.   2d Mo. Vols. now stationed at Pardew Bridge will upon the receipt of these orders, proceed to St. Louis with the command under him, and report to the Commanding Officer, at St. Louis Arsenal. He will give a certificate of the number of his command transported to the Conductor of the Road. This order is given on the representation that the troops under your command, are out of rations and that their term of [se]rvice has expired, and the Bridg. Genl. being absent. Should you be in possession of Goverment arms, and other property of the United States, you will turn the same in to the proper Officer, and get his receipt."—Copy, DNA, RG 94, 21st Ill., Order Book.

1861, JULY 29. USG Special Orders No. 7, addressee unknown. "On the morning of the 30th ult. (Tuesday,) you will hold your command in readiness to move to St. Charles via N. Mo R R, there to report to Bridg Genl Pope. Should Genl Pope have not arrived, you will await his arrival, and then report for escort duty to this Encampment. You will have issued three days rations to your command, and have the same delivered at Depot of North Mo R. R. Mexico, Mo. at, 9.o.clock a.m. to-morrow (Tuesday.)"—Copy, DNA, RG 94, 21st Ill., Order Book.

1861, JULY 29. USG Special Orders No. 27. "Corporal E. B. Stevens of Co. "H." 21st Regt Inft Ills Volts. for disobedience of orders, and absenting himself from his Camp and his duties in the night of the 28th inst is hereby reduced to the ranks as a private."—Copy, DNA, RG 94, 21st Ill., Order Book. The order was marked "Null & withdrawn." Stevens was a corporal at the time of his death, March 4, 1864.

1861, JULY 30. USG Special Orders No. 8 for "Officer Comdg Co A, Capt Nortons Command." "You will proceed immediately to removing all of your Camp equippage, and deliver the same at Depot of North Mo. R R Mexico, Mo. at 4 ½ o.clock P. M. this day, and embark with remainder of Company, and rejoin your Company at St. Charles, Mo. on the 5 ½ o.clock, P.M train this day"—Copy, DNA, RG 94, 21st Ill., Order Book.

1861, JULY 31. USG Special Orders No. 29. "Corporal Geo W. Stevens of "A" Co 21st Regt Ills Volts. for intemperance, and common street drunkenness, is hereby reduced to the ranks as a private soldier to take effect from this date. The Commander of his Company will make the proper note of the fact on his muster Roll."—Copy, DNA, RG 94, 21st Ill., Order Book.

1861, AUG. 2.   USG Special Orders No. 30." " C̶" I and "G" companies under their respective commanders, will hold themselves in readiness to move from this place at 12 o.clock (noon) this day. They will be provided with two days rations, without Camp or Garrison equippage All such persons as in the opinion of their Commander are not able to march will be left behind. Capt J̶. W̶. C̶l̶a̶r̶k̶ Geo. W. Peck will command the expidition"—Copy, DNA, RG 94, 21st Ill., Order Book. On Aug. 2, by Orders No. 3, Brig. Gen. John Pope sent Peck to Troy and Warrenton, Mo., to implement Special Orders No. 3 designed to prevent further raids on the railroads by holding the citizenry responsible.—Copy, *ibid.*, RG 393, District of North Mo., General Orders. *O.R.*, I, iii, 417–20.

1861, AUG. 8.   Capt. Franklin D. Callender to USG enclosing "an invoice of Ordnance and Ordnance stores. Requests return of duplicate receipts."—DLC-USG, V, 10; DNA, RG 393, USG Register of Letters Received.

1861, AUG. 9.   USG General Orders No. 8.   "You will forthwith inform the different company commanders, of your Regt. that company Provision Returns should be given to the Regtl Adjutant, in order to be compared with his morning Report, and consolidated as per form No. 14 Subsistence regulations. All Requisitions on the Depot at Pilot Knob must be examined, and approved, of by the commanding Officer before issued upon. All requisitions for Stores must be made through the Depot at Pilot Knob, where the necessary blanks can be obtained." —Copy, DNA, RG 94, 21st Ill., Order Book.

1861, AUG. 9.   USG General Orders No. 10. "All Regimental, and Detachment commanders, will hold their respective commands, not absent on duty, under arms, on their respective Parade Grounds, tomorrow from 9 o.clock, A.M. until, visited by the commanding officer of the Post. This notice must be published this evening to each Regiment and Detachment, so that there shall be no absentees."—Copy, DNA, RG 94, 21st Ill., Order Book.

1861, AUG. 9. USG special orders. "The Officer in command of the troops en route from St. Louis to Ironton will distribute four companies of his command at such points on the Iron Mountain Railroad as may be designated by Colonel H. Kallman to whose orders they will be subject whilst on this detached service"—Copies, DLC-USG, V, 15, 16, 82; DNA, RG 393, USG Special Orders. The troops were part of the 15th Ill.

1861, AUG. 12. USG General Orders No. 15. "Hereafter, on Wednesdays, and Saturdays, at 10 o.clock, A. M., the commands at this point will be marched out by companies to the places already designated for each command for the purpose of firing one round each at a target. All firing must cease at 11 o.clock."—Copy, DNA, RG 94, 21st Ill., Order Book. This order was announced to the troops in a humorous way. "Hereafter on Wednesdays and Saturdays, at 10 A. M., firing by target by companies is permitted. Accordingly I hereby notify Hardee, Jeff Thompson, and such other of the rebels as may be near by, that it is a target we are firing at, not them, so they may not unnecessarily take to their heels and flee to parts unknown, before we even get a sight of them."—Reported in letter of "Orion," Aug. 12, 1861, in *Missouri Democrat*, Aug. 13, 1861.

1861, AUG. 12. USG General Orders No. 16. "A general Court-Martial is hereby appointed to meet at Ironton, Mo. on the 13th day of August 1861, or as soon thereafter as practicable, for the trial of private Henry Schupback of K. Company, 24th Ills. Vol. and such other prisoners as may be brought before it.

Detail for the Court:

1 Col Fr Hecker	4 Capt. Leopold Becker
2 Maj. W. E. McMakin	5 " J. S. Temple
3. Capt. A. M. Peterson	6 " F. A Bragg

7th Lieut August Gahenty.

2d Lieut. J. L. Bowman Judge Advocate. No other Officers than those named can be assembled without manifest injury to the public service."
—Copy, DNA, RG 94, 21st Ill., Order Book.

1861, AUG. 12. USG special orders for Lt. Col. John W. S. Alexander. "Lieutenant Colonel Alexander, commanding 21st Illinois Volunteers, will detail from his command, one commissioned, two noncommissioned officers and twenty five privates, to report without arms, to Major Krout, tomorrow morning at seven o'clock for fatigue service."—Copies, DNA, RG 393, USG Special Orders; DLC-USG, V, 15, 16, 82.

1861, AUG. 12. Maj. Gen. John C. Frémont to USG. "The resignation of First Lieutenant Louis M. Habich of Co. C. 6th Regiment Mo. Volunteers, transmitted through Col. P. E. Bland and yourself, is hereby accepted."—Copies, DNA, RG 393, Western Dept., Letters Sent by Gen. Frémont; *ibid.*, Letters Sent (Press).

1861, AUG. 13. USG special orders for Col. Peter E. Bland. "Colonel P. E. Bland, 6th Missouri Volunteers, will immediately upon receipt of this order, send one commissioned officer and twenty privates to report to Acting Assistant Quartermaster Joel, for duty at Pilot Knob."—Copies, DNA, RG 393, USG Special Orders; DLC-USG, V, 15, 16, 82.

1861, AUG. 13. USG special orders for 1st Lt. Charles H. Fuller. "1st Lieutenant and Adjutant C. H. Fuller, 21st Illinois Volunteers, will proceed without delay to Saint Louis, Mo. and superintend the drawing of clothing, camp and garrison equipage, ordnance &c, for the use of his regiment. He will rejoin his regiment as soon as practicable."—Copies, DNA, RG 393, USG Special Orders; *ibid.*, RG 94, 21st Ill., Order Book; DLC-USG, V, 15, 16, 82.

1861, AUG. 14. USG General Orders No. 18. "The same instructions will be observed to morrow as to day, as to drill, firing guns Teams &c &c Citizen teamsters, will draw rations from the command, to which they are attached. To morrow morning at as early an hour as possible, each regiment will double their pickets."—Copy, DNA, RG 94, 21st Ill., Order Book.

1861, AUG. 16. USG special orders for Capt. Joshua C. Winters, 9th Mo. "Captain Winters with the three companies of his command, is hereby temporarily attached to the 6th Missouri Volunteers. They will draw rations from the commissary of the 6th Missouri Volunteers, and be subject to detail for duty from it"—Copies, DNA, RG 393, USG Special Orders; DLC-USG, V, 15, 16, 82.

1861, AUG. 17. USG General Orders No. 21. "Hereafter provision returns sent to brigade headquarters for approval must be accompanied by a morning report of the regiment, company, or detachment for which it is drawn. The Post Commissary will issue no rations except upon returns approved at these Headquarters or upon orders issued from the same."—Copies, DNA, RG 393, USG General Orders; DLC-USG, V, 12, 13, 14.

1861, AUG. 20. Hd. qrs. of Brig. Gen. John Pope to USG. "The General commanding directs me to inform you that the bearer John E. Cone, is a competent instructor of Infantry and Cavalry drill and to direct you to assign him to such Regiment as you think most needs his services."—Copy, DNA, RG 393, District of North Mo., Letters Sent. This is probably the John E. Cone who later served as col., 54th U.S. Colored Inf.

1861, AUG. 21. Capt. Thomas M. Vincent to USG. "For resignation of Vols. see par. sixteen hundred forty seven (16.47)."—Telegram, copies, DNA, RG 393, USG Hd. Qrs. Correspondence; DLC-USG, V, 7. "Officers of the volunteer service tendering their resignations, will forward them through the intermediate commanders to the officer commanding the department or *corps d'armée* in which they may be serving, who is authorized to grant them honorable discharges. This commander will immediately report his action to the Adjutant-General of the Army, who will communicate the same to the Governor of the State to which the officer belongs. A clear statement of the cause will accompany every resignation."—*Revised Regulations for the Army of the United States, 1861* (Philadelphia, 1861), p. 497.

1861, AUG. 22. To Maj. Gen. John C. Frémont. "Requesting the order given for the transfer of Lieut. Peas, Irish Brigade, be not confirmed."—DNA, RG 393, Western Dept., Register of Letters Received. 2nd Lt. Henry Pease of Chicago remained with the 23rd Ill. until mustered out, Oct. 31, 1864.

1861, Aug. 28.   Col. Thomas A. Marshall, 1st Ill. Cav., to USG from Tipton, Mo. "My command is nearly a mob—The rear is committing many depredations. I have issued the strictest orders, but am unable to catch the culprits—My train is terribly in my way. We marched hard & make but 12 miles yesterday, but that was owing to delay in procuring forage which we had to stop for on the road. I learn enough to know there are considerable forces between here & Lexington, perhaps as near as George town though I think not—I wish you would send the Artillery to me by R. R to Syracuse, & then by a forced march. I shall most likely want artilery of some kind. I am working my self like a turk, of course pretty green, as are all with me My great trouble is that so many officers & men are bent on plunder. I wish I had more regular infantry. Parsons is reported at Versailles, but the report is not probably true."—ALS, DNA, RG 94, Generals' Papers and Books, Stephen A. Hurlbut. For the outcome of the Lexington expedition, see Robert Underwood Johnson and Clarence Clough Buel, eds., *Battles and Leaders of the Civil War* (New York, 1887), I, 313; *O.R.*, II, i, 320–21.

1861, Aug. 29.   Capt. John C. Kelton to USG. "The General Commanding can only permit the companies to be temporarily attached to 23rd, Ill. Regt. till an opportunity offers for them to become component part of a new Regiment. Till that time they may be attached to Col. Mulligan's Regt."—Copy, DNA, RG 393, Western Dept., Endorsements. Written on a letter of Col. James A. Mulligan, Aug. 26, requesting that two cos. be attached to the Irish Brigade.

1861, [Aug.?].   USG special orders. "Lieutenant Wickfield, of the ——— Indiana cavalry, having on this day eaten everything in Mrs. Selvidge's house, at the crossing of the Ironton and Pocahontas and Black River and Cape Girardeau roads, except one pumpkin pie, Lieutenant Wickfield is hereby ordered to return with an escort of one hundred cavalry, and eat that pie also." This order appears frequently in nineteenth century biographies of USG, e.g., P. C. Headley, *The Hero Boy; or, The Life and Deeds of Lieut.-Gen. Grant* (New York, 1864), p. 42. Since no Lt. Wickfield can be identified, USG cannot be placed at the scene of the incident, and no such order appears in USG's book records, the order is probably spurious.

1861, SEPT. 4. Capt. Chauncey McKeever, asst. adjt. gen. for Maj. Gen. John C. Frémont, to USG. "The Major General Commanding directs that you will order a Genl. Court Martial to convene at Cape Girardeau or such other point within your district as you may select, for the trial of Captain Frisbie 20th Ills. Volunteers, and such prisoners as may be brought before it. I herewith enclose you charges against Captain Frisbie."—Copies, DLC-USG, V, 4, 5, 7, 8, 81; DNA, RG 393, Western Dept., Letters Sent; *ibid.*, USG Hd. Qrs. Correspondence. On Sept. 12, 1861, Capt. William S. Hillyer for USG drafted special orders appointing a court-martial for Frisbie on Sept. 14. This was marked "not carried into effect."—Copy, DLC-USG, V, 80. Capt. Orton Frisbie, 20th Ill., was dismissed for neglect of duty on Nov. 16, 1862.

1861, SEPT. 5. Hd. qrs. of Maj. Gen. John C. Frémont to USG. "The Commanding General directs that if the 2 companies of Colonel Bissell's Engineer Regiment sent to Cape Girardeau for special service in erecting fortifications and mounting guns, have completed their labors, they be ordered to return to the Head Quarters of their regiment at the Saint Louis Arsenal."—Copies, DNA, RG 393, Western Dept., Letters Sent; DLC-USG, VIA, 1.

1861, SEPT. 6. Maj. Gen. John C. Frémont to USG. "A. Kim is on our side. You can trust his words."—Telegram, copy (Hungarian), DNA, RG 393, Western Dept., Telegrams. The meaning of this message is unknown.

1861, SEPT. 7. Col. Michael K. Lawler, 18th Ill., to USG. "I have some 4 or 5 officers in my Regt who are utterly worthless for the service and I would be pleased to be rid of them. I can find excellent material in the Regt to replace them. with these changes my officers would be efficient. Can you not enable me to get rid of them by appointing a board of officers to examine them. or my be by a shorter process? My Regt is improving rapidly in health and is pretty well drilled. I can put in the field 500 men at a moment's notice and would be gratified to be put in active service Our Guns are the old Flint lock changed Can you funish us with a better gun in whole or in part for our Regt?"—LS, DNA, RG 393, District of Southeast Mo., Letters Received.

1861, SEPT. 9.   Capt. William S. Hillyer to Brig. Gen. John A. McClernand. "I am directed by Gen Grant to inform you that the steamer W.H.B will go to Paducah this afternoon. If there are any men at this post or Birds Point belonging to any of the Regiments stationed at Paducah you can send them up, except those sick in hospital. The Co belonging to Col Pughs regiment, which are here unarmed had better be sent up—"—ALS, McClernand Papers, IHi.

1861, SEPT. 10.   USG pass. "All ferry boats at this place and government transports plying between St. Louis Mo. and Paducah, Ky., will pass Dr. G. Aigner . . . he being on public service"—Parke-Bernet Sale No. 2004, Feb. 6, 1962. On Aug. 2, President Abraham Lincoln wrote to Maj. Gen. John C. Frémont. "Godfrey Aigner, M. D. has been selected by the Sanitary Commission to visit the camps of a portion of your department, to report upon circumstances affecting their health, and to advise the officers in regard to means for sustaining and improving the sanitary condition of their men."—Lincoln, *Works*, IV, 469.

1861, SEPT. 10.   Capt. William F. Brinck to USG. "I have the honor to inform you that the Magazine at Birds Point is not sufficient in size nor condition for the ammount of ammunition that should be kept on hand I respectfully request that you will issue such order as may be necessary. I would suggest that Capt Houghtaling with a sufficient detail of men can build one"—ALS, DNA, RG 393, District of Southeast Mo., Letters Received.

1861, SEPT. 11.   Capt. William S. Hillyer to Capt. Reuben B. Hatch. "I am instructed by Brig Genl Grant Commanding to inform you that if you can procure row boats with men to man them, you will detail one to be stationed at Fort Holt and one at Birds Point subject to the order of the commanding officer. Also one at this post for the special use of Gen Grant The one to be stationed at Birds Point is of the most immediate necessity The detail of men should be from the troops"— Copies, DLC-USG, V, 1, 2, 3, 77; DNA, RG 393, USG Letters Sent.

1861, SEPT. 11.   Capt. William S. Hillyer to Capt. S. A. Turner, commanding steamer *Meteor*. "You will proceed with the troops on board your vessel without unnessesary delay to Paducah Kentucky and report yourself to Brig Genl Smith Commanding Post"—Copies, DLC-USG, V, 1, 2, 77; DNA, RG 393, USG Letters Sent.

1861, Sept. 12.   Col. Eleazer A. Paine to USG. "The bearer Mr. James Enlow shipped from Murray the County seat of Calloway County in Kentucky to this place, a number of Hogsheads of tobacco, consigned to shippers here to be forwarded to Boston Mass. The Steam Boat Jefferson now at Cairo, owned by secessionists contained this tobacco at the time she was seized by the Gun Boat, and the Boat was running up the Tennessee instead of down, at the time of siezure. The ownership of the Boat and the fact that she could easily have run up the Tennessee River to intersect a Rail Road running south determined me to hold the tobacco and send it to Cairo to be libeled in the U. S. Court in Illinois, although I am very doubtful if it can be held as contraband. If you can decide the matter will you do so. And if you can release the tobacco you will oblige a very worthy gentleman the owner and also your corespondnt. Mr. Robert Lockhard goes to see you on the same business."—ALS, McClernand Papers, IHi.

1861, Sept. 15.   Brig. Gen. John A. McClernand to USG transmitting report of inspection of ordnance stores.—DLC-USG, V, 10; DNA, RG 393, USG Register of Letters Received.

1861, Sept. 15.   Capt. William S. Hillyer to Commodore Barton S. Able. "The men brought down by the J D Perry to work on the boats here refuse to do any other work than taking a boat back to St Louis saying that was the only purpose for which they shipped They will therefore be returned to St Louis as we have no such use for them— We want men to work on the boats here."—Copies, DLC-USG, V, 1, 2, 3, 77; DNA, RG 393, USG Letters Sent. On the same day, Hillyer wrote to the capt. of the *J. D. Perry*. "You will convey the 25 men brought by you from St Louis to ship here as roust abouts back to St Louis & report to Commodore Able—"—Copies, *ibid.*

1861, Sept. 16.   Capt. John A. Rawlins for USG, special orders for Surgeon John H. Brinton. "In consequence of the lack of capacity of the Hospital at this post to hold the sick unfit to remain in Camp Brigade

Surgeon Brinton will proceed by boat this evening to Saint Louis in charge of such sick as may be put under his charge by the Medical Director of the Post. On his arrival at Saint Louis Dr Brinton will report to the Medical Director of the Department of the West, Dr DeCamp Upon being relieved of his sick he will return to this post without delay. A list of the sick so disposed of together with the company and Regiment to which they belong will be furnished to this office in order that the Gen Comdg may cause to be made out and furnished to the proper Medical Director in Saint Louis a description roll of them"—Copies, DLC-USG, V, 15, 16, 77, 82; DNA, RG 393, USG Special Orders. See *Personal Memoirs of John H. Brinton* (New York, 1914), pp. 38–39.

1861, SEPT. 17.   To Col. Leonard F. Ross. "Your orders meet with entire approval. I hope you will see them enforced." The orders concerned discipline at Camp Crittenden, Ky.—Anderson Galleries Sale No. 1565, March 14, 1921. See *ABPC*, 1928, p. 702; *ibid.*, 1944, p. 605; *ibid.*, 1958, p. 458.

1861, SEPT. 17.   Brig. Gen. John A. McClernand to USG. "As you have already taken measures in connection with the orders from the Head Quarters of the Western Department herewith inclosed; and as I am not fully advised of what has been done or what is intended to be done, I beg to refer said orders to you."—ADfS, McClernand Papers, IHi.

1861, SEPT. 17.   Brig. Gen. John A. McClernand to USG. "A communication is received from Col. M. K. Lawler of the 18th, in which he refers to Special Order No. 320, issued from these Head Quarters, Sept. 14, summoning a general Court Martial to meet at your Head Quarters on the 16 inst., and reports that Captain Cooper of his regiment died at Cairo on the 12 inst, that Captain Hunter of his regiment is absent on detached service for several weeks, and that Major Eaton is present very sick and therefore is unable to attend."— Copy, McClernand Papers, IHi. On Sept. 17, Capt. John A. Rawlins for USG ordered Lt. Col. Thomas H. Burgess, Capt. Jabez J. Anderson, and Capt. Richard R. Hopkins, 18th Ill., "detailed as members of a General Court Martial to convene at Cairo Illinois on Wednesday the

18th day of Sept Inst, at 10 o.clock A. M. to take the place of members who cannot be present"—Copies, DLC-USG, V, 1, 2, 3, 77; DNA, RG 393, USG Letters Sent.

1861, SEPT. 17.   Lt. S. Ledyard Phelps to USG. "The following are the articles of value found on board the Prize Steamers Stevenson and Gazelle...."—ALS, DNA, RG 393, District of Southeast Mo., Letters Received.

1861, SEPT. 18.   USG special orders. "The Commanding officer at Fort Holt will cause a search to be made through and about the Camp for axes wheelbarrows and other Public Property pertaining to the engineer Department reported missing. He will have all such property returned to Capt Schwartz."—Copies, DLC-USG, V, 15, 16, 77, 82; DNA, RG 393, USG Special Orders.

1861, SEPT. 18.   Capt. John A. Rawlins for USG, special orders for Col. Gustav Waagner. "Capt McAlister will proceed with forty men of his company to Fort Holt Ky to take charge of the heavy Guns there under the instructions of Captain Schwartz. On the arrival of Capt McAllister at Fort Holt the detachment from Capt Houghtalings will be releived and join their compy at Birds Point. A Sergeant and eight men will be left with the peice above the Mill."—Copies, DLC-USG, V, 15, 16, 77, 82; DNA, RG 393, USG Special Orders; McClernand Papers, IHi. On Sept. 18, Maj. Mason Brayman wrote to USG. "A copy of a Special order from your Head Quarters, addressed to Col. Waagner, relating to change in the disposition of artillery is received. Genl. McClernand desires to learn, if Gen. Grant desires him to issue the proper order, or if the order has been already issued."—ADfS, *ibid.* On the same day, 1st Lt. Clark B. Lagow wrote to Brig. Gen. John A. McClernand. "I am directed to say by Genl Grant the order to Col Waagner has been allready issued—a copy of which sent to you"—ALS, *ibid.*

1861, SEPT. 18.   Augustus DeLange to USG. "I have eight recruits for Capt. Hasie's engineers at Cape Girardeau, Mo. Order transportation."—Telegram received (punctuation added), DNA, RG 393, Dept. of the Mo., Telegrams Received (unarranged).

1861, Sept. 20. USG General Orders No. 7. "Commandants of the different Posts under this command will observe the Following instructions The Post Adjutant at Cairo will ~~also~~ send consolidated reports of all forces stationed at that post. The Post Adjutants at Norfolk and Fort Jefferson will each send consolidated reports of the forces under their respective commands. Commanders at Cape Girardeau and Ironton will send their reports to the A. A. Genl 'Western Dept' furnishing a copy to these Head Quarters. These reports will be required weekly showing the exact condition of each command on Monday the 23d inst and each succeeding Monday thereafter"—Copies, DLC-USG, V, 12, 13, 14, 80; DNA, RG 393, USG General Orders; (Printed) McClernand Papers, IHi. On Sept. 20, 1861, Capt. John A. Rawlins wrote to Capt. Reuben B. Hatch. "Enclosed you will find copies of General Orders No 7 and 8 which you will have printed immediately. (50 copies each)"—Copies, DLC-USG, V, 1, 2, 3, 77; DNA, RG 393, USG Letters Sent.

1861, Sept. 20. Brig. Gen. John A. McClernand to USG. "Being informed that a man by the name of Hogan—(lately agent or clerk on the Wharf Boat of the Central Rail Road Company at this landing—) was employed as a guide of the movements from Fort Holt to Forts Jefferson and Crittenden, and perhaps beyond those points, I write to advise you in regard to him. Yesterday I learned that he is a man of questionable loyalty—that he was at Columbus at the time the Steamer Cheney was seized by the rebels, and by his intimacy and whisperings with the leaders in that measure, excited suspicions against himself— That at another time, having seen two men from Columbus get out of thier Skiff on to the Wharf Boat Mentioned, he in two or three days afterwards identified one of them to a Mob who came in search of the same man, and charged him with taking Secession arms to Cairo and holding communication with the enemies of the rebels there."—LS, McClernand Papers, IHi.

1861, Sept. 20. Col. Napoleon B. Buford to USG "in reference to transferring Private George W. Sears Co. C. 2d. Iowa Infty Vols. to the 27th. Ills."—DLC-USG, V, 10; DNA, RG 393, USG Register of Letters Received.

1861, Sept. 20.   Maj. Joseph D. Webster to USG. "I submit herewith my account current to date, by which it will appear that the funds in my hands, applicable to the defensive works at this post will be soon exhausted.—Indeed there is a demand of $1860.72 which although not directly incurred by myself, I yet deem to be a just charge against this Department, and which, knowing most of the circumstances relating to it, I am desirous of paying.—The weekly expenses for the present working force of assistants, mechanics and laborers is in round numbers $1500. There are also considerable bills outstanding for materials.—The force of laborers now Employed should be at once increased; as it is to deficiency in this respect that the slow progress of the works up to this time has been almost entirely due.—The season is now approaching when laborers when laborers can be procured if funds can be furnished to pay them promptly.—During the very hot weather of the latter part of summer it was very difficult to induce laborers to come here.—Some were also deterred by fear of an impending attack by the enemy.—At this present time, I think there will be no difficulty in procuring from Chicago or elsewhere all the laborers it may be thought best to Employ.—Several heavy guns have recently arrived, and of course should be at once mounted in positions already designated.—To accomplish this additional force must be employed, and for efficient prosecution of the work at this place and at Bird's Point, the lowest estimate of the amount required weekly would be two thousand dollars—and twenty-five hundred could be usefully employed.—I shall therefore need the sum of eight thousand dollars applicable to current expenses, and five thousand applicable to payment of existing liabilities—making thirteen thousand dollars. (—$13000.)"—LS, DNA, RG 393, District of Southeast Mo., Letters Received.

1861, Sept. 20.   John Belser to USG or Brig. Gen. John A. McClernand. "Man named Cash left Jefferson County yesterday avowdly for Texas with nine horses & his family. He will cross river at Metropolis or Paducah tonight or tomorrow. Has in his possession sixty (60) or 70 letters from secessionists in Jefferson & Williamson County to the south & to Illinoisans in rebel army—above is perfectly reliable. Cash should be stopped, letters searched & horses taken."—Telegram received (punctuation added), DNA, RG 393, Dept. of the Mo., Telegrams Received (unarranged). See letter to Julia Dent Grant, Aug. 15, 1861, note 6.

1861, SEPT. 21.   Capt. John A. Rawlins for USG, special orders for Capt. Adolph Schwartz. "Captain Schwartz of the Artillery, will as soon as practicable, move his company, with the exception of one piece and sufficient men to ~~man~~ tend it, from Fort Holt to Cairo"—Copies, DLC-USG, V, 15, 16, 77, 82; DNA, RG 393, USG Special Orders. On the same day, Rawlins wrote to Brig. Gen. John A. McClernand. "I am instructed to inform you that Capt. Swarts of the Artillery with a part of his command has been ordered from Fort Holt to Cairo in your command."—ALS, McClernand Papers, IHi. On Sept. 24, Rawlins for USG issued special orders for Schwartz. "That portion of Capt Schwartz Light Artillery now at Fort Holt immediately rejoin the remainder of the company to which ~~they~~ it belongs at Cairo. Capt Schwartz act Chief of Artillery will supply to Fort Holt such ordnance as may be required for the defence of that Post."—Copies, DLC-USG, V, 15, 16, 77, 82; DNA, RG 393, USG Special Orders.

1861, SEPT. 21.   Capt. Thomas J. Haines to USG. "Two hundred and fifty thousand rations were yesterday turned over to the Quartermaster, for transportation to Paducah."—Telegram, copies, DLC-USG, V, 4, 5, 7, 8; DNA, RG 393, USG Hd. Qrs. Correspondence.

1861, SEPT. 22.   Brig. Gen. Charles F. Smith to USG. "In answer to yr. letter of this date, just recd., I have to state that the *Troy* referred to is on the Mobile and Ohio Rail Road, at or near the Obion river and just where the Paducah R. R. prolonged would would strike the Mobile & Ohio R. R. The Bridge to which I referred passes over the Swamp S. E. of Troy, is built on tressels, and three-fourths of a mile long. I can have it destroyed, ~~I believe~~, without a military demonstration of any kind. Should the rebels be driven from Hickman & Columbus on the Mobile Road they would undoubtedly destroy this bridge on their retreat. Please see the enclosed map of this part of the country which I have cause to be prepared and believe reliable. I send by this mail a similar copy to Genl Frémont. Please telegraph the substance of this to Genl. Frémont."—ALS, DNA, RG 393, District of Southeast Mo., Letters Received.

1861, Sept. 23. Capt. John A. Rawlins for USG to George W. Graham. "The Steamer Chancellor on its arrival at Paducah will be subject to the order and direction of Lewis H. Hall Esqr Speaker of the Senate of Pennsylvania and will not leave that place untill he directs P. S. The Steamer Chancellor will not start for Paducah untill Lewis H. Hall Esqr above named comes on board"—Copies, DLC-USG, V, 1, 2, 3, 77; DNA, RG 393, USG Letters Sent. See *O.R.*, I, lii, Part 1, 188–89.

1861, Sept. 24. Brig. Gen. John A. McClernand to USG. "I am informed that there are a number of water crafts, consisting of skiffs, wood boats, etc., at Hacker's Bend on the Mississippi a few miles above Cairo, which are liable to be used, through the complicity of disaffected persons in that vicinity, for the purpose of conveying rebels with hostile purposes across the river. Would it not be well to cause these boats to be brought down and left in charge of the officer having command of the 'Trade water Belle,' lying at the water tank, at the head of the levee on the Mississippi?"—DfS, McClernand Papers, IHi.

1861, Sept. 25. Brig. Gen. John A. McClernand to USG. "At our interview last Evening, I understood that the order issued yesterday, directing requisitions for supplies &c. did not refer to my Brigade at Camp McClernand, consisting of the 27th 29th 30th & 31st Regiments. The letter accompanying that order, however, might bear a different construction. For reference, a copy is herewith given. The orders have already been issued to all under my command with the exception of my Brigade. Please advise me, on this point."—Copy, McClernand Papers, IHi.

1861, Sept. 25. Capt. Reuben C. Rutherford to USG. "In answer to yours of this date, I am able to report five days rations in store, with a considerable quantity in the hands of Q. M's of the various regiments, and 200,000 rations ordered to arrive on the 1st October. The C. S. at Paducah having bee received liberal supplies from St Louis a few days ago, I do not anticipate being called upon to supply that post, at least for the present. Our present store room is insufficient for storing so large a quantity as you mention. The issuing Clerk informs me it will receive about 300,000 rations. If you think it important to hasten the arrival of the supplies already ordered, please inform me"—Copy, DNA, RG 393, Western Dept., Letters Received. On Sept. 25, 1st Lt. Clark B. Lagow wrote to Rutherford. "I am directed by Genl Grant to say to you that you will hurry up the 200,000 rations ordered for 1st of October and order 200,000 rations more for delivery the same time" —Copies, DLC–USG, V, 1, 2, 3, 77; DNA, RG 393, USG Letters Sent.

1861, SEPT. 26.   Capt. William F. Brinck to USG. "Considering it my duty I very respectfully report that in pursuance with your order, I proposed to turn over to the QuarterMaster department some ammunition to be transported to Paducah Ky. Mr Dunton refused to be troubled with it. Again being unable to obtain men to move the centre pieces for the Columbiads sent to Paducah as our last Artillery Company had been ~~ordered~~ sent to Paducah I ordered the Frieght agent at the Stone Depot to have them put on the Wharf Boat—This was Friday the 20th inst and requested Capt Graham to have the Paducah Boat stop and load them on her next trip up. Satturday I went to the Depot and found them still there the Depot Master informing me that Capt Hatch had ordered him not to ship them without an order from him— neither Capt Hatch nor the Frieght Agent informed me of such an order and the centres might have remained there a month had I not gone to the Depot—Brig General McClernand then issued an order to the Quarter Master to ship the centres on the first trip up which order was not complied with until yesterday morning and then only after the order had been repeated several times by Brig General McClernand—And several excuses made by Employees at the Quarter Masters department. My conception of the great necessity of promptness in the Quarter Masters department has forced me to enter this complaint"—LS, DNA, RG 393, District of Southeast Mo., Letters Received.

1861, SEPT. 27.   USG special orders for 2nd Lt. Uzziel P. Smith sending him to Chicago on recruiting service.—Copies, DLC–USG, V, 15, 16, 77, 82; DNA, RG 393, USG Special Orders. Smith served with McAllister's Battery, later Battery D, 1st Ill. Light Art. On Oct. 7, Smith telegraphed to USG from Gilman, Ill. "Send passes to Gilman for twelve men want to start on train tonight"—Telegram received, *ibid.*, Dept. of the Mo., Telegrams Received.

1861, SEPT. 27. Maj. Joseph D. Webster to USG. "I have the honor to acknowledge the receipt of Capt Schwartz's letter of the 25th ins. referred by you to this Department. The several matters mentioned in that letter have long engaged the careful consideration of this Department. As a means of strengthening the position of Fort Holt, the fortifying the line of the creek in the rear would be useful.—But as there is a practicable road by which an enemy could approach from the North, it would be necessary to make a line of defences across from the creek to the river North of the Fort, making the whole line probably over a mile in length.—It would be better to throw up a line of intrenchment with a strong profile directly in rear of the fort itself enclosing a semicircular space within the fort in the centre on a radius of say 500 yards.—Orders are now in force, and have been for some weeks for the establishment of a battery of heavy guns at or near the 'Stone Depot' for the purpose of sweeping the open space between that point, and the shore of the Mississippi opposite.—I had the honor sometime since to represent to Major General Fremont, the desirableness of giving this battery such strength and construction as to enable it in addition to its inland purpose, to control the Kentucky shore opposite.—I have selected the point for it, so as to give it also a flanking fire along the levee southward, and a long reach up the Ohio river.—I have made a requisition for funds to enable me to proceed with the work.—I have also heretofore often suggested the necessity of a stronger interior line of defence from river to river North of this city, which would be attained by a battery on the Mississippi opposite the one last referred to, and an intermediate one,—the three having defensive relations to each other. I have been informed by Col. Waagner verbally, that these views have been approved by Major Gen. Fremont, commanding the Western Department—but am not otherwise advised on the subject.—The letter of Capt. Schwartz is herewith returned.—"—LS, DNA, RG 393, District of Southeast Mo., Letters Received.

1861, SEPT. 28. William M. Gross and William S. Miller to USG. "We were intimidated from staying longer to endeavor to obtain our property as you will perceive from our Depositions. We take it as granted that the Government troops had use for our horses or else they would not have been absent when we left. We presume that our property will be worth its value to the Government. And Should our affidavits justify you in granting pay to us, and you giving us a demand on the Government payable at St Louis this Shall be evidence that we received through you the amount of our said claims Any communication that you may have the goodness to make to us on the subject please direct to the Post Master, Farmington St Francois County Missouri" —DS, RG 109, Records of the U.S. War Dept. Relating to Confederates, Union Provost Marshal's Citizens File. Attached is their deposition. "Be it remembered that on this 28th day of September AD 1861. Personally appeared before me the Subscriber a justice of the peace within and for the County of St Francois aforesaid, William M Gross and William S Miller residents of said County well known by me to be young Men of good moral characters who being by me first sworn according to law, Upon their Oaths declare, That on or about the 22nd day of August 1861 they were boath arrested in Bolinger County State of Missouri and taken to the City of Cape Girardeau in Cape Girardeau County Missouri, and were there delivered up as prisoners to the United States troops Stationed at said place Colonel Marsh then in command, that they each of them had with them a gun and a horse that they each had an examination before General Grant and that they were acquitted, that they the said Gross & Miller were liberated from said arrest, But at a time when Colonel Smith intimated to them that they had better leave—their horses were absent, having been ridden away by some of the troops of the place, they therefore left in consequence of the intimation of Colonel Smith, and without getting their horses or guns, Colonel Irvine stated to them and others in like situation that if their horses could not be obtained there would be other arrangements made in their favor. Colonel Irvine gave an order for several horses, on Sargent Brach Wagon Master, each owner of a horse was required to give a Seperate receipt, what came of the Order deponents know not, but they neither of them obtained either their horses or their guns, nor did they reciept for them or any part thereof, said deponents believe that their horses and equipage which they have lost, were worth One hundred and twenty five dollars each, General Grant stated to deponents and others, that they should have all their property and that they should not be deprived of their property in consequence of their having been arrested"—DS, *ibid.*

Index

All letters written by USG of which the text was available for use in this volume are indexed under the names of the recipients. The dates of these letters are included in the index as an indication of the existence of text. Abbreviations used in the index are explained on pp. xxvi–xxviii. Individual regts. are indexed under the names of the states in which they originated.